AF587456

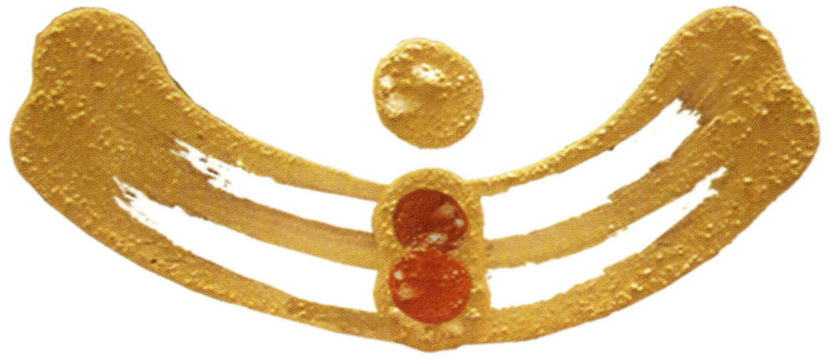

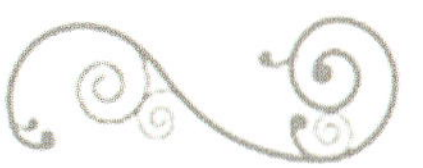

Anant Koti Brahmand Nayak Rajadhiraj Yogiraj Parabramha
Shri Satchidanand Samarth Sadguru Sai Nath Maharaj Ki Jai

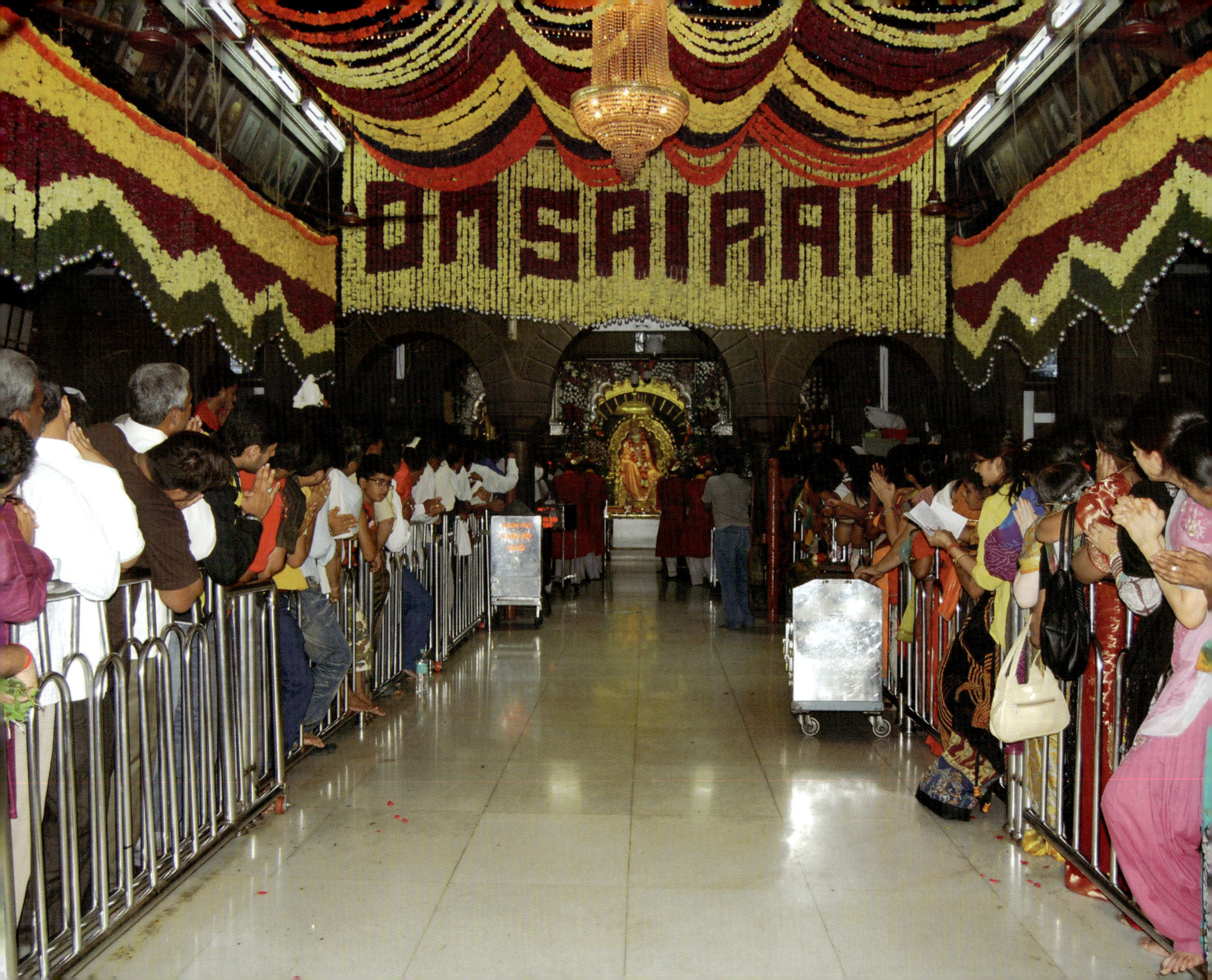
OMSAIRAM

SHIRDI

within & beyond

A collection of unseen & rare photographs

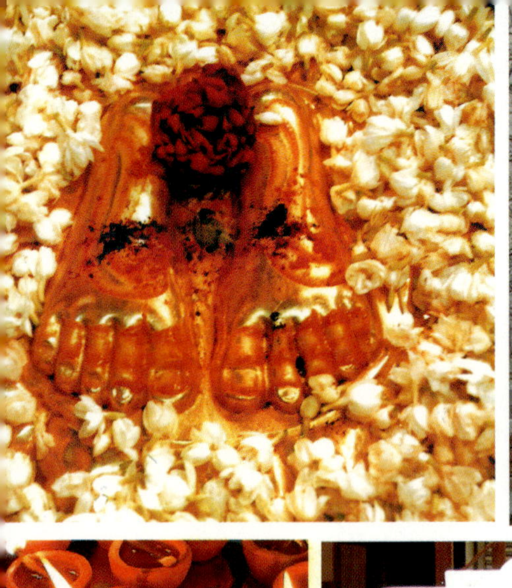
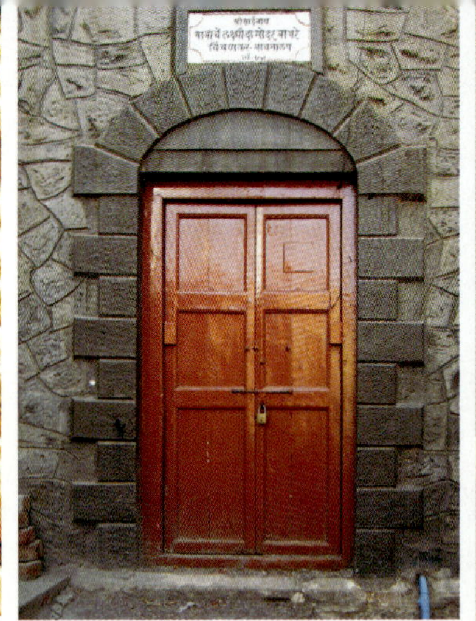
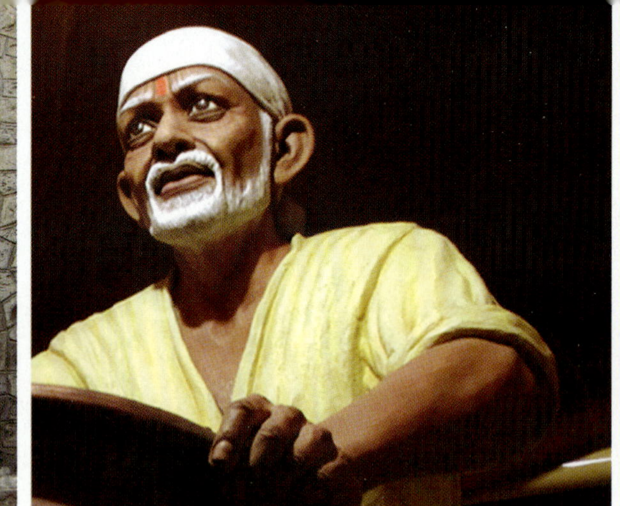
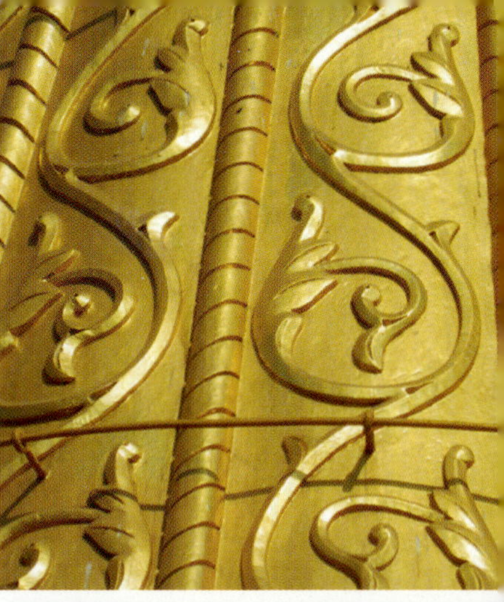
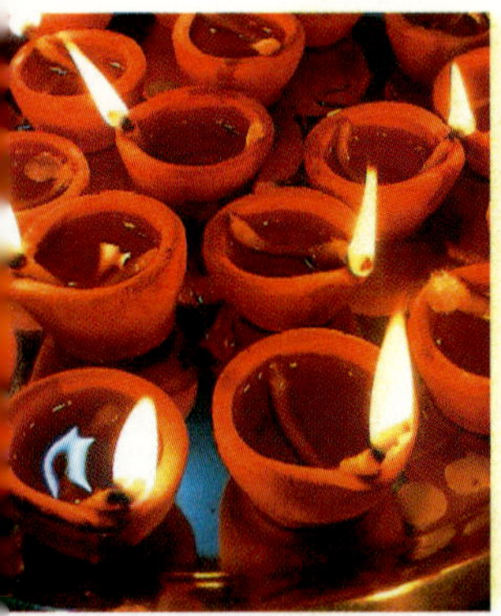
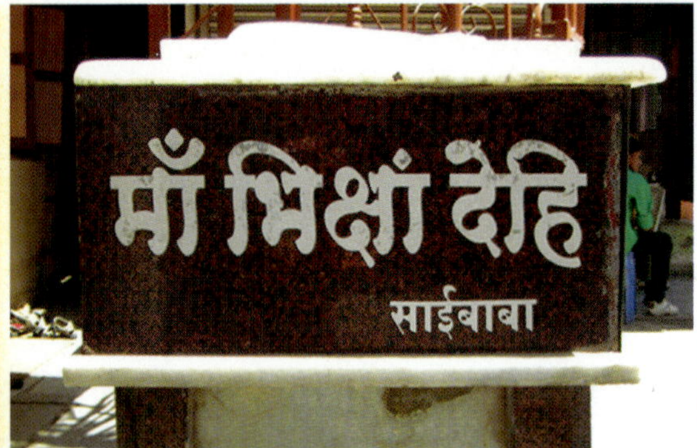
माँ भिक्षां देहि
साईबाबा
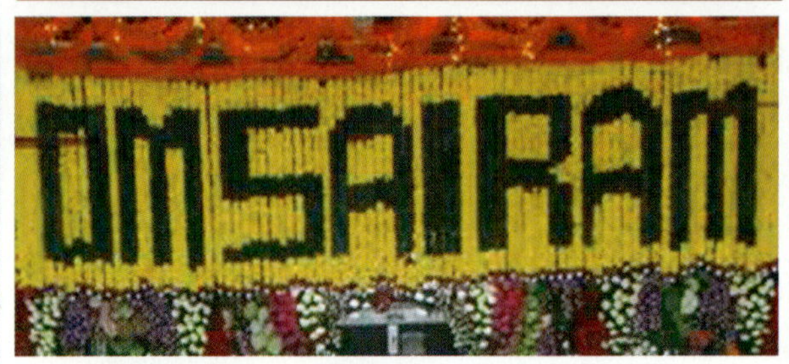
OMSAIRAM
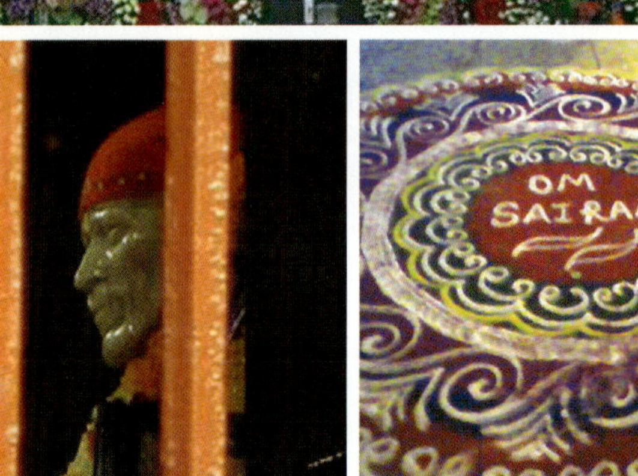
OM SAIRAM
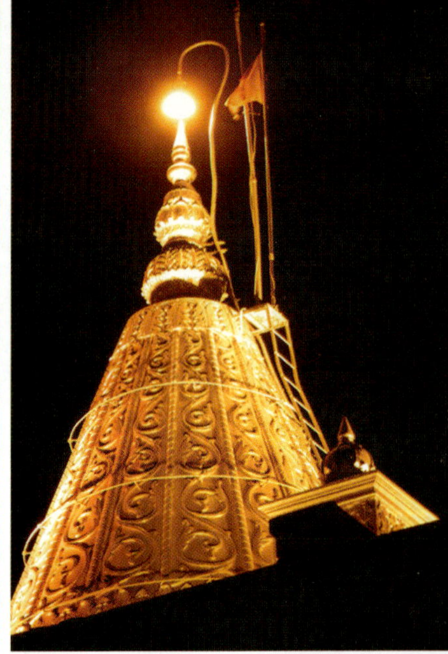
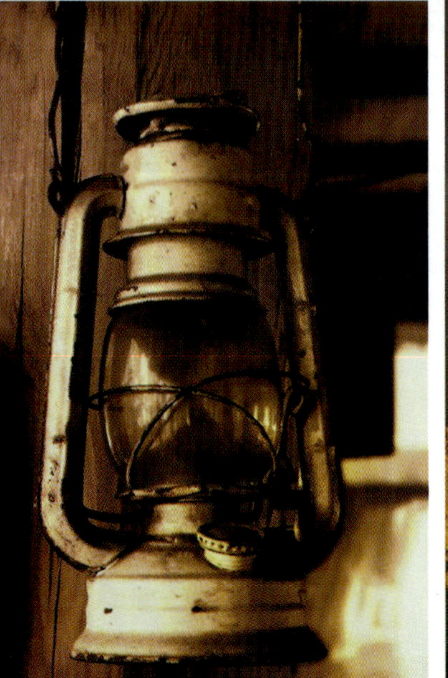
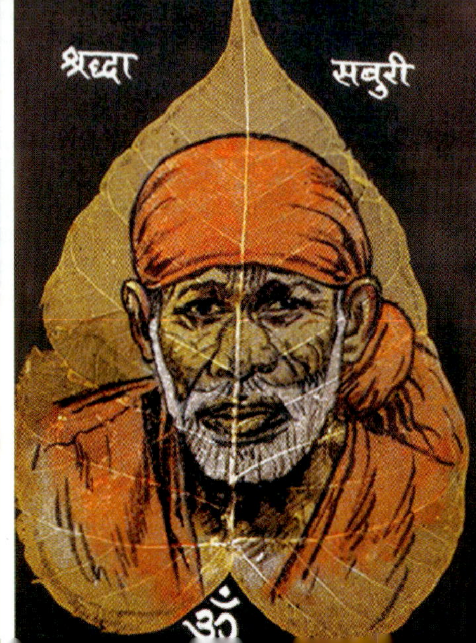
श्रद्धा
सबुरी
ॐ
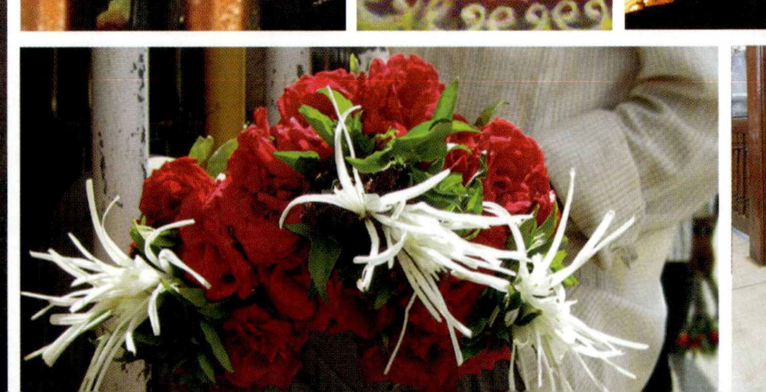

SHIRDI

within & beyond

A collection of unseen & rare photographs

Dr. Rabinder Nath Kakarya

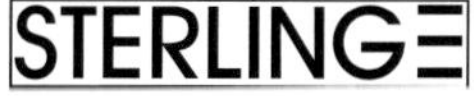

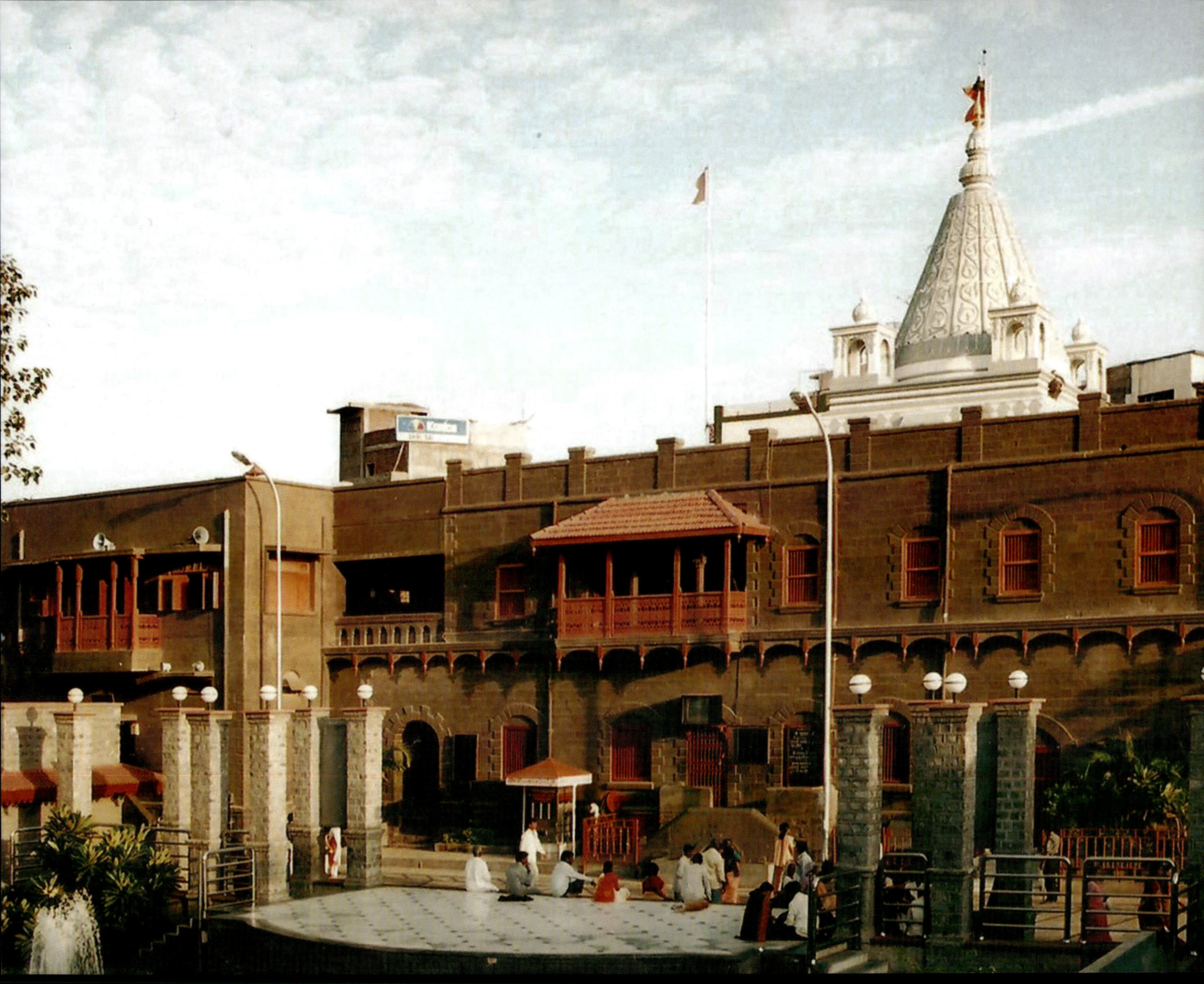

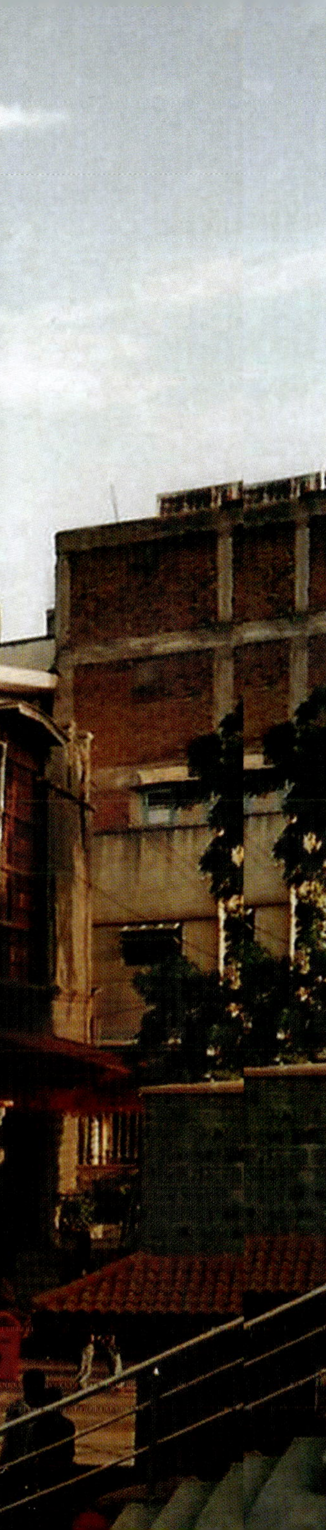

CONTENTS

ACKNOWLEDGEMENTS

A photo-essay of this magnitude has borne fruit with the diligent efforts and unconditional support of my friends and Baba's devotees. I express my profound appreciation and genuine gratitude to all concerned and would like to mention a few whose contributions were absolutely critical in transforming this venture into a success. First and foremost, I am thankful to Shri Sai Baba Sansthan Trust, Shirdi, whose immaculate handling of Baba's treasured artifacts and pictures has contributed vastly to this pictorial collection.

I am delighted to acknowledge my cherished association with Dr. Vinny Chitluri of Shirdi who has been my most reliable and inexhaustible source of information. I express my sincere admiration for Sh. Mohit Suneja, an extraordinarily gifted artist, who conceptualised and designed this pictorial tribute to Baba. I am fortunate to have friends like Smt. Vandana Rastogi and Sh. Mukesh Rastogi who, despite being based in Nigeria, edited and supplemented the script along with providing some memorable montage of Baba. I am indebted to Smt. Mayuri Kadam (Mumbai), Sh. Sanjay M. Padia (Kolkata), Sh. H.P. Sharma (Shirdi), Sh. Dilip Sankalecha (Shirdi), Sh. Saurabh Singh (Shirdi), Sh. Nitin Gautam (Delhi) and Sh. Jai Sinh Nimbalkar (Gujarat), Sh. Rajiv Harish Talim (Mumbai) for their invaluable contribution in the form of rare photographs. I am deeply touched and shall forever be obliged to my dearest friends Smt. Neeru Saigal and Smt. Archna Dogra for the midnight oil they burnt in finalising the manuscript of this epic creation.

I submit my salutations to my parents Sh. Surinder Nath Kakarya and Smt. Sudharna Kakarya, my father-in-law Sh. Inder Sain Pandhi who have moulded and guided my character and destiny. I am delighted and proud of my sons Raunak and Raghav for giving me the innovative input regarding the photo album. I express my deepest admiration for my wife Neelam, my pillar of strength in life. I offer my sincere regards to Sh. Surinder Kumar Ghai, Chairman, Sterling Publishers Pvt. Ltd., for his unstinting support throughout the compilation and publication of this book.

I humbly offer my devotion at the sacred feet of the divine sage, His Holiness Shri Ashutosh Maharaj Ji, Founder and Head of Divya Jyoti Jagrati Sansthan, for chartering me through the untested waters of life.

Sterling Publishers Private Limited
Regd. Office: A1/256 Safdarjung Enclave, New Delhi-110029
Cin: U22110DL1964PTC211907
Phone: +91 82877 98380/ +91 120-6251823
e-mail: mail@sterlingpublishers.in
www.sterlingpublishers.in

ISBN: 978 81 207 7806 1
First Edition: January 2013
Reprint: 2013, 2022
Printed at Sterling Publishers Pvt. Ltd

Every effort has been made to trace the copyright holders and we apologise in advance for any unintentional omission. We would be pleased to insert the appropriate acknowledgement in any subsequent edition.

Most of the photographs are clicked by the author himself.

Designed by: Mohit Suneja

PREFACE

The world is transforming at a rapid pace and Shirdi is no exception. As modernisation swamps this once dusty township, there is an anxious endeavour by one and all to preserve its structures, ambience and heritage. This pictorial biography of Shri Sai Baba's legend and legacy is a humble attempt in this direction.

A lovingly compiled photo album, it comprises of rare and awe-inspiring photographs of Baba, His beloved Shirdi and everything associated with Him. Every devotee of Baba, whether a newly baptized child or a veteran in dotage, is aware that Baba is omnipotent and omnipresent. His presence permeates every living moment of Baba's followers. Shirdi is a blessed land where every living being can sense and bask in the physicality of the aura of His Holiness, Shri Sai Baba. It is this essence of Shirdi and the associated innocence and sublime faith of the worldwide diaspora of Baba's devotees, which our book has attempted to capture and reflect in its pages.

We hope that this offering of ours at the portals of the earthly domain of His Benevolent Grace, Shri Sai Baba of Shirdi, finds a worthy place in the home of every Sai bhakta.

Om Sai Ram

Dr. Rabinder Nath Kakarya

236, Jahaz Apartments
Plot No.6, G-17 Area
Rohtak Road,
New Delhi 110 087, India.
Mob: +91 9560211156
Email: rnkakarya@gmail.com

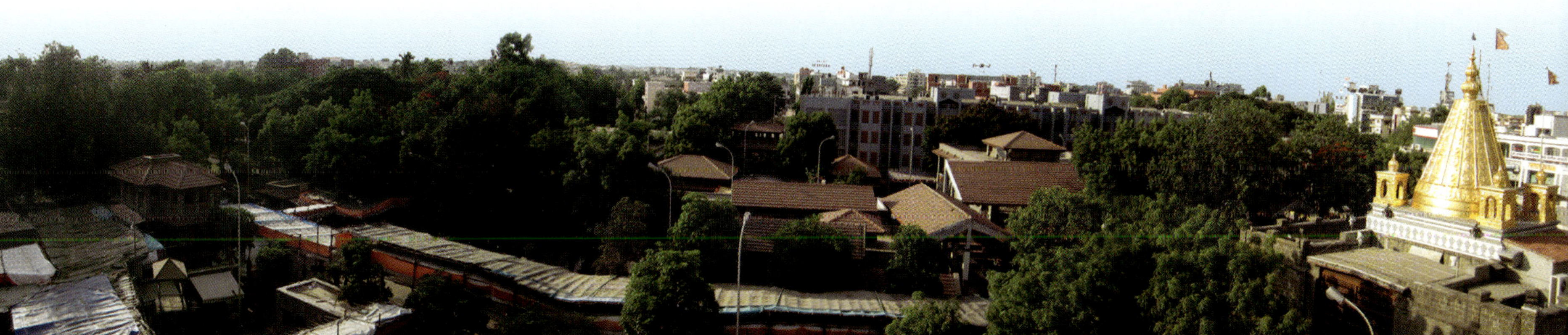

INTRODUCTION

Shri Sai Baba has immortalised the once tiny hamlet of Shirdi into a world renowned pilgrim town. He appeared under a neem tree one day as a young lad and was heartily welcomed by the local populace. He taught them the gospel of religious tolerance and unflinching faith in the Almighty. Sai Baba spent His entire life in Dwarkamai (the mosque), retiring there every alternate night. Every inch of Dwarkamai mosque is blessed by Baba's halo and grace. Here, Baba ground the sins, troubles and arrogance of His devotees in the form of wheat in His hand mill. He lit the eternal dhuni, the holy fire, which burns to incinerate the miseries of those who come to Him for succour. He distributed the sacred ash (udi) from the dhuni among His followers, which acted as a panacea for all maladies. The udi still heals thousands and imparts health and well-being to those who smear it upon themselves.

People came to seek Baba's permission when they wanted to depart from Shirdi. He met them in Dwarkamai and gave them udi. Today, devotees prostrate before Baba's portrait in Dwarkamai and seek His blessings for a safe journey. Baba led the simple life of a mendicant. He asked for food from five chosen homes in Shirdi and collected the offerings in a cloth bag (*jholi*) and tin pot (*tumrale*). He offered the food in an earthen pot to wandering animals and birds, inculcating the spirit of sharing in one and all. He slept in Chavadi on alternate days. It served as a meeting place for the village folk during the daytime. He maintained a garden in a small plot and named it Lendi Baugh. Sanctified by Baba's feet, the garden blooms till this day. Baba lit an eternal lamp, Nanda Deep, within this garden, which burns effervescently even today.

Baba took Mahasamadhi on 15 October, 1918. His mortal remains were consigned to a Samadhi in the mansion built by Gopalrao M. Butti. This mansion is now known as Samadhi Mandir. Baba had said, "My tomb shall bless and address the needs of my devotees". Millions will vouch for the fact that Shri Sai Baba has been taking care of their lives from His Samadhi, His eternal abode of rest and peace. Baba's assurance to His devotees rings true to this day, "Whoever steps on Shirdi's soil, his sufferings would come to an end".

Baba was the living embodiment of supreme divinity, encompassing the simplicity that envelops every worldly miracle. His resplendent personality reflected peace and piety, the virtues still associated with His Samadhi. Thousands revere Him, hold Him in the highest esteem and turn to Him to seek spiritual guidance.

Let us forget our troubles by consigning them to His sacred dhuni and commit ourselves to purposeful lives, adhering to the principles of Dharma. The moral, social and spiritual renaissance ushered in by Baba is the beacon which has guided and steered us so far, and will continue to show the light of true Karma to one and all.

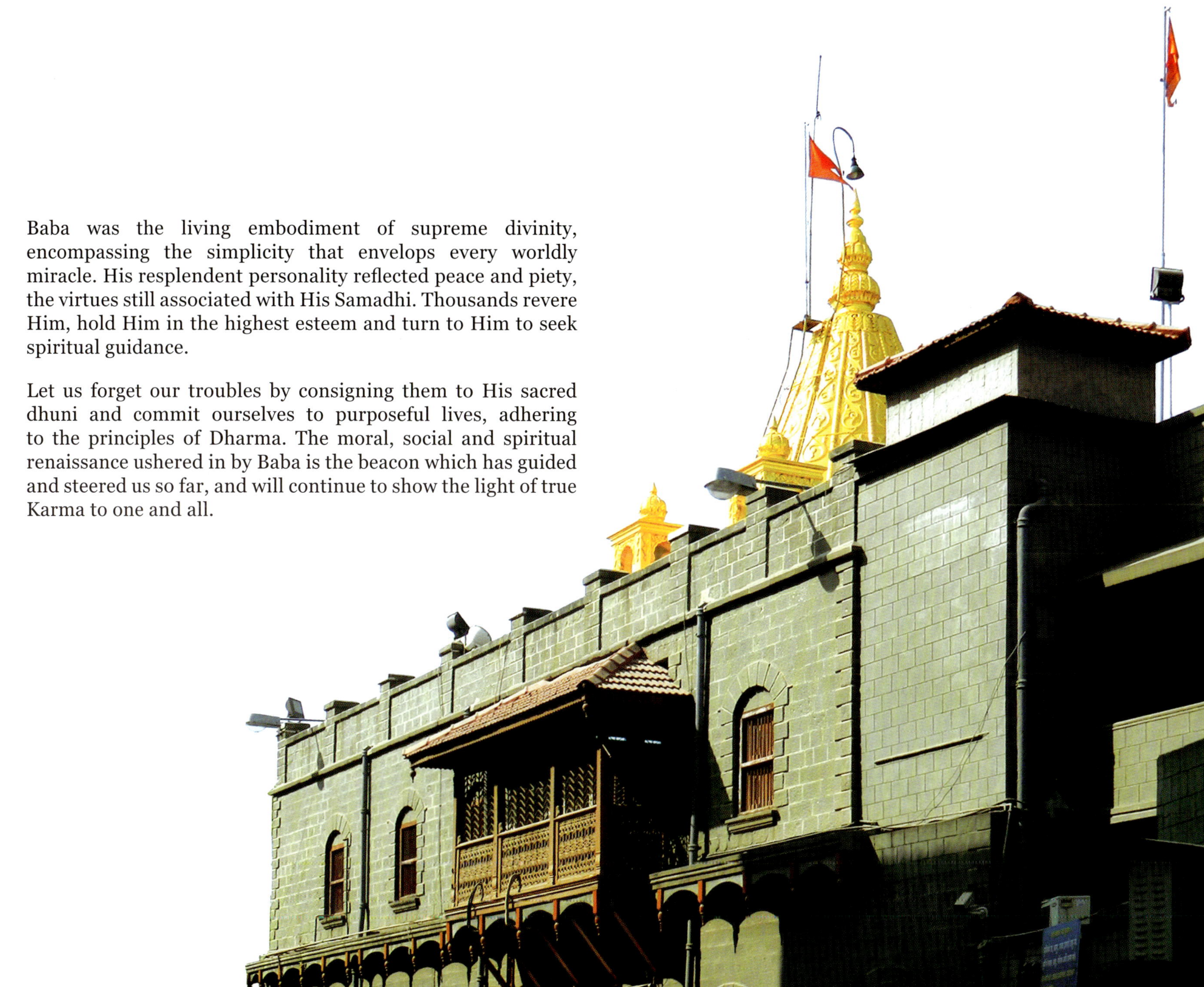

SAMADHI MANDIR
(BUTTI WADA)

Gopalrao Mukund Rao Butti, a humble philanthropic millionaire from Nagpur, has achieved immortal fame throughout Baba's realm. He built a mansion for his family in Shirdi which stood ready in 1917. Baba's fondness for this humble abode was conveyed to Shama in His desire to be there when the house *(wada)* would be complete.

When His Holiness Shri Sai Nath Maharaj shed the trappings of His mortal shield on 15 October, 1918, a Tuesday, in Dwarkamai, His shell-shocked followers fell prey to attritions regarding His last rites. The matter was finally resolved on Thursday, 17 October, 1918. Baba's mortal remains left Dwarkamai for the last time in a procession and He was laid to rest in His preferred abode, the Butti Wada. The Butti Wada has transformed into Samadhi Mandir, bonding Butti with his Baba till eternity. The Samadhi Mandir of today emerged after a gradual metamorphosis of the Butti Wada. In the initial days after Baba's Mahasamadhi, a black and white photograph was kept behind the Samadhi. The Sansthan, after judicious deliberations involving inspection of five model sculptures by different artists, commissioned Balaji Vasantrao Talim to sculpt a five and a half foot stone idol of Baba. His masterpiece was ready in 1954 and the idol was installed *(Pran Pratishtha)* in an emotional ceremony on 7 October, 1954. The idol was seated on a silver throne which had two carved lions perched on the arm support. People's devotion and fervour saw this throne being replaced by a gold throne. The bare-footed fakir, who collected food from five different homes everyday, now sits surrounded by gold trappings. Baba had told His devotees that He would accept whatever they would offer. The grateful masses share their material achievements at Baba's feet, who smiles understandingly.

His idol faces east and its head is tilted towards north-east, a direction dedicated to Lord Vishnu as per Hindu mythology. Baba's idol is bathed every morning *(Mangal Snan)* and the morning aarti *(Kakad Aarti)* is performed thereafter. The rose water that flows off the body is sought after by devotees as prasad. The Mandir resonates with Baba's name being chanted by the resurgent throngs throughout the day. The afternoon aarti *(Madhyaan Aarti)* at 12.00 is followed by the evening aarti *(Dhup Aarti)*. Baba is lovingly put to sleep after the night aarti *(Shej Aarti)*. His heavy robes are taken off and a mosquito net is lowered around Him. The idol is considered a living embodiment of Baba. Millions are convinced that they received personal communion with Baba, each one having gazed into Baba's glittering divine eyes. Samadhi Mandir brings people into the presence of GOD Himself; an experience created by the life-size and lifelike idol.

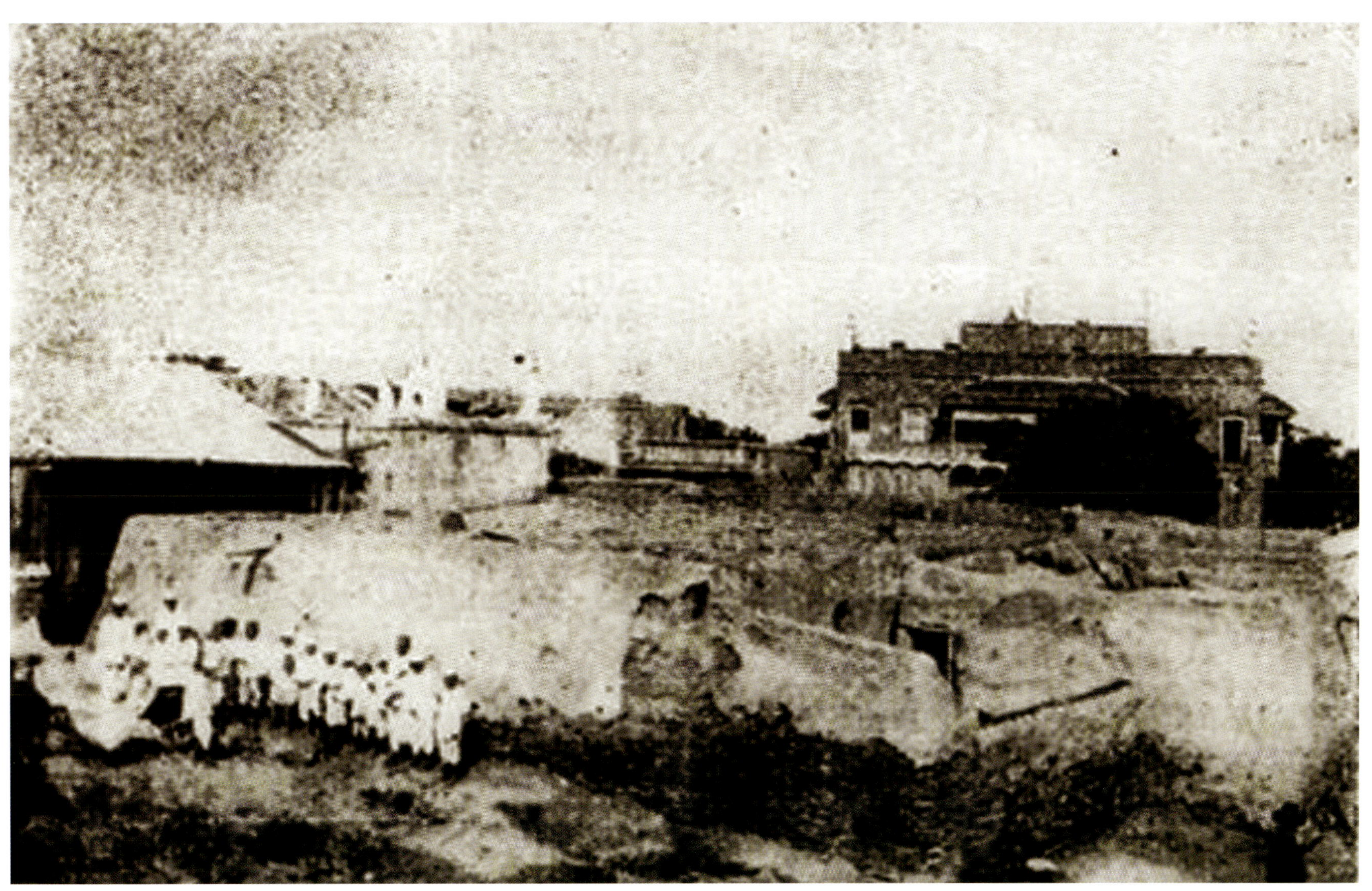

Old Shirdi Village – Butti Wada dominates the landscape. School children from the neighbourhood gather against the wall in the foreground. *(1917)*

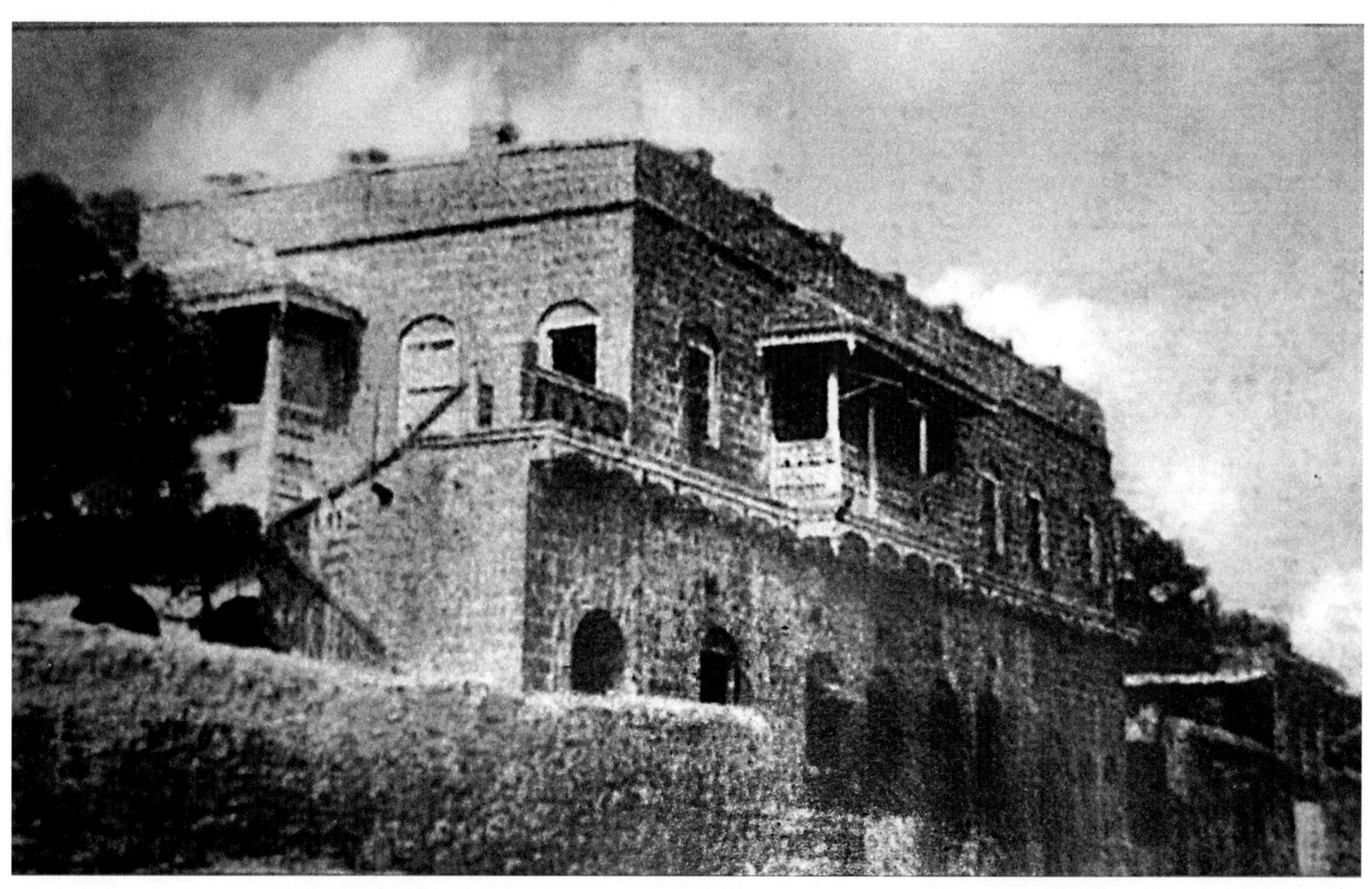

Butti Wada seen from the west side. The balcony, arched alcoves and stairs are visible. *(1947)*

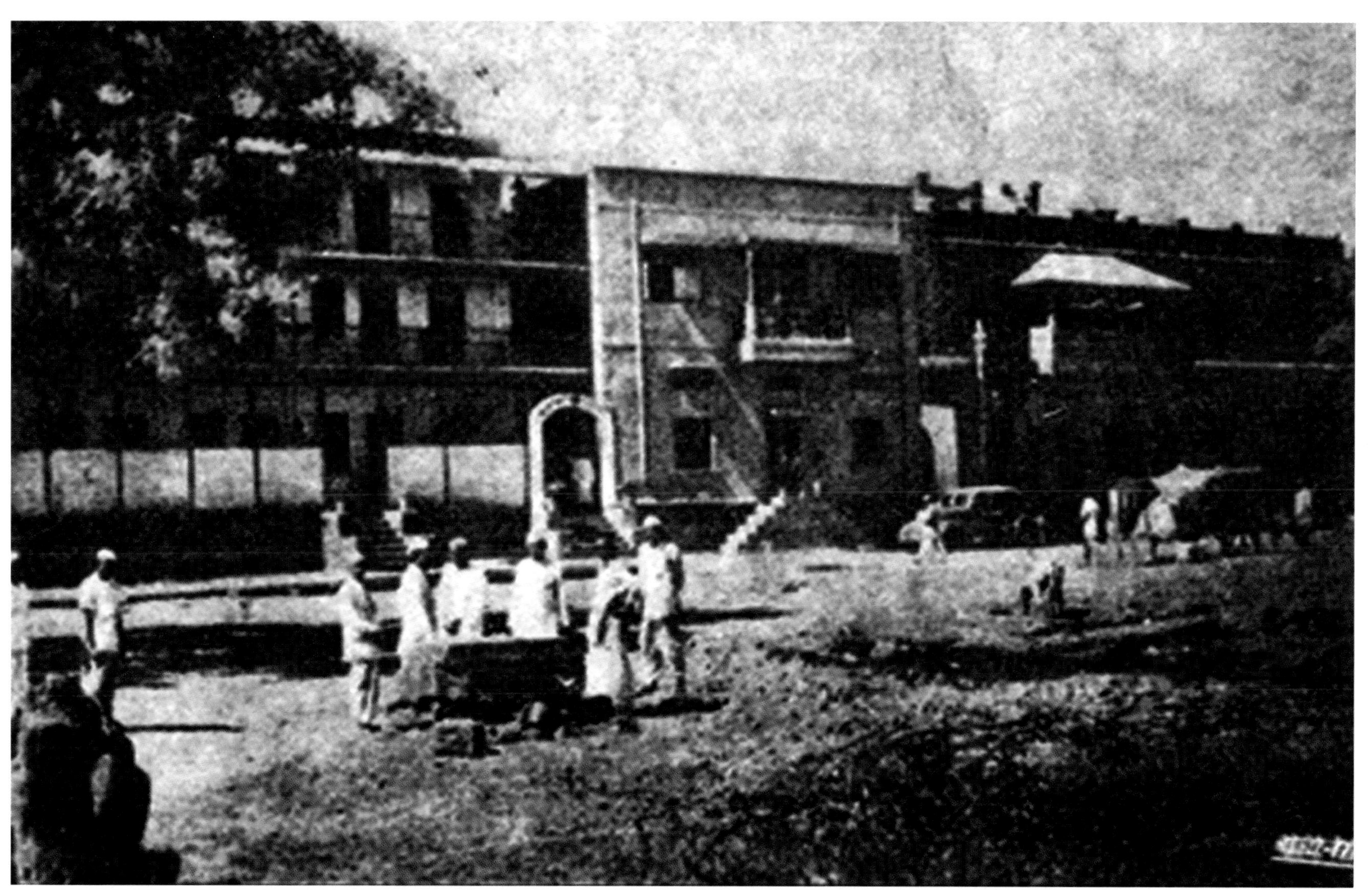

Butti Wada seen from the north side. A vintage car stands near the stairs, close to the entrance. *(1960)*

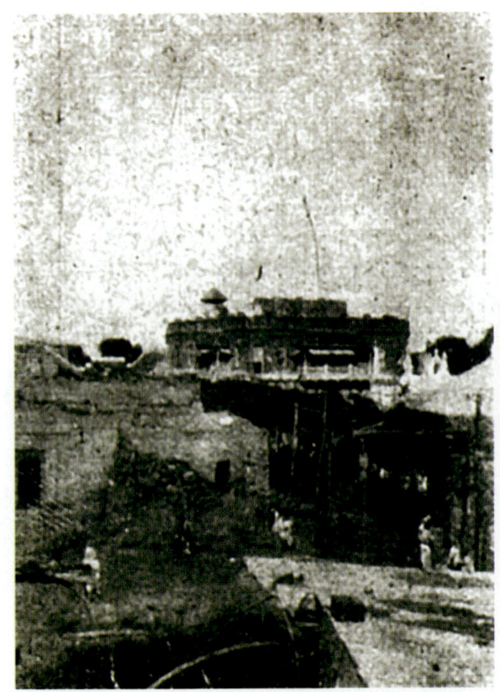

Samadhi Mandir rare photograph

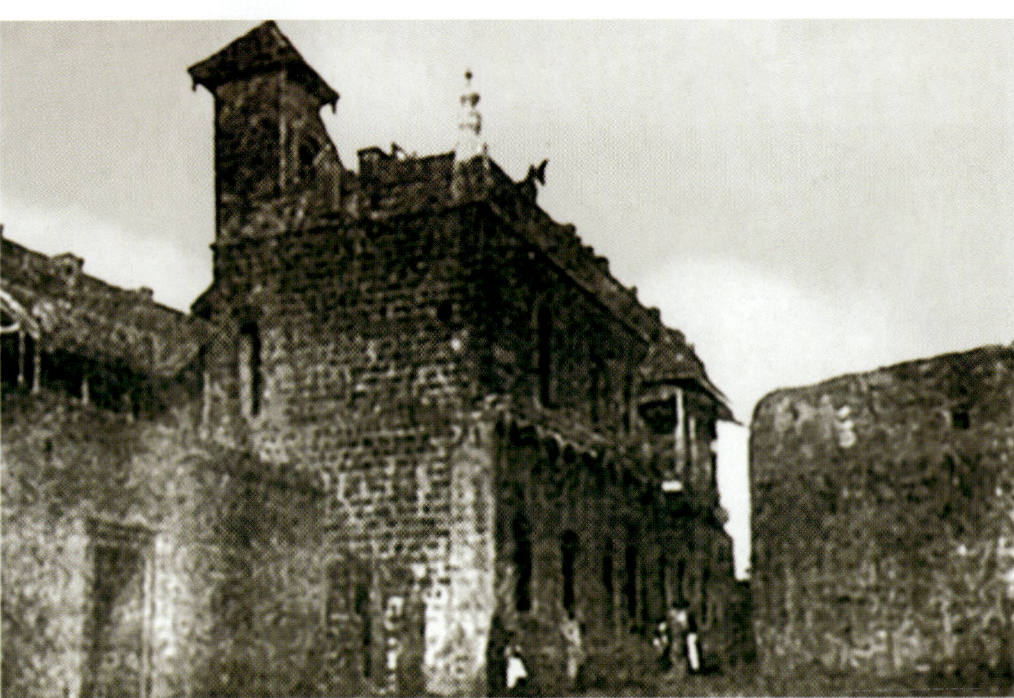

Samadhi Mandir from north

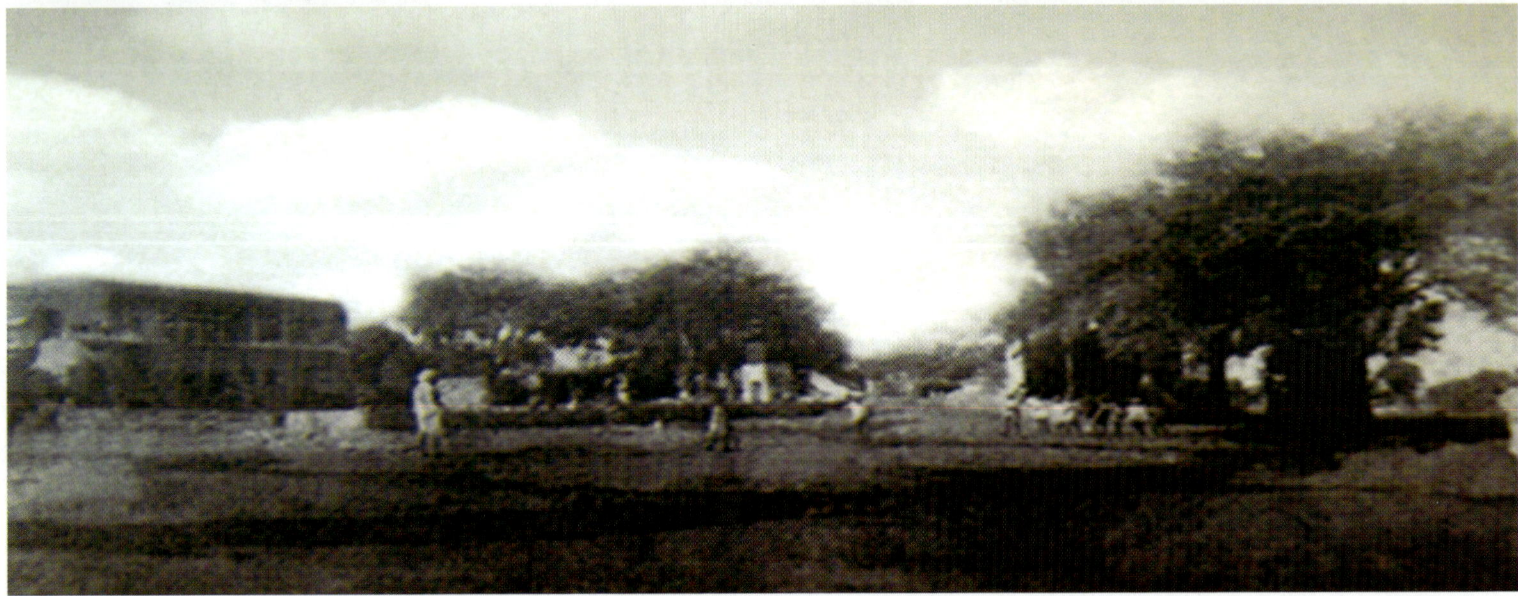

On the extreme left is Samadhi Mandir without its dome. Nearby, an open space and some devotees can be seen. *(1920)*

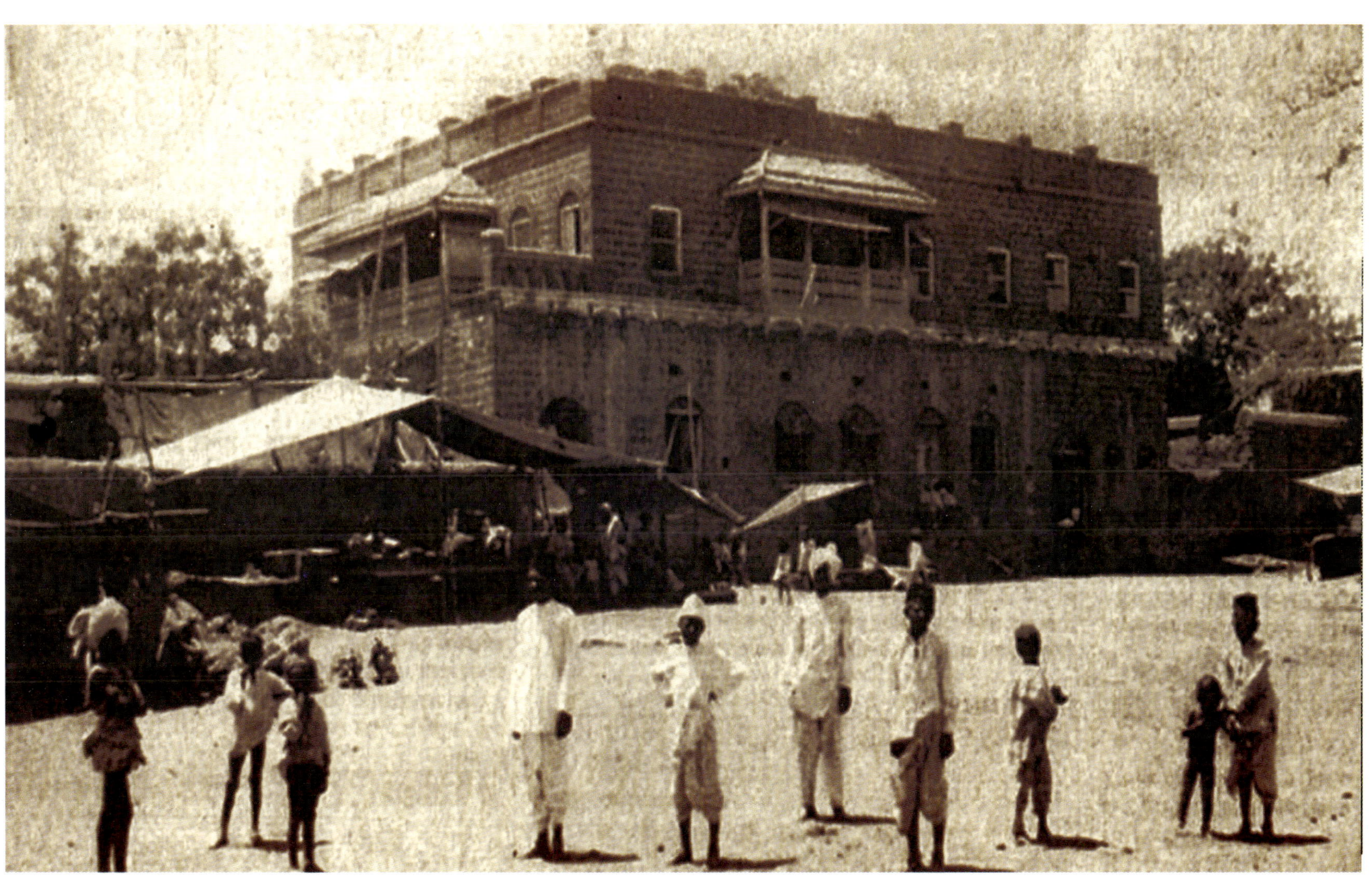

The open ground in front of Samadhi Mandir was frequented by pilgrims at all times. Tented shops did brisk business right next to Samadhi Mandir. *(1947)*

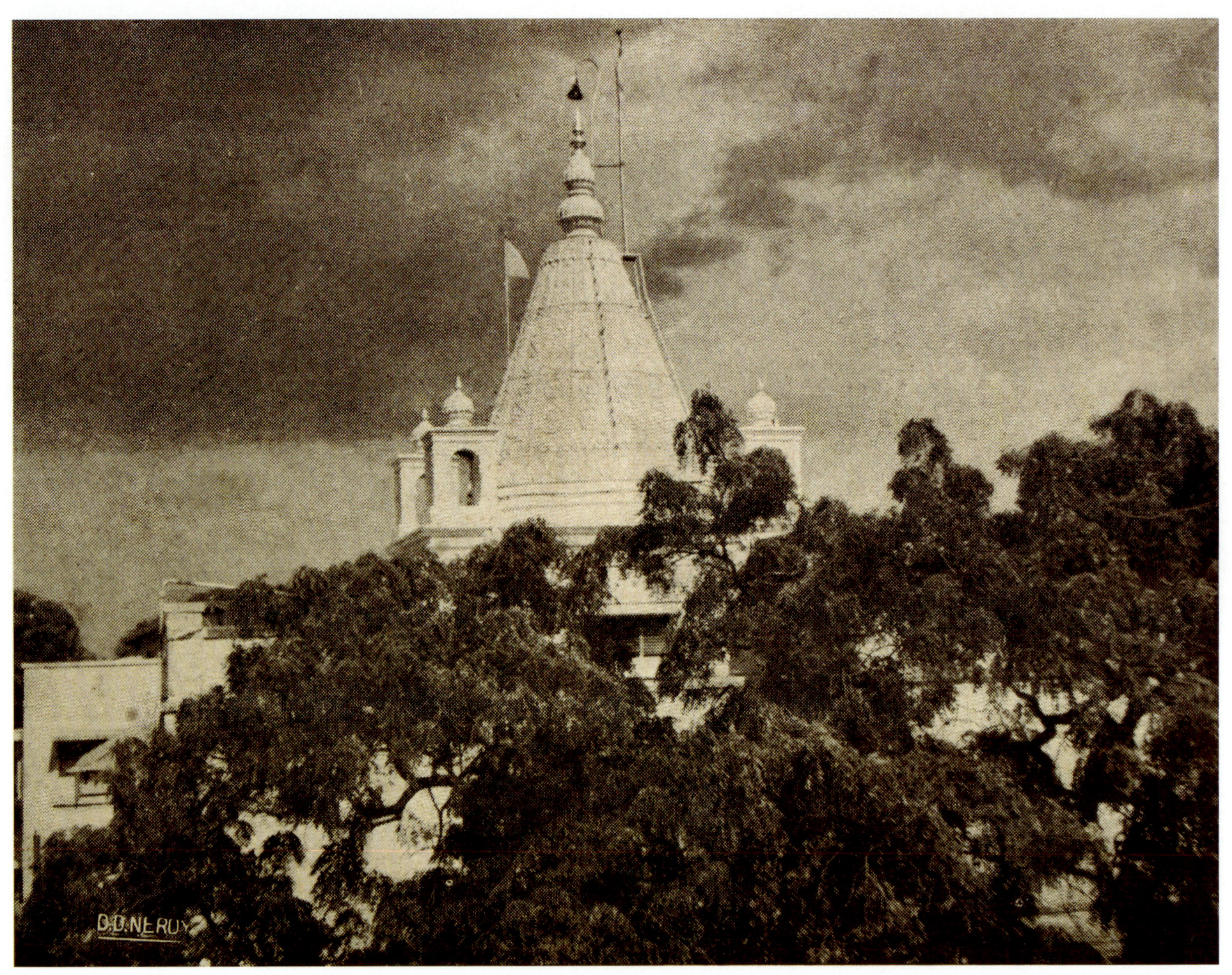

The majestic dome *'Kalash'* of Samadhi Mandir towers above the trees. *(1975)*

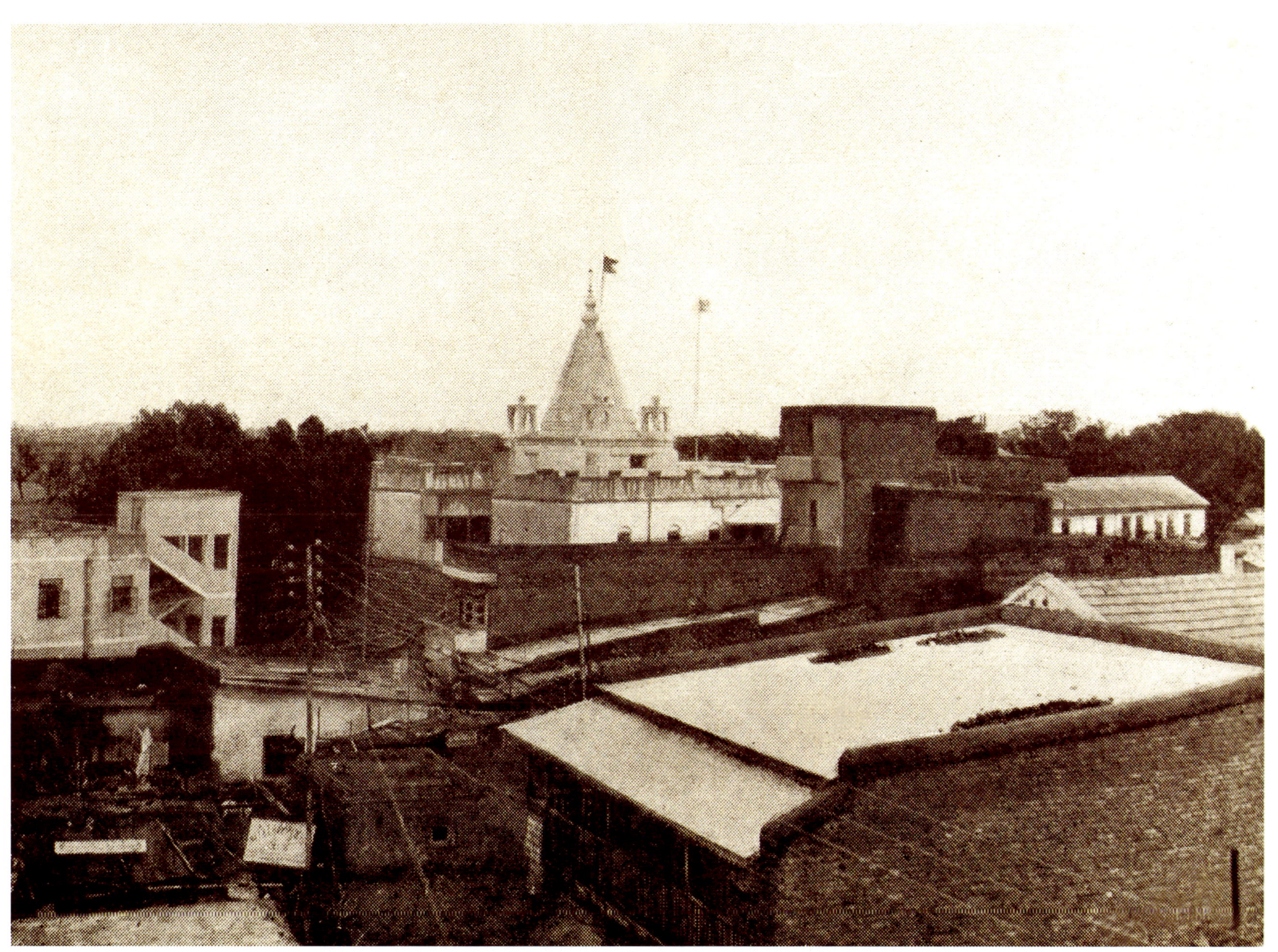

A long view of Samadhi Mandir showing the gradual rise in density around the temple. *(1976)*

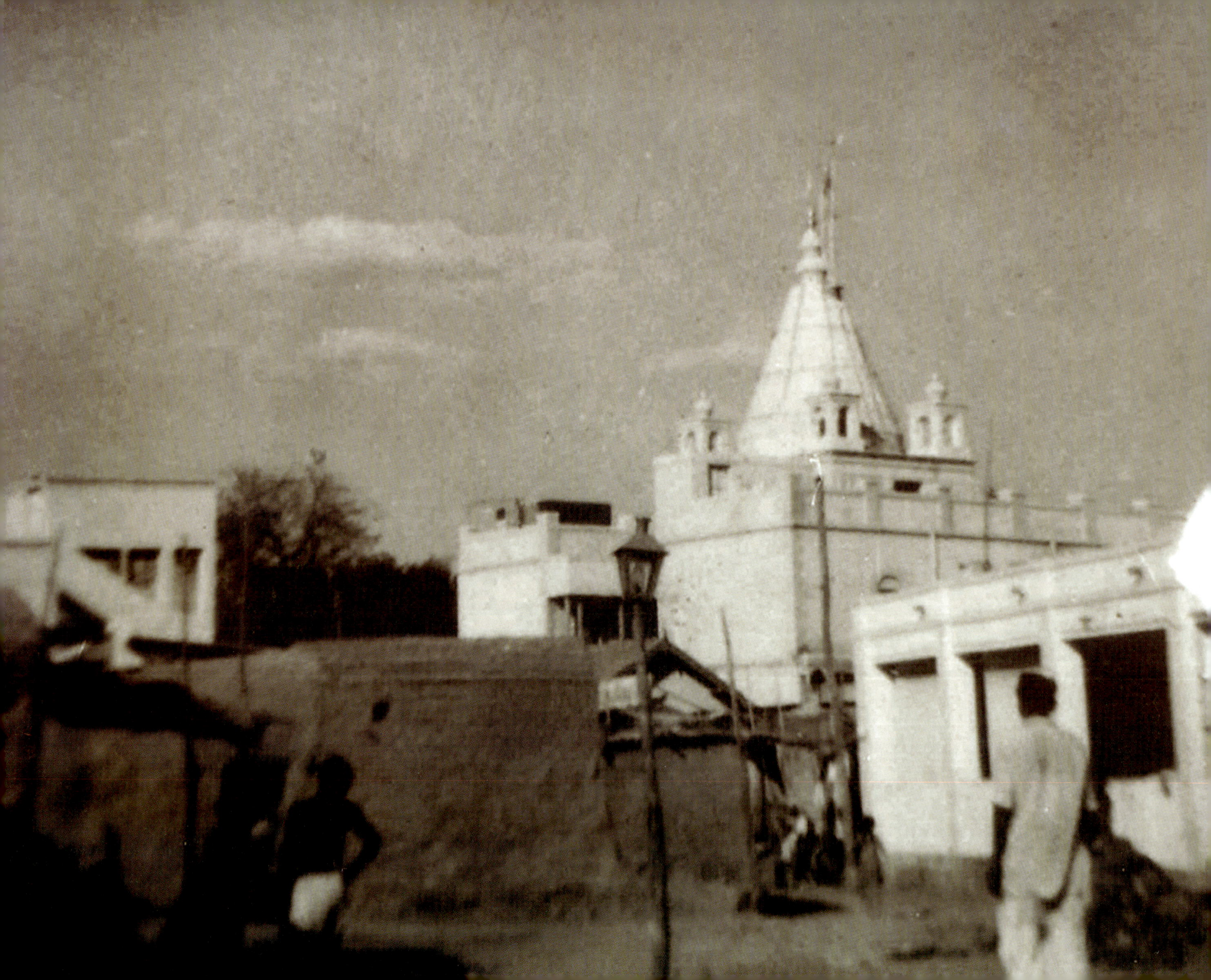

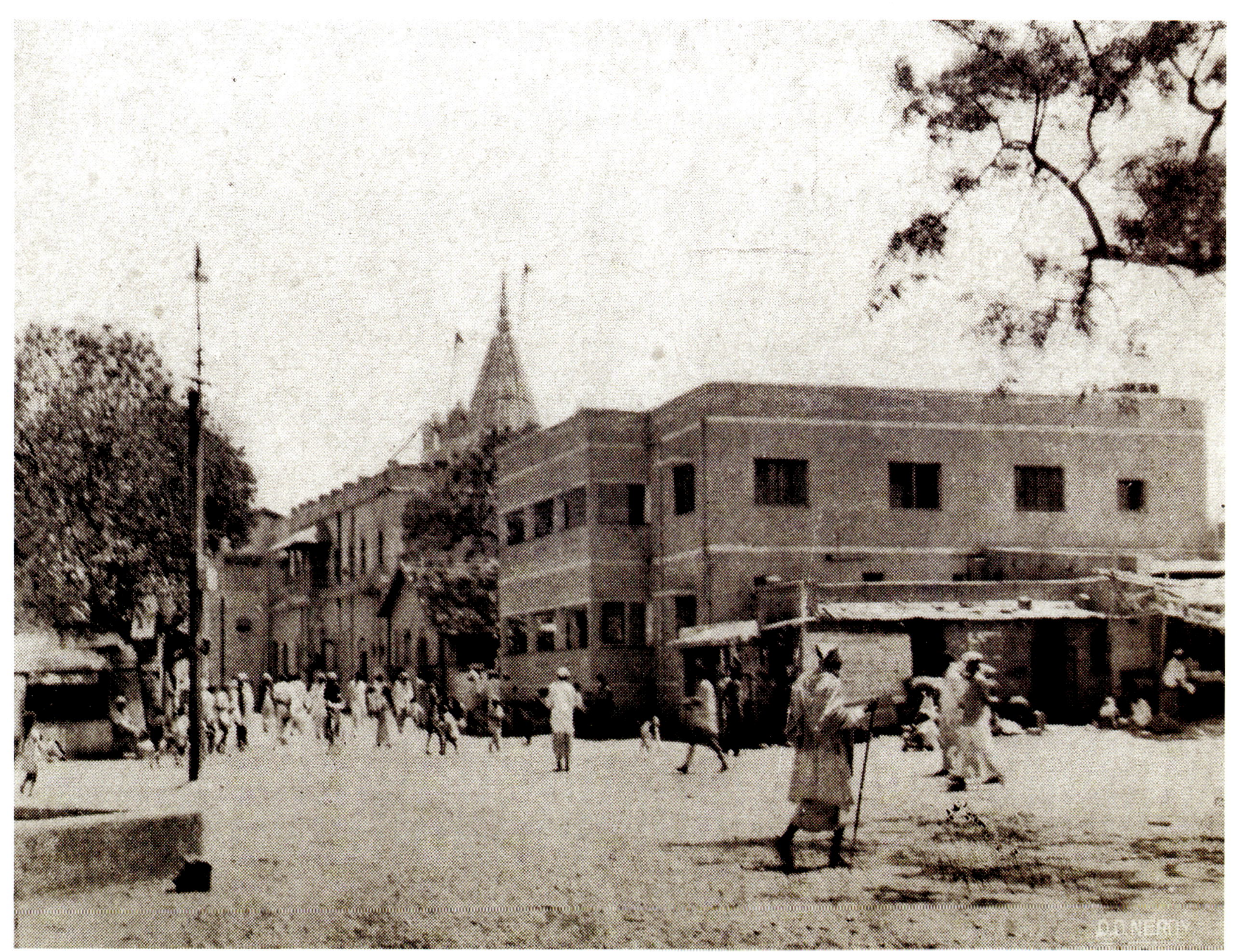

The neighbourhood construction is a barometer of congestion in Shirdi.

← Samadhi Mandir at different stages of development.

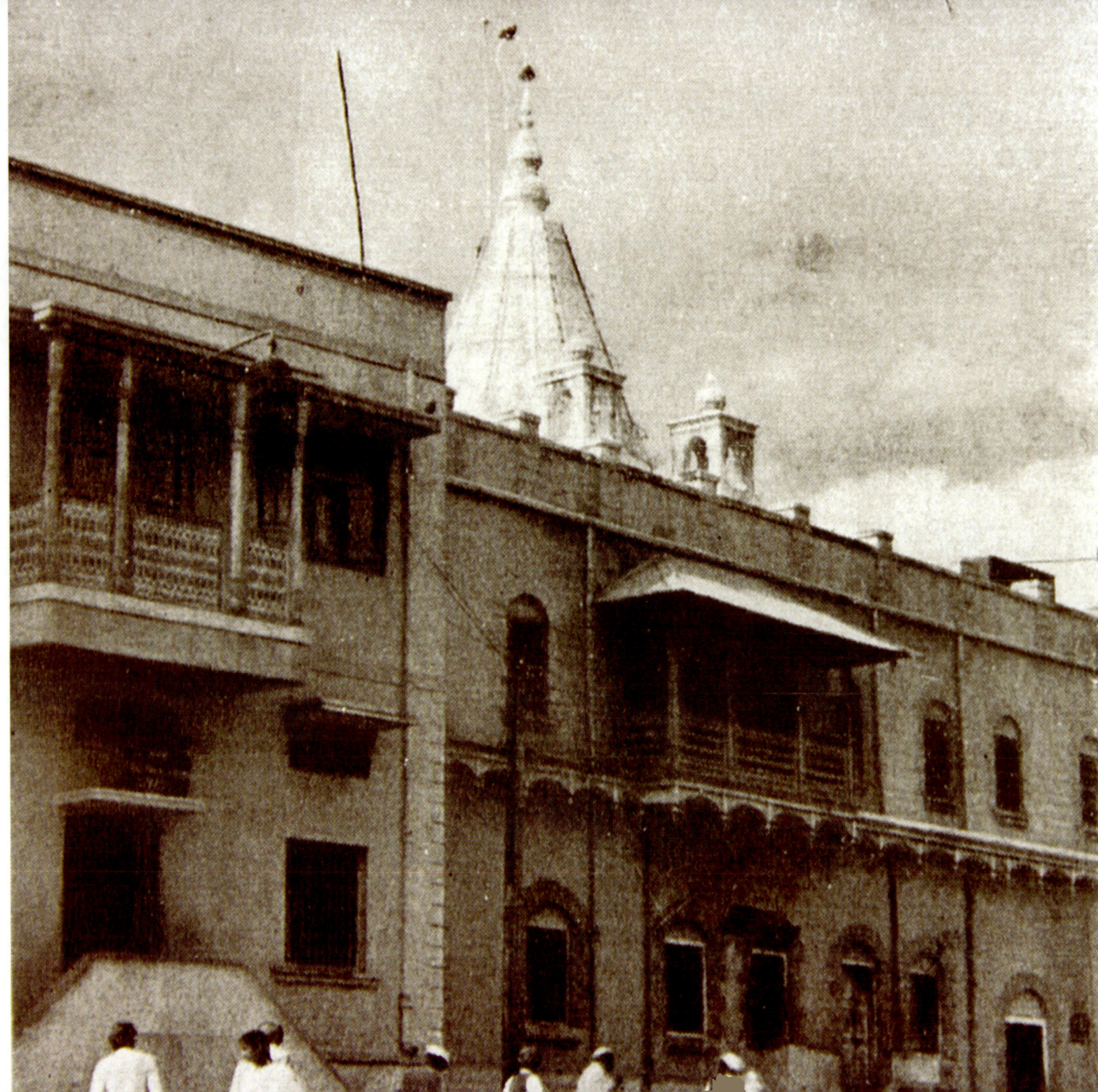

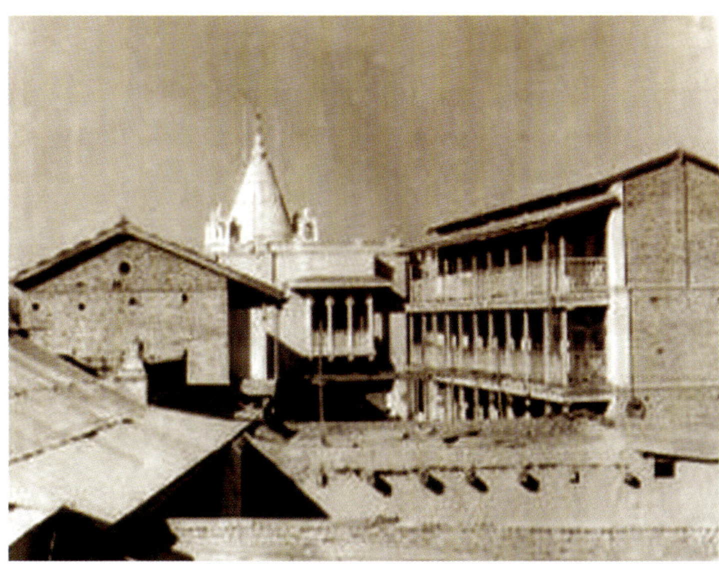

Samadhi Mandir and near by construction

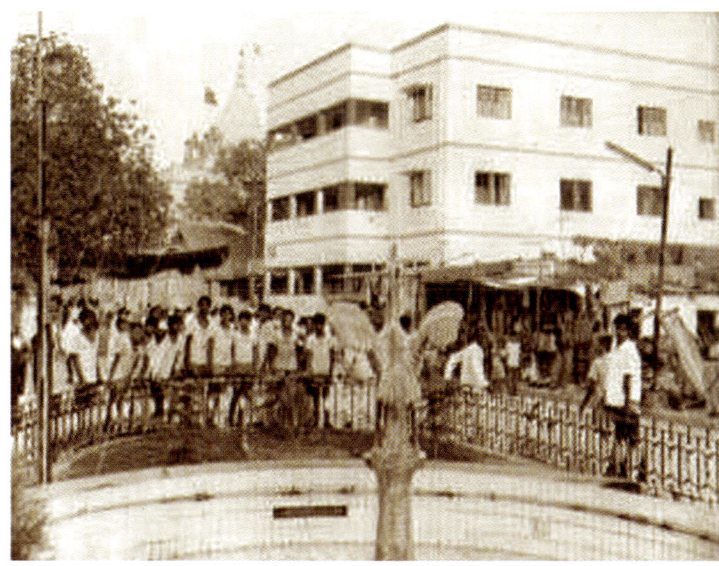

Fountain near Samadhi Mandir *(1975)*

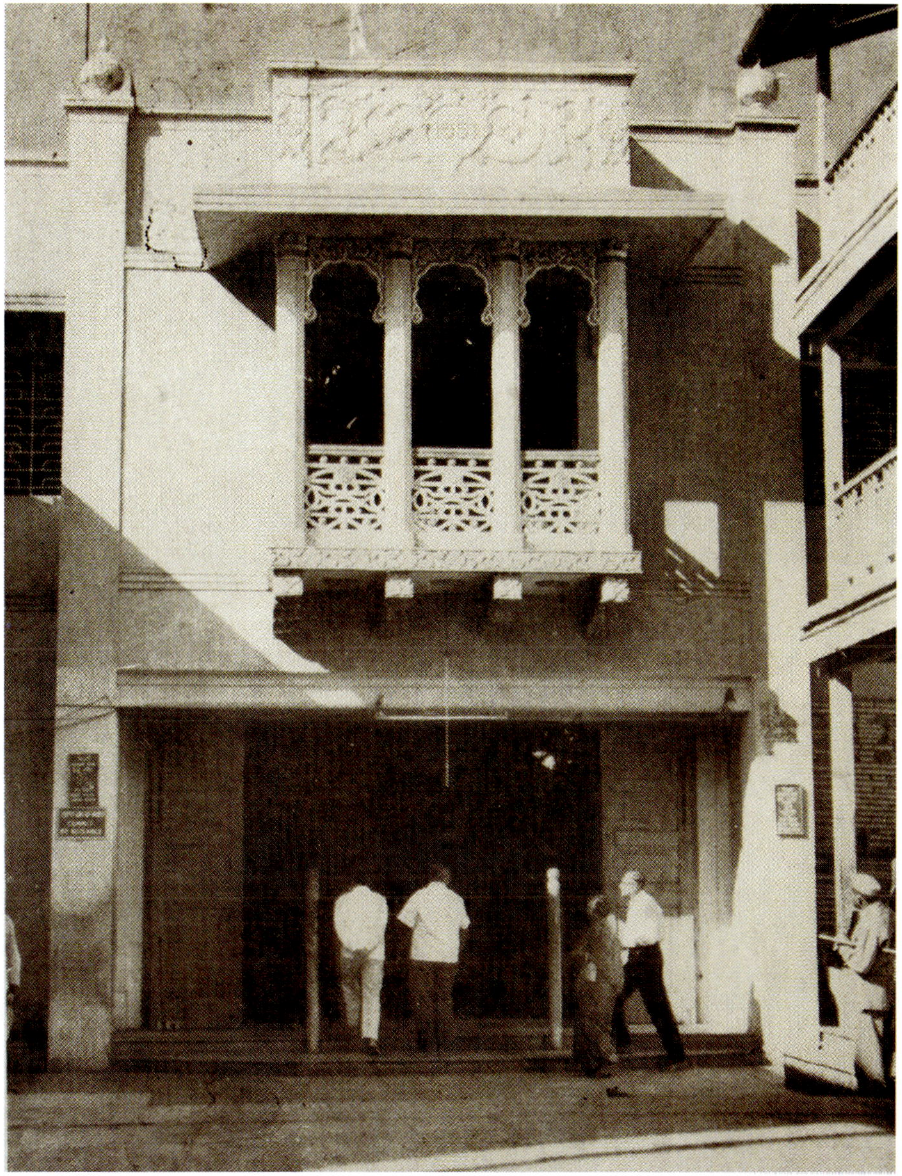

Wooden door entrance which was used to enter Samadhi Mandir before the construction of the Sabha Mandap. *(1975)*

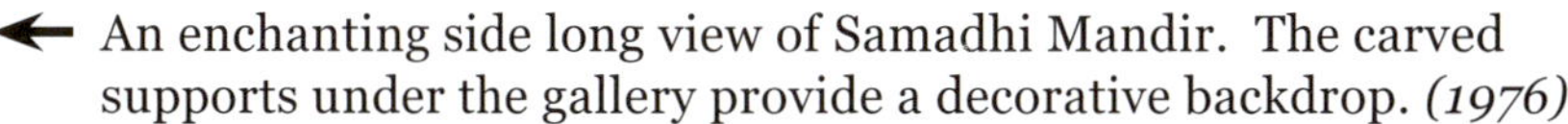

← An enchanting side long view of Samadhi Mandir. The carved supports under the gallery provide a decorative backdrop. *(1976)*

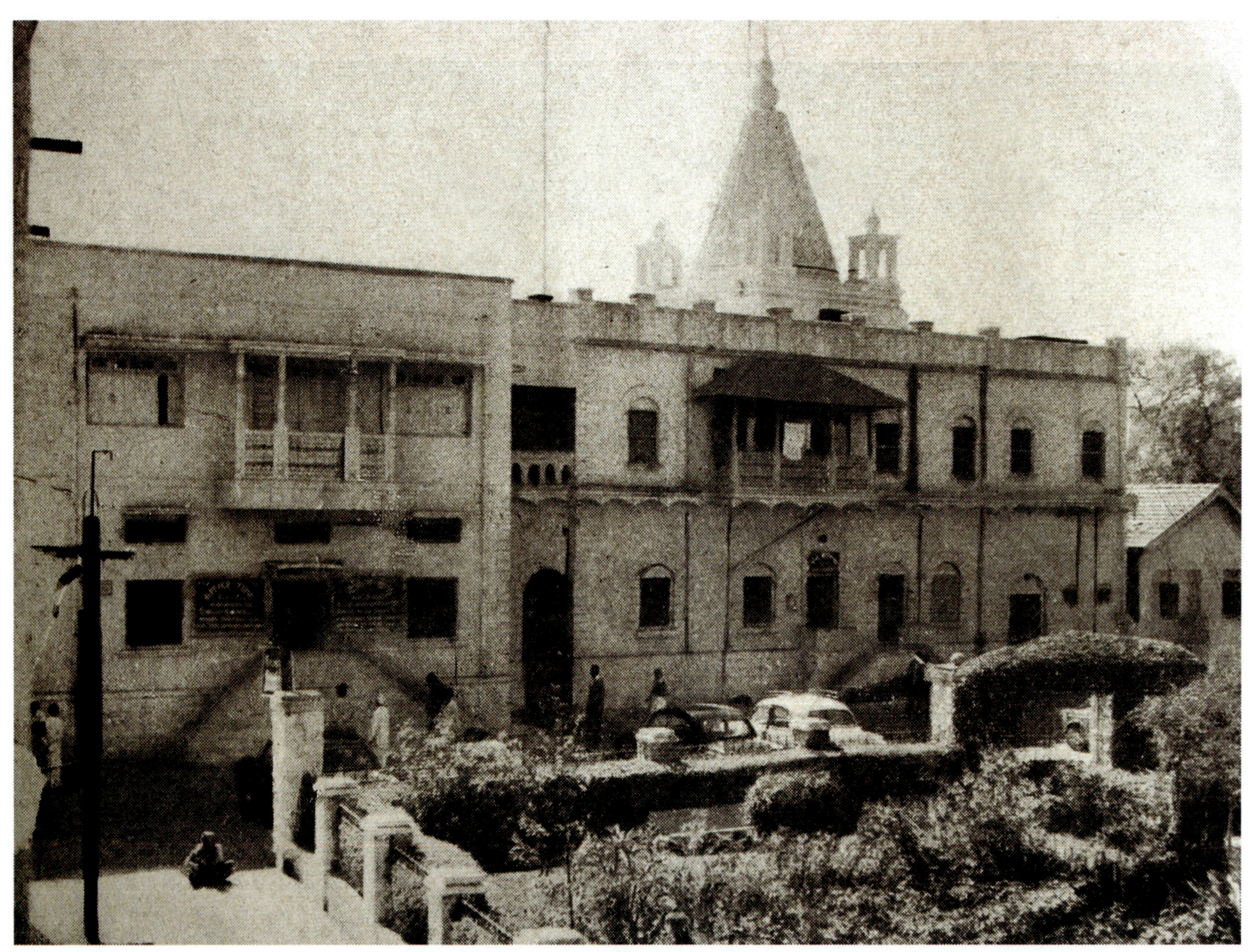

Samadhi Mandir from across the garden. The adjoining building housed the administrative network of the Sansthan. The cars parked in front of the Mandir complex reflect the uncongested state of Shirdi; a sight quite unimaginable now. *(1975)*

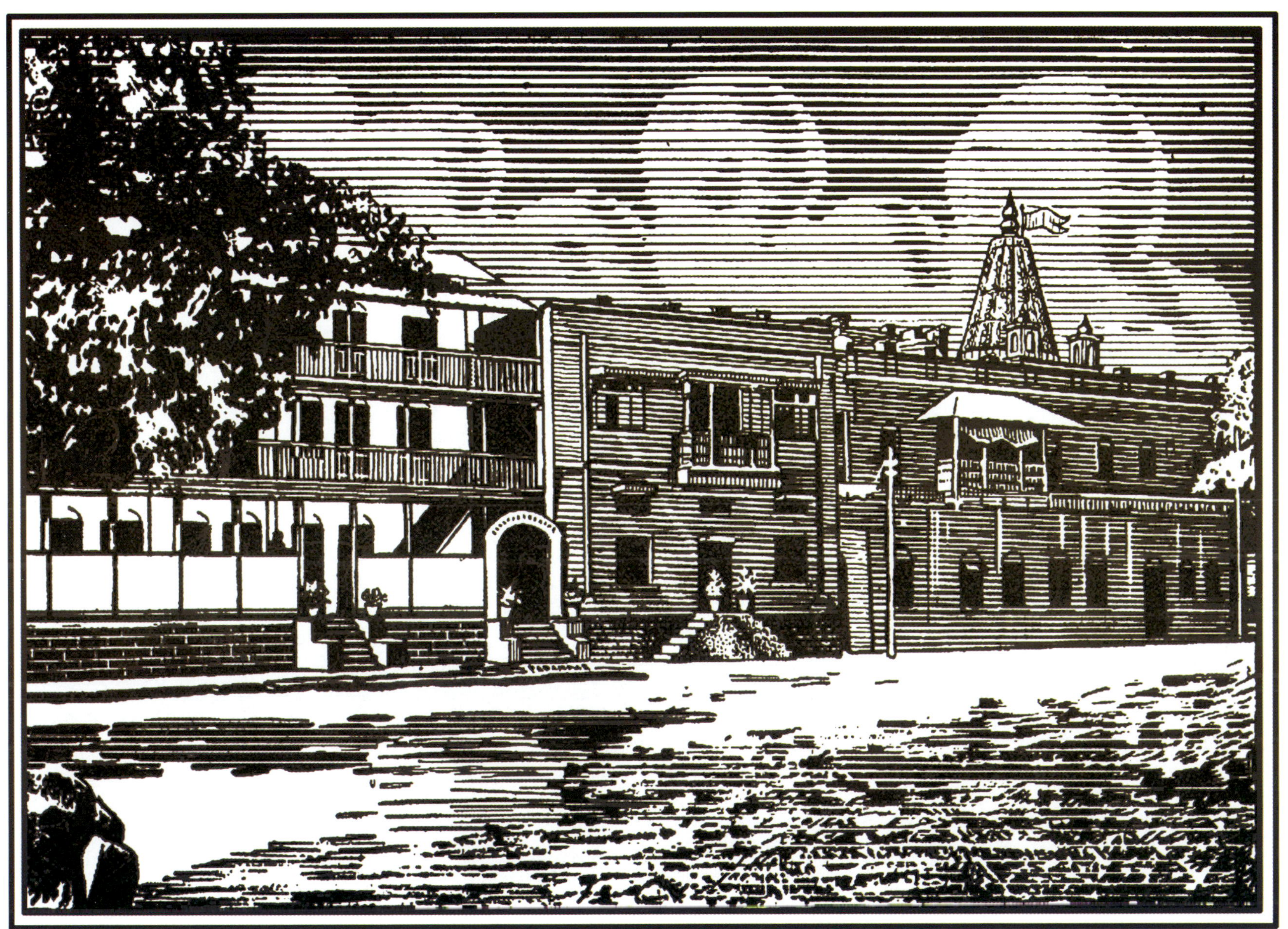

A rare wood cut print artwork of Samadhi Mandir *(1970)*

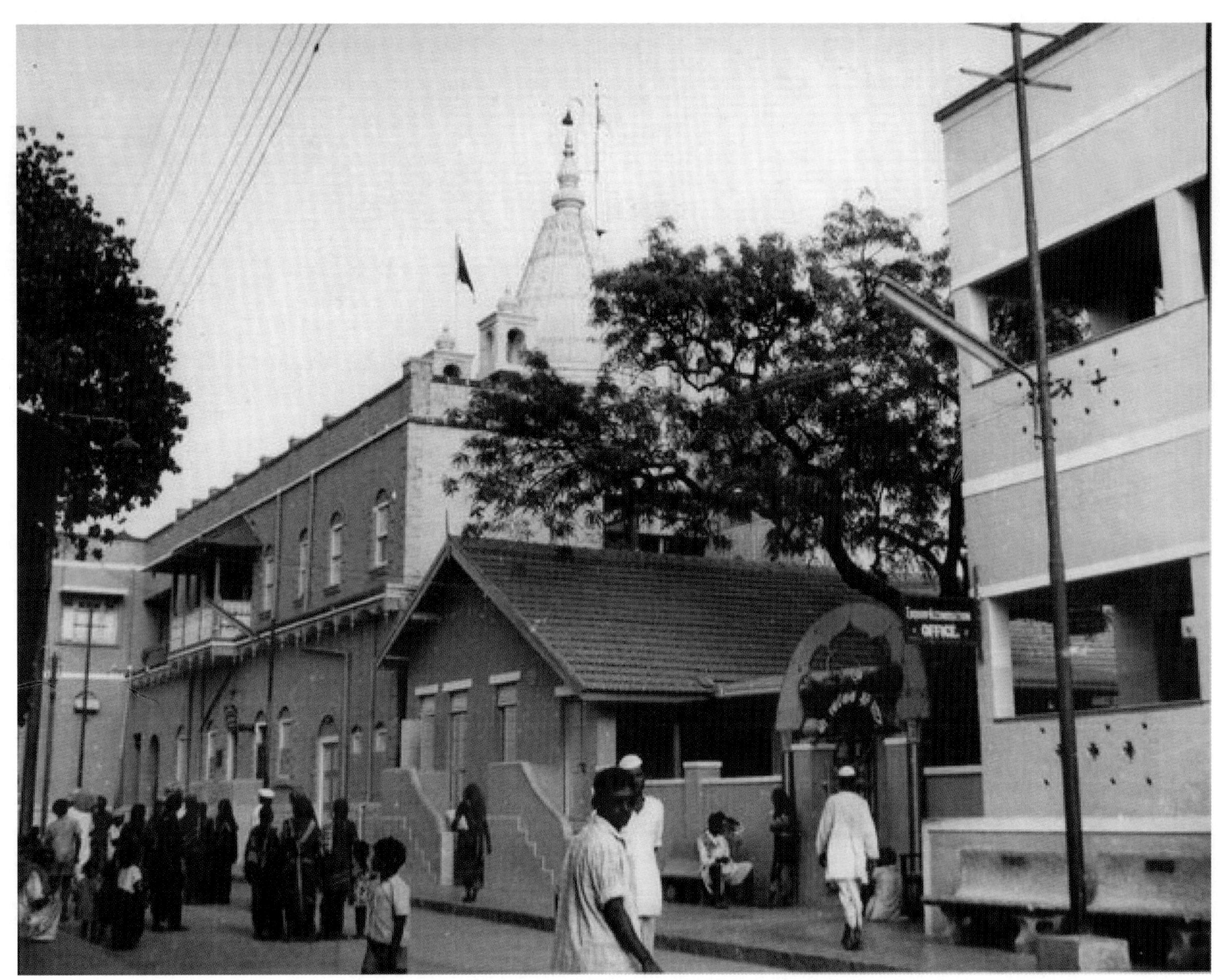

Sathewada with an inclined shed, built by Shri Hari Vinayak Sathe for accomodation of devotees can be seen standing between Samadhi Mandir and Gurusthan's neem tree. *(1980)*

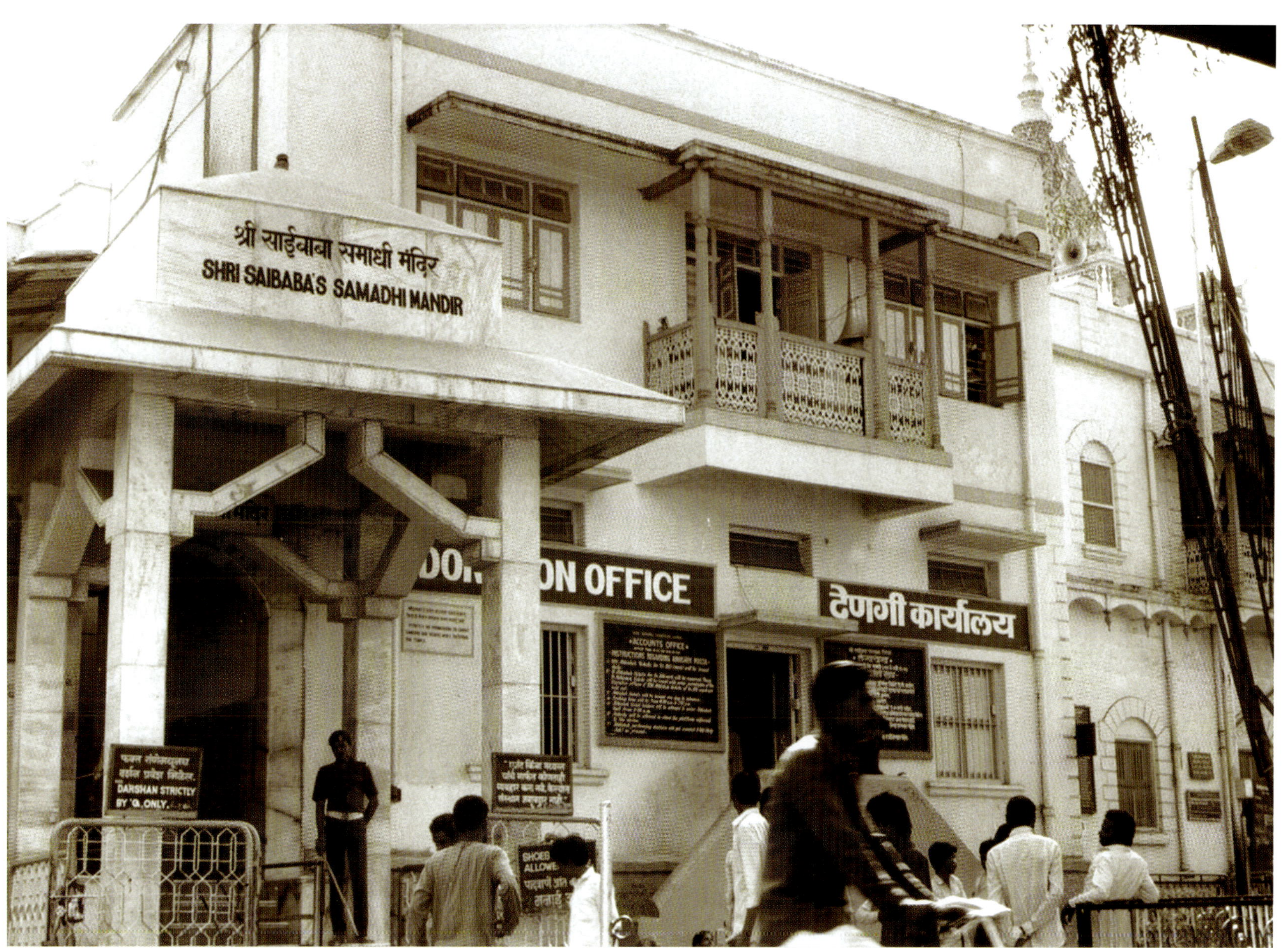

Samadhi Mandir surrounded by the administrative support network. A security guard stands at the main entrance.

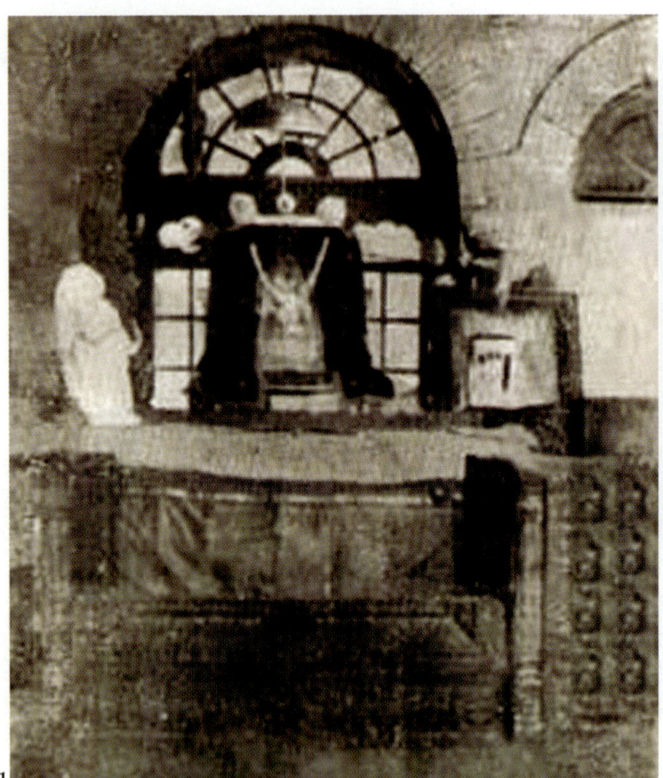
1

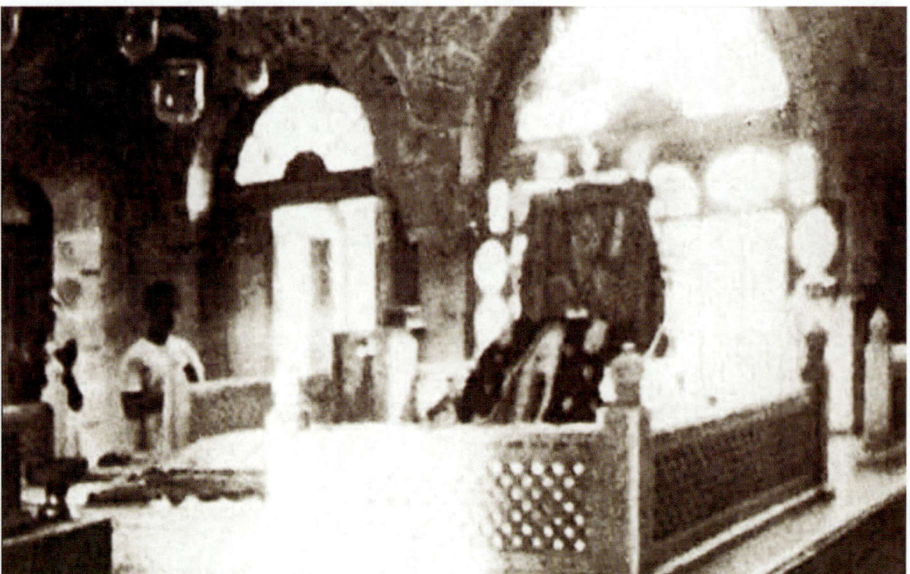
2

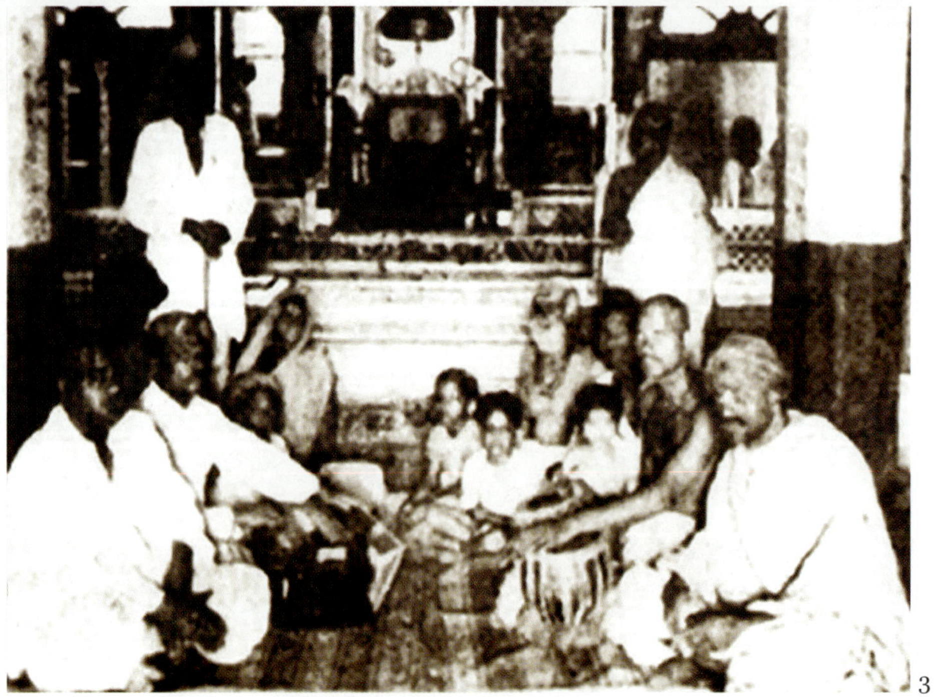
3

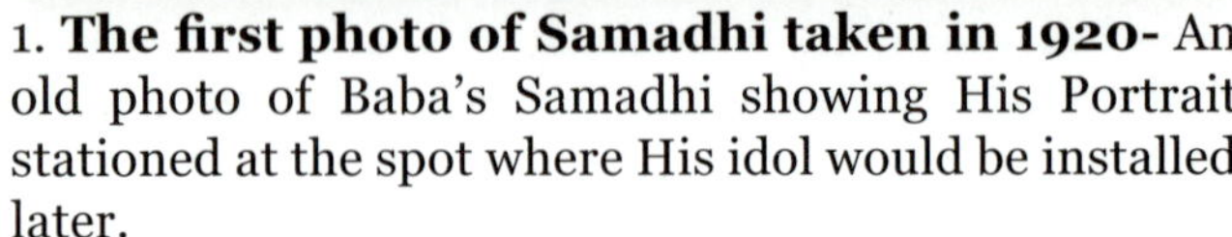

1. **The first photo of Samadhi taken in 1920-** An old photo of Baba's Samadhi showing His Portrait stationed at the spot where His idol would be installed later.

2. Samadhi after the installation of marble railing *(1926)*. Baba's Samadhi can now be seen surrounded with a marble latticework boundary.

3. Devotees offering devotional songs at the Samadhi.

4. Baba's original photograph in an ornate silver frame is placed on a silver throne *(sinhasan)*. Here, Baba is seen sitting on a stone. The silver sinhasan is embossed with peacocks and apsaras on either side. There is a silver umbrella above the photograph. A fly-whisk *(chowri)* with a silver handle is placed in front of it. Baba's caparisoned photo is festooned with garlands. A floral sheet is spread over the Samadhi.

4 →

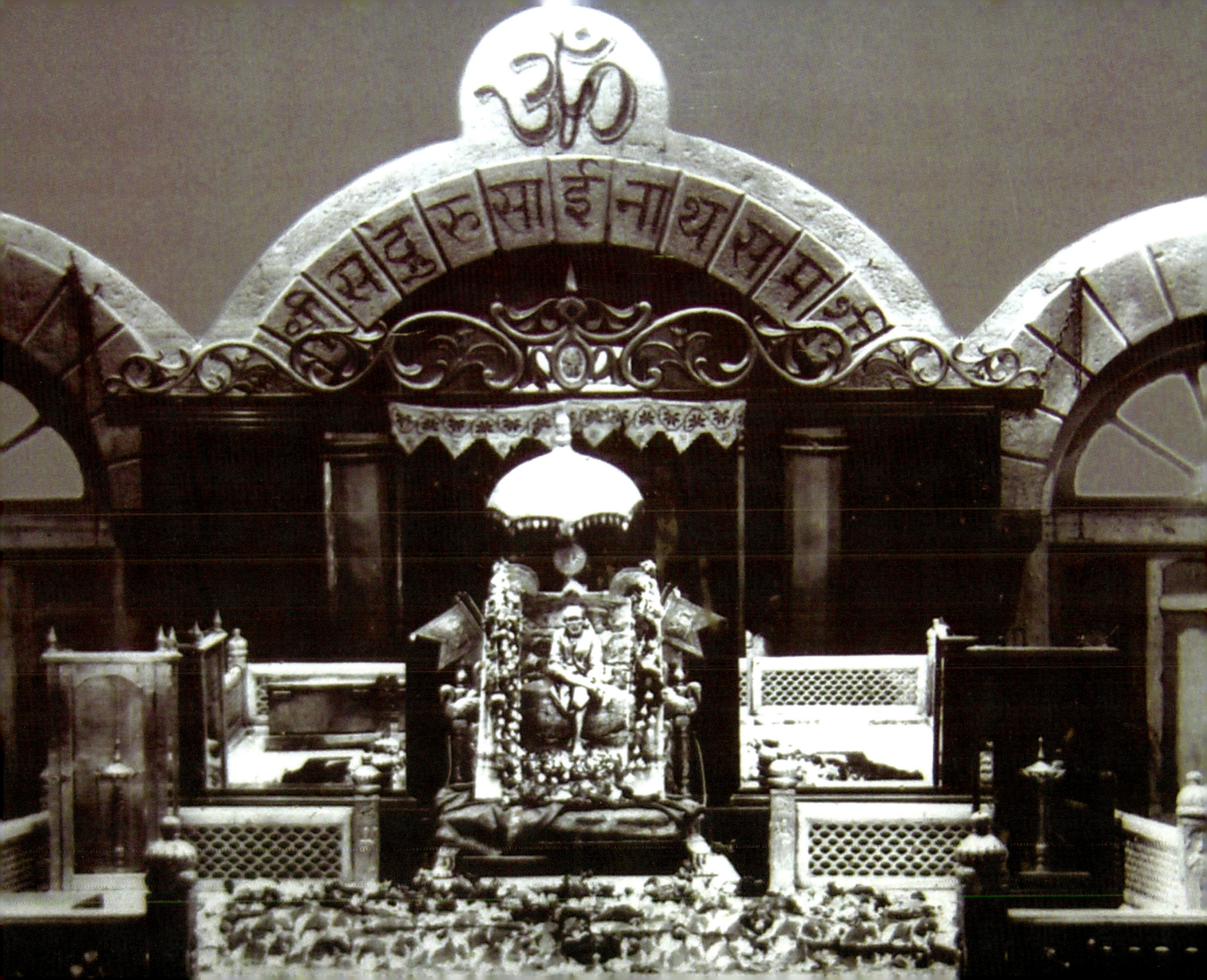
ॐ
श्री सद्गुरु साईनाथ

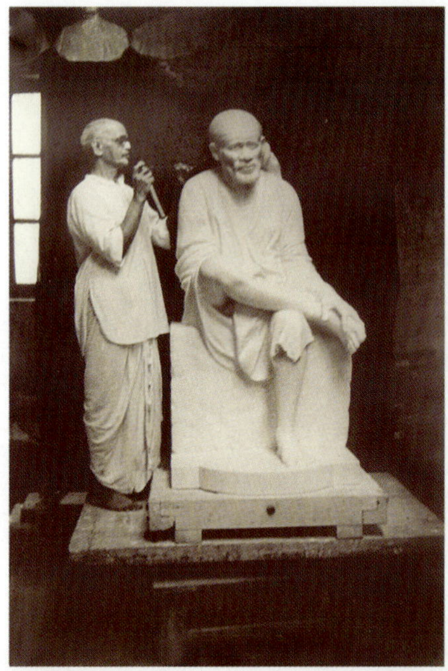

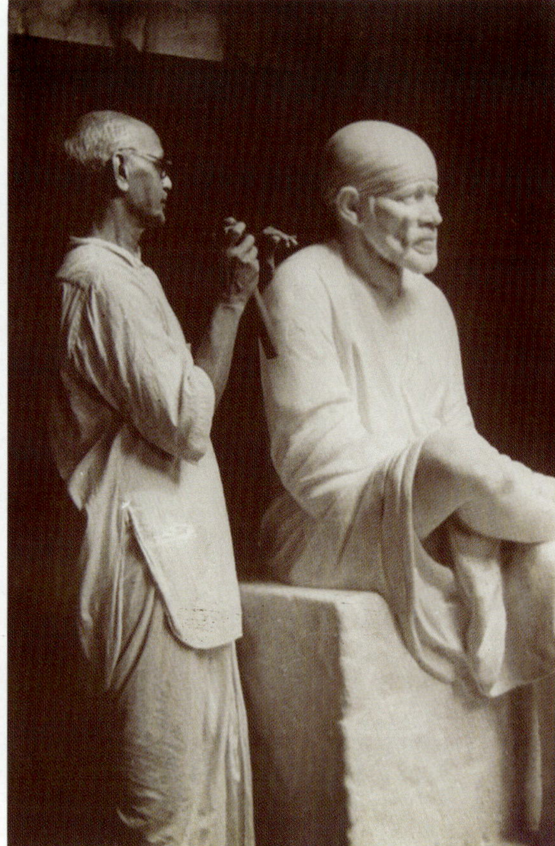

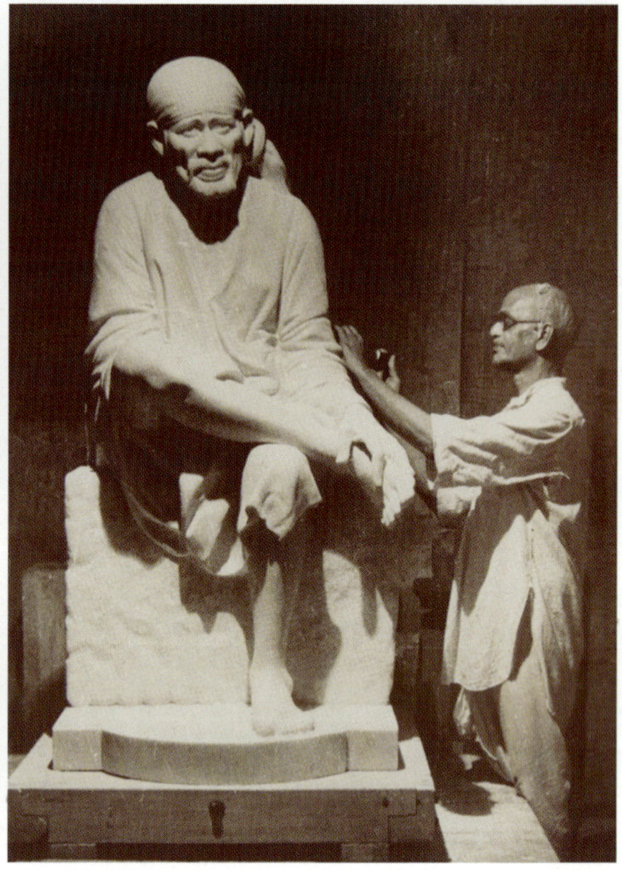

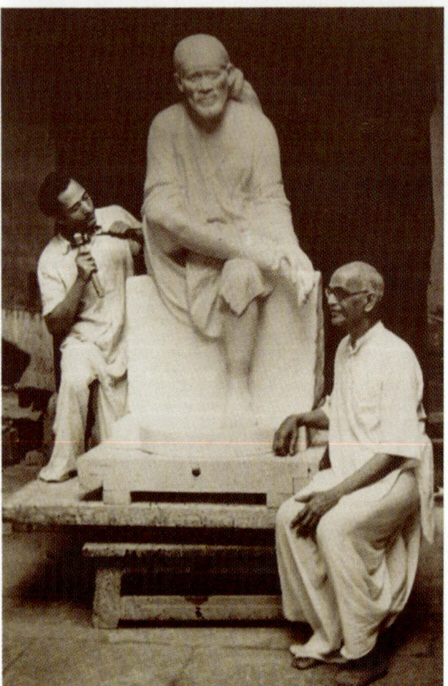

Above : Shri Balaji Vasant Rao Talim in his studio sculpting Baba's Idol. The five and a half feet statue was carved out of single marble block costing Rs. 22,000 in the year 1952. The astonishingly life like Idol reflecting Baba's stone pose was installed on October 7, 1954. The idol faces east and the face is tilted towards Ishanya disha (north-east).

Balaji graduated from J.J. School of Art, Mumbai and established 'Talim Art Studio' in 1918. The British appreciated his work and assigned him numerous prestigious assignments. At the age of 82, on 25th December 1970, Talim breathed his last.

Opposite page : On October 7, 1954, the idol was installed next to the western wall, on the platform behind Baba's Samadhi. →

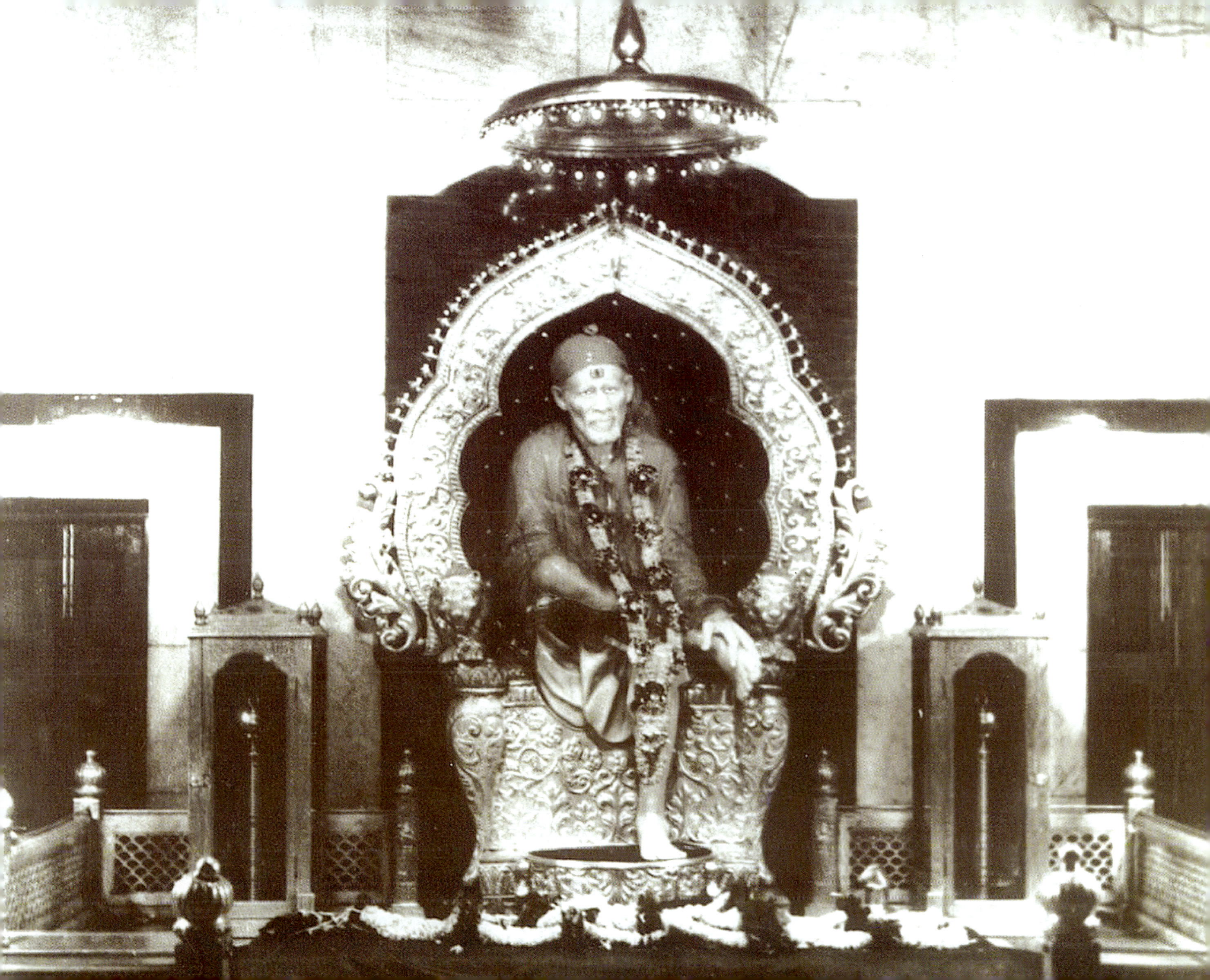

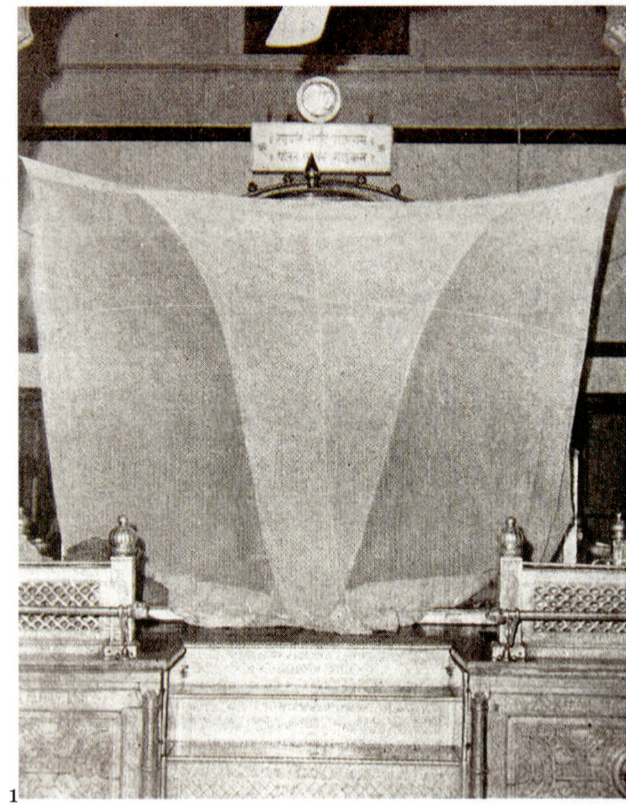
1

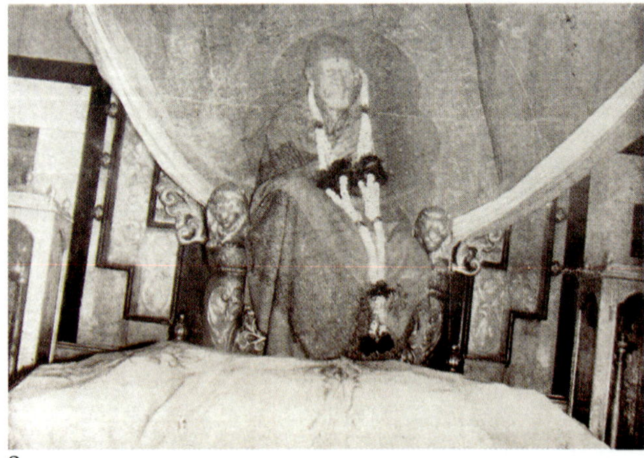
2

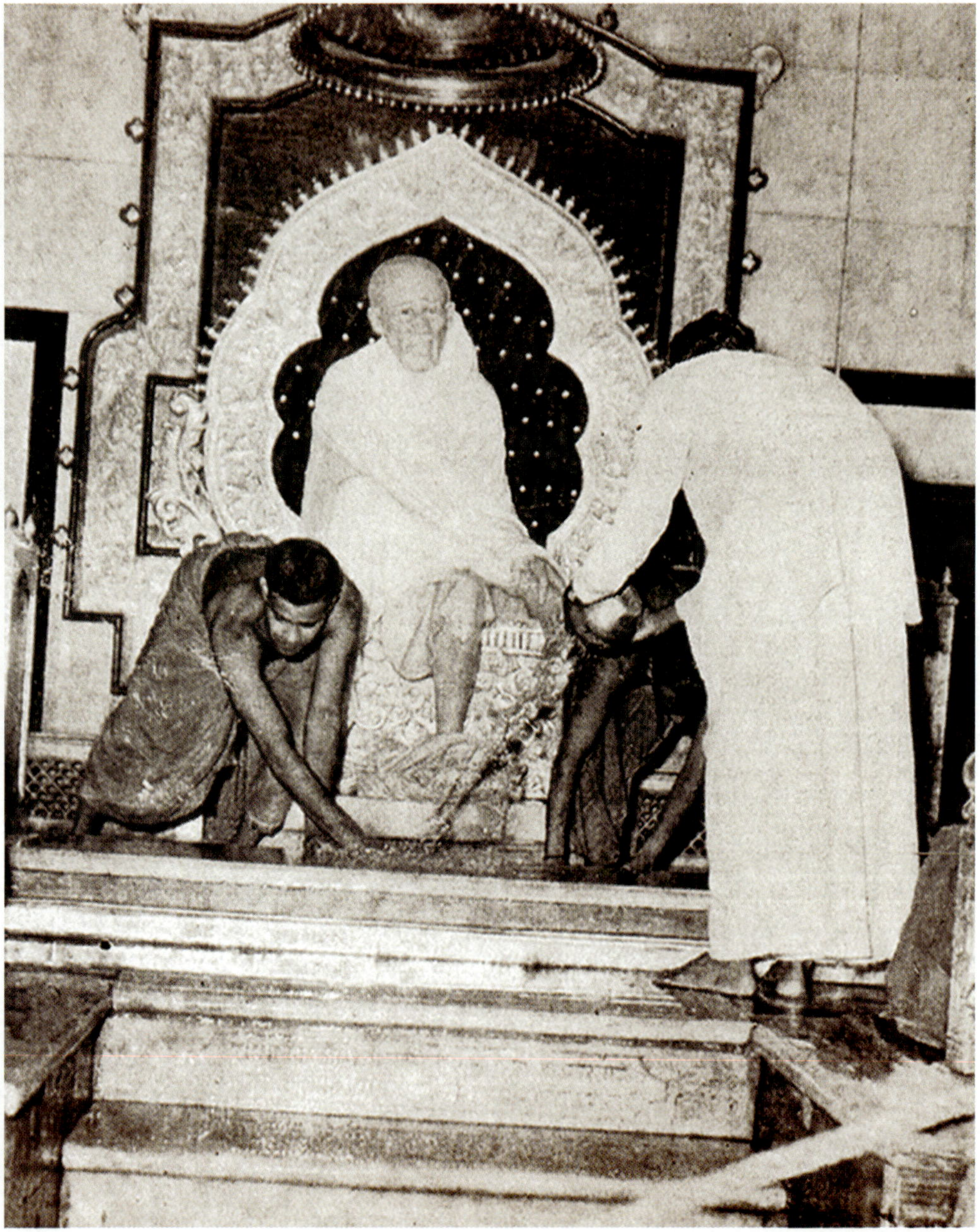

3

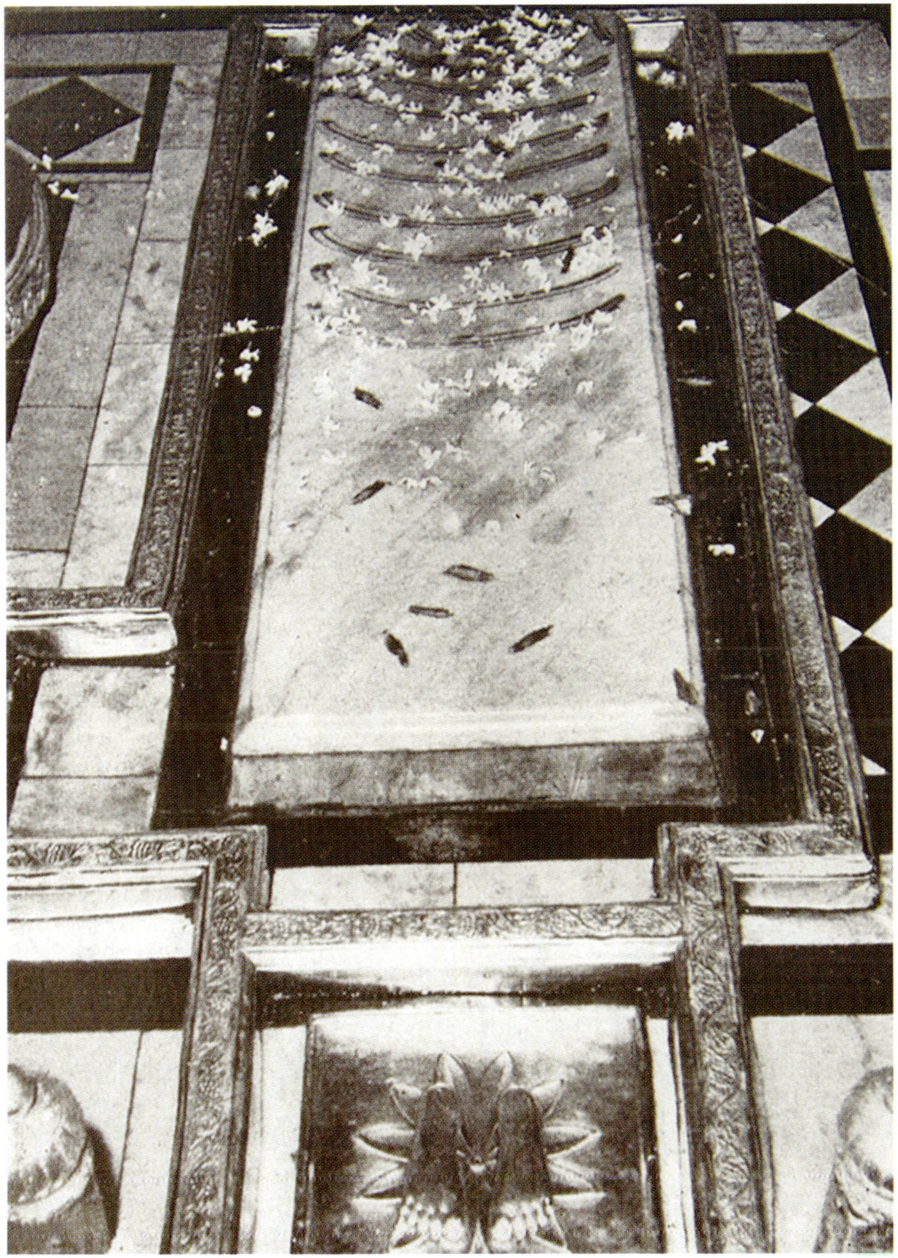

4

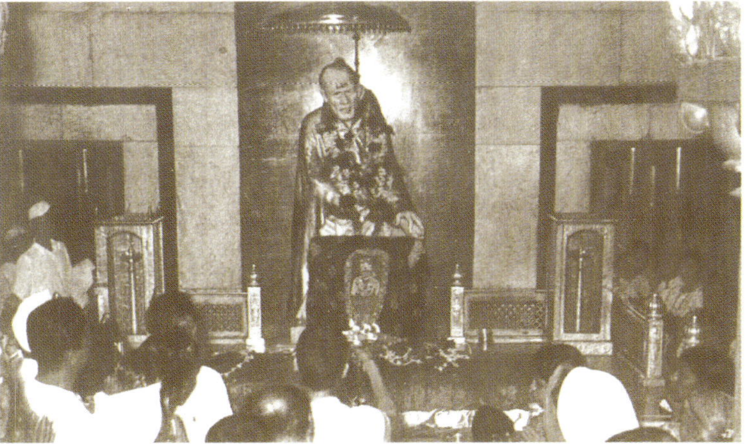

5

Baba's daily routine in different stages:

1. Baba's idol and Samadhi are cocooned inside a mosquito net.
2. Early morning, the net is lifted.
3. The Samadhi is uncovered and Baba's idol is made ready for the ritual bath.
4. Baba's Samadhi is smeared with the fragrant ashtagandha paste and flower petals are showered on it after the bath. The etched silver feet sparkle in the foreground.
5. Fresh clothes and garlands are draped over Baba's idol and the morning aarti is offered to His Grace.

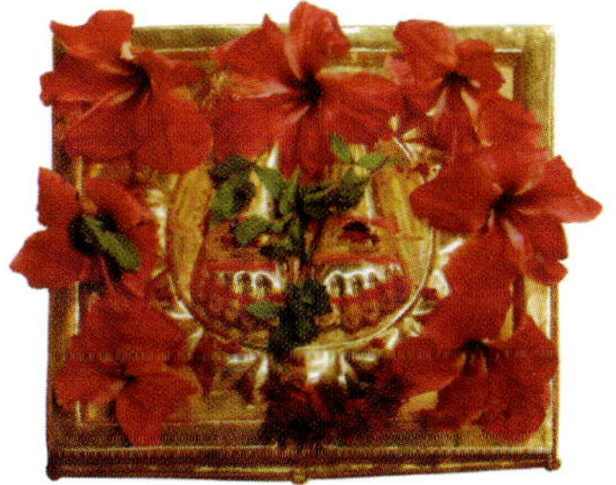

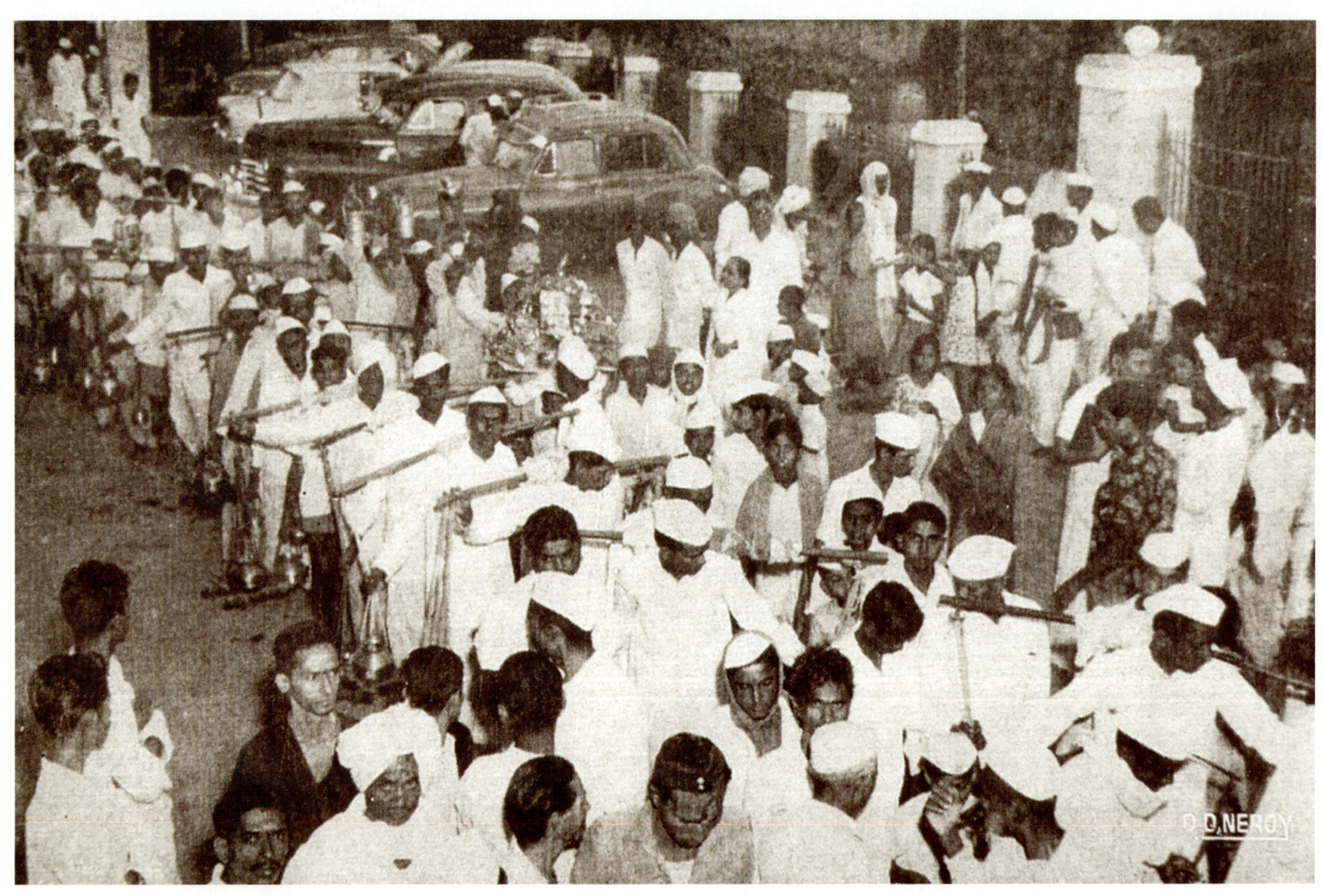

Devotees carry holy water of river Godavari in pitchers hung on bamboo poles. The water is offered for Baba's bathing ritual.

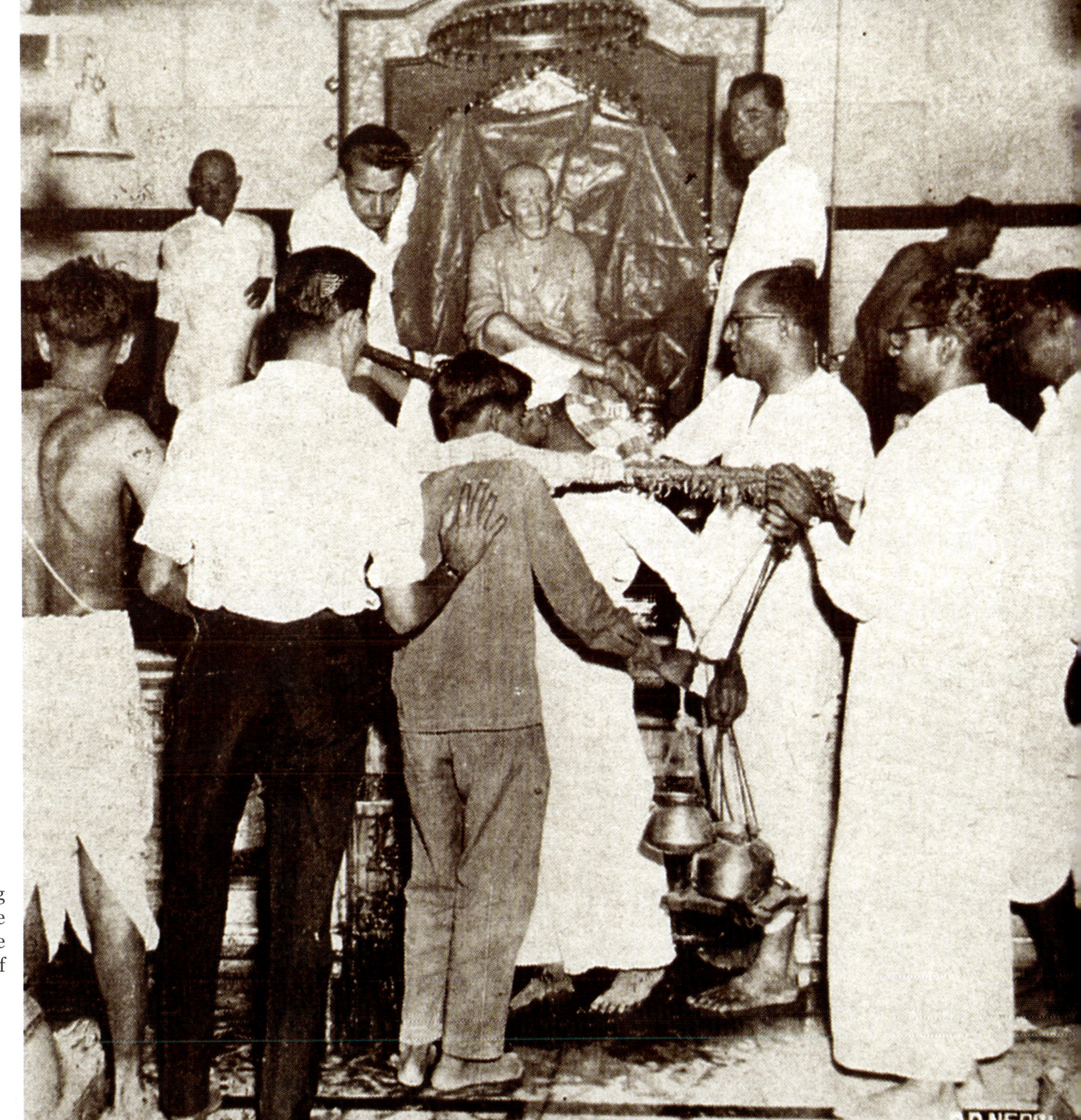

The Godavari water being gathered for Baba's bath. The velvet seat of Baba's throne is protected by a waterproof sheet draped over it. *(1974)*

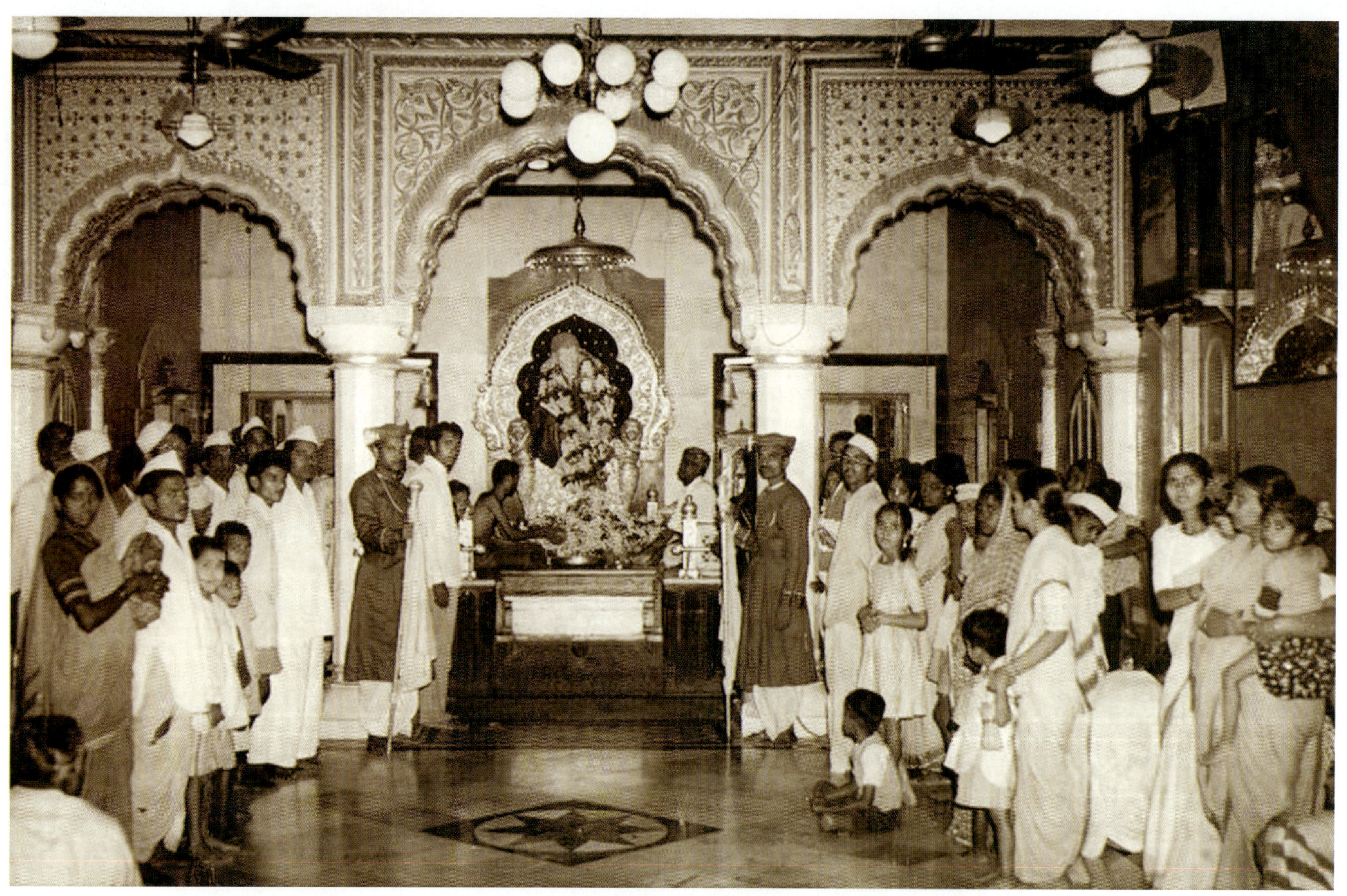

A wide angle view of the Samadhi and the idol presiding over it. The chopdars, bearing a silver staff each, flank the two pillars in the hall. The chandeliers suspended from the ceiling highlight the starred pattern on the floor. *(1970)*

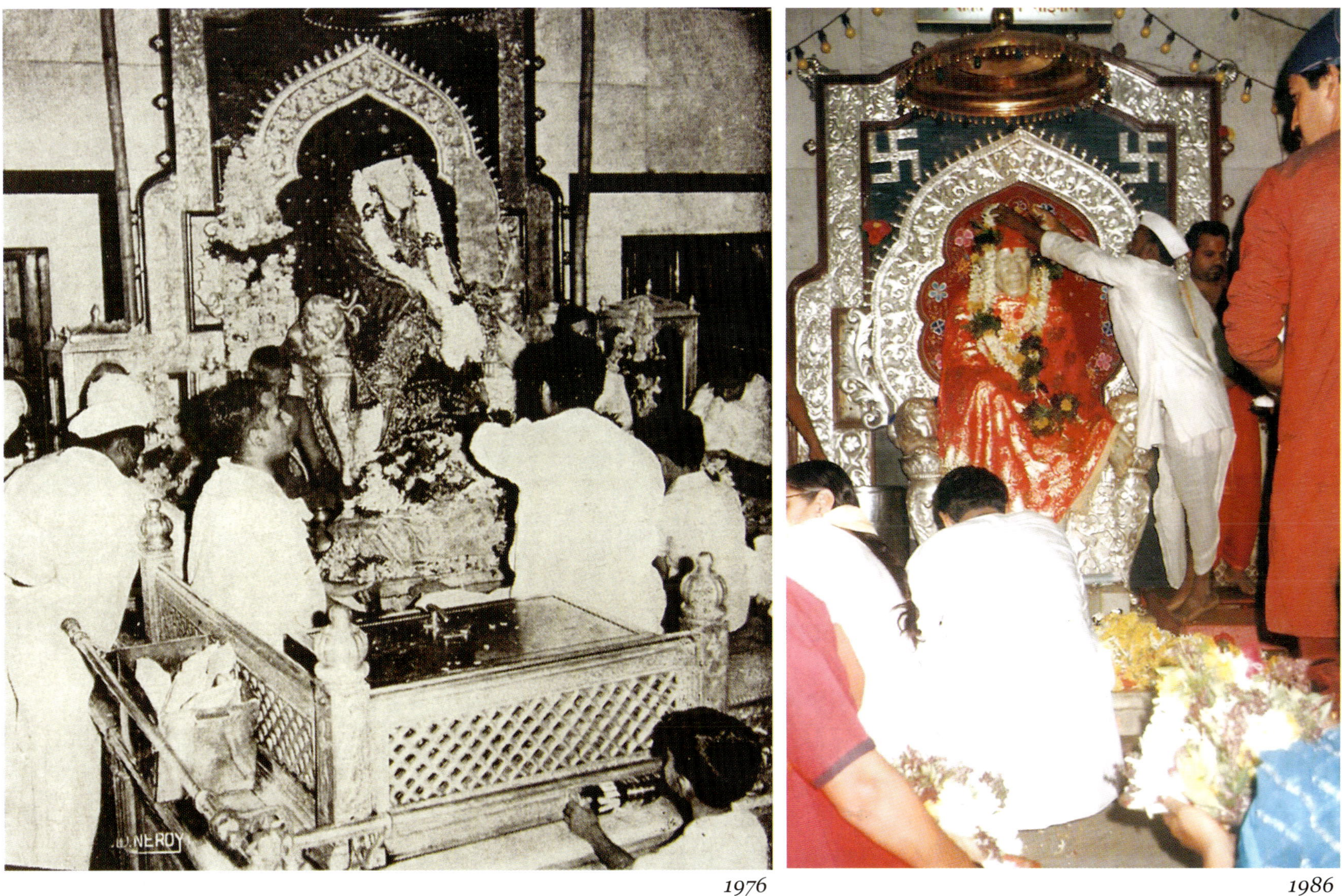

1976 *1986*

Baba's idol is considered a living embodiment of the Immortal Soul Himself. Physical proximity to the idol provides solace and succour to the distressed. These two pictures show glimpses of the time when devotees actually clambered up to the idol, touched it and performed rituals. The rising throngs now have restricted access to the marble enclosure.

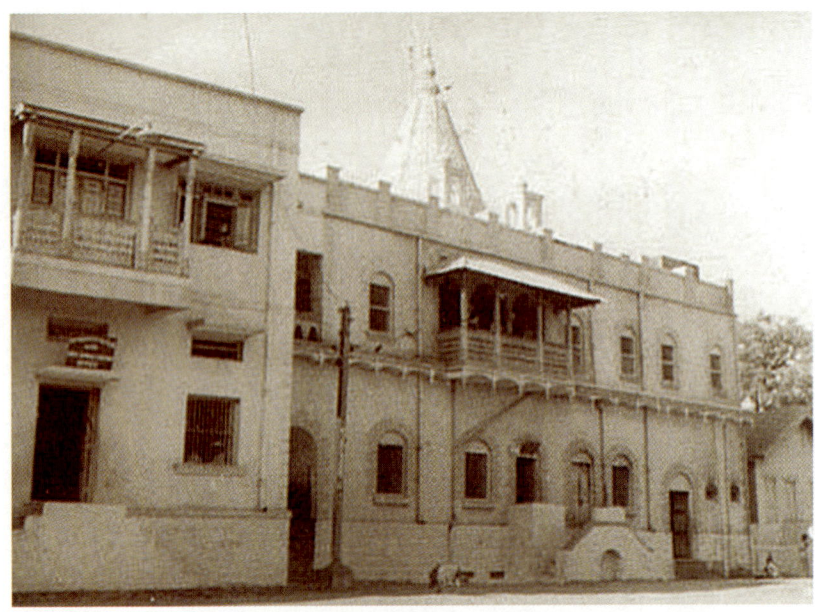

Samadhi Mandir from the northern side *(1975)*

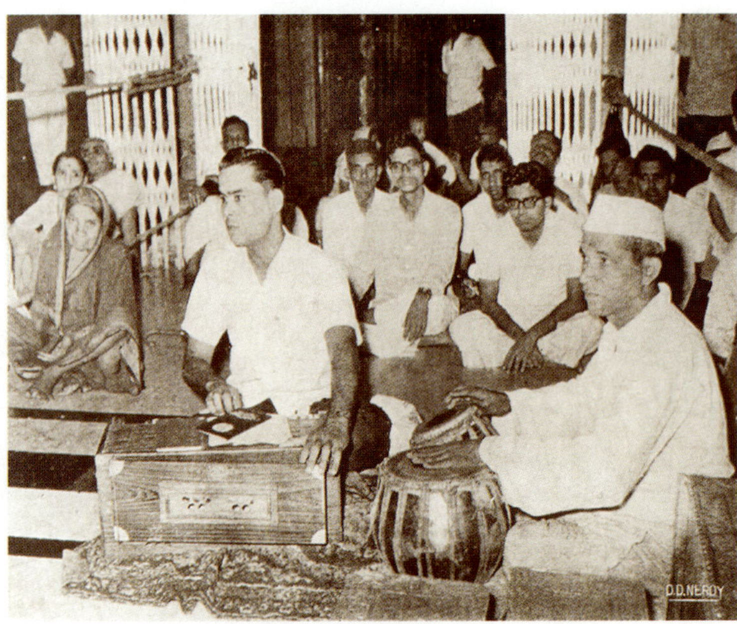

Devotees singing hymns. *(1976)*

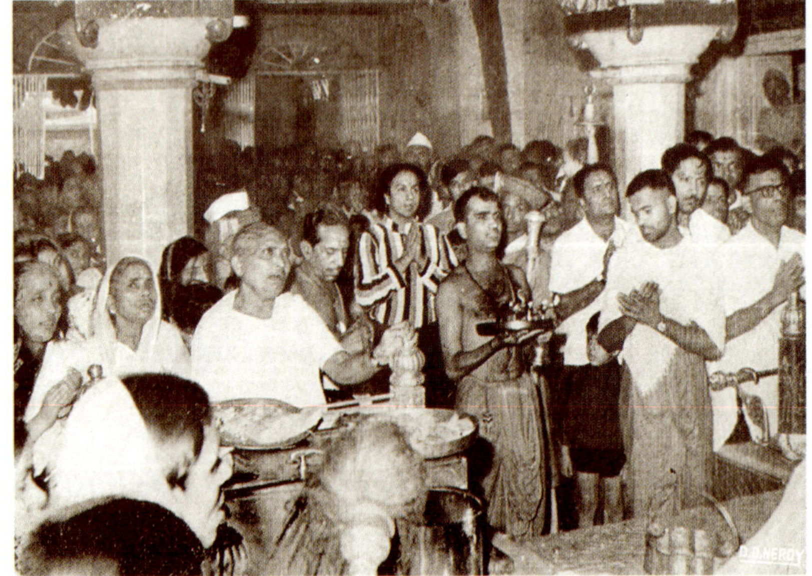

Panchaarti with lights and camphor being waved around Baba. *(1975)*

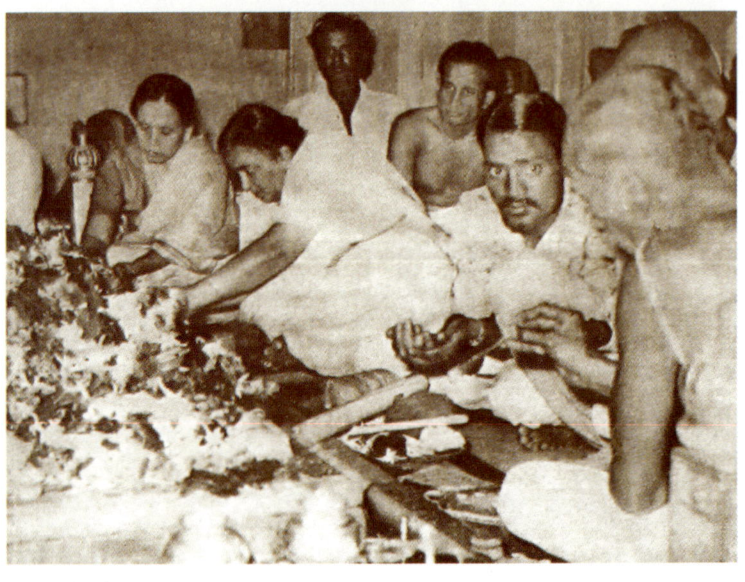

Religious rituals being performed at the Samadhi. *(1976)*

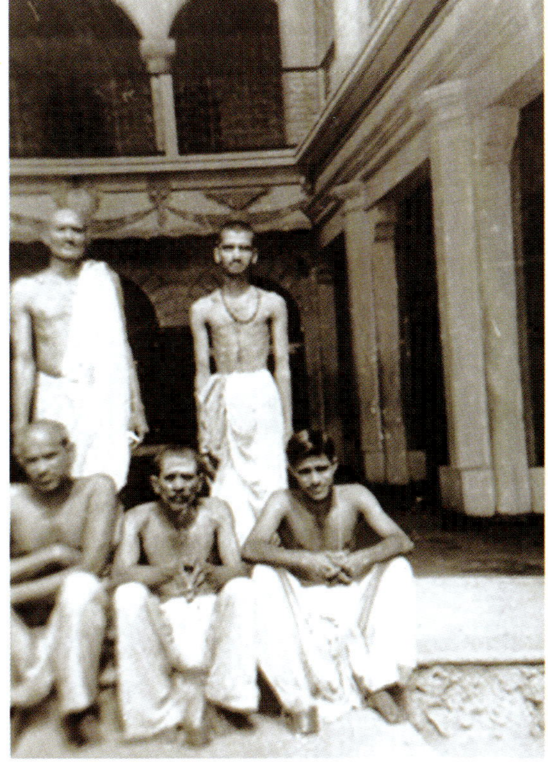

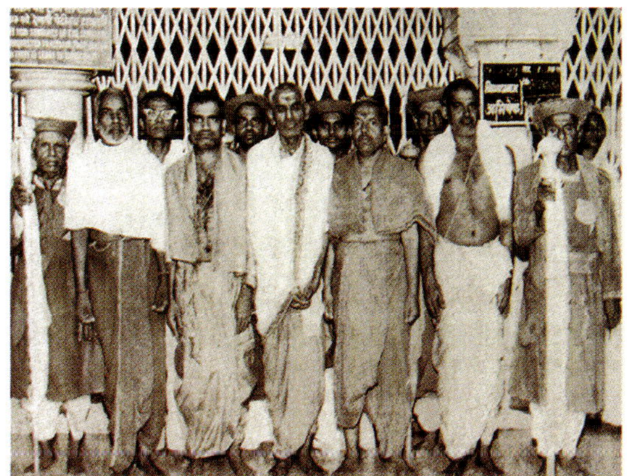

Priests and chopdars of Samadhi Mandir in traditional garb outside the entrance.

A profile view of Baba on His magnificent silver throne. A lion carved out of silver sits next to Baba, accompanying Baba in His silent contemplation. →

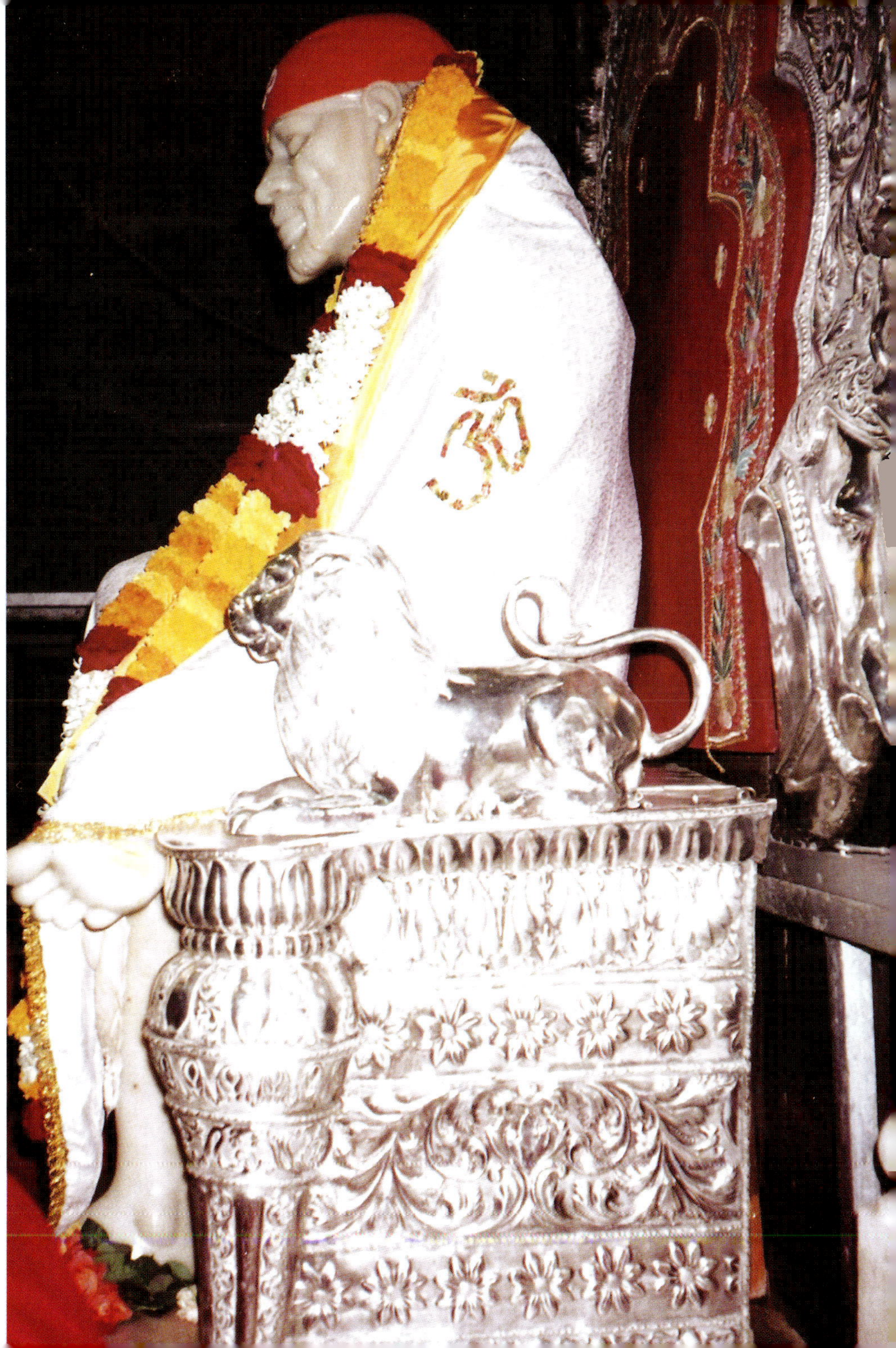

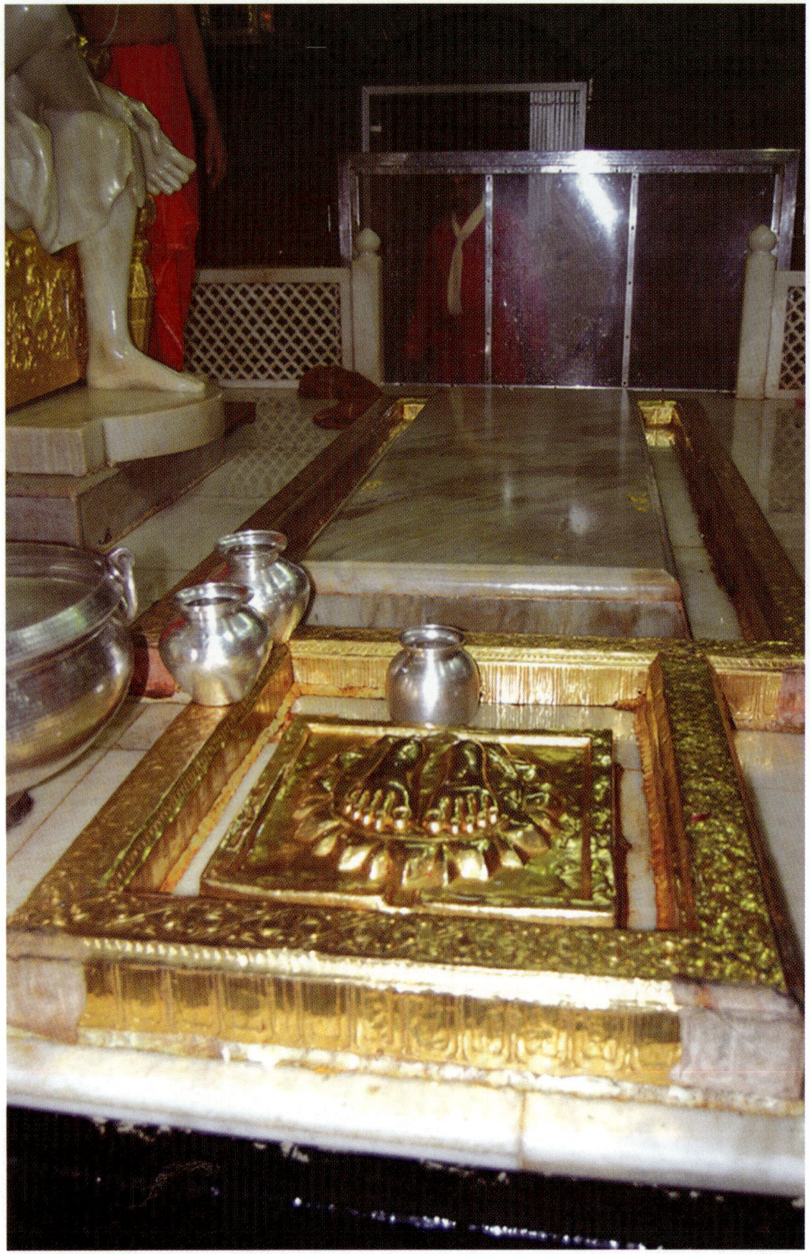

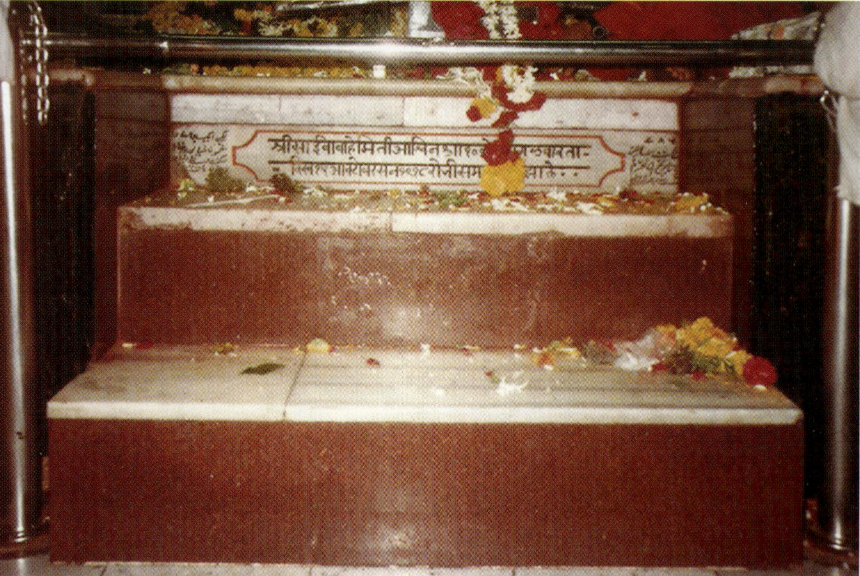

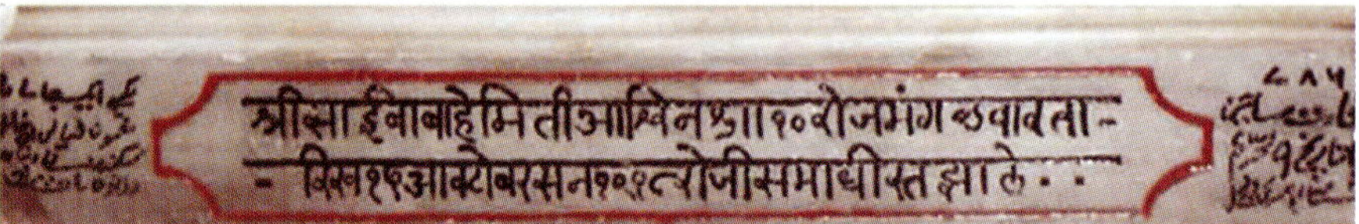

Three steps lead to this altar. On the third step, a Marathi inscription is etched. The Marathi inscription visible at the base of the raised altar, informs all about the time and date of Baba's Mahasamadhi. Inscriptions on either side are etched in Urdu.
(Roughly translated) In the month of *Ashwin Sudh*, tenth day, on Tuesday, October 15, 1918, Shri Sai Baba took Mahasamadhi.

← The Samadhi is 6 ft long and 2 ft wide. Surrounding it is an altar 9 ft by 9 ft in dimensions, with a height of 3 ft.

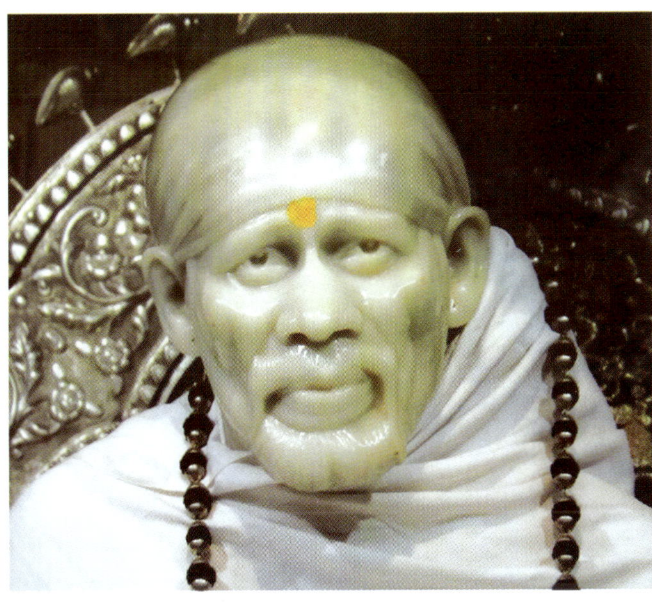

Baba being readied for the morning bathing ritual. The idol is draped by a simple white sheet and Baba's only ornament is a long rosary of "*Rudraksha*" beads where every seed is held encased in silver crescents on top and bottom. Baba's headgear (the patka) is also set aside before the commencement of the daily morning bath. *(Mangal Snan)*

Baba is ready for the Supreme Bath, His rosary bead and clothes having being kept aside.The simple white sheet which covers the Samadhi, has been removed for the bath. Lukewarm water brought in a silver cauldron is used to pour water over Baba and His Samadhi through silver tumblers. Precious little water is used for Baba's bath these days to protect the idol which is carved out of porously configured marble.

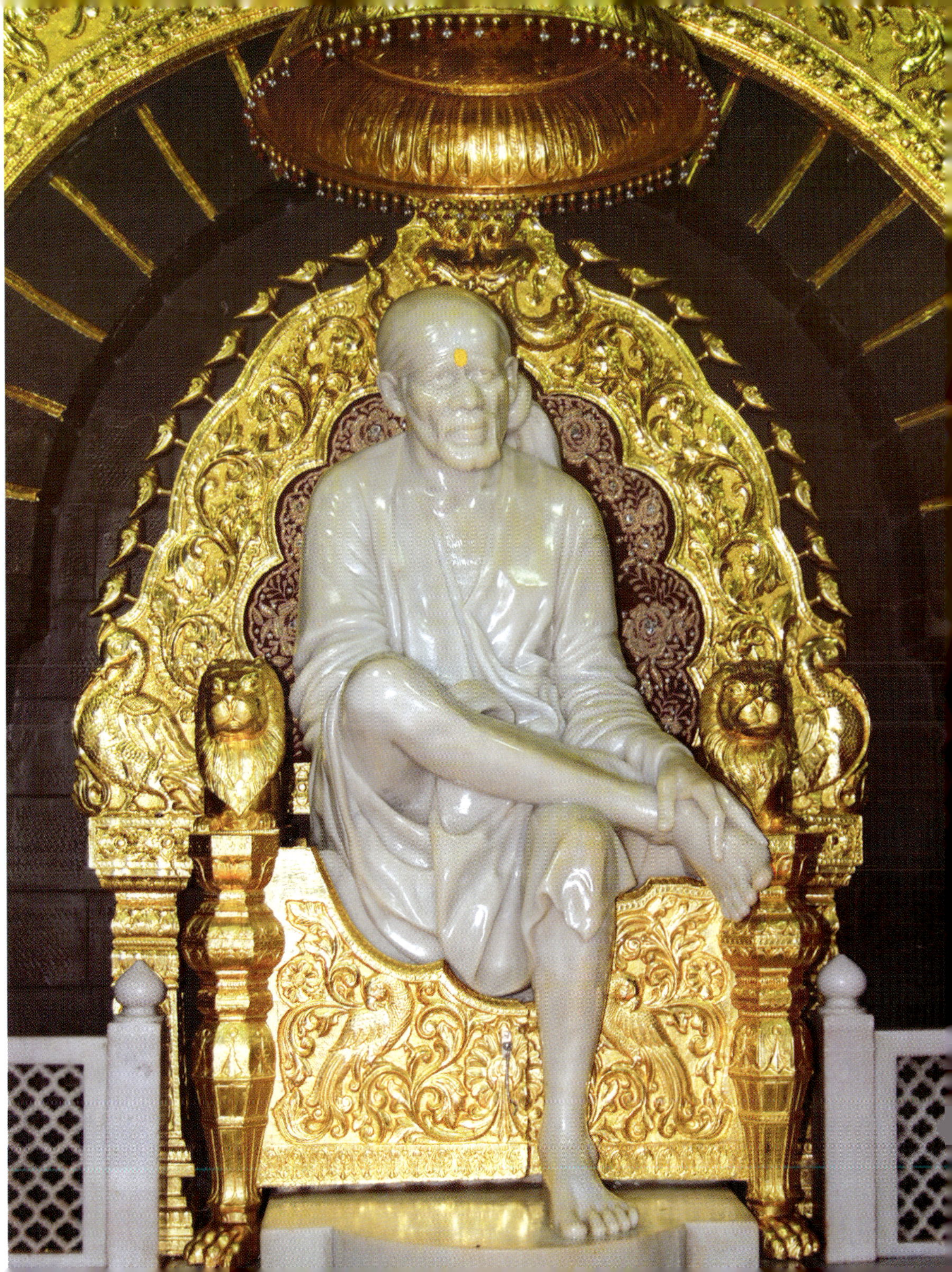

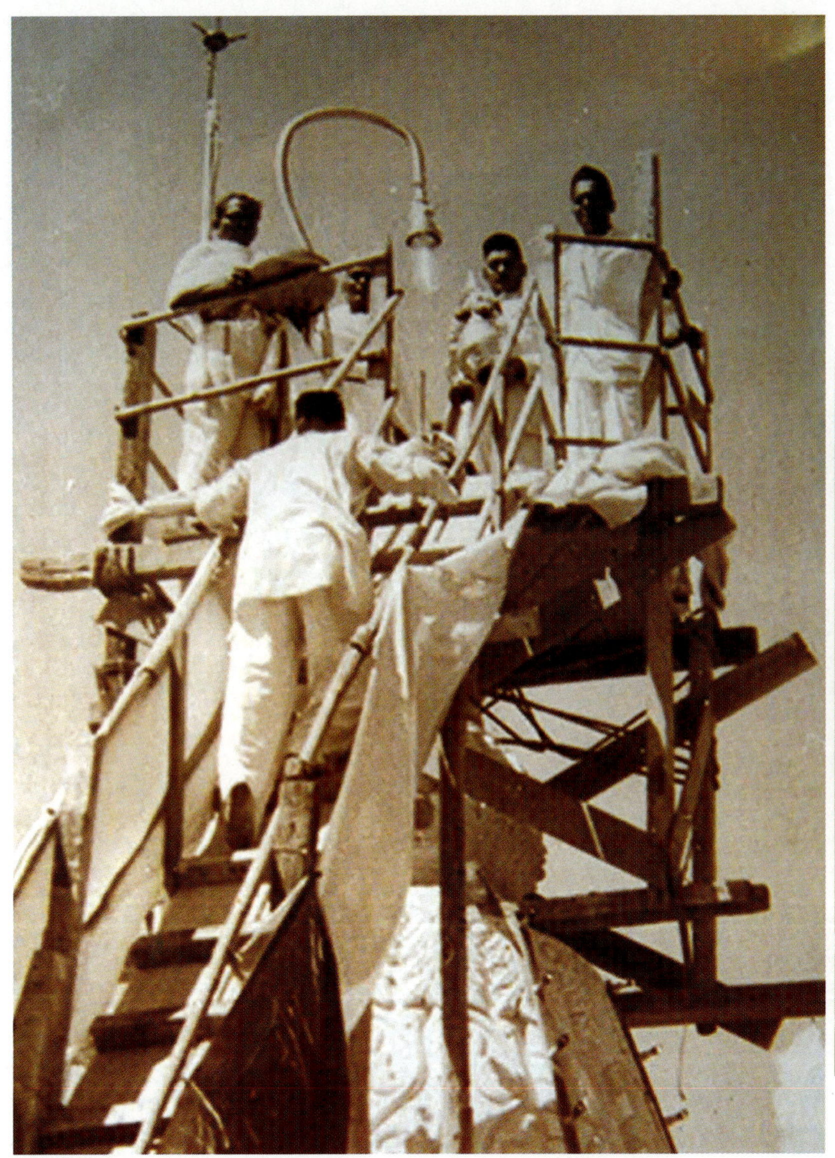

Grand ceremony of fixing of the golden spire *(Kalash Sthapana)* on the Gopuram by Dr. Ramchandra Prahlad Parnekar and the members of the Sansthan. *(Sept. 29, 1952)*. A huge ochre coloured silk flag was brought by Shri N.A. Savant and was fixed next to the Kalasha.

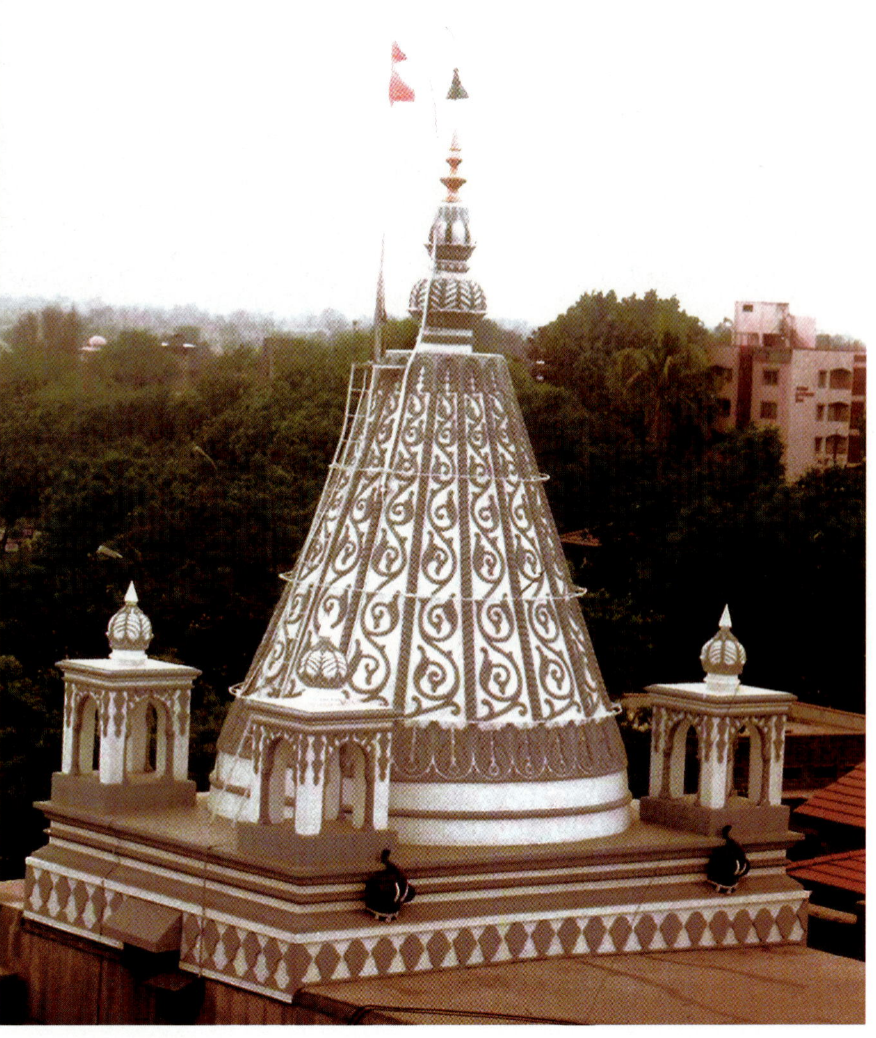

Top view of Samadhi Mandir- The Kalash and the flag enhance the majesty of Baba's Samadhi in this photograph of Samadhi Mandir. (*2001*)

Golden Gopuram (2011): The golden top of Samadhi Mandir pierces the darkness of the surrounding night with its brilliance. The supporting illumination from the lights around the temple complex makes this an enchanting view.

→

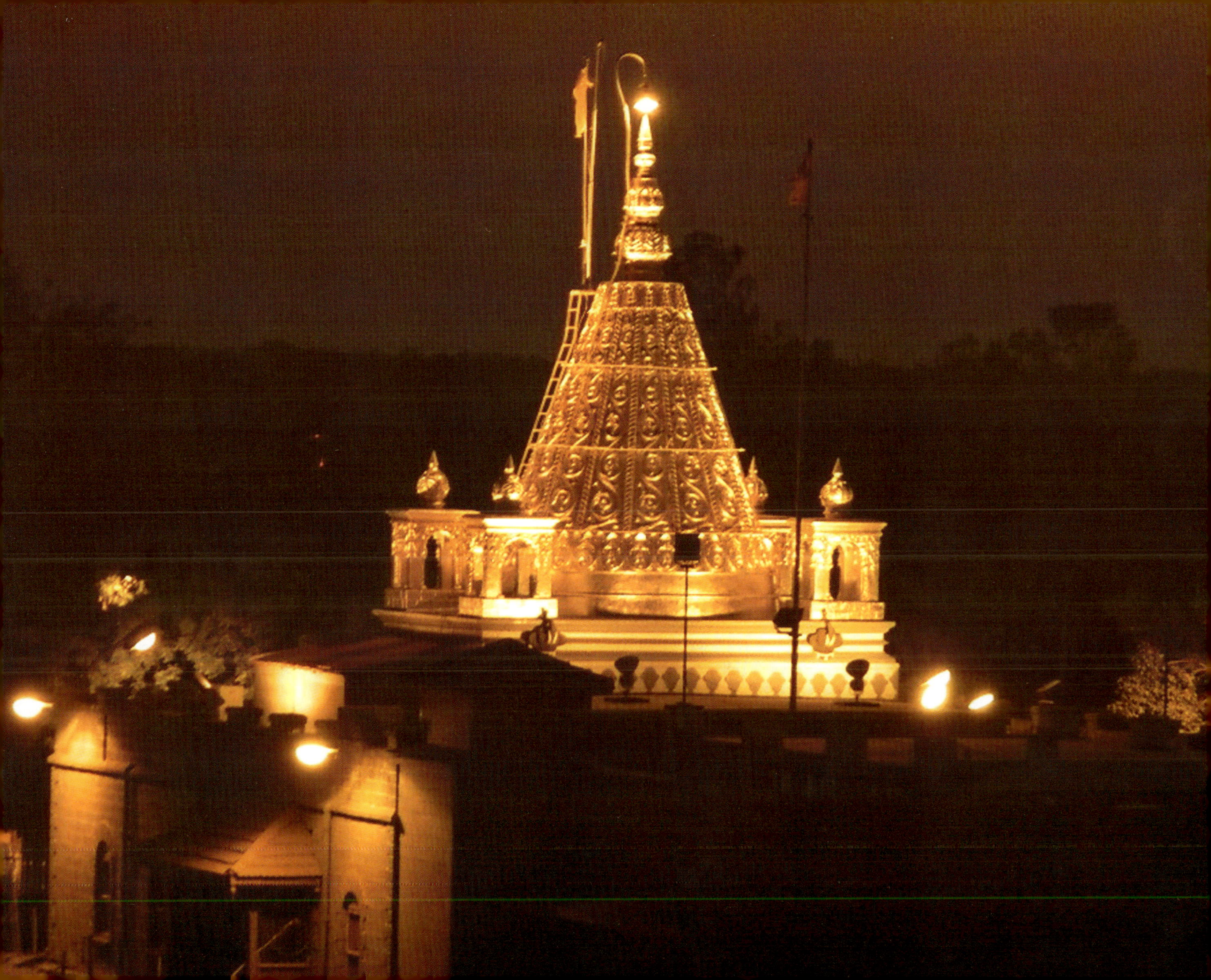

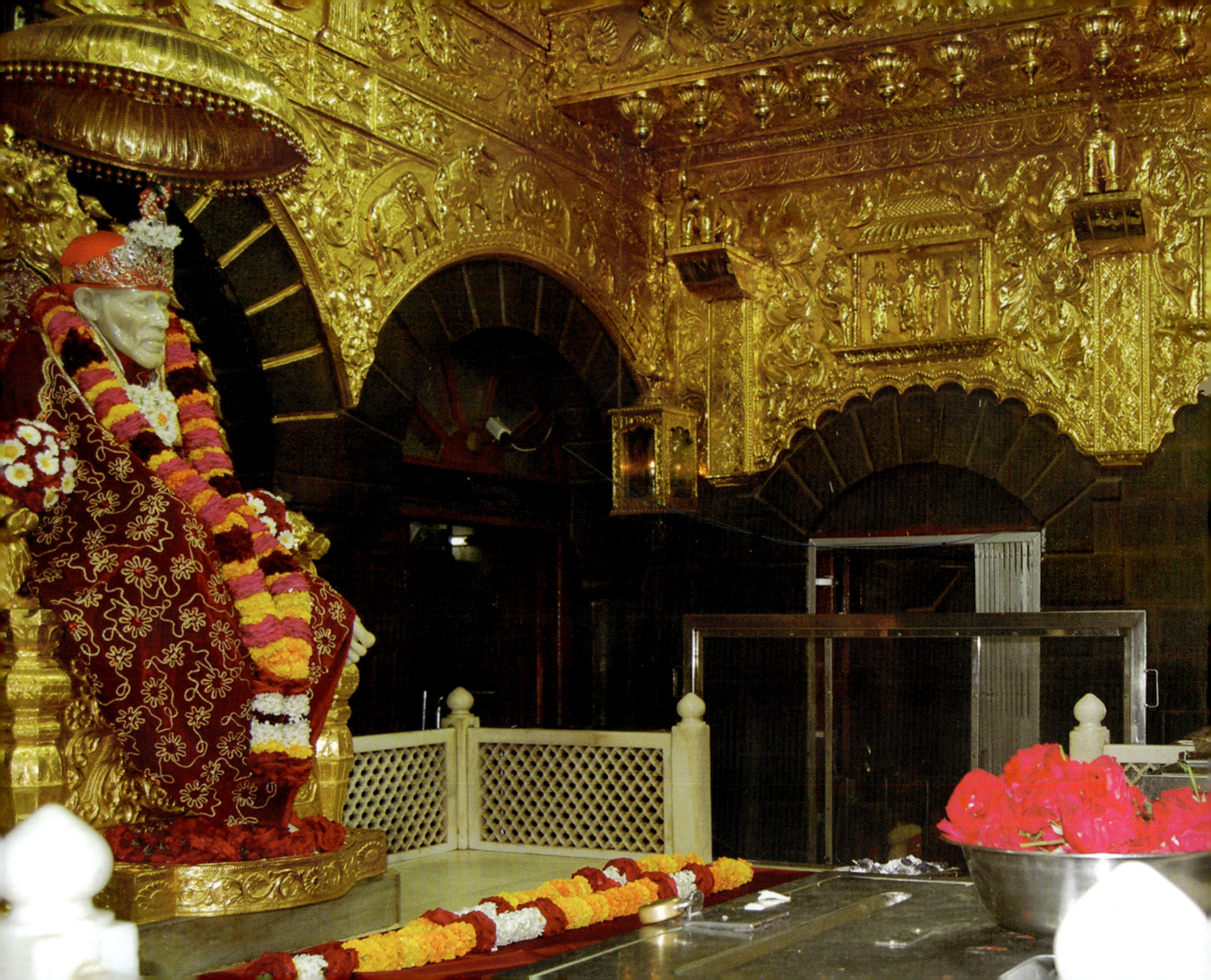

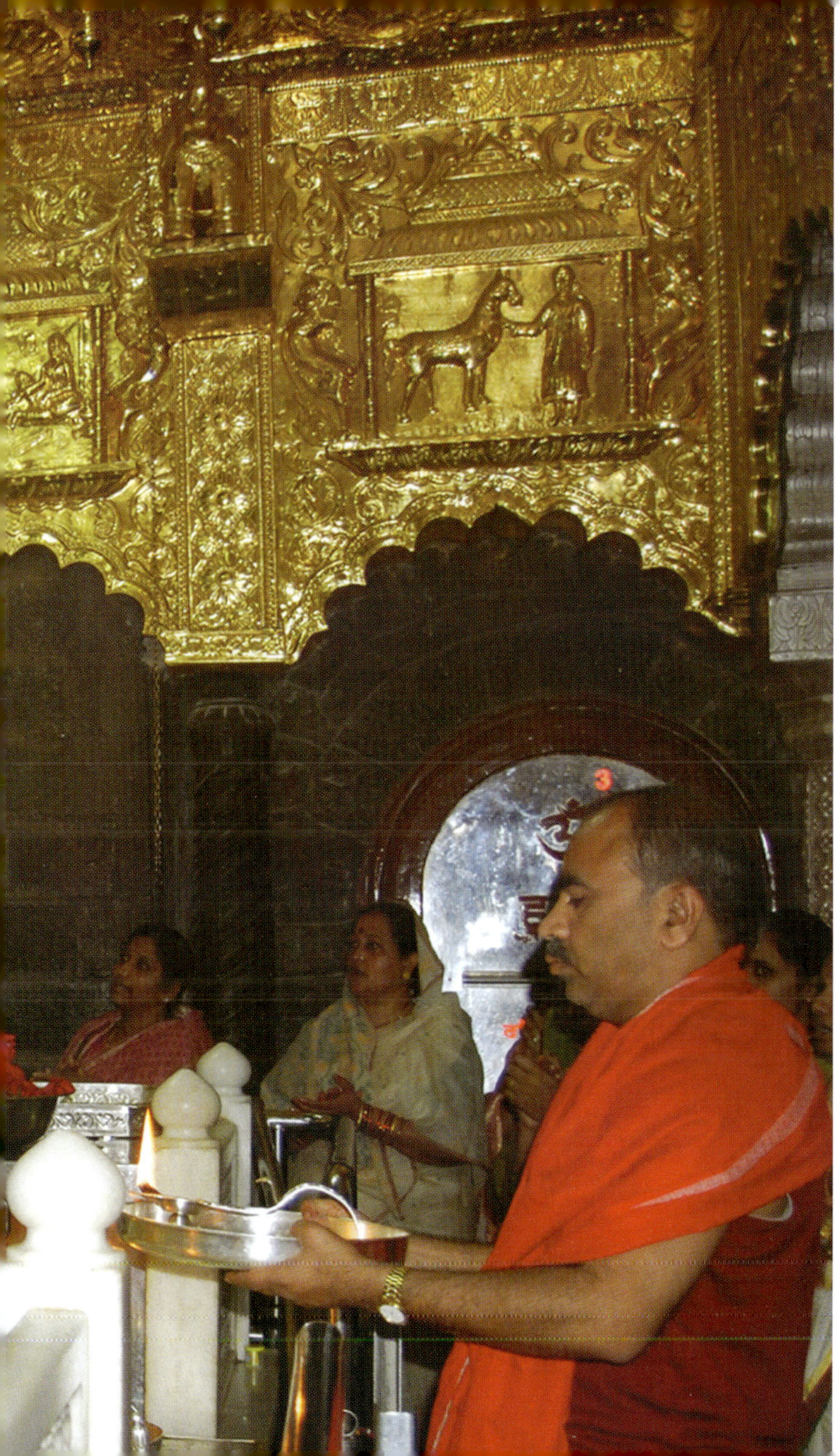

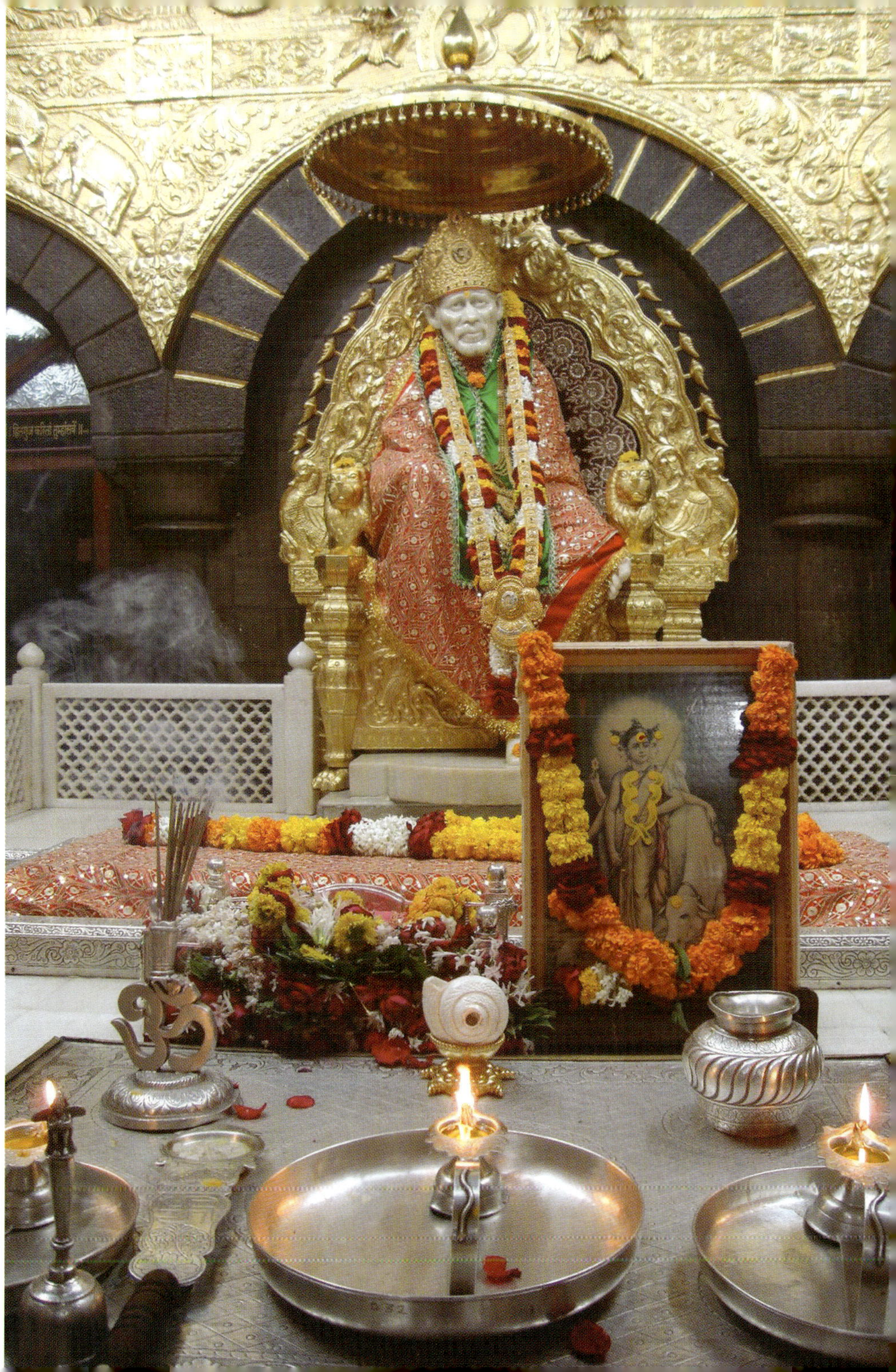

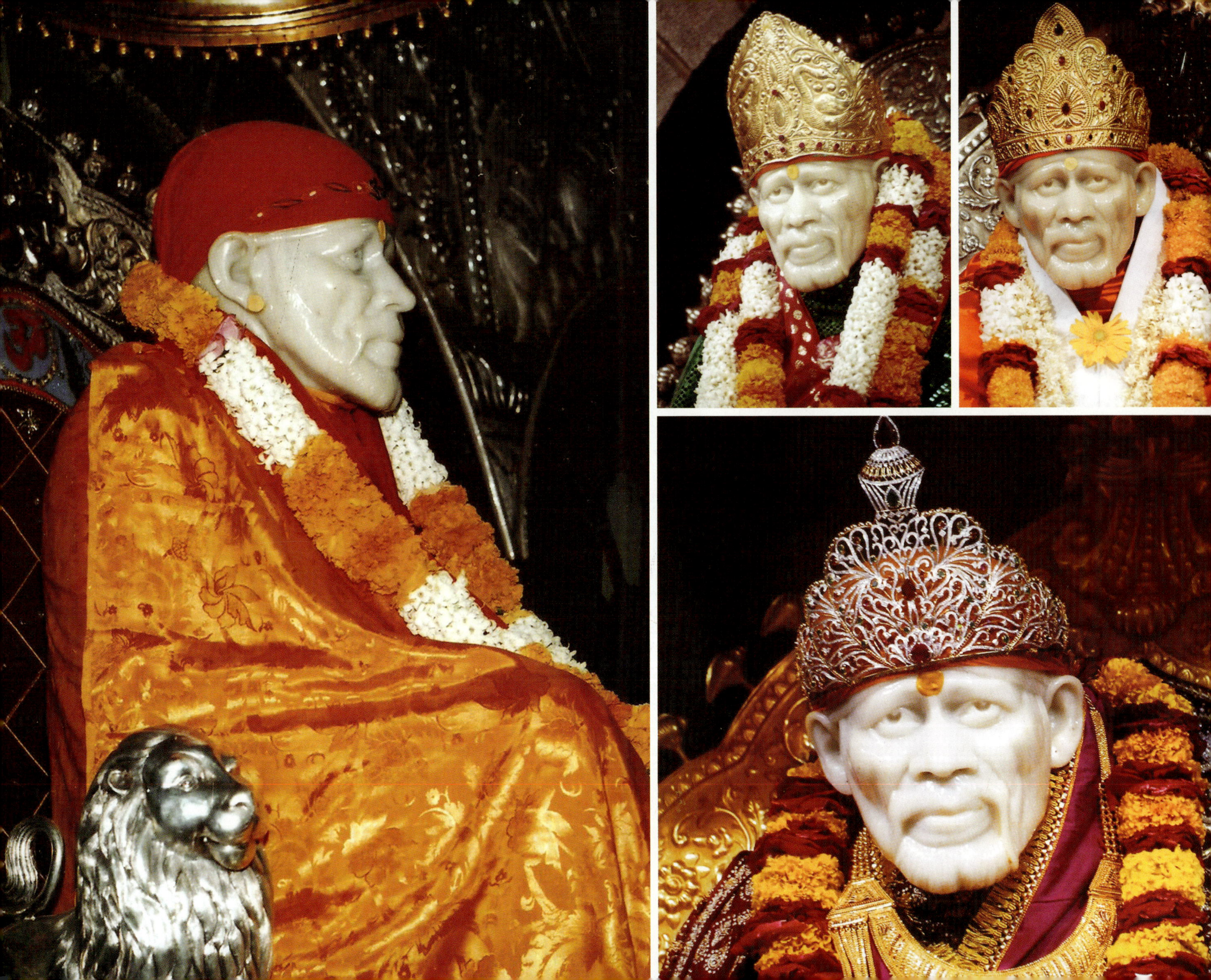

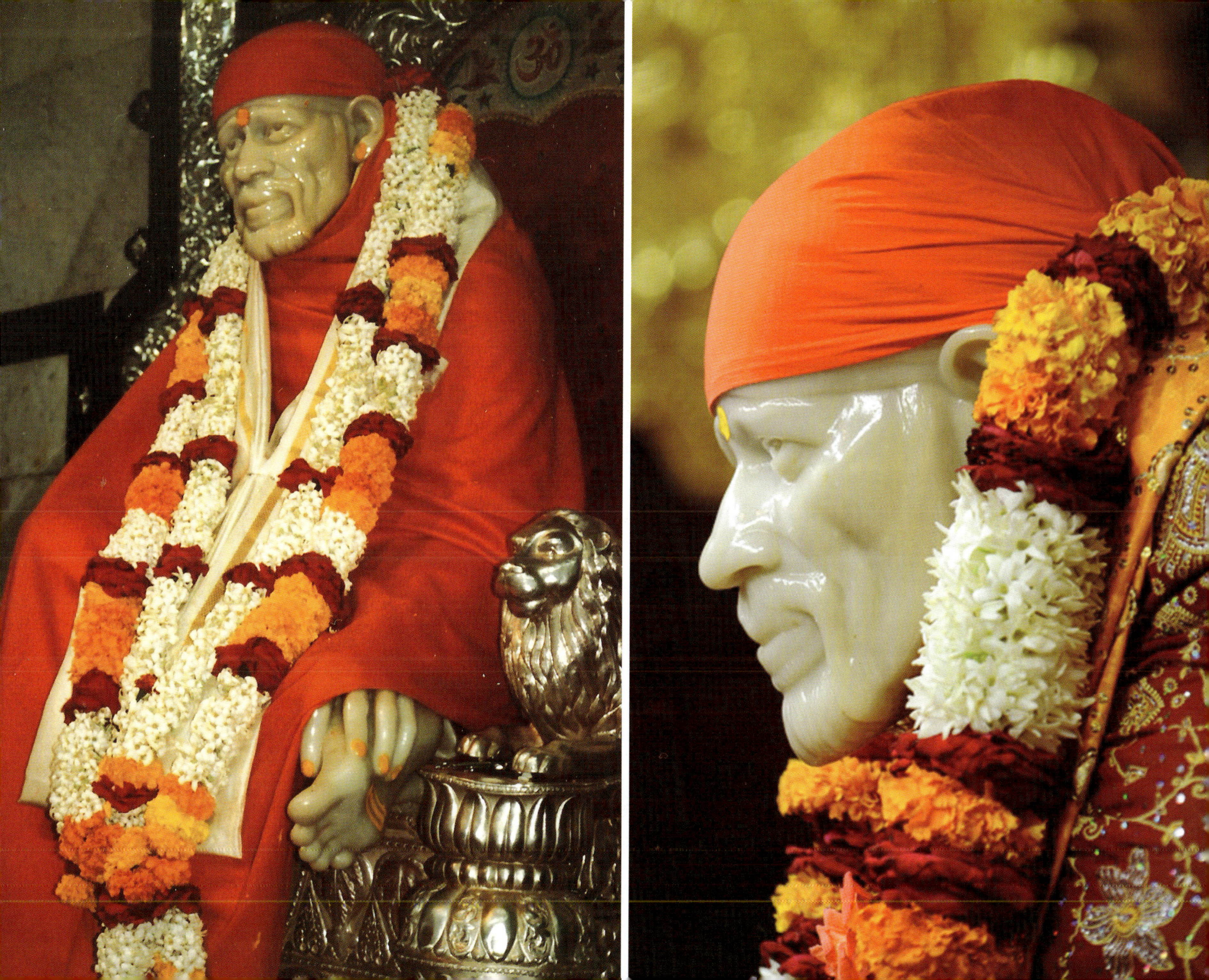

DWARKAMAI

Dwarkamai, as the name suggests, refers to a place called Dwarka, which is as dear to the residents and visitors as a mother or *mai*. A mother is the epitome of the worldly compassion and heavenly refuge that a living being can receive from any other soul on this earth. Baba believed that this old mosque (*masjid*) offered a similar sanctuary to the harried multitudes that thronged Shirdi. The believers also called it Masjidmai. Like the legendary city of Dwarka, established and blessed by Lord Krishna, this old masjid is said to grant Baba's devotees what they wish.

Baba spent around six contented decades in this small building. When Baba took up residence here, it was a ramshackle structure with an uneven floor and a leaky roof. In fact, so precarious was the condition that people feared for Baba's safety during severe storms. It was after a particularly violent storm that He relented to public pressure and established the routine of spending every alternate night in Chavadi. The dirt filled mosque of yore did not deter Him or His devotees from putting down roots here. Unmindful of His surroundings, Baba stayed here, accompanied by His meagre belongings which comprised primarily of His tattered garments, His smoking pipes (*chillums)* and a few pots. He left the masjid daily to seek alms in the form of food and fluids from five houses in Shirdi. He partook of whatever was offered and shared it with the strays that flocked at His door. Baba was revered for His special powers. The divinity aspect dawned gradually on the simple villagers who were witness to the daily miracles performed by Him. The masjid is full of articles and artifacts that transport people back in time. The lamps, the stove, the red wooden pillar, the cupboard, the net, the pots, and the stone on which Baba used to sit are still there, mute witnesses of the time when Baba sanctified this humble structure by His presence. The sacred fire lit by Baba called Dhunimai, burns eternally inside the modern mosque. Lit over 150 years ago, it was fed by logs, cut and carried by Baba Himself. The task is now managed by Sansthan which has carried out repairs and alterations from time to time. The udi from the fire is distributed as prasad among devotees who reverently smear it on their forehead.

Dwarkamai is broadly divided into two parts – one, the inner Sanctum Sanctorum which has a portrait of Baba installed in a pavilion opposite Dhunimai, and the Sabha Mandap or assembly hall where His stone-pose portrait gazes down at the gathering. The portrait is hung behind the stone on which Baba sat and which has His silver footprints etched on it. Stone idols of a tiger and Baba's beloved equine devotee, Shyama Karan, are erected next to the stone. Every brick in Dwarkamai is testimony to Baba's benign presence which is experienced by all to this day. Devotees come to the mosque before leaving Shirdi, seeking Baba's grace and permission before commencing their return journey. The haze from Dhunimai adds to the aura of this abode of Baba which comforts all those who enter its portals.

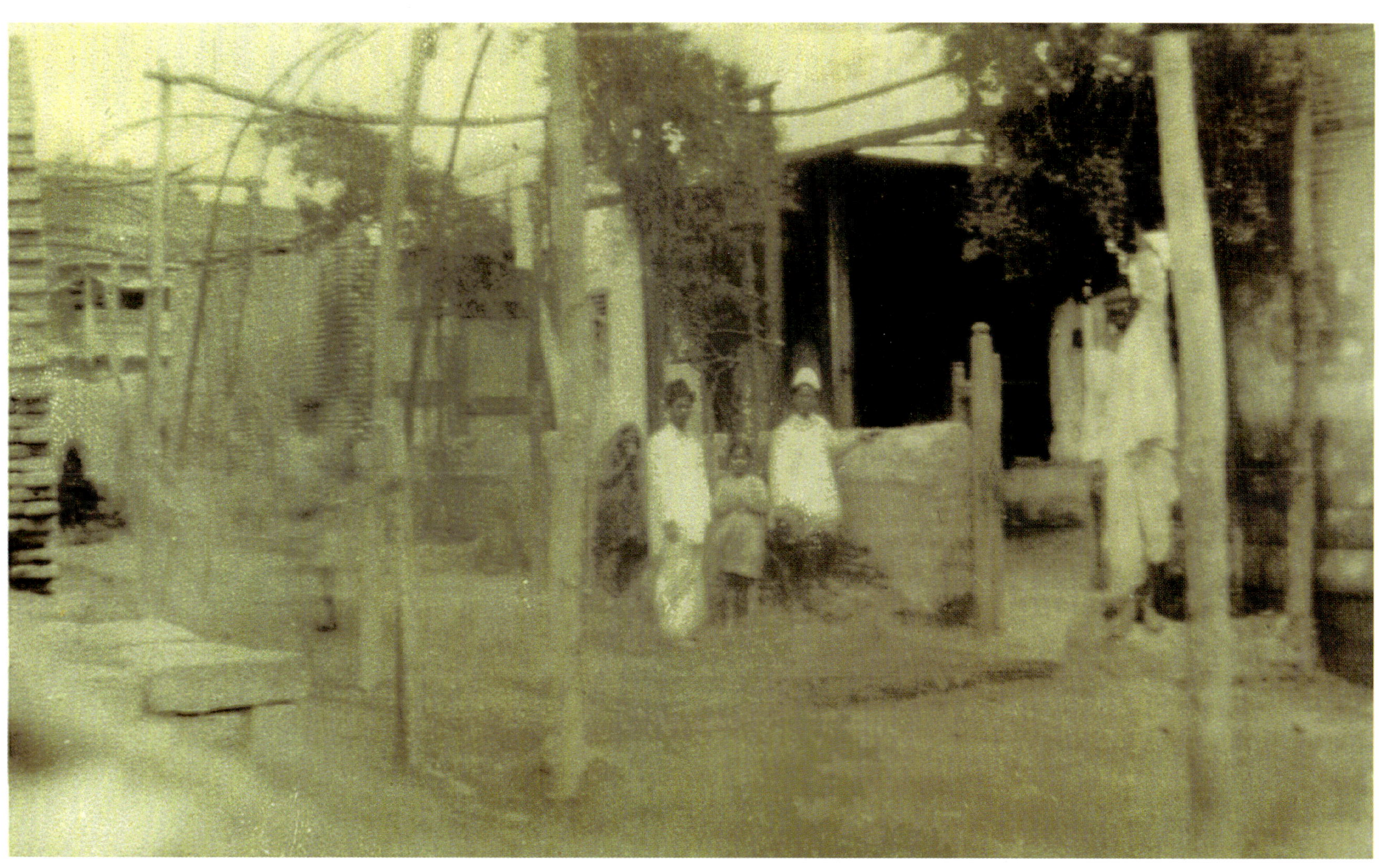

Dilapidated old Dwarkamai Masjid front view. *(1920)*

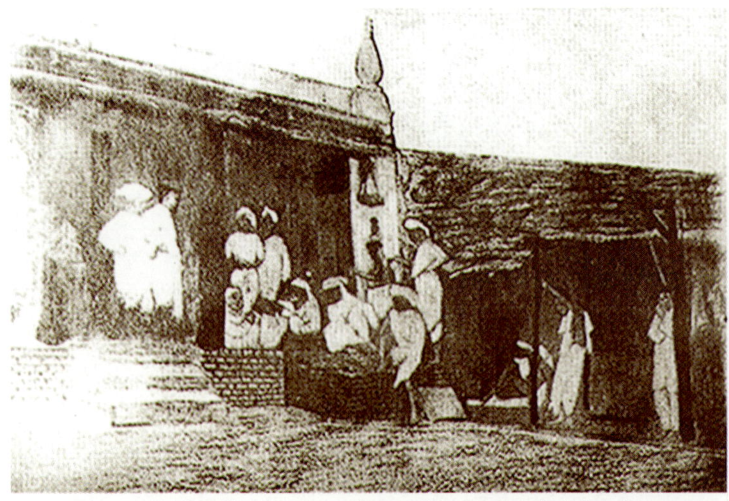

A rare image of Baba in Dwarkamai surrounded by devotees. It was Baba's custom to interact regularly with the locals.

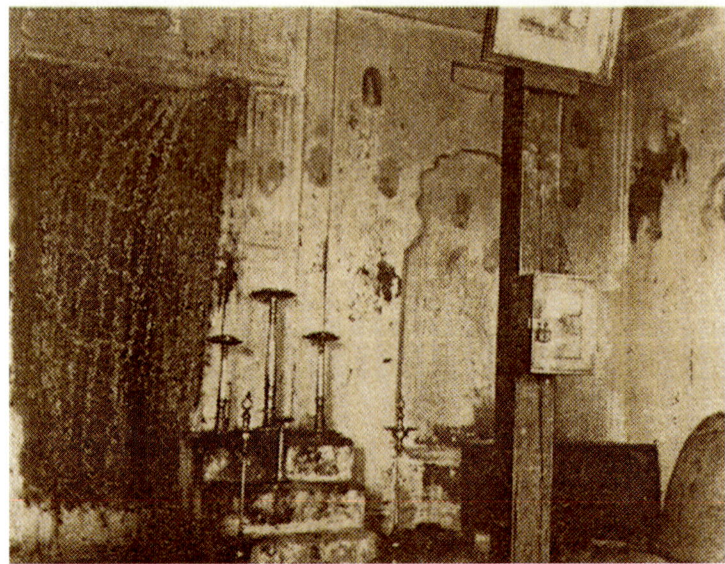

Inside photograph of Dwarkamai *(1920)*. Visible next to the carved design in the wall *(Nimbar)* is Baba's bolster against which He used to recline. Decorative lamps can be seen to the left of the pillar which stands till date.

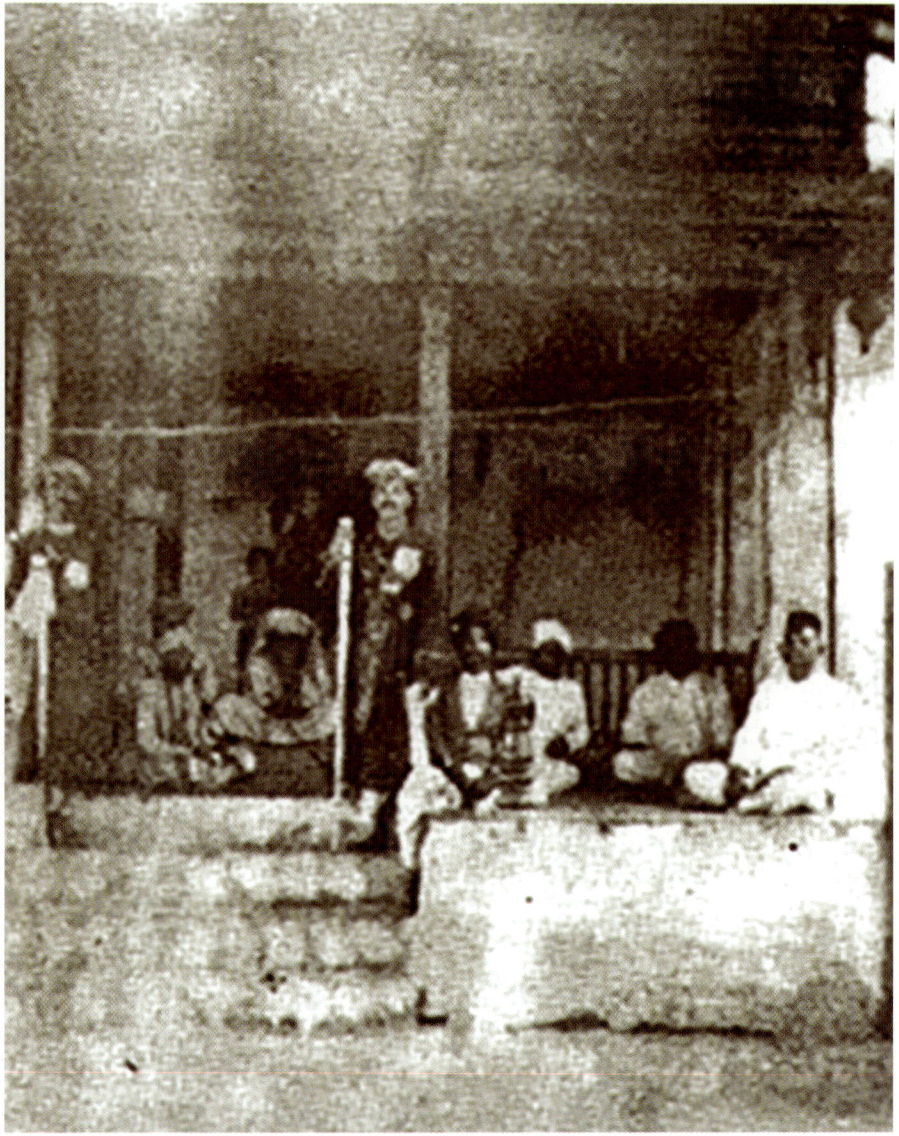

This picture of Dwarkamai was taken three days after Baba's Mahasamadhi on 15 October, 1918.

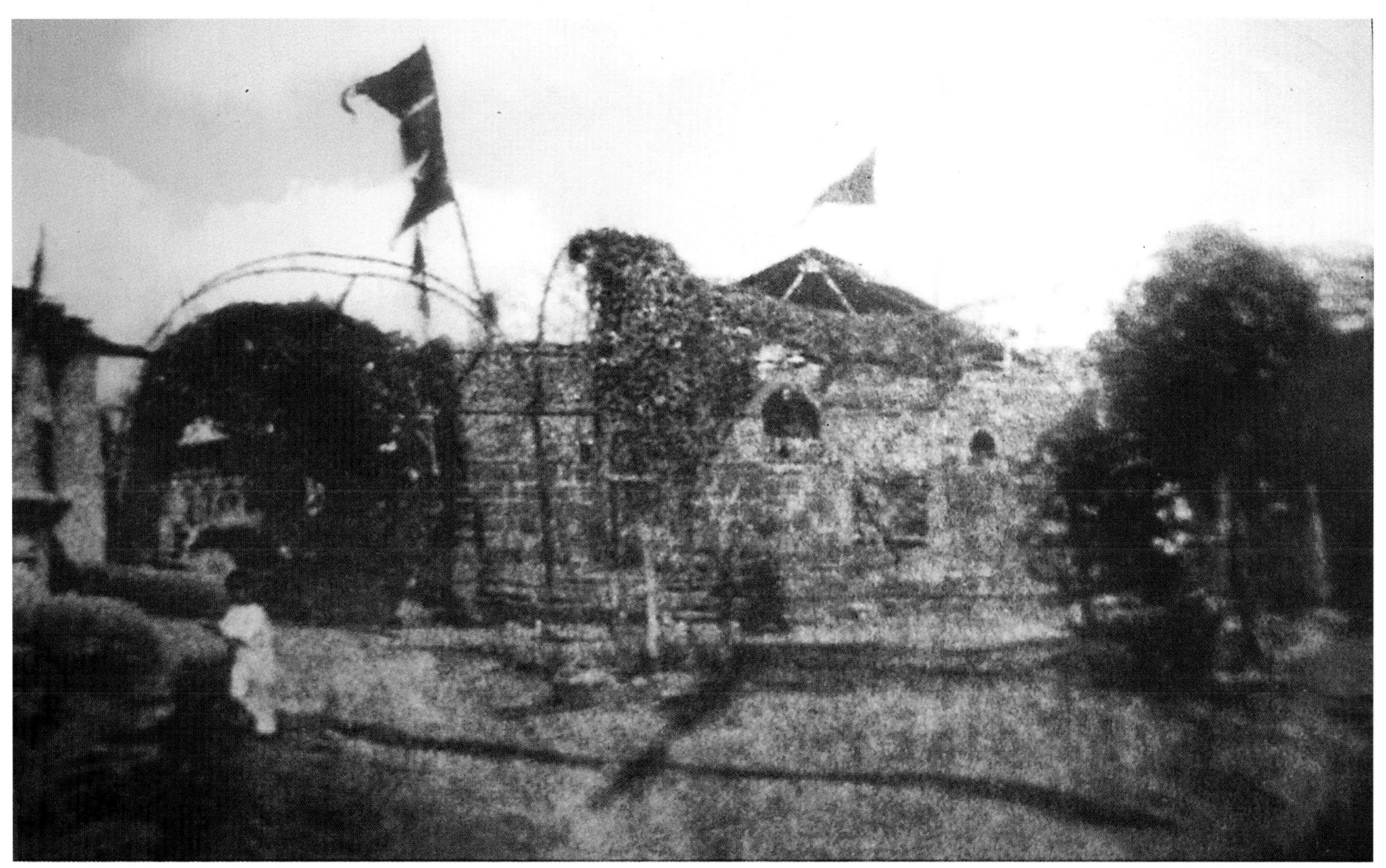

Dwarkamai and its surroundings- Flag hoisted atop the roof of Dwarkamai and neighbourhood structures can be seen. *(1920)*

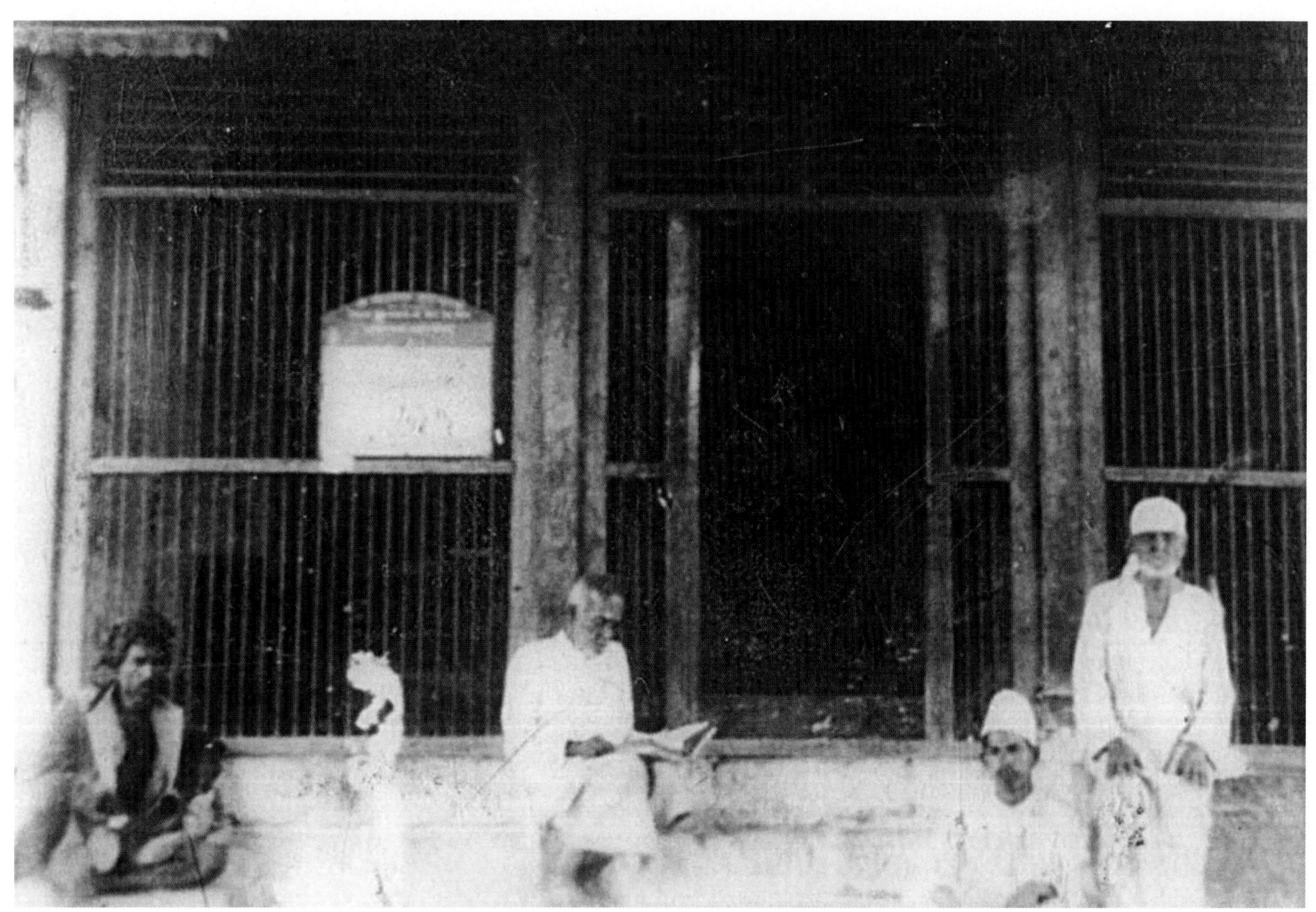

Devotees and villagers sitting outside the Dwarkamai. Grilled doors of Dwarkamai can be seen. *(1920)*

Sanctum Sanctorum of Dwarkamai- An old devotee holding a stick in his hand is sitting on the entrance of Dwarkamai. Two devotees can be seen inside. *(1950)* →

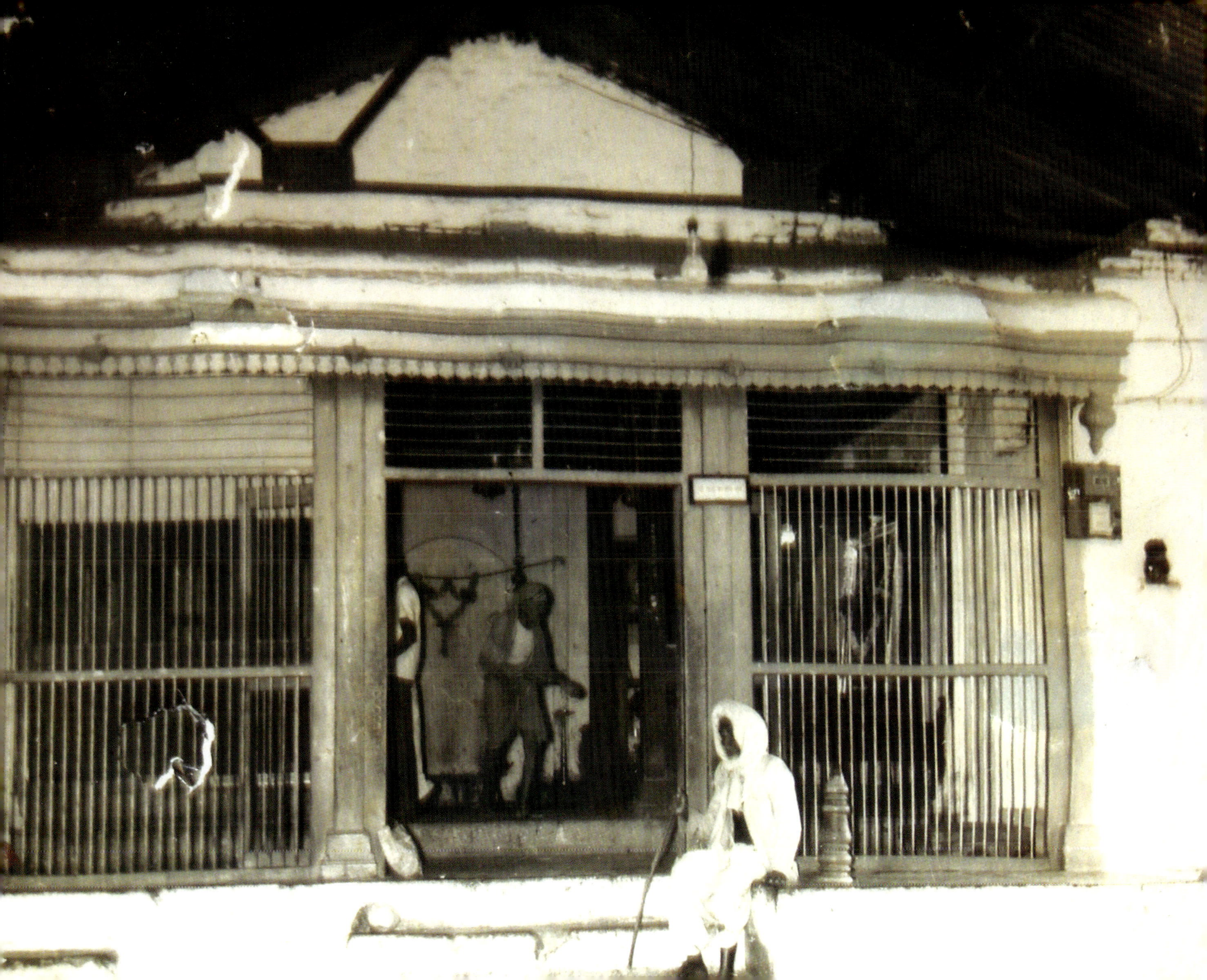

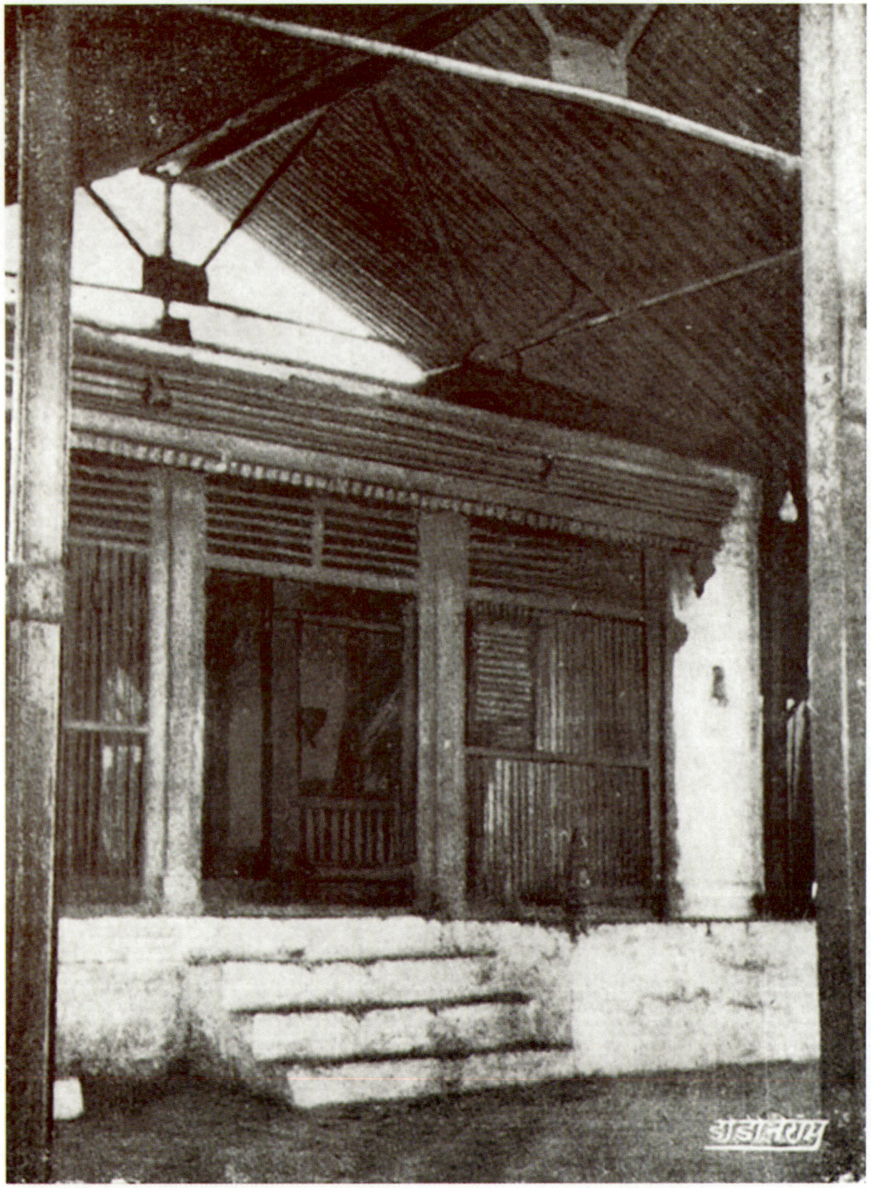

A long shot of Sanctum Sanctorum facing the Sabha Mandap (prayer hall) in Dwarkamai. The asbestos roof can be seen clearly. *(1975)*

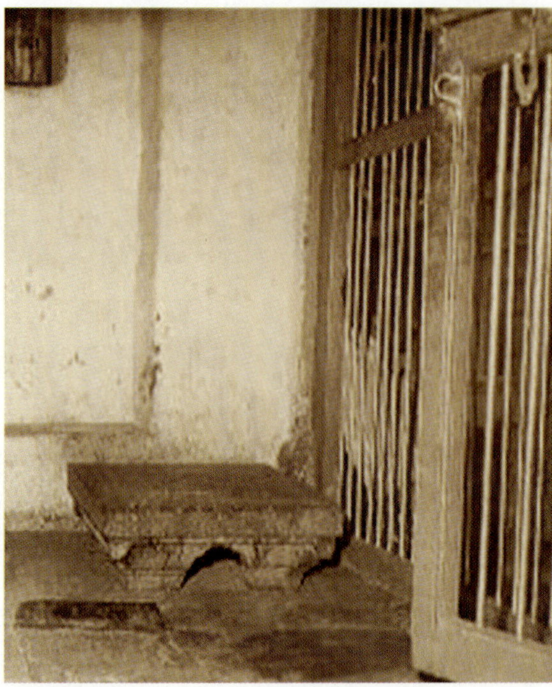

Baba's bathing stone- Rambaji of Nasik, a simpleton who was devoted to Baba, bathed in the water which flowed off Baba after He took His bath. Rambaji miraculously recovered his faculties and made a humble offering of this square stone stool to Baba on which Baba sat and bathed.

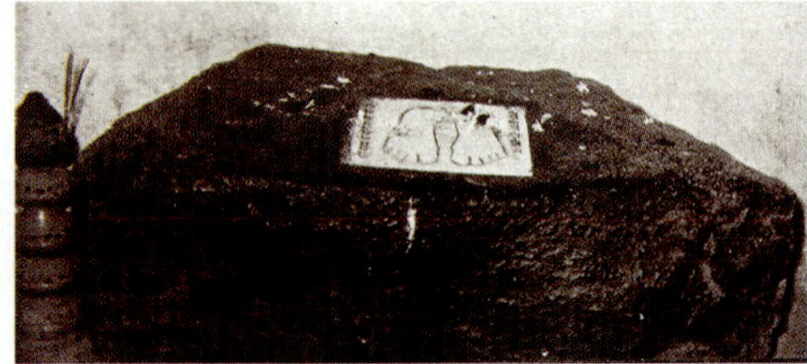

Footprints carved on the sacred stone. Next to it, the incense sticks are seen burning.

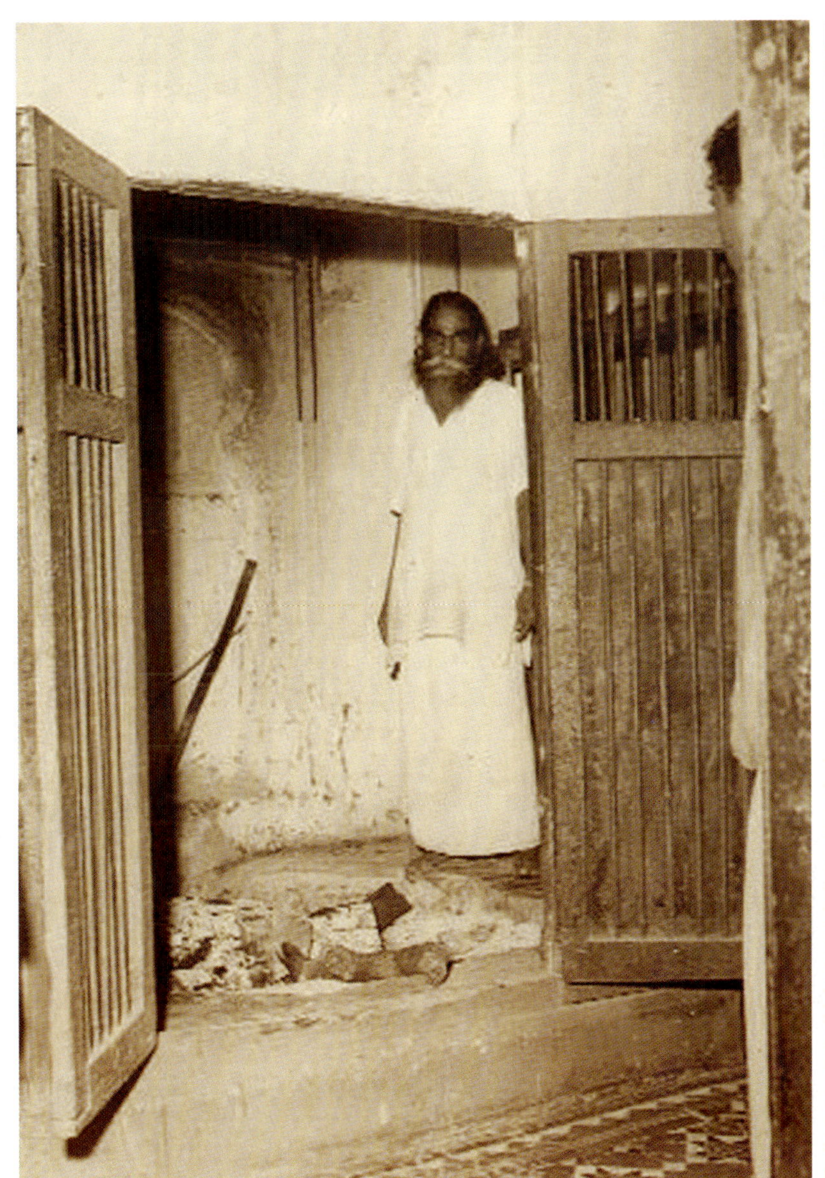

Swami Shivneshan, who selflessly took care of Dhunimai all his life, is seen standing inside the grilled doors. *(1980)*

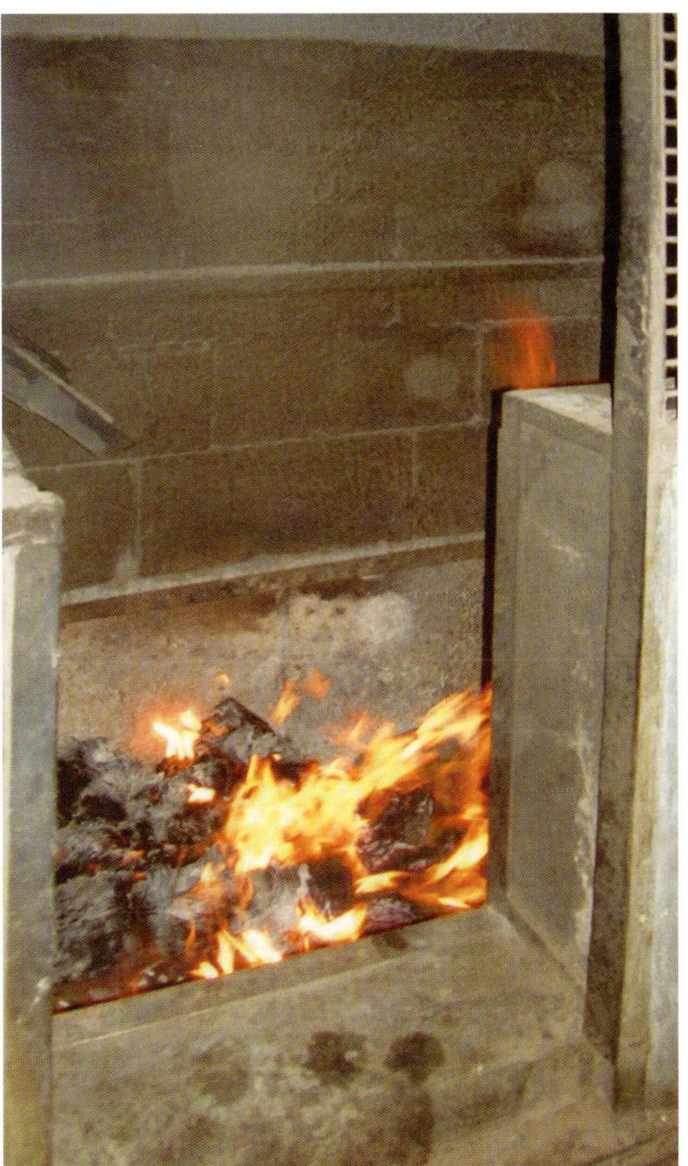

Sacred Dhuni *(2010)*

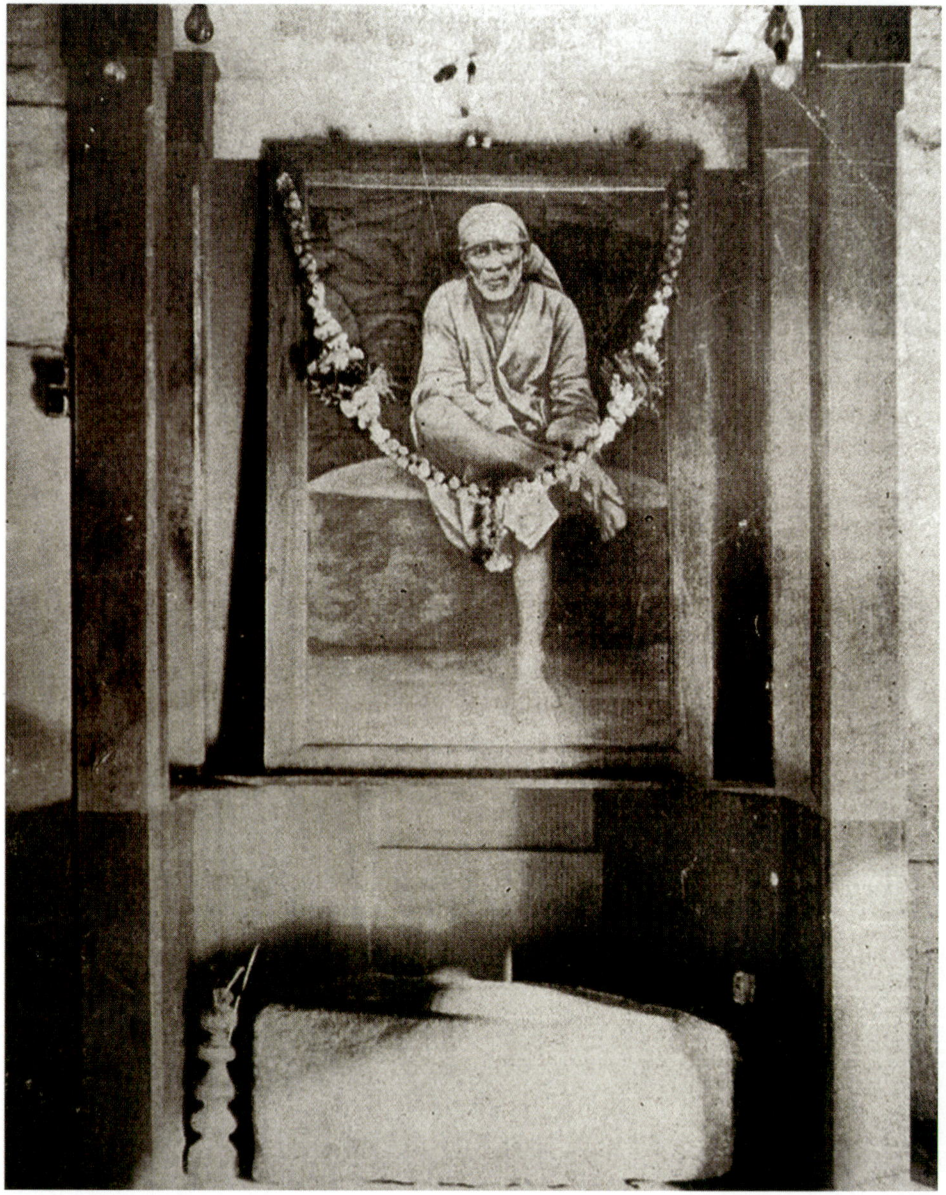

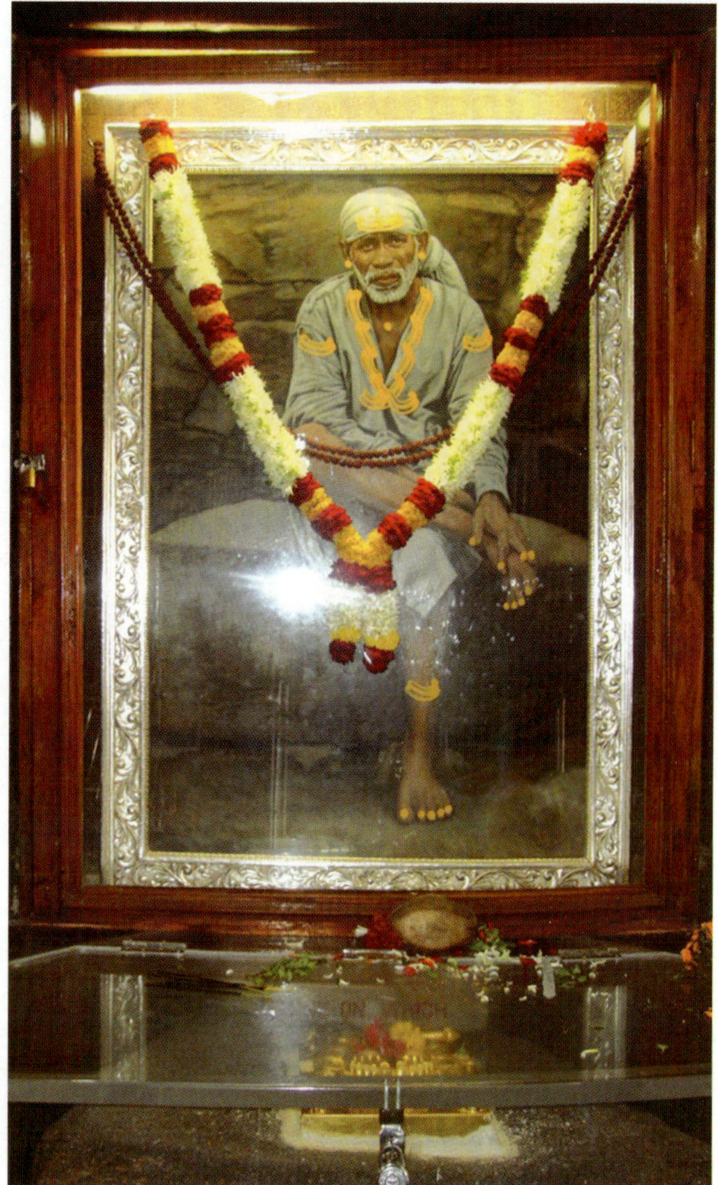

(1975) *(2012)*

The Saint and His Stone- This oil painting by Shri. D.D. Neroy is displayed in Dwarkamai, above the original stone on which Baba sat.

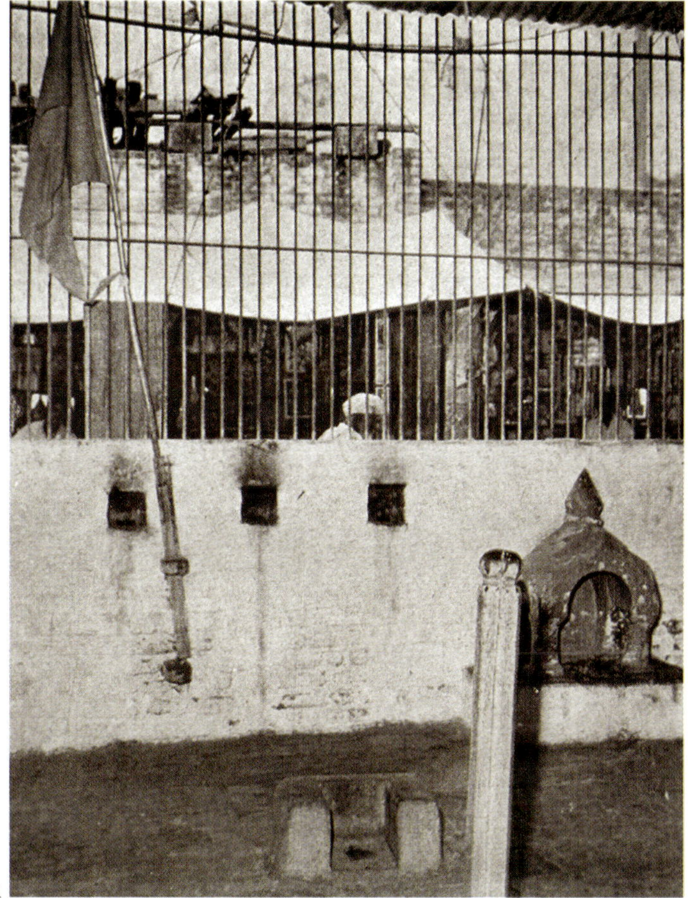

1

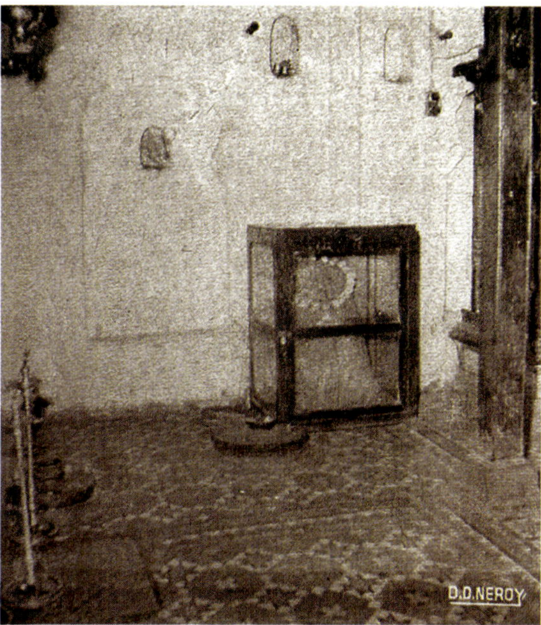

2

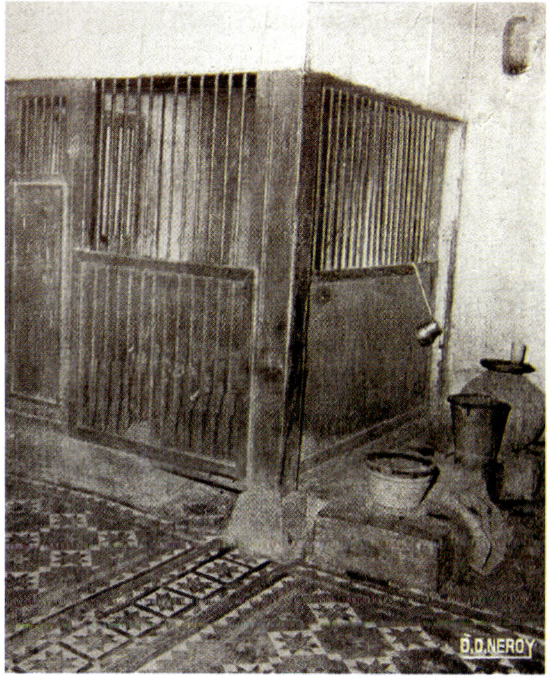

Inside view of Dwarkamai-

1. The visual shows the mud stove or oven (*chulha*) on which Baba cooked food for His devotees. Next to it is the wooden pillar against which Baba rested and His sandal imprints (*padukas*) are carved on the extreme left. These structures are on the extreme left side of Dwarkamai.
2. Housed in the glass case is the wheat sack offered by Balaji Patil Nevaskar to Baba. A garland is placed on top and the hand mill (used by Baba) lies in front.
3. As one moves into the Sanctum Sanctorum, Dhunimai can be seen. Placed outside are the stone pot *(Kolamba)* and the earthern pot used for storing water. The intricate floor design reflects the art of the country side. On the extreme right, is a small alcove in the wall at the top.

D.D.NEROY

3

The Painting of Baba in front of Dhunimai (Dwarkamai pose)

This is an oil painting by the famous artist Shyam Rao Ramchandra Jaikar. Moreshwar Pradhan brought Jaikar to Shirdi and requested him to make two portraits of Baba. After meeing Baba Jaikar made more than one painting on his own accord.

This painting was presented to the Sansthan after Baba's Mahasamadhi. It was installed at the very place where Baba sat. As the painting was created with Baba's consent, it has this incredible feature that when a devotee looks at it with love and devotion, he gets the 'living experience' of Baba in it. The devotees could not leave Shirdi without Baba's permission. When they wanted to leave they came to see Baba in Dwarkamai and sought his permission. Baba gave them udi and his blessings and they had a safe journey. Even today devotees go to this painting, prostrate and ask for permission. Then they take udi and have a safe journey home. At present, Jaikar's original painting of Baba is kept in the museum. The one in the Dwarkamai is a copy of the same.

This famous and beautiful painting is a masterpiece and is widely known as 'The Dwarkamai Pose'.

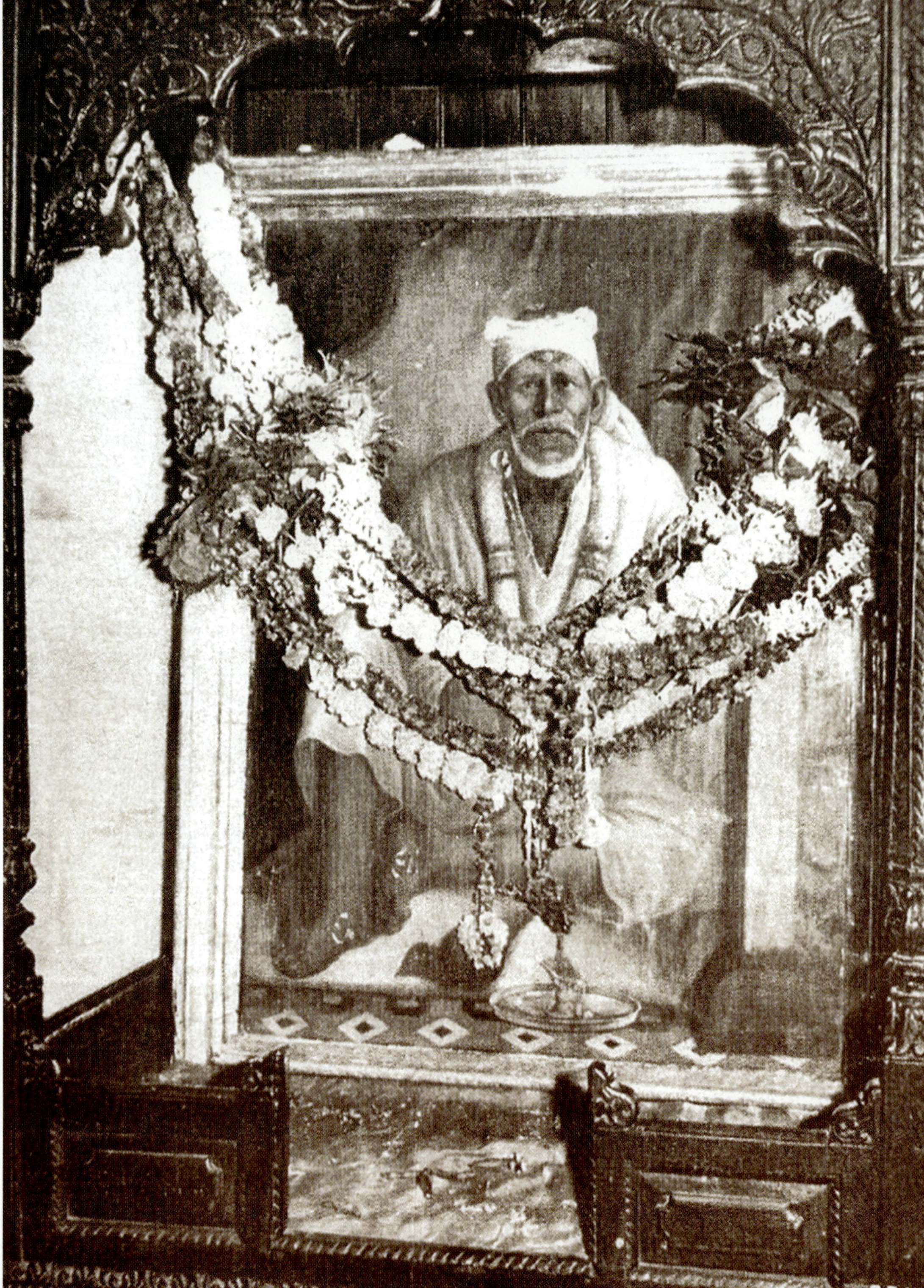

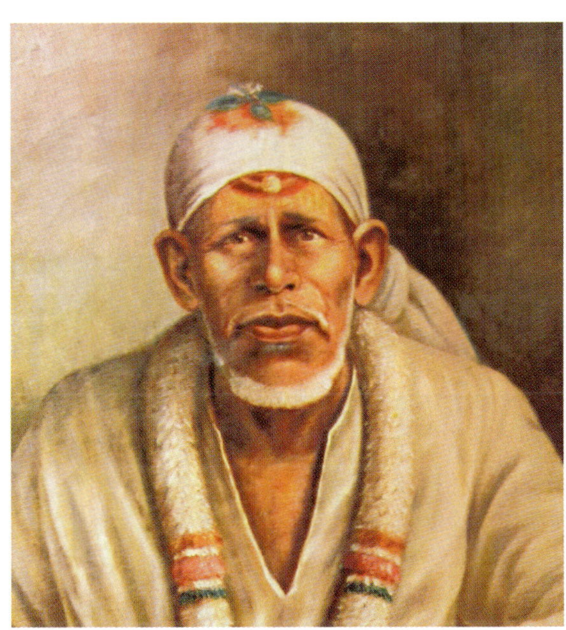

This famous portrait of Baba is known as 'The Dwarkamai Pose'. Sadguru Sainath Maharaj gazes beatifically and offers salvation to those who behold him.

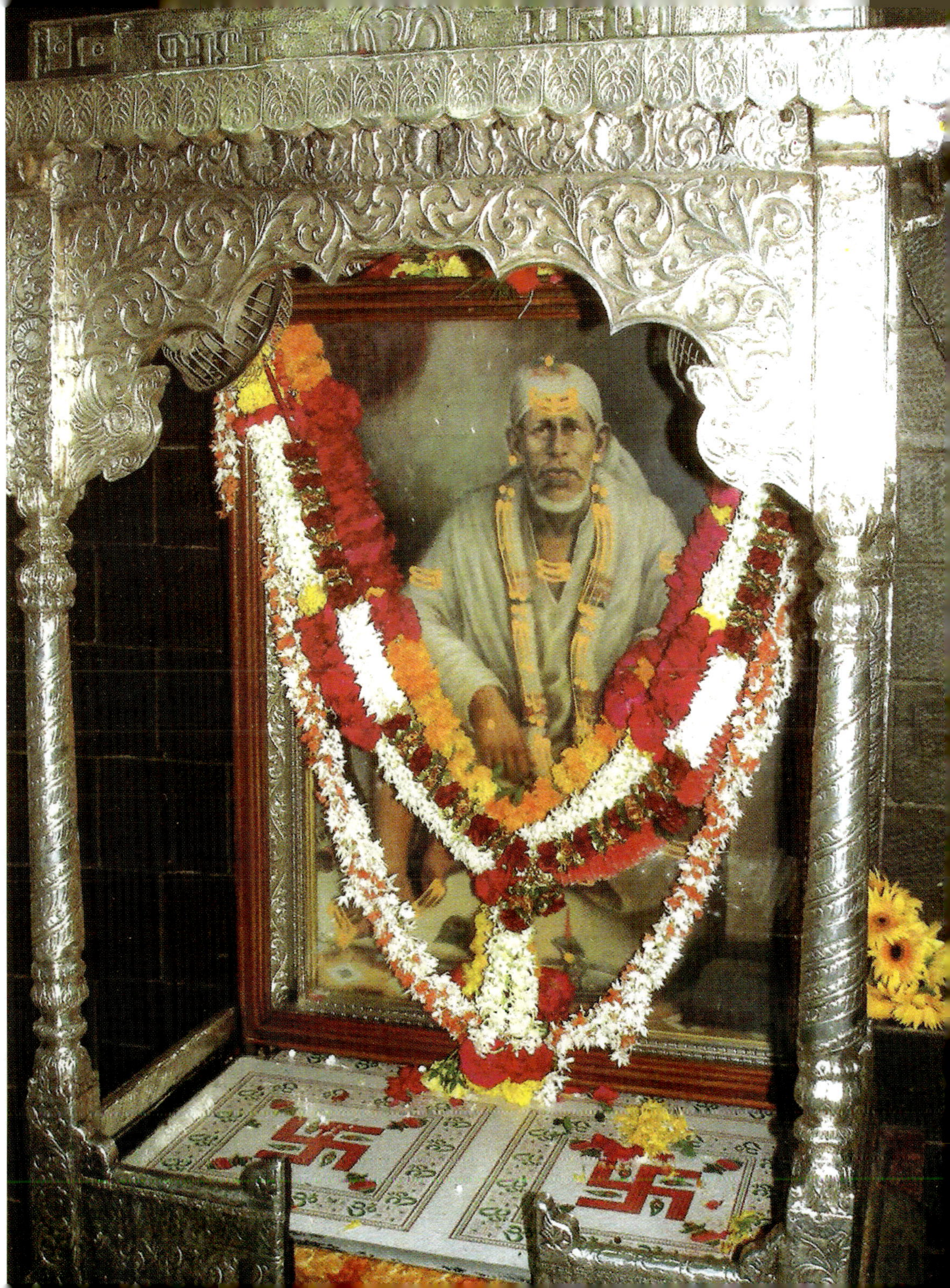

A FIRE PLACE
BABA USED TO

1

2

3

तीर्थ-जल
पावित्र्य राखा.
TEERTHA-JAL
MAINTAIN SANCTITY

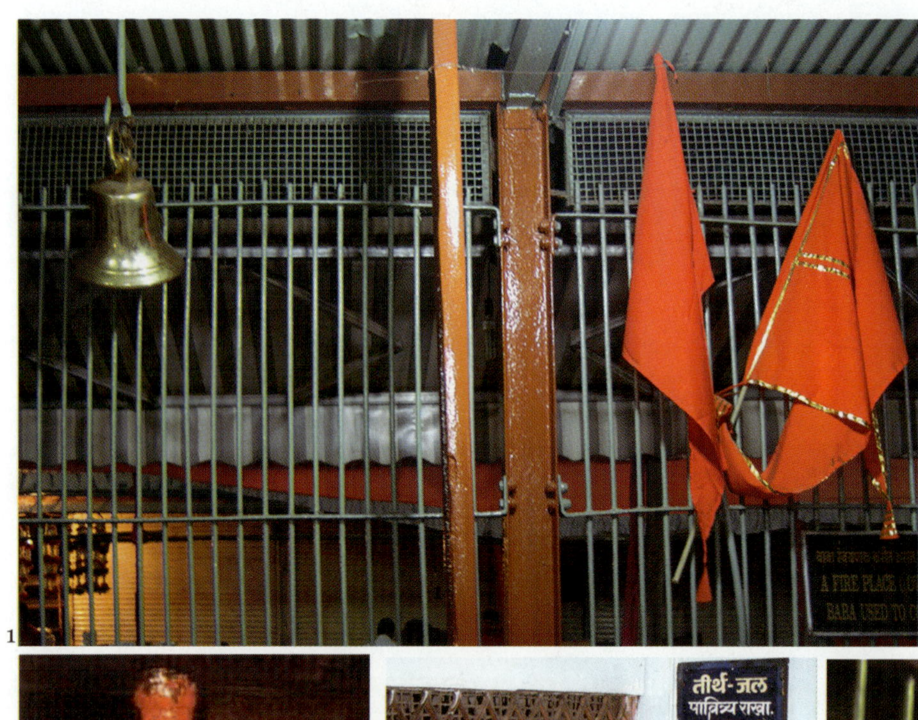

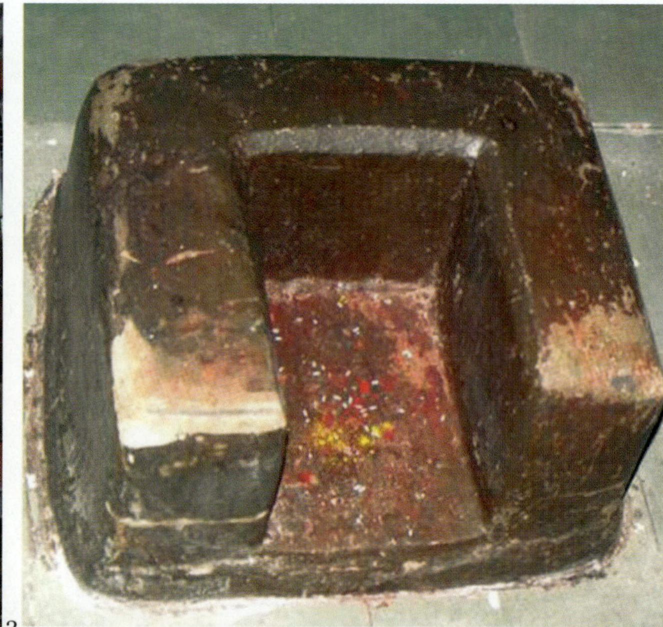

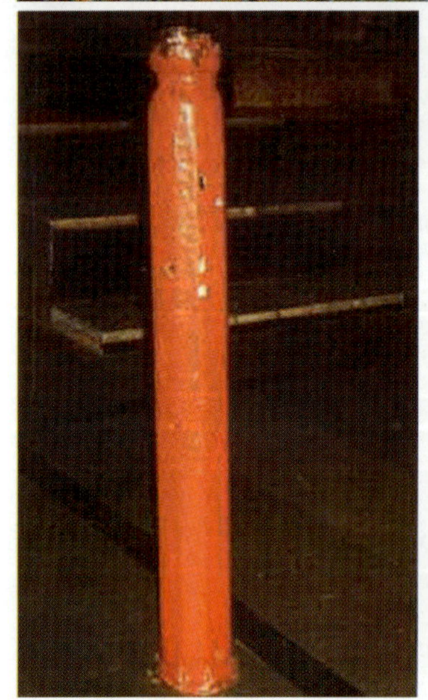

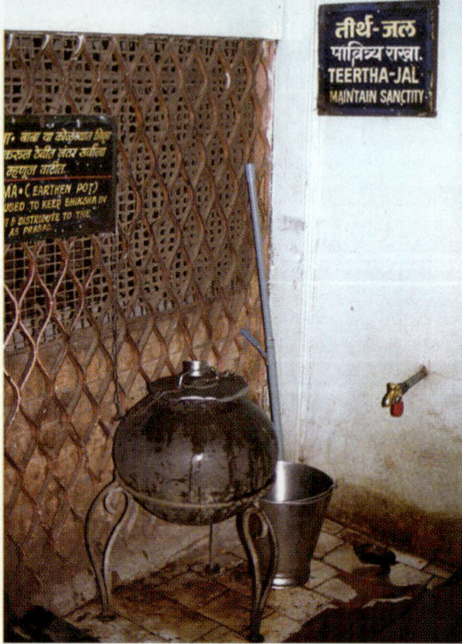

4

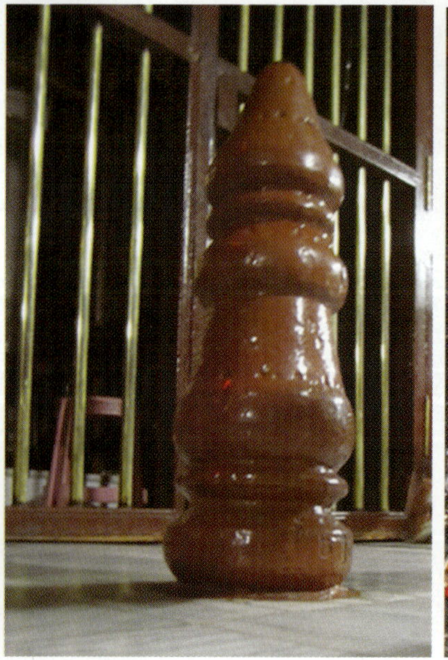

5

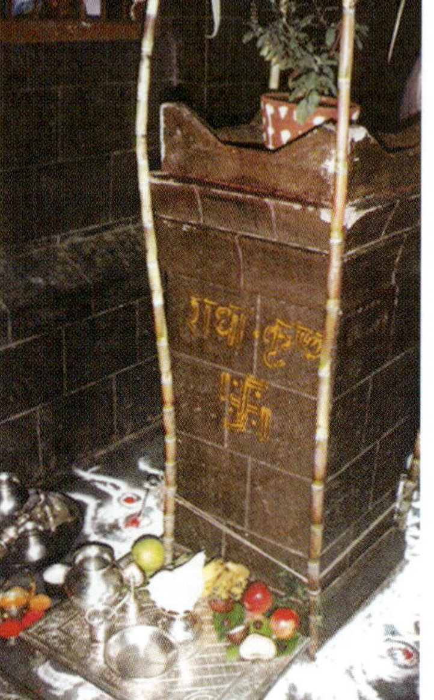

6

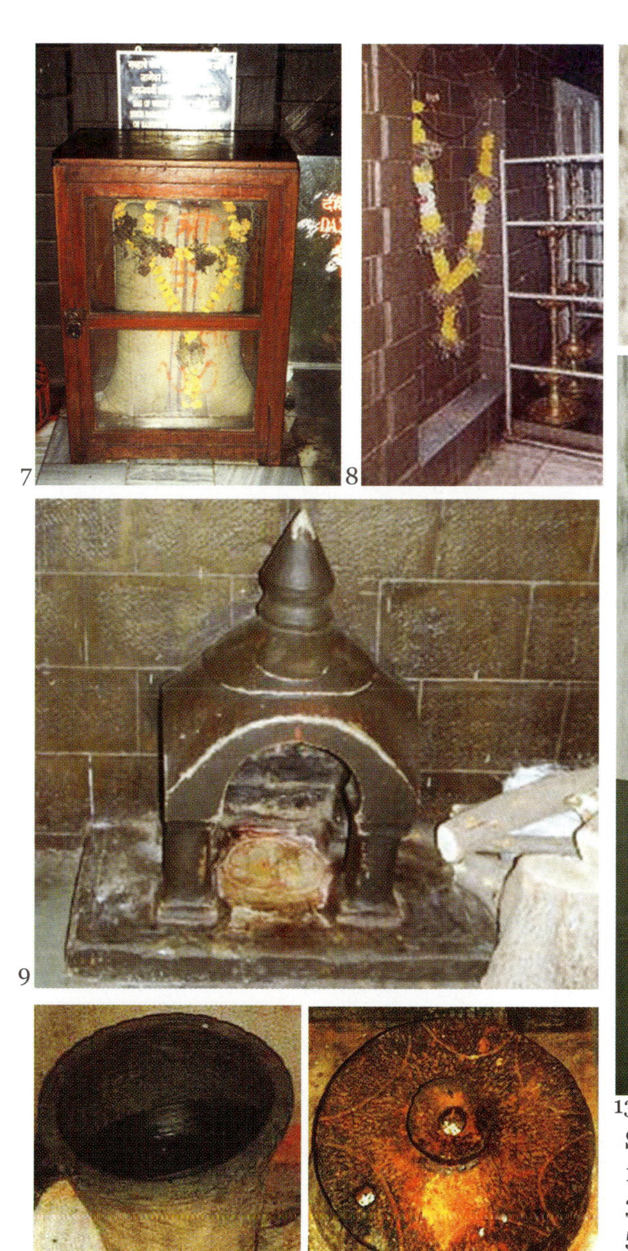

7 8 9 10 11 12 13

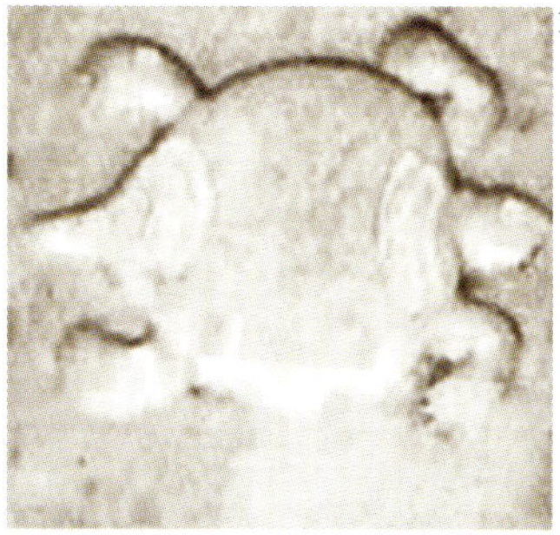

Sacred relics blessed by Baba's touch-

1. Brass bell and saffron flags, 2. The chulla inside Dwarkamai,
3. The wooden pillar painted in ochre, 4. Replica of earthen pot,
5. Incense stick stand fixed to the floor, 6. Holy basil plant in its stone pot,
7. Wheat sack in display case, 8. Nimbar, 9. Etched footprints, 10. Kolamba,
11. Hand mill, 12. Stone carved tortoise, 13. Flags donated by Rasane and Nimonkar family.

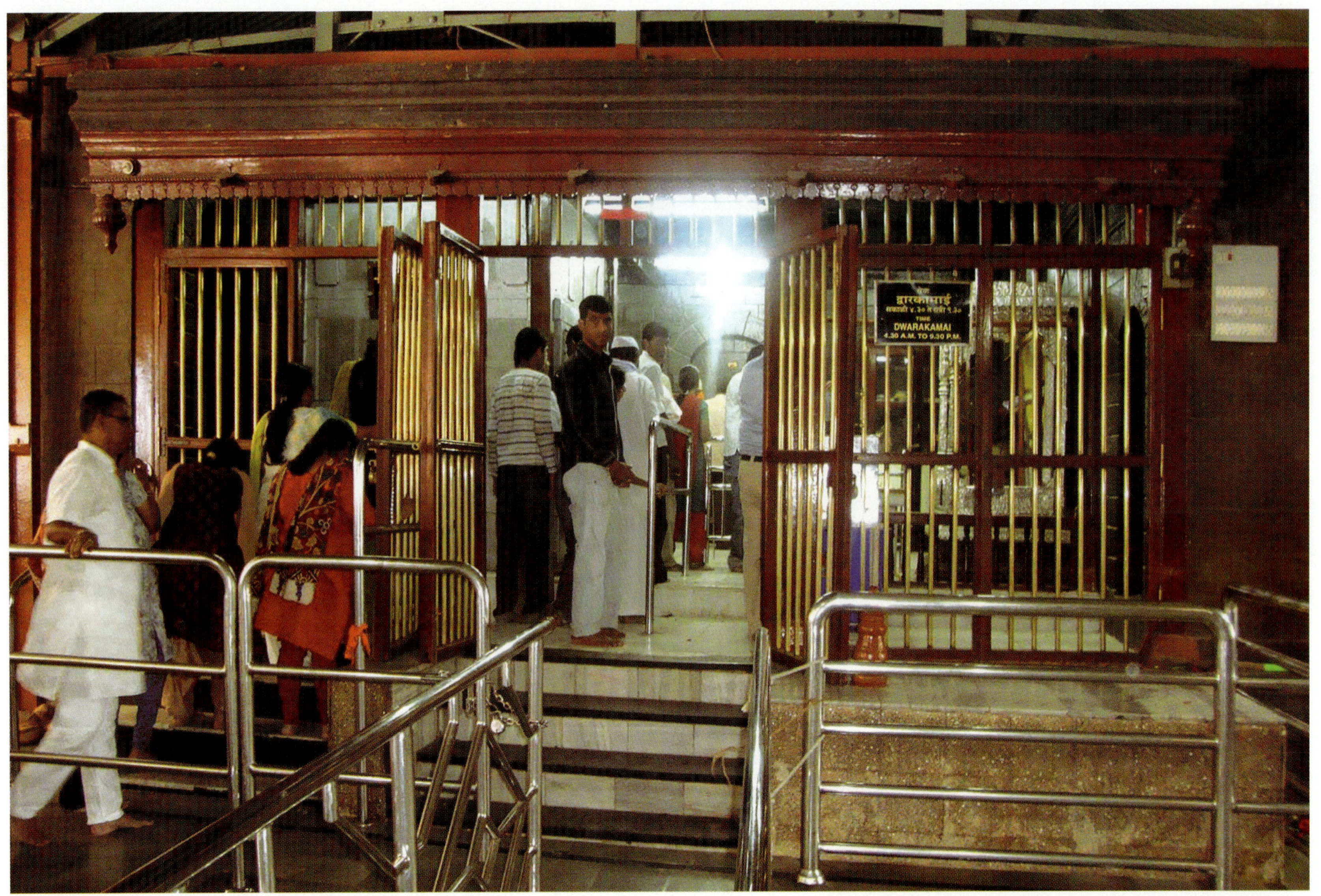

Long shot of Sanctum Sanctorum: Devotees queue up to prostrate in front of Baba. The haze from the ever burning Dhunimai imparts a halo to the surroundings of Dwarkamai. The intricate carvings on wood panels are visible.

A panoramic view of the 'Stone pose' of Baba- D.D. Neroys's oil painting is displayed against the backdrop of Baba's favourite stone on which he sat for long hours. On either side of Baba's feet are the stone idols of Shyama Sunder, Baba's horse and a tiger. The long suffering tiger had laid down its life in Baba's august presence.

→

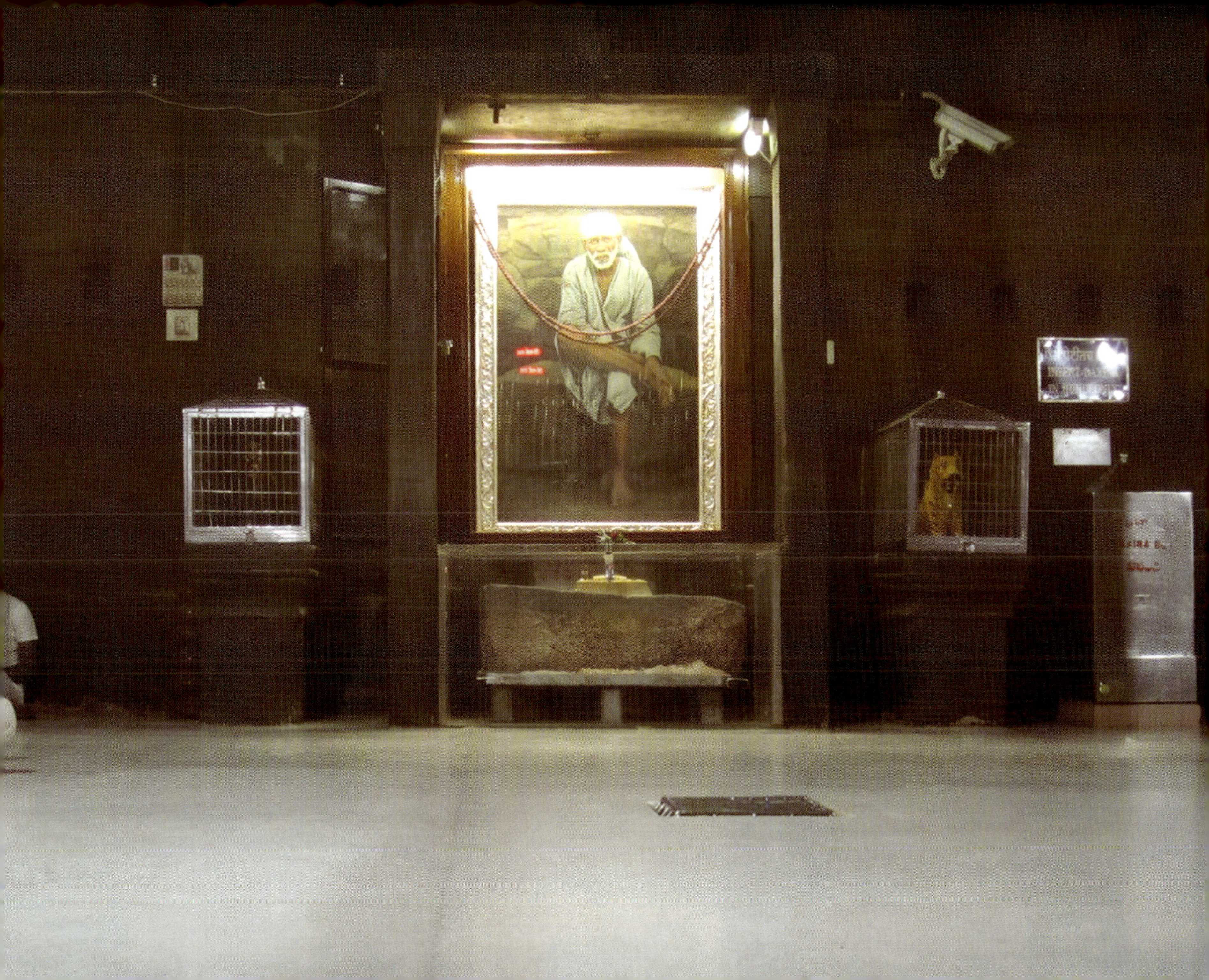

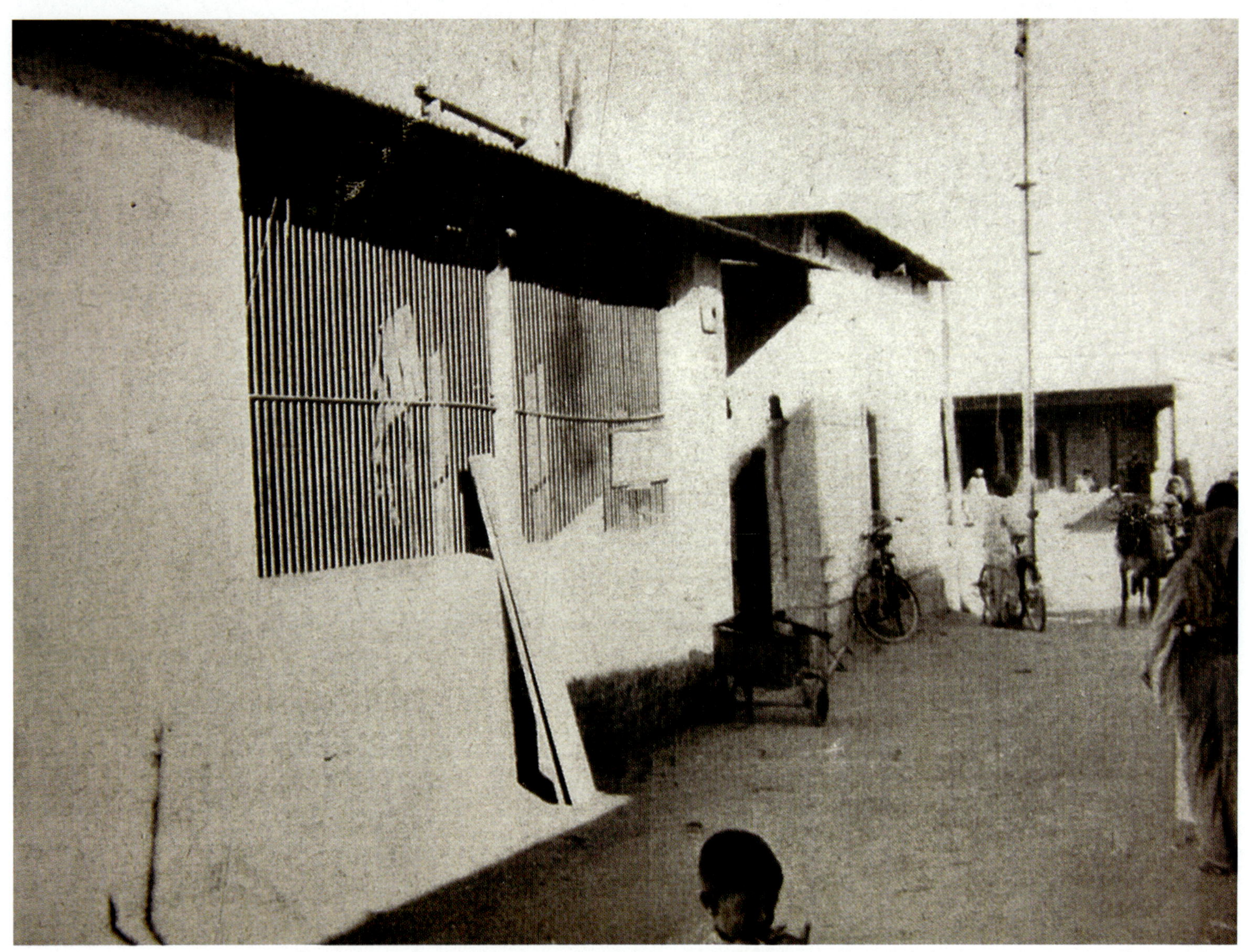

Dwarkamai- *Vaikunth* (Heaven on Earth) where Shri Sai Samarth dwelt. *(1974)*

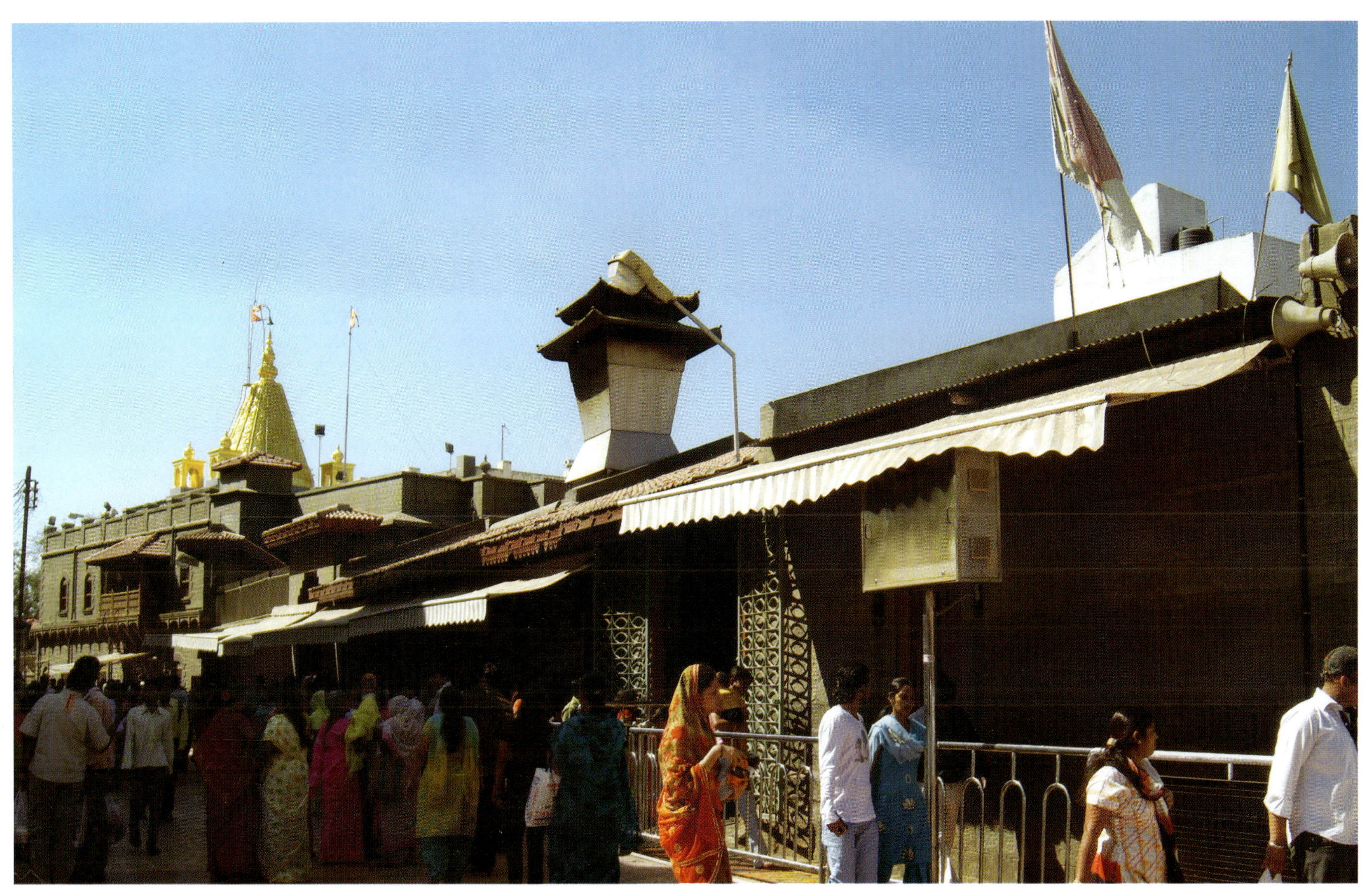

A wide angle recent view of Dwarkamai- The picture shows flags atop the masjid along with the chimney above the Dhunimai chamber. The gold plated dome of Samadhi Mandir glitters in the background. *(2011)*

CHAVADI

The word Chavadi means a meeting place for the villagers. Baba used this south-facing Chavadi for discourses with His disciples and devotees. One day, perturbed by a particularly violent storm, the devotees entreated him to shift from the crumbling and leaky Dwarkamai to the relatively sturdier Chavadi. Baba refused initially, but succumbed to the love and concern of His devotees. Thereafter, He slept in Chavadi every alternate day and stuck to this routine.

On entering Chavadi, one can see a plaque bearing the name of Chinchanikar family. The issueless couple was devoted to Shri Sai and had offered the proceeds of a favourable court verdict for repairing Chavadi. With Baba's grace, the family's name has been immortalised by being eternally linked to Baba's Chavadi.
The Chavadi has a bifurcated entrance, the left one being exclusively reserved for females with the males going through the right entrance. The enclosure on the left is graced by the oil painting of artist Ambaram of Navasari who put his dream about Baba on a canvas. In the enclosure on the right, Baba gazes out of a black and white portrait, encased in a glass box with its border laced with silver. This photograph is known as the '*Raj Upachar pose*'.

This photograph is taken out every Thursday with great reverence in an elaborate ceremony that leaves the milling audience spellbound. The procession is telecast live in the Shirdi temple complex. It begins from Samadhi Mandir where the Raj Upachar photograph has been transferred. Tilak and Naivedya are applied and offered to the photograph and it is taken in a procession through Samadhi Mandir and placed on the bedecked palanquin in Dwarkamai. The cavalcade, led by dancing troupes, lazium players and drum playing cadres, bands of musicians and flag bearing devotees, presents a thrilling spectacle and halts in front of Chavadi. The photograph is then carried back into Chavadi, accompanied by a phalanx of staff-bearers (*chopdars*). A chillum is offered to Baba and aarti is performed. Entire Shirdi watches with bated breath, every eye riveted on various facets of Baba.

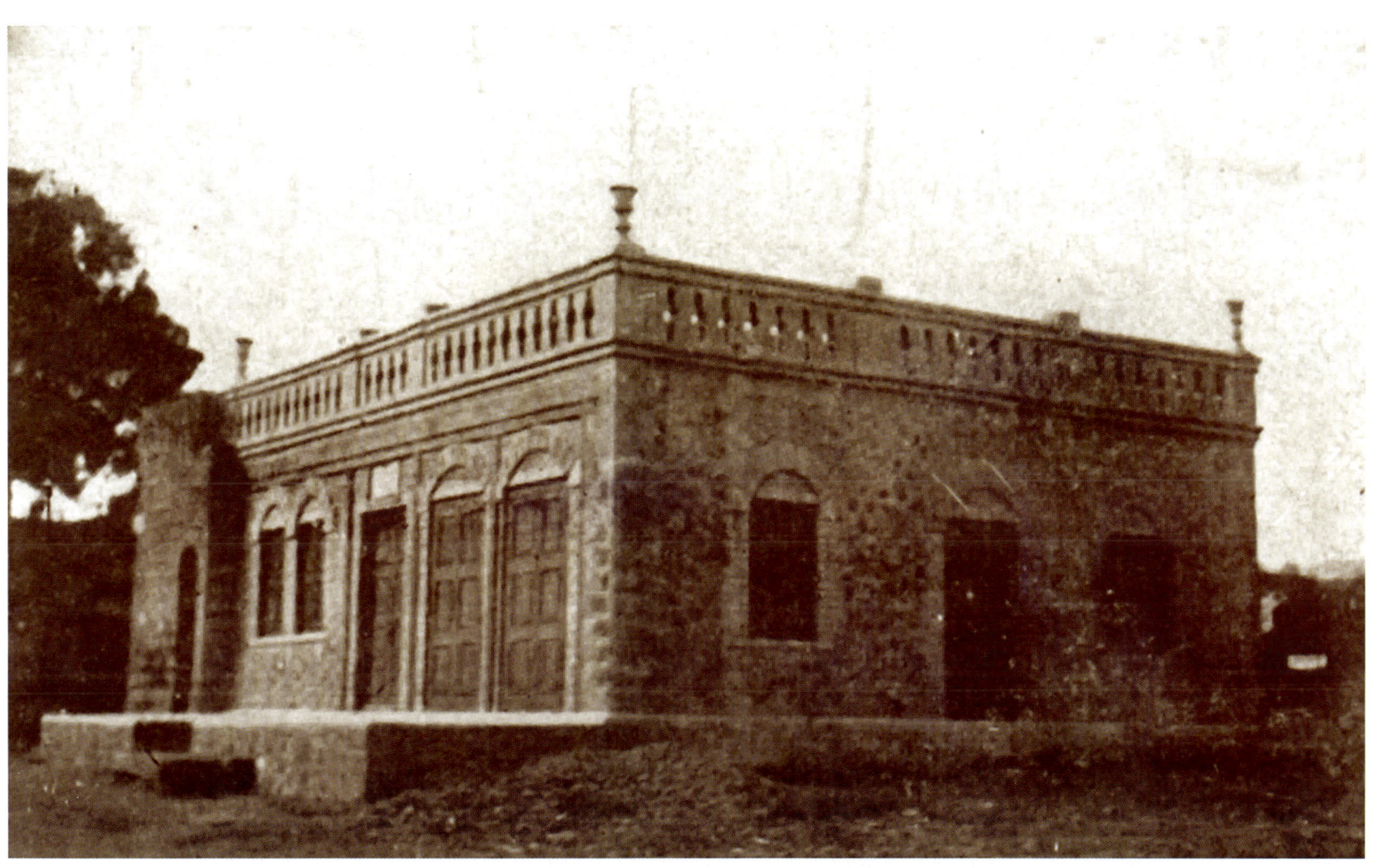

A landscape view of the old Chavadi which showed arched entrances and windows. The terrace has patterned tiles on the boundary along with miniature minarets on the four corners. *(1920)*

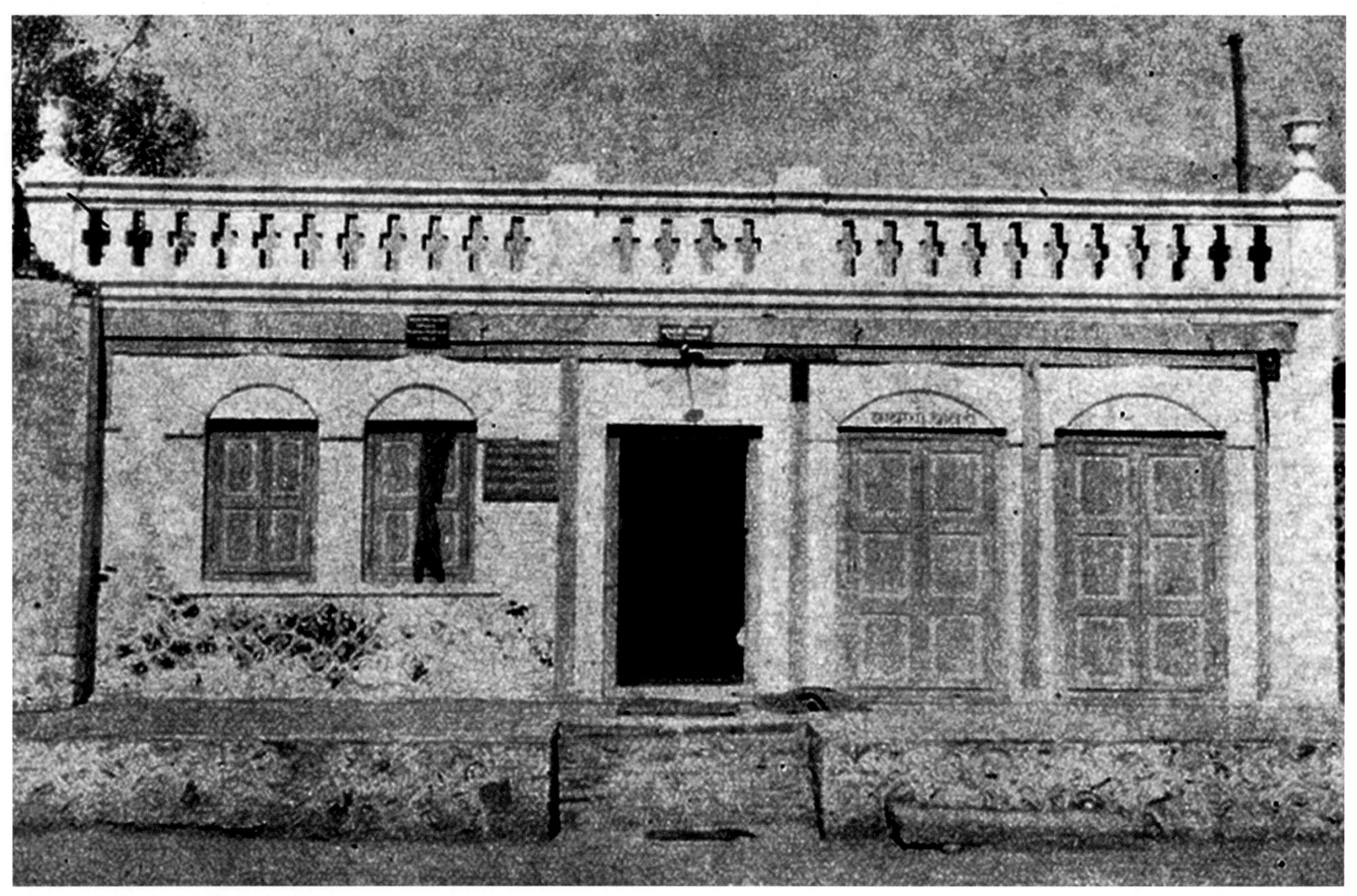

Old Chavadi's frontal view- Every pattern on the terrace wall, the grilled windows, the canopy inside and the stairs are visible.

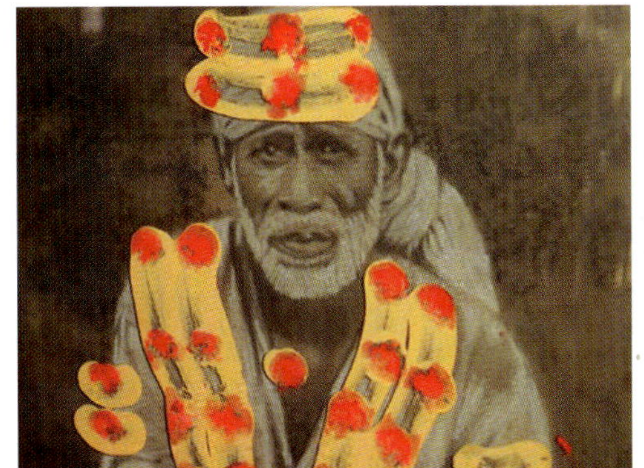

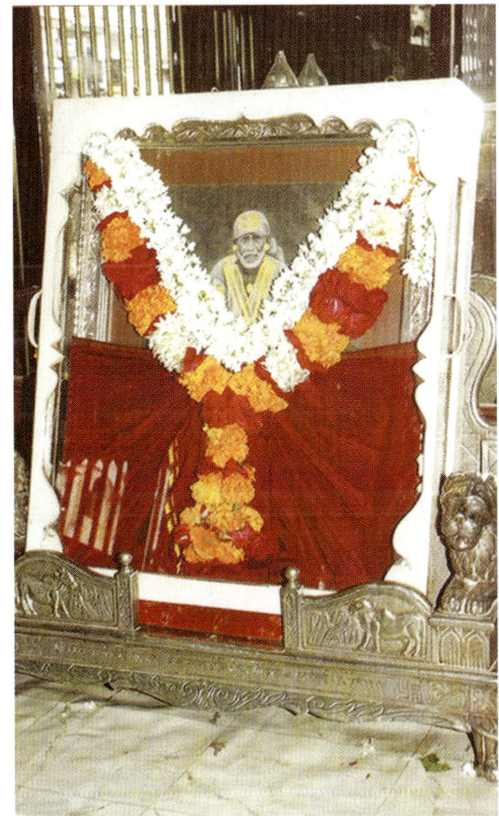

A small photograph of Baba on the silver throne. *(Raj Upachar photograph)*

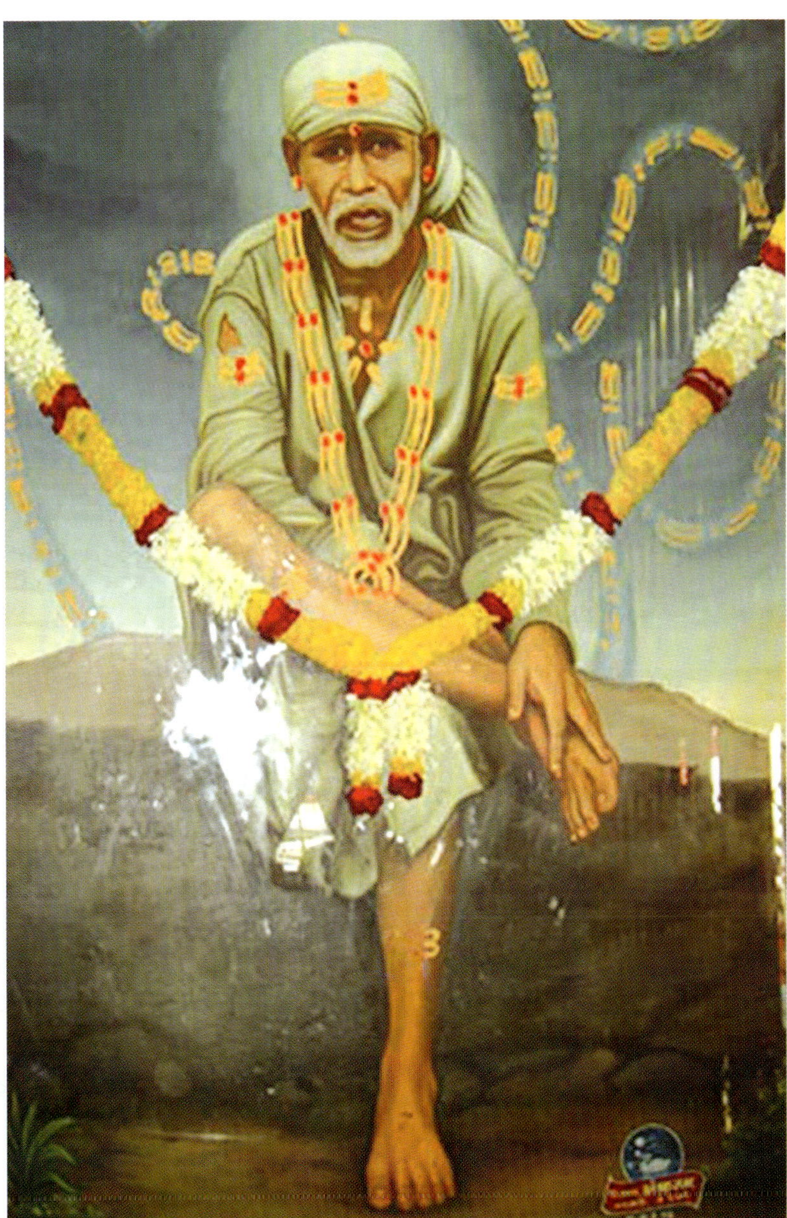

Oil painting of Baba, painted by artist Ambaram Lalbhai Kahar of Navasari according to his dream vision in year 1953.

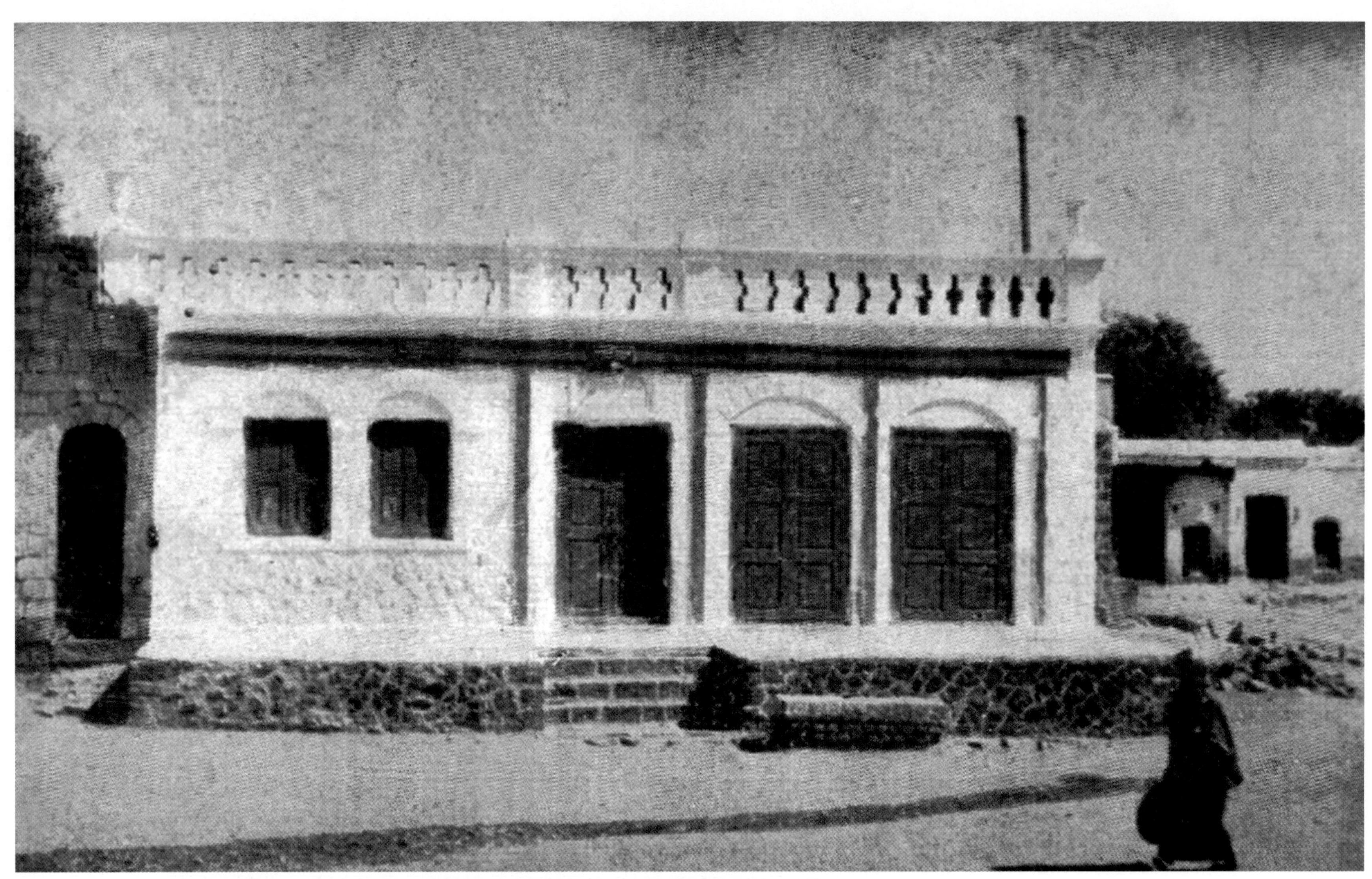

Photograph of Chavadi by Sir G.G. Welling, Poona. *(1970)*

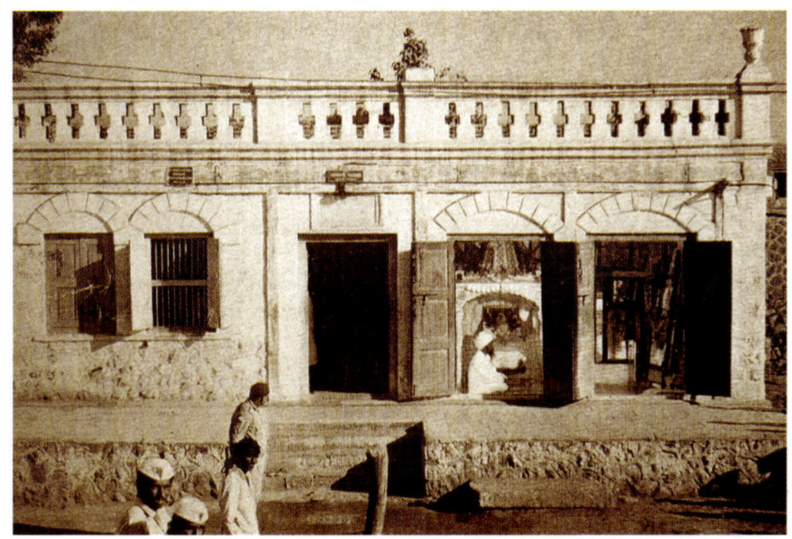

Front view of Chavadi

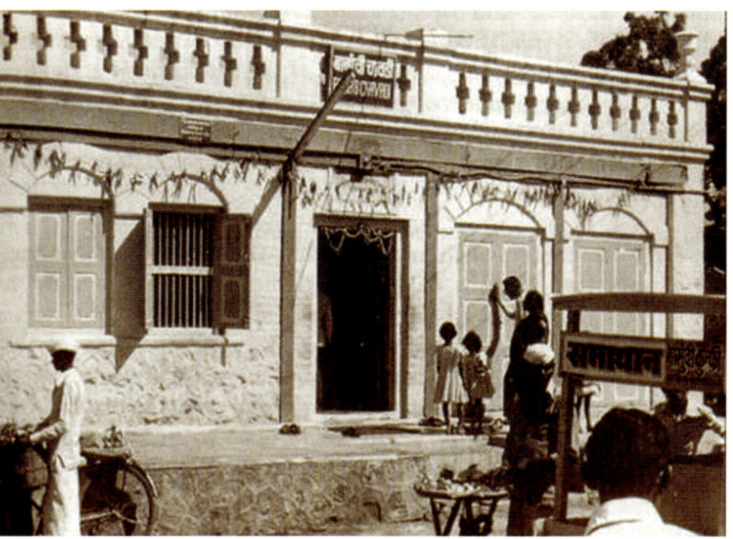

Local villagers outside Chavadi *(1960)*

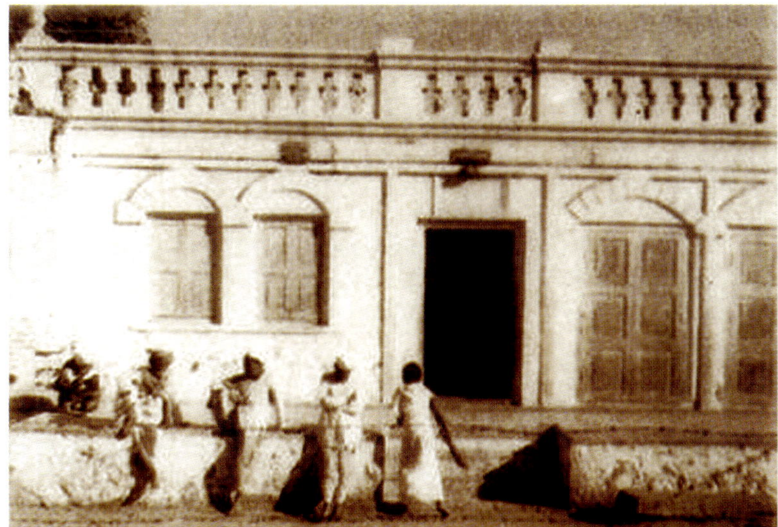

Some local people of Shirdi sitting on the platform outside Chavadi

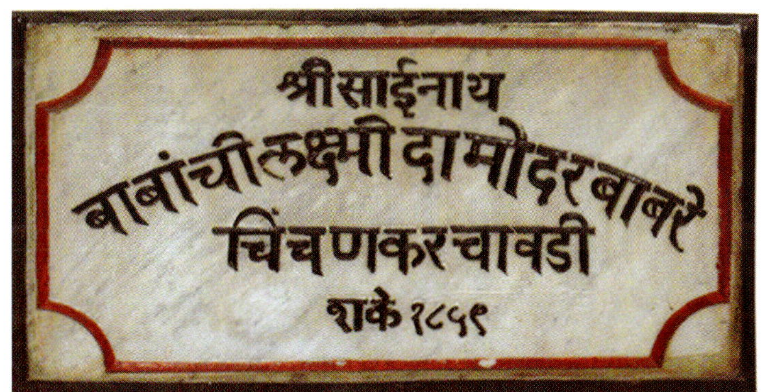

The plaque outside Chavadi, forever linking the Chinchanikar family with Baba on which "*Shri Sai Nath, Babanchi Lakshmi Damodar Babre, Chinchanikar Chavadi, Saka 1859.*" is inscribed.

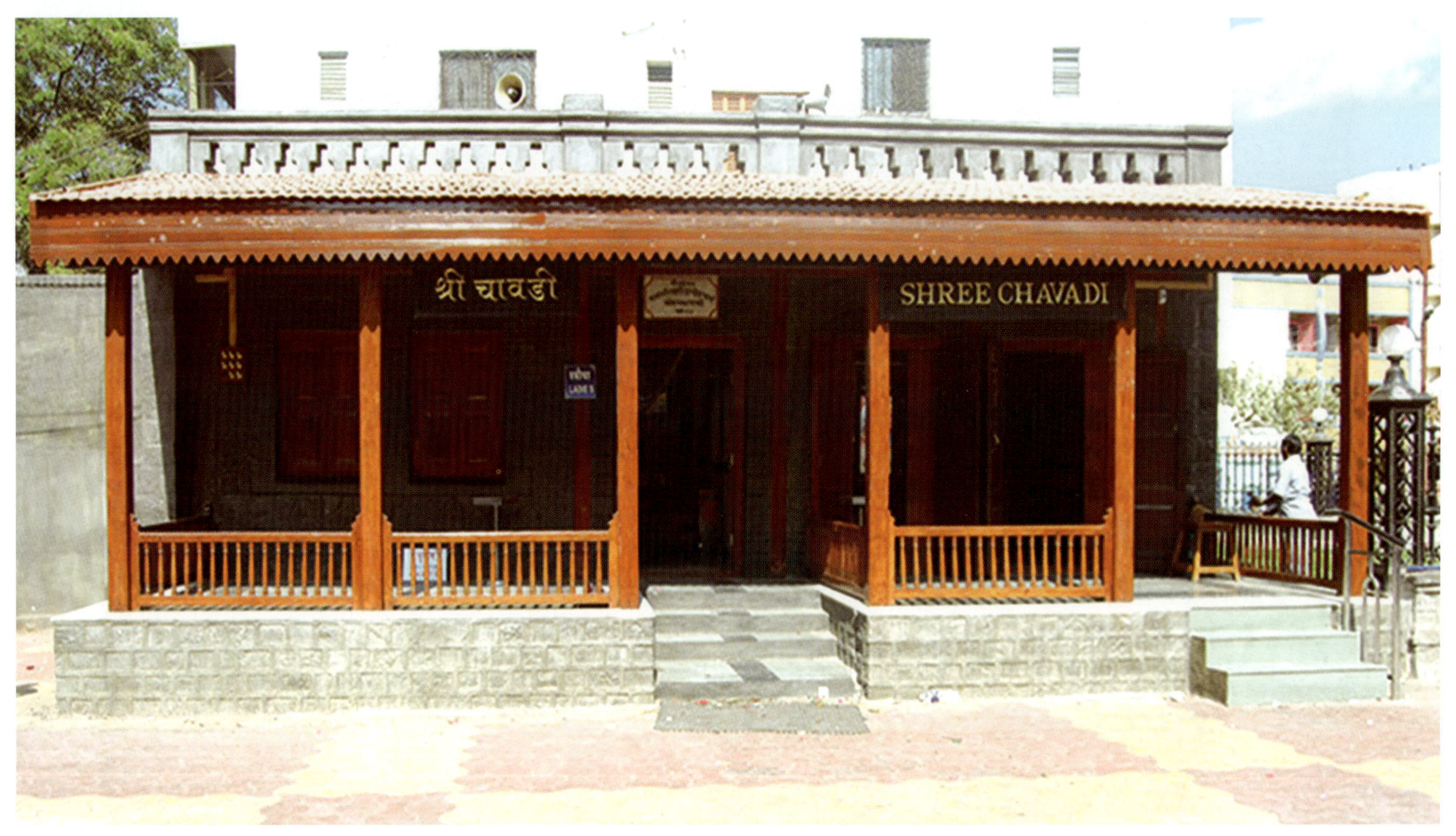

A refurbished Chavadi with a newly constructed wooden facade in front. The left enclosure admits only female devotees. The right enclosure, with separate steps leading to it, is the exclusive worship area for men. The rising throngs at Shree Chavadi have necessitated this bifurcation of devotees. *(2011)*

A rare photograph of the culmination of the Thursday procession of Baba's Palki in December 2011. The blessed crowd watches in mesmerised silence as Chopdars in red outfit stand outside Chavadi while the priests inside offer chillum to Baba. The Palkhi stands in the centre, its occupant, the Raj Upachar photograph of Baba, now resting back in Chavadi. The proceedings are being telecast live in the temple complex. →

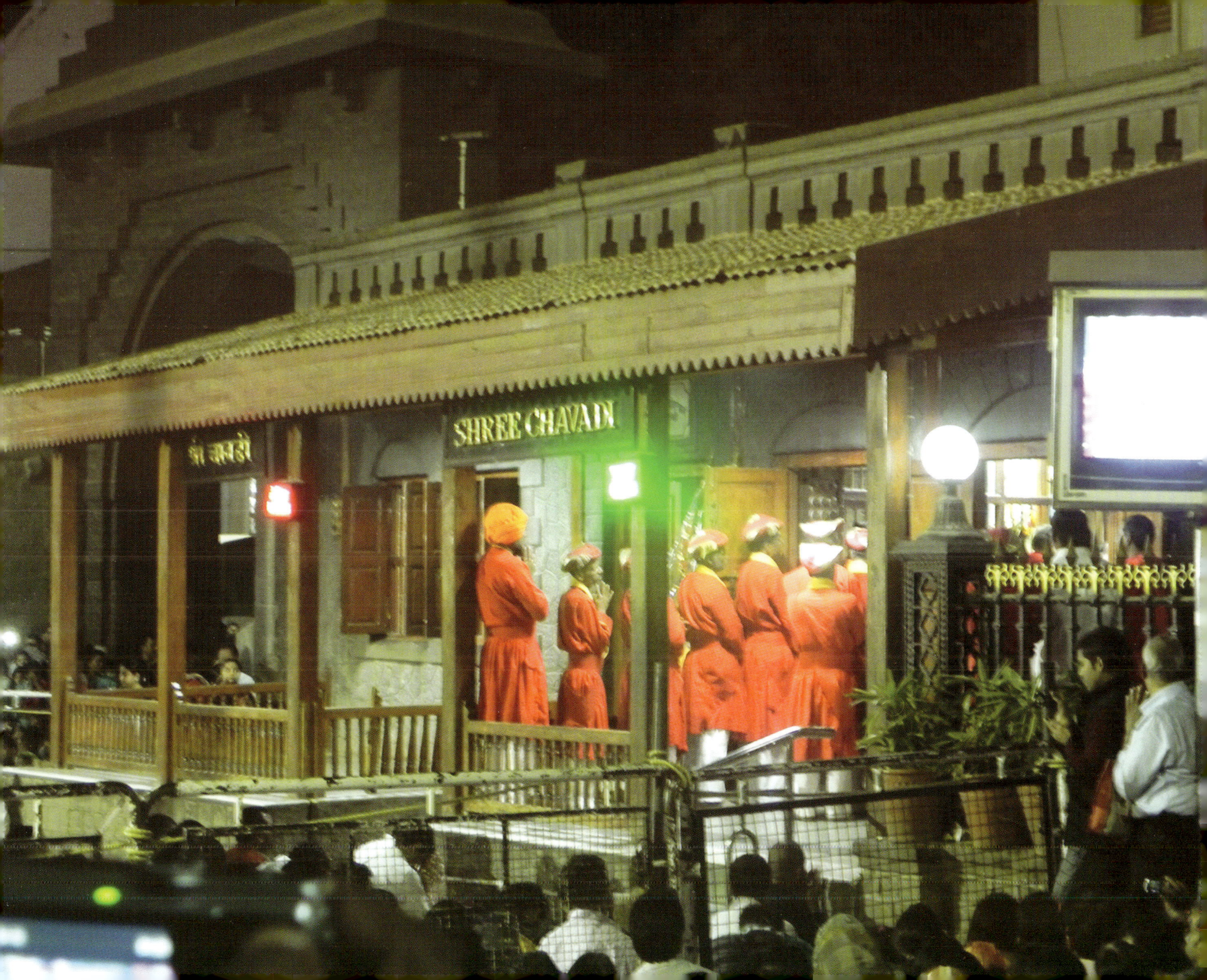
SHREE CHAVADI

GURUSTHAN

Baba had appeared for the first time in Shirdi as a young lad of 16 without any physical ties to the outside world. His blazing countenance made people flock to the neem tree where the young wandering soul sat in splendid isolation. This tree is said to surpass the magic and mystique of the *kalpa vriksha* which, scriptures say, flourishes in heaven. People from all over the world strive to possess a leaf of this holy tree which can relieve their ailments.

No knowledge can be imparted or imbibed without the benign guidance of a teacher, called 'Guru' by most. In fact, beyond material pursuits, philosophical and spiritual nirvana is the exclusive domain of a Guru. On their own, ignorant selves just move around in ever widening circles in the desert of life. Cognizant of this universal truth, Shri Sai Baba meditated under this neem tree and offered prayers to His Guru, Venkusha. He did penance under this neem tree inspired by His Guru. He established the truth, once again, that communion with God can be effected only through a Guru, who opens the right channels of communication with the Almighty.

It was the devotion, exemplified by His meditation and penance, which gave the spot its name 'Gurusthan'. He once said, "This is the place of my Divine Teacher (*Sadguru Maharaj*). Anyone who applies a coat of slurry of cow dung on this area, on Thursday and Friday, and burns incense and offers prayers will receive my Lord's blessings." This place was sanctified by His penance for 12 years. Devotees have continued to receive His benefaction by offering fragrant myrrh and incense sticks in the vicinity of this spot.

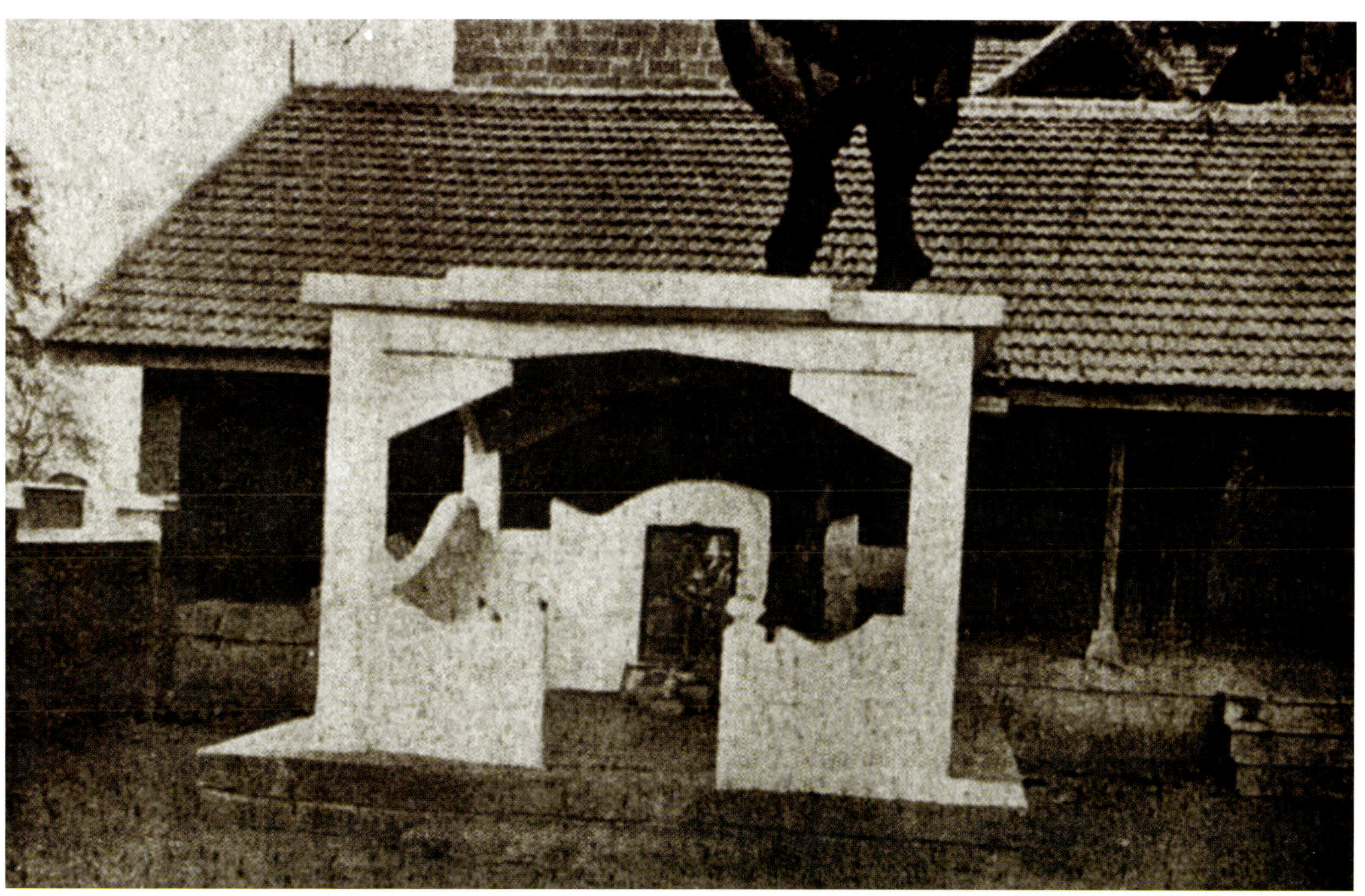

An amazing photograph of the old and modest structure surrounding Gurusthan. Baba's portrait occupied the central space. His favourite companion, the neem tree towers above Sathewada, a tiled-roof mud complex adjacent to Samadhi Mandir. The complex, visible between Gurusthan and Samadhi Mandir's wall, now stands demolished. *(1930)*

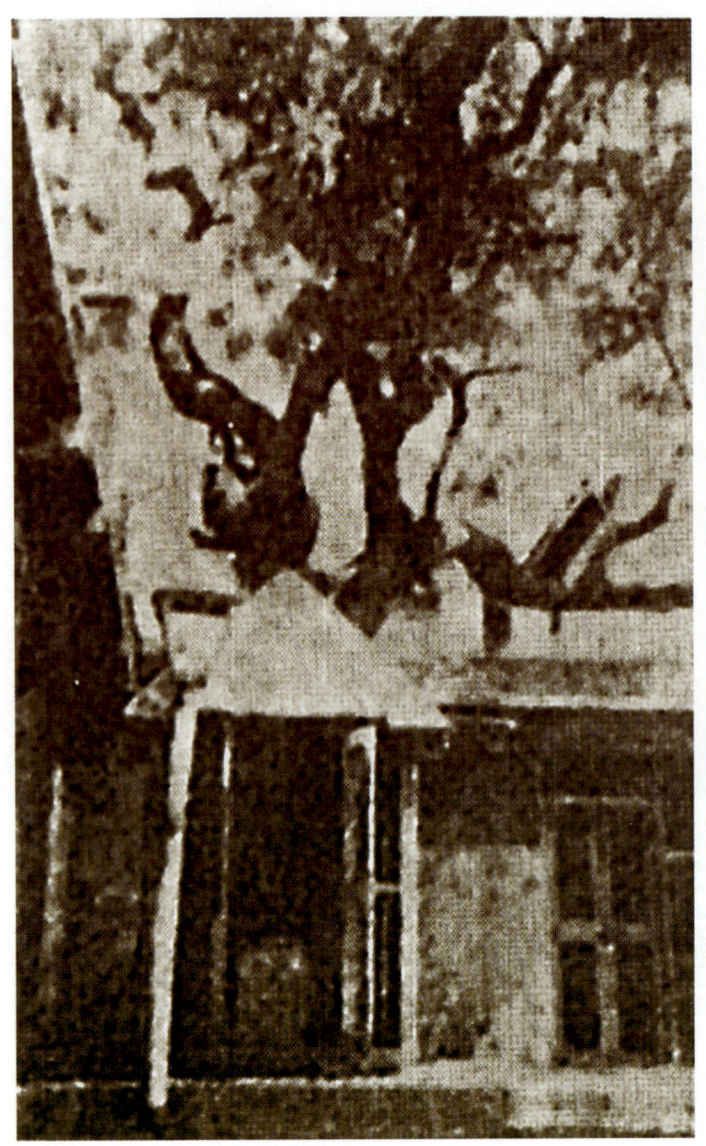

Gurupaduka sthan. *(1920)*

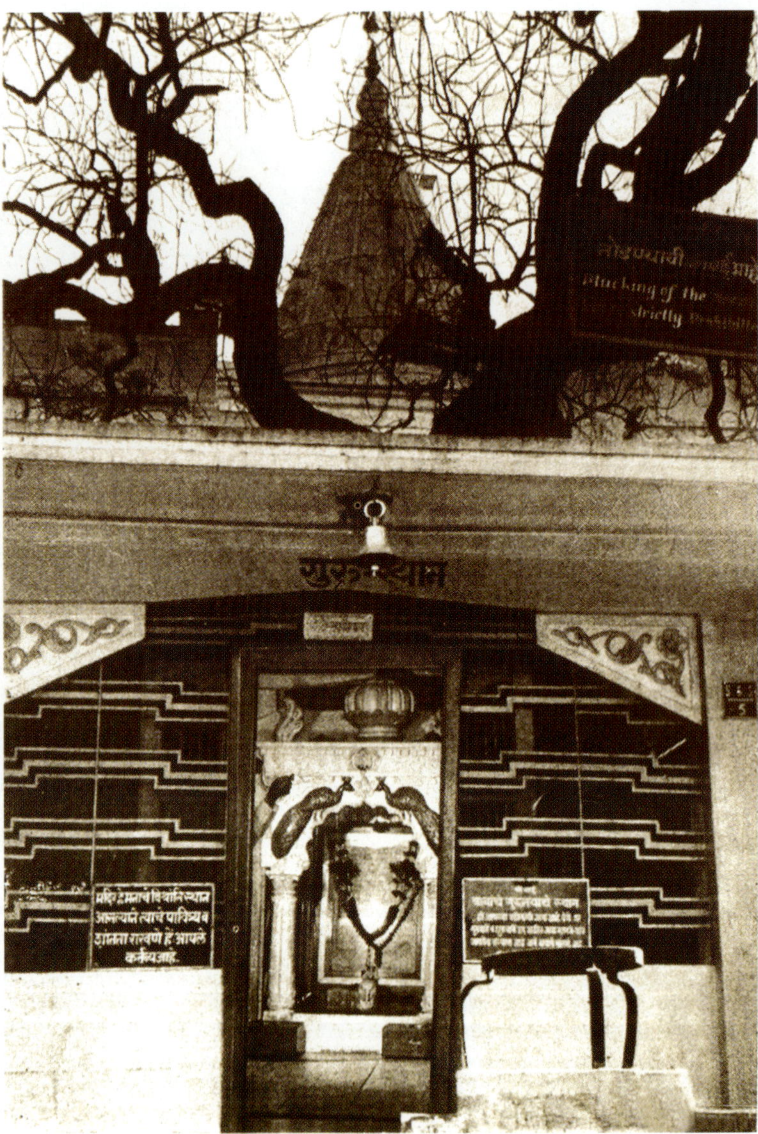

Samadhi Mandir dome peeping through the branches of the neem tree above the temple at Gurusthan. *(1974)*

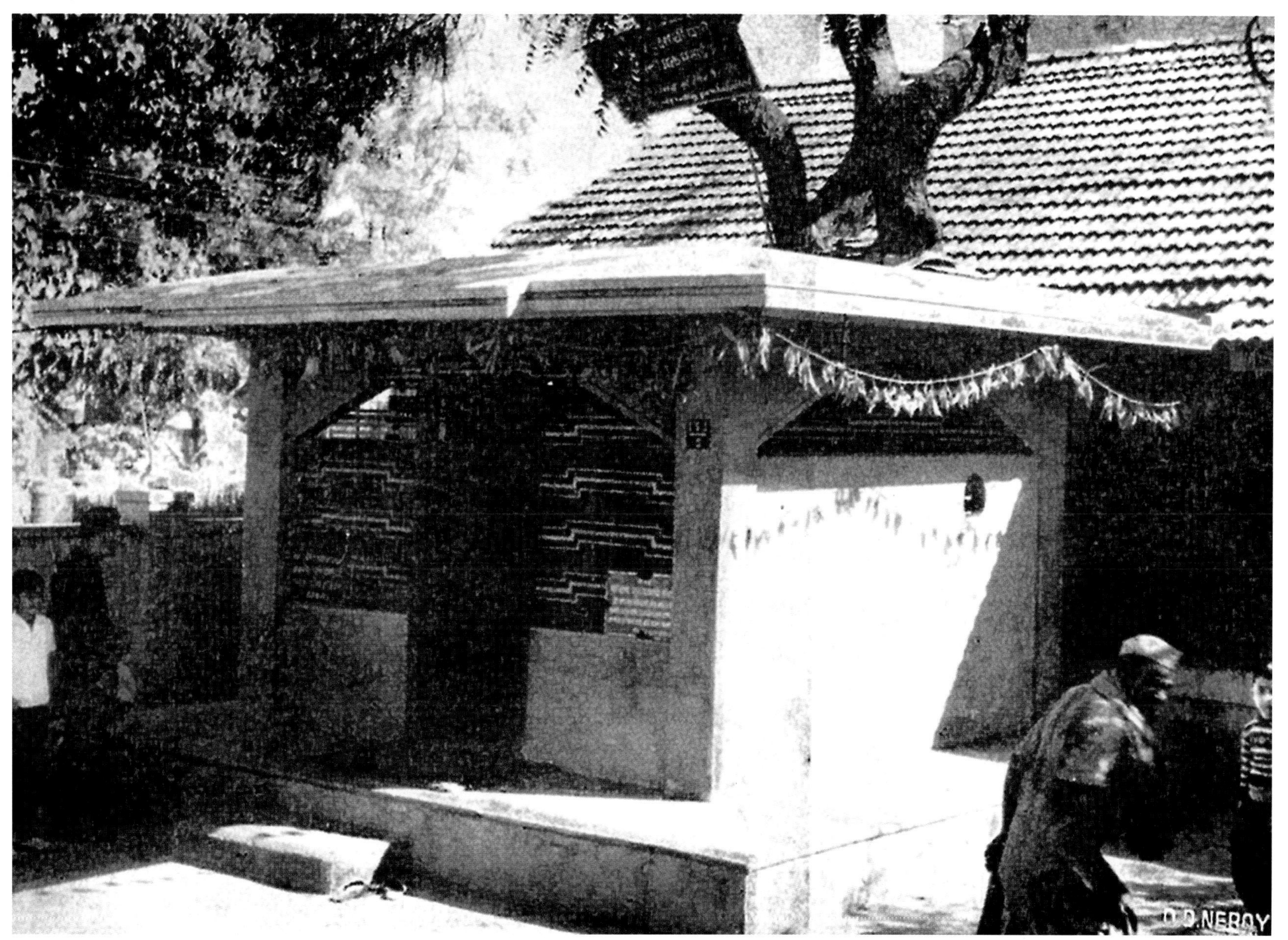

A plaque atop the neem tree requesting devotees not to pluck leaves from the tree. Gathering of fallen leaves is permitted. *(1974)*

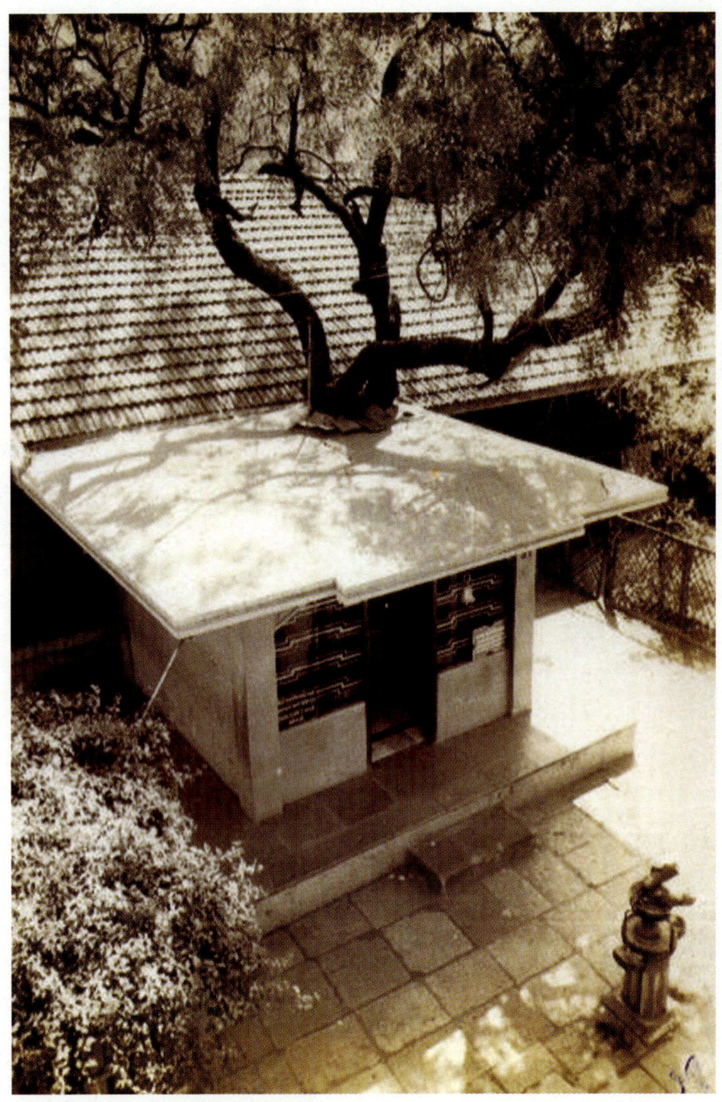

A magnificient view of Gurusthan. The neem tree looms out of the roof of the little west facing temple. Sathewada provides the backdrop and the permanent receptacle stand (built for receiving myrrh and incense sticks) is seen facing the temple. *(1974)*.

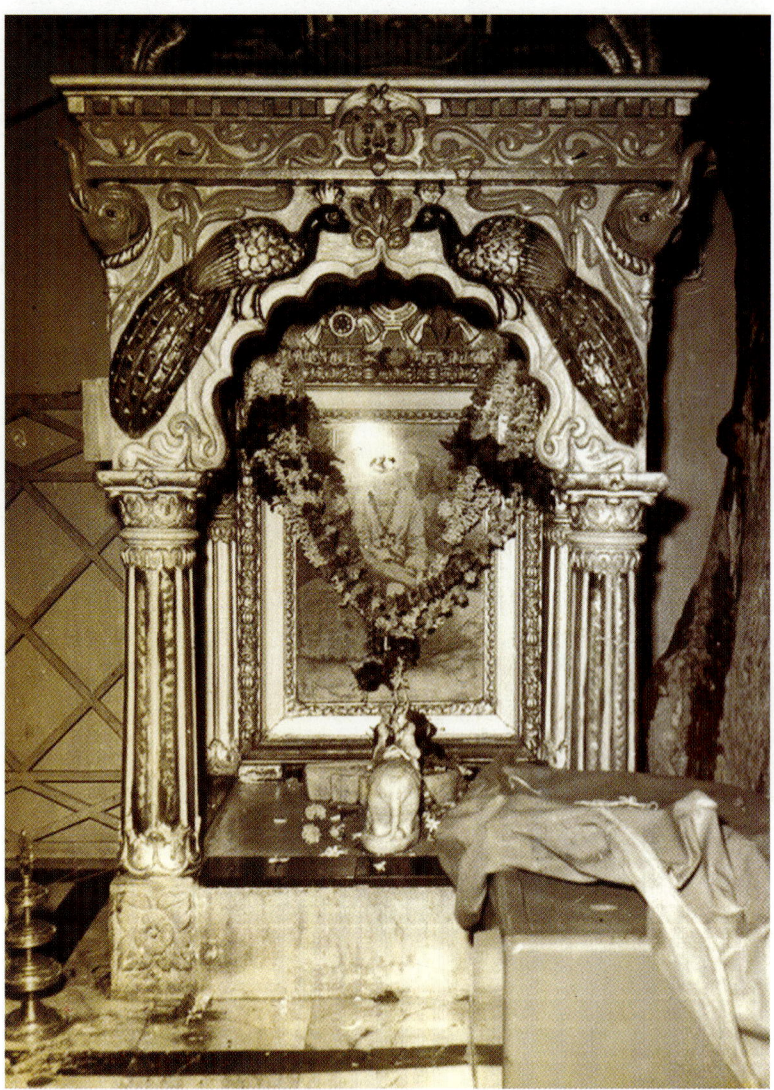

Baba's photograph, adorns this small pavilion which was specially built to house this portrait. It has an intricately carved roof, showing peacocks in bass relief, atop four exquisitely carved pillars. A marble statue of Nandi, Shiva's sacred bull was installed opposite the Shivling. The Shivling was gifted by Baba to one of his favourite disciples, Megha.

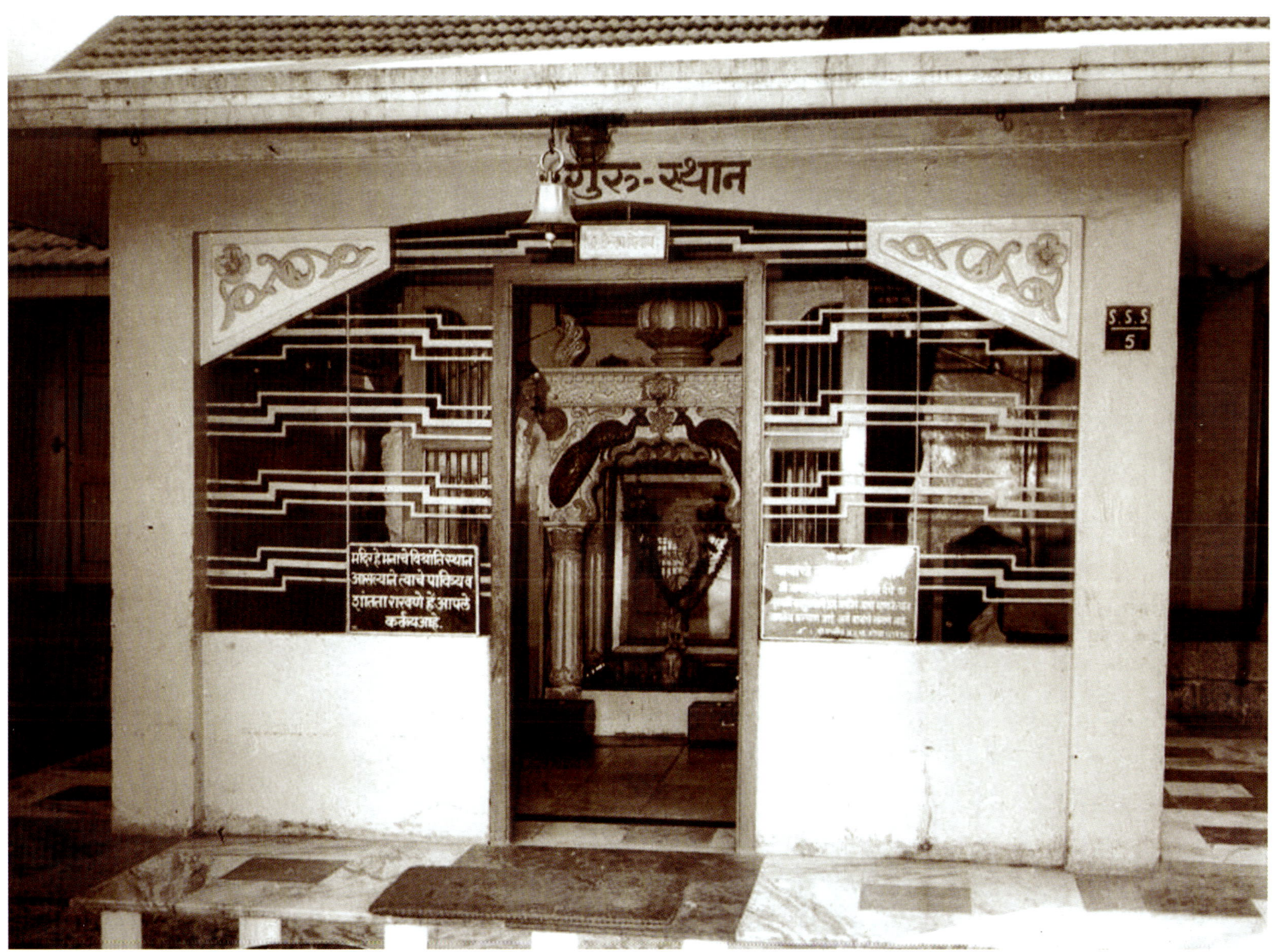

A front view of *Turbat*, the Samadhi of Baba's Guru erected at the foot of Neem tree. The temple built above it bears the inscription of Shirdi Sai Baba Sansthan. *(1975)*

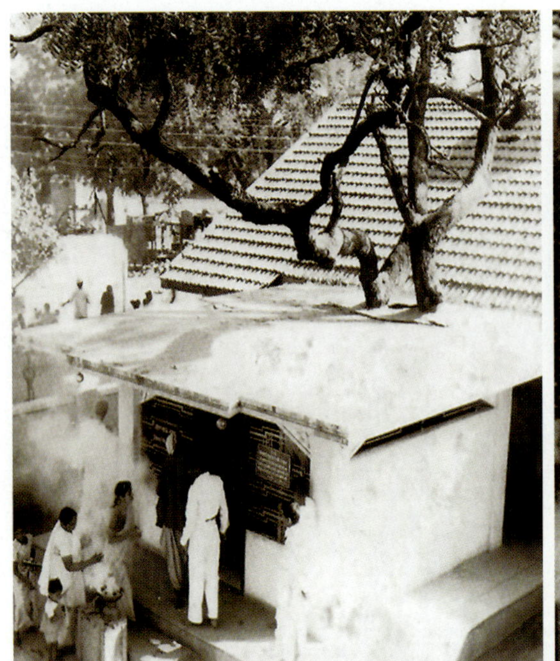

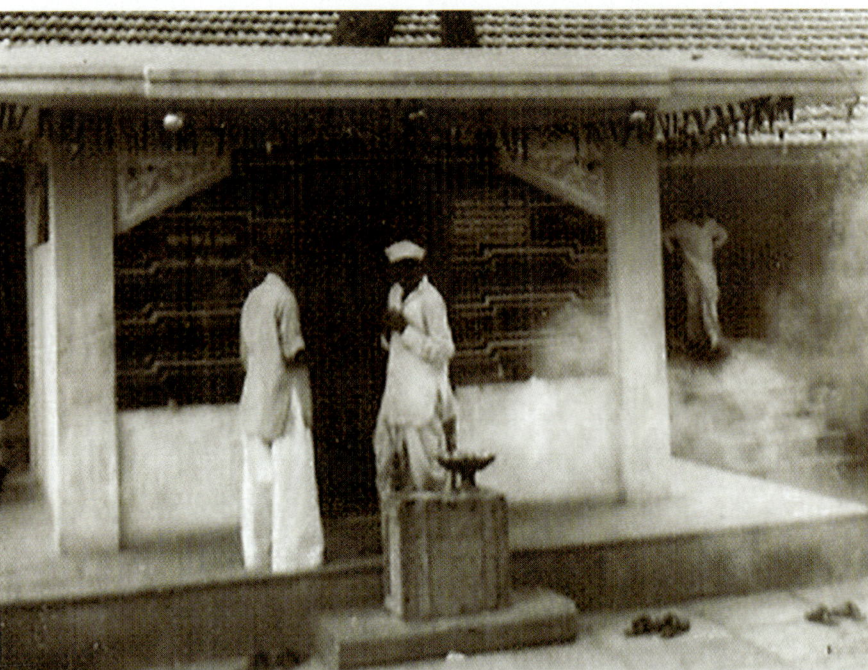

The majestic neem tree gazes down at devotees who are offering myrrh and *lobaan* at the receptacle.

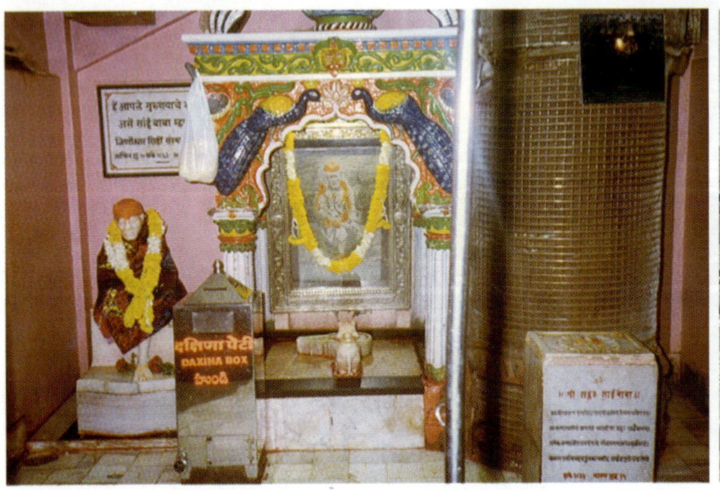

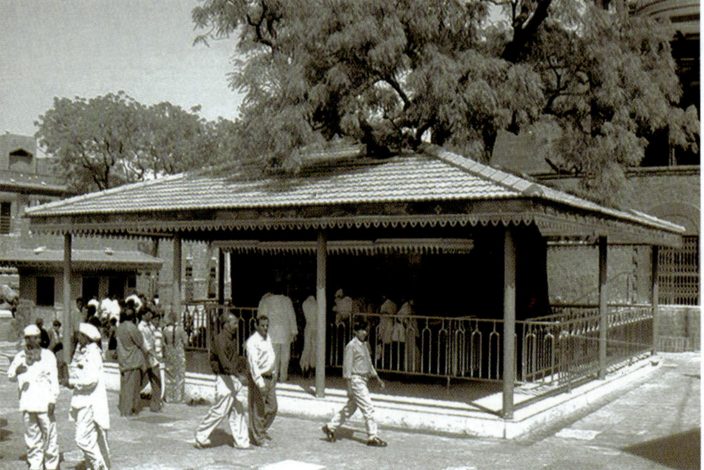

Baba's marble idol was installed next to His portrait in 1974. The trunk of the neem tree is encased in a steel mesh. In the front, Baba's footprints have been etched on a stone block. On the front panel, the fourth verse of Shri Sainath Mahima Stotra, written by Upasani Maharaj, has been inscribed.

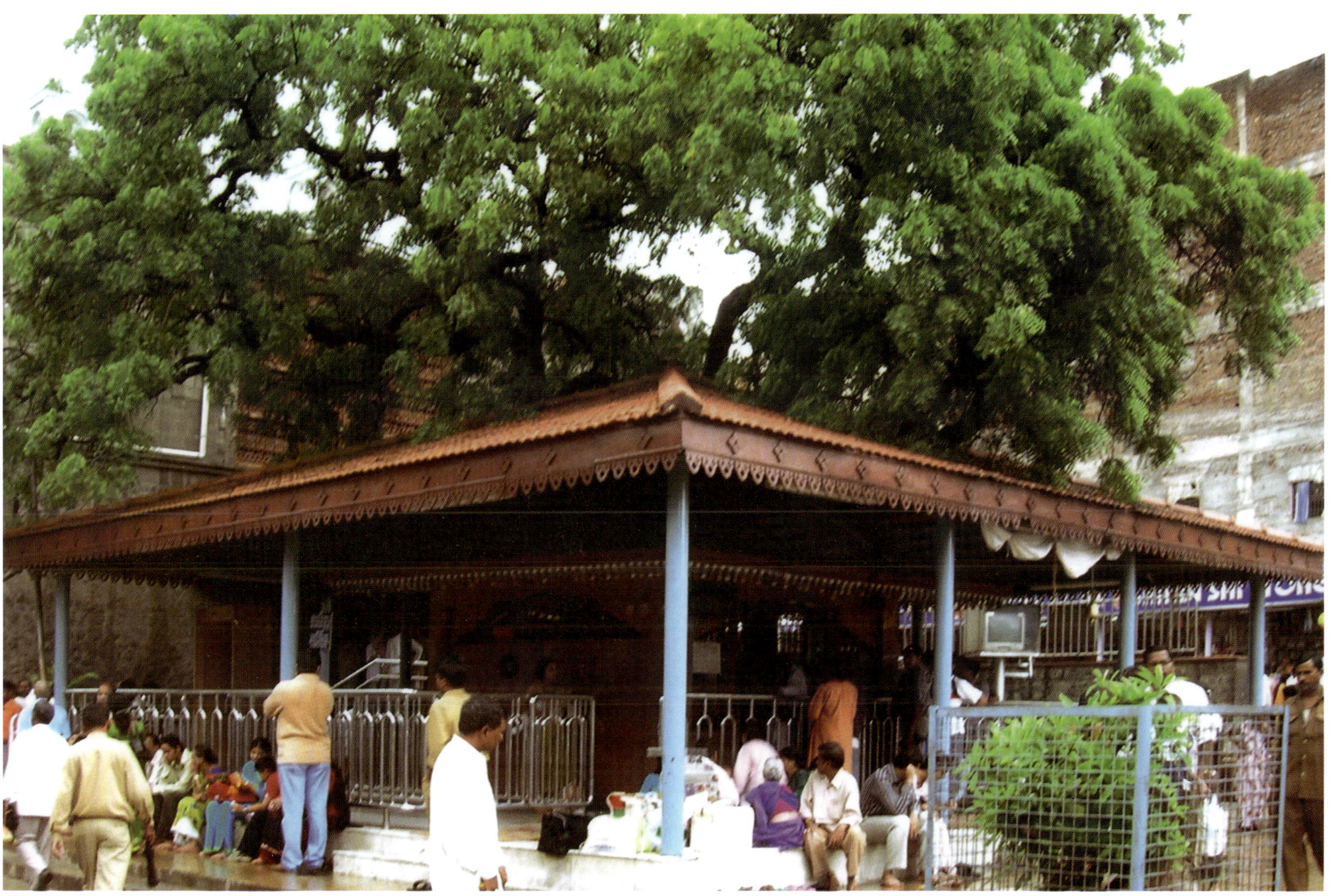

A rcconstructed Gurusthan- A bigger temple was constructed around the original small temple in 1974. The neem tree dominates the compound. People circled the shrine inside the grilled enclosure. The channel gate of Samadhi Mandir is visible since Sathewada had been demolished earlier in 1998-99. Lobaan is now offered at a bigger structure away from the temple.

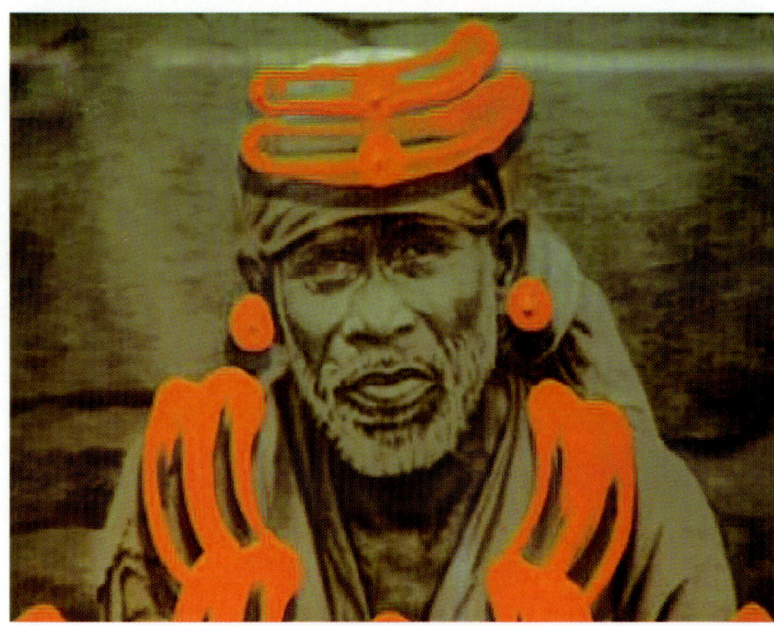

Shri Sai Baba's Photograph at Gurusthan.

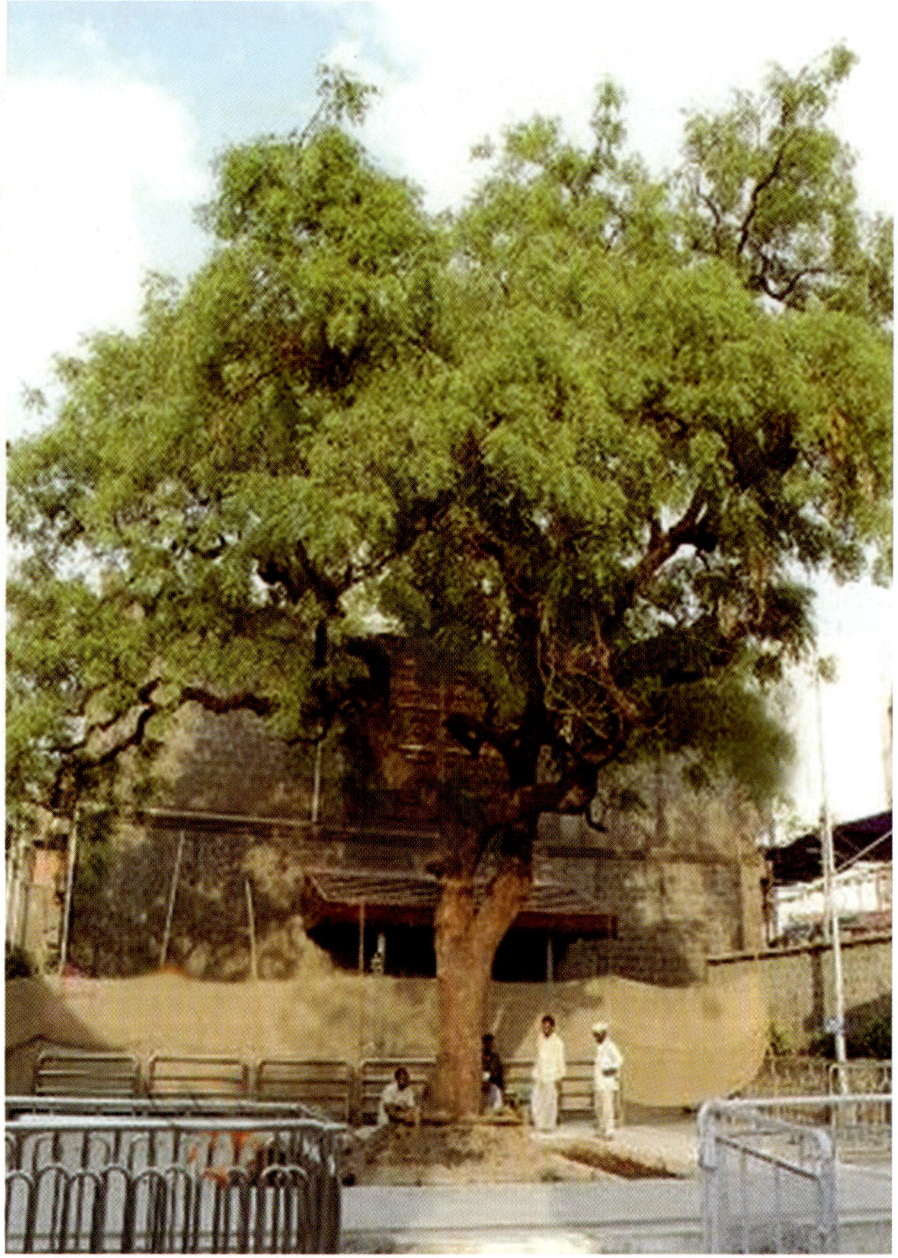

Notice the halo around Baba in the Photograph! This halo appeared out of the blue on the photograph, reflecting the divine aura of His Holiness Shri Sai Baba. Today the portrait sits in the lap of greenery, replicating His desire to commune with nature. Baba's grooming of Lendi Baugh establishes the credo that a healthy mind needs a healthy environment.

Alarm bells rang at Sansthan when the neem tree began to wither around April 2007. Consultations with the Horticulture Department pointed to rising temperatures around the tree due to influx of devotees. The existing structure was torn down and Baba's idol was transported to the Museum and covered. With Guru Purnima approaching fast, hectic efforts were made to install Baba's black and white portrait in a small pavilion. The area around the neem tree was left open, facilitating flow of oxygen to its sprawling roots. Devotees now walk around on a marble path, laid at a distance from the tree.

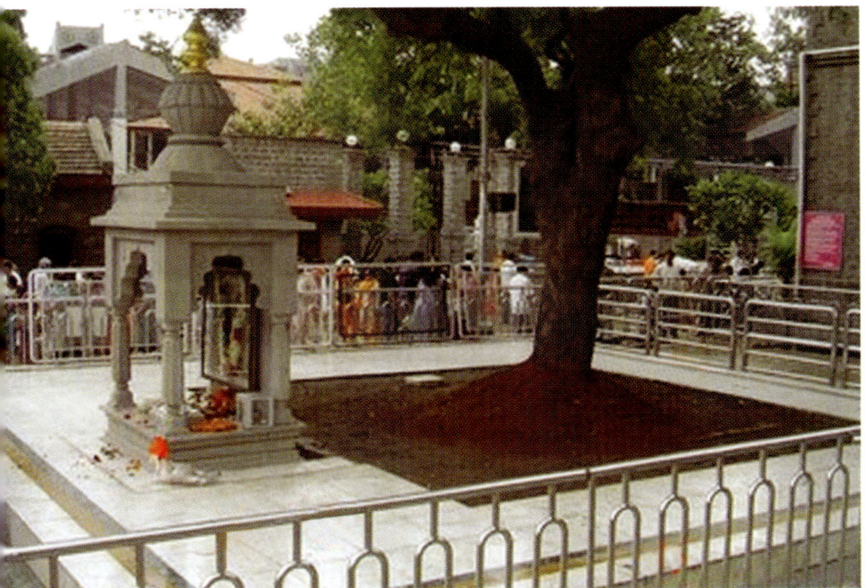

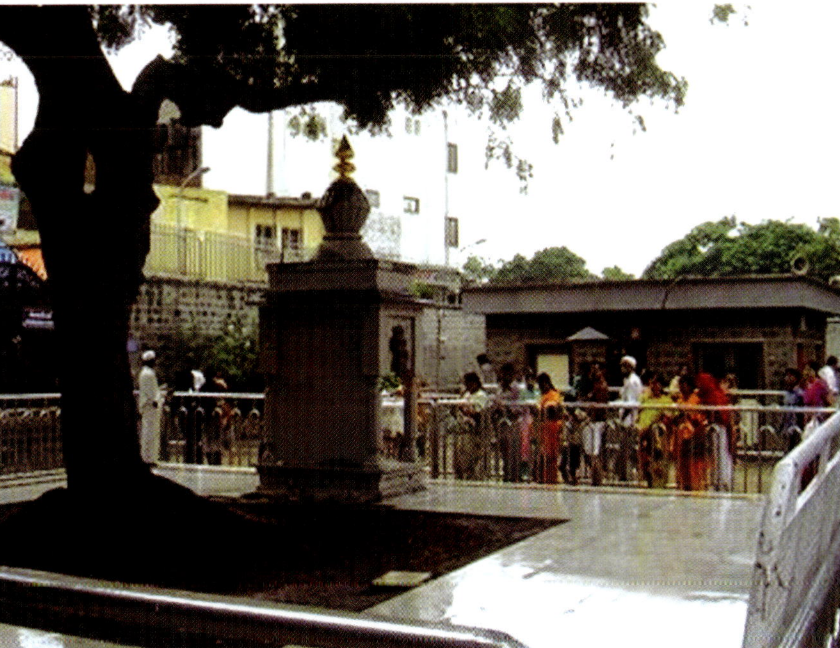

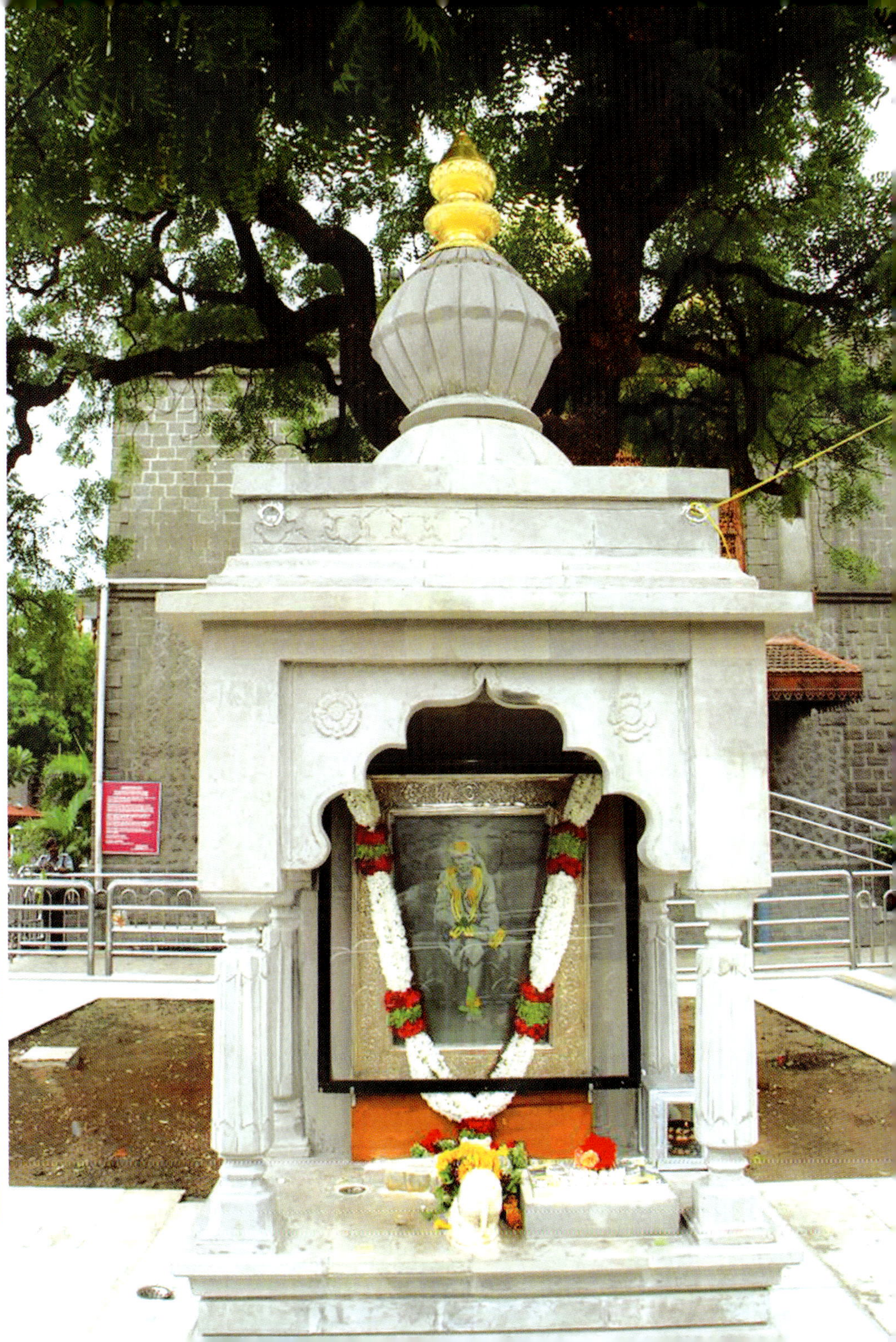

LENDI BAUGH

Baba's love for nature was reflected in His desire to be close to flora and fauna. He adopted strays, fed the birds and groomed the plants. Shirdi had been blessed by a small stream, Lendi, passing through it since long. It flowed underground and then emerged in a green stretch of land, called Lendi Baugh. The river bisected this park into two parts. Baba developed fondness for this green patch and groomed it into a garden. He went there twice a day. He sprinkled water in the four directions, for the amelioration of the sufferings of His devotees. Abdul Baba carried this water in pitchers. Later, His devotees started taking out a procession to the accompaniment of musical bands. They waited patiently at the gates of the garden while Baba spent contented hours in the peaceful environs of the Baugh. It was here that He lit Nanda Deep, the eternal lamp of life which shows the ray of light to those struggling in the dark. Lendi Baugh's front facade shows a bougainvillea which flourished till 1980s. The garden is full of trees and flowering plants like peepul (*ashwathha)*, neem, marigold, jasmine etc. The gate to this garden faces east. This piece of land was sanctified by Baba's feet and is referred to as 'Vaikunth', i.e. Heaven on earth.

Lendi Baugh is home to Samadhi of Shyama Karan, also known as Shyama Sunder, Baba's black horse. The horse was a gift from a horse merchant and Baba treated it like His soulmate. He never sat on this horse as He took the horse to be a reincarnation of a beloved devotee. The horse reciprocated Baba's affection in an almost human manner. It used to stand patiently in Dwarkamai, waiting for aarti to begin. Baba used to apply udi to the horse first and then to others. The bedecked horse danced with joy during the aarti, adorned with anklets and other finery. After Baba left for His heavenly abode, it would attend the aarti in Samadhi Mandir and bow in front of Samadhi. It used to be taken out in a procession on Vijaydashami Day. The horse, after breathing its last, was buried in Lendi Baugh. Its statue stands testimony to its immortal bond with Baba.

Baba used to throw coins into the Lendi river daily. Yet, His devotees were never tempted or got diverted from Baba's august presence. His devotees are still guided by His mantra of Patience and Devotion and are content to develop spiritually.

Lendi Baugh *(1975)* →

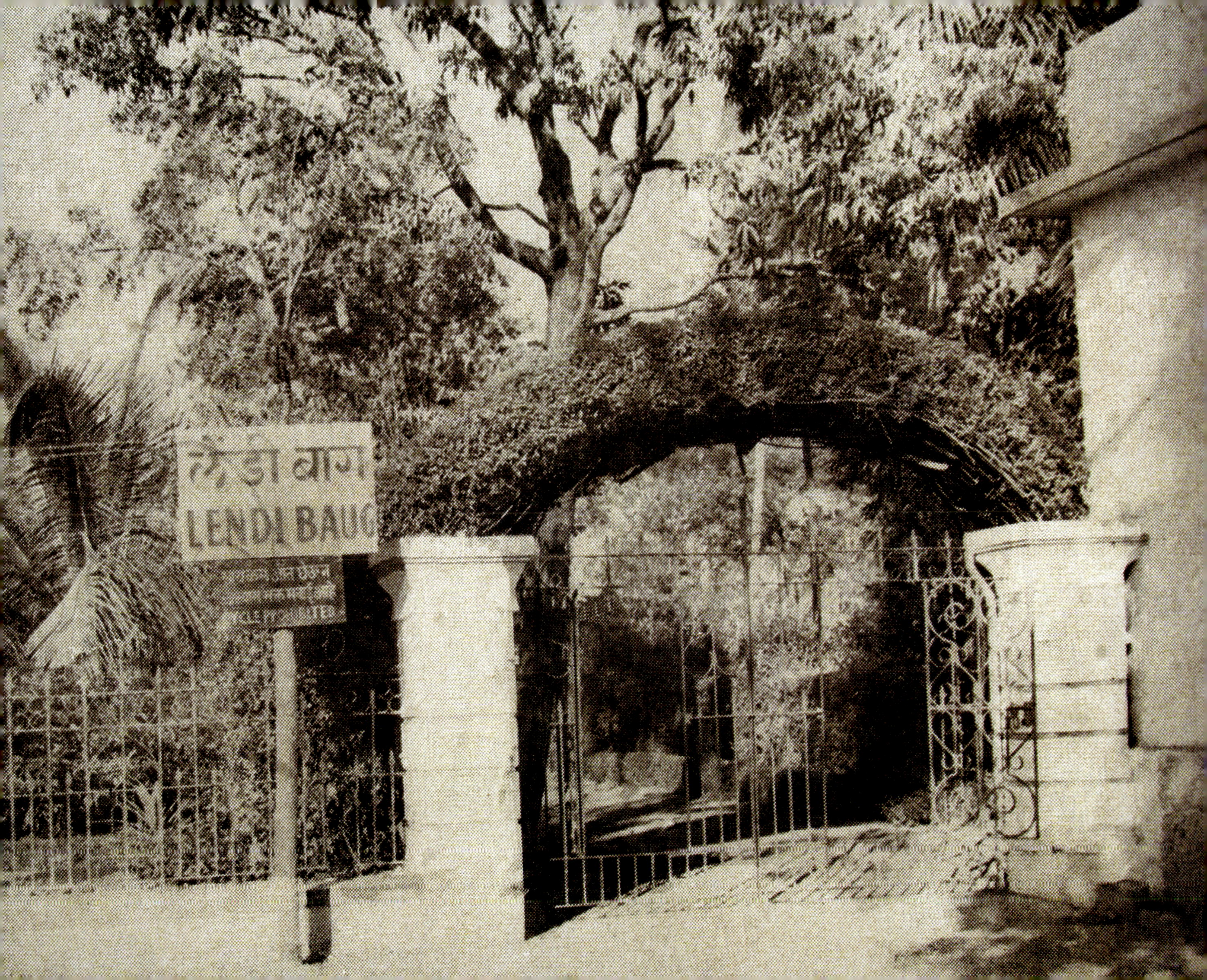
लेंडी बाग
LENDI BAUG

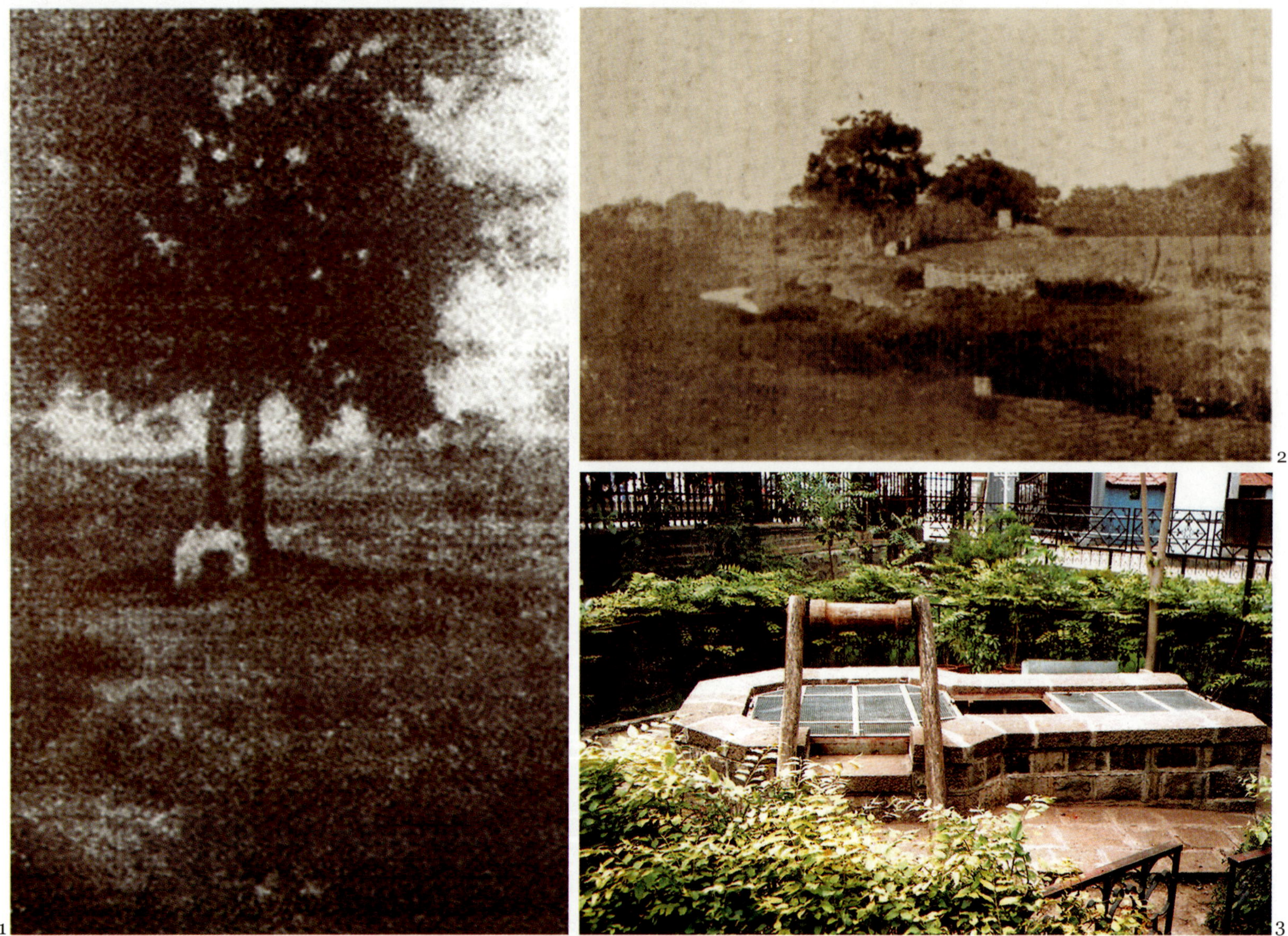

1. Old Lendi Baugh's long view, 2. Nanda Deep burning bright under the shade of two trees, 3. The well dug by Baba and His devotees in the middle of Lendi Baugh. Baba called this well Budki. People credited the water of this well with healing power which could drive away fever and various maladies. The well is covered with an iron mesh to ensure sanctity of water. The well had dried up but was revived in 1983 when it was dug deeper and abundant water sprang up.

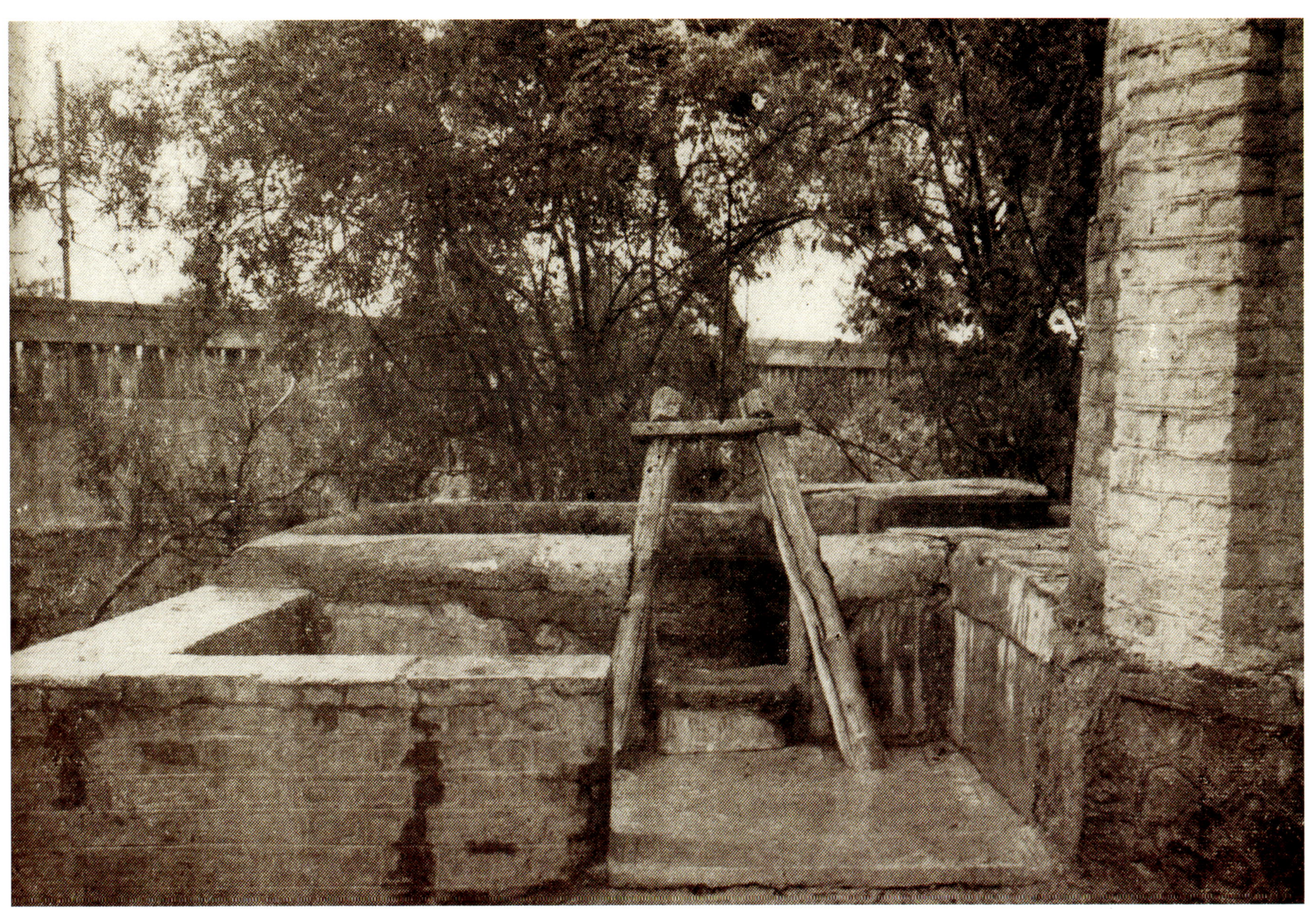

The old well with a workable pulley that was used by the devotees to draw water from the well, a practice now suspended. *(1974)*

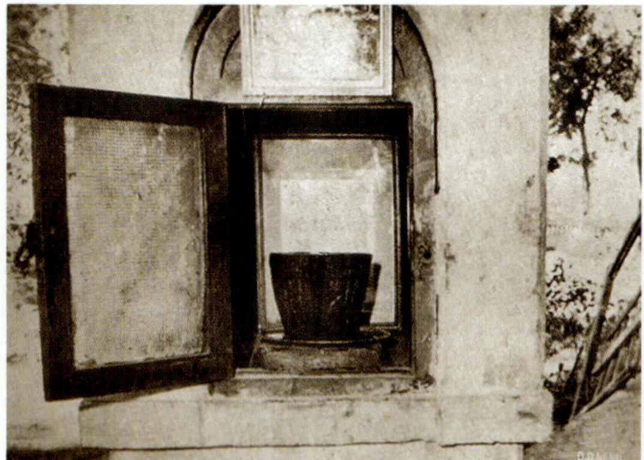

Nanda Deep *(1970)*

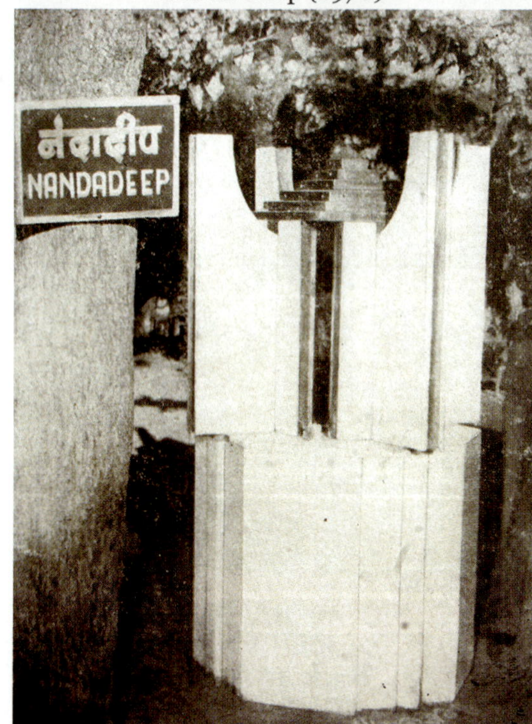

Nanda Deep, nestled in an alcove with a glass panel.

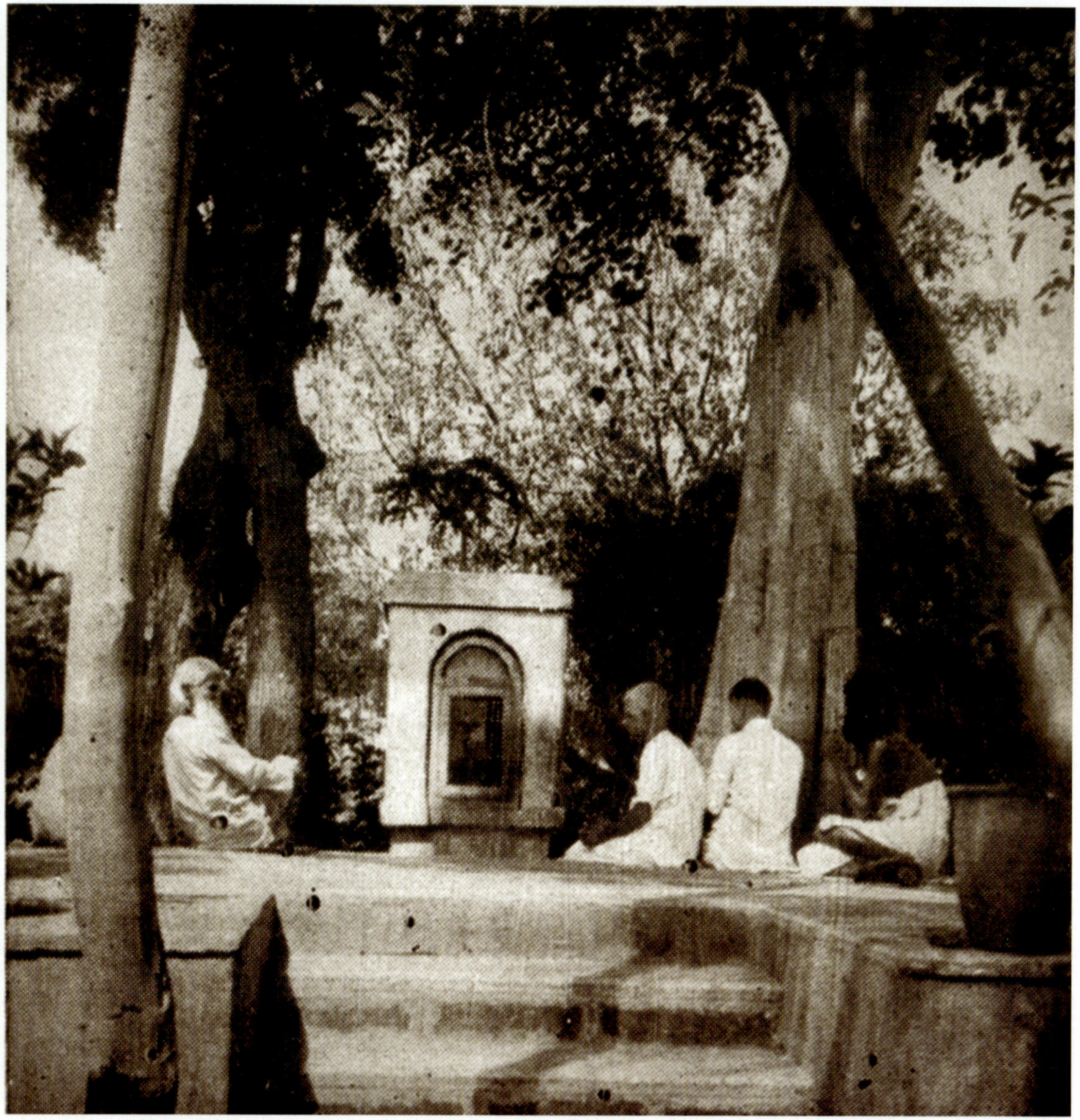

Devotees, resting on a platform around Nanda Deep. To the left of the lamp is a peepul tree and, to its right, the two neem trees planted by Baba can be seen. Photo by Sir G.G. Welling of Poona. *(1970's)*

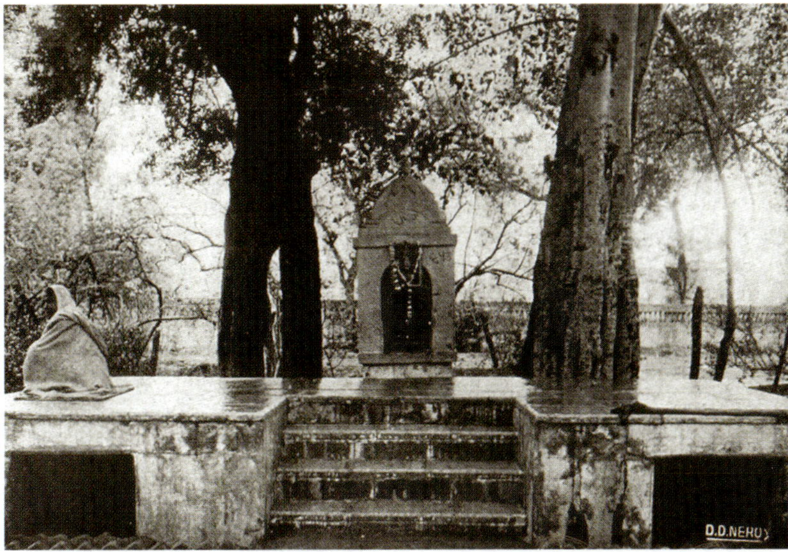

The view shows the Nanda Deep in an isolated structure *(1975)*.

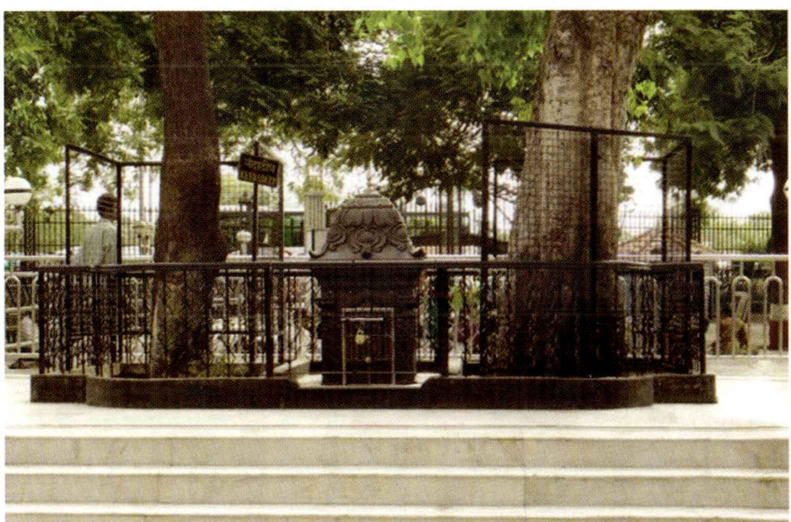

Nanda Deep in a grilled enclosure *(2011)*. One of the two neem trees has been cut at ground level.

The intricate carvings on the roof of the pavilion can be seen. The eternal lamp burns brightly in every picture. →

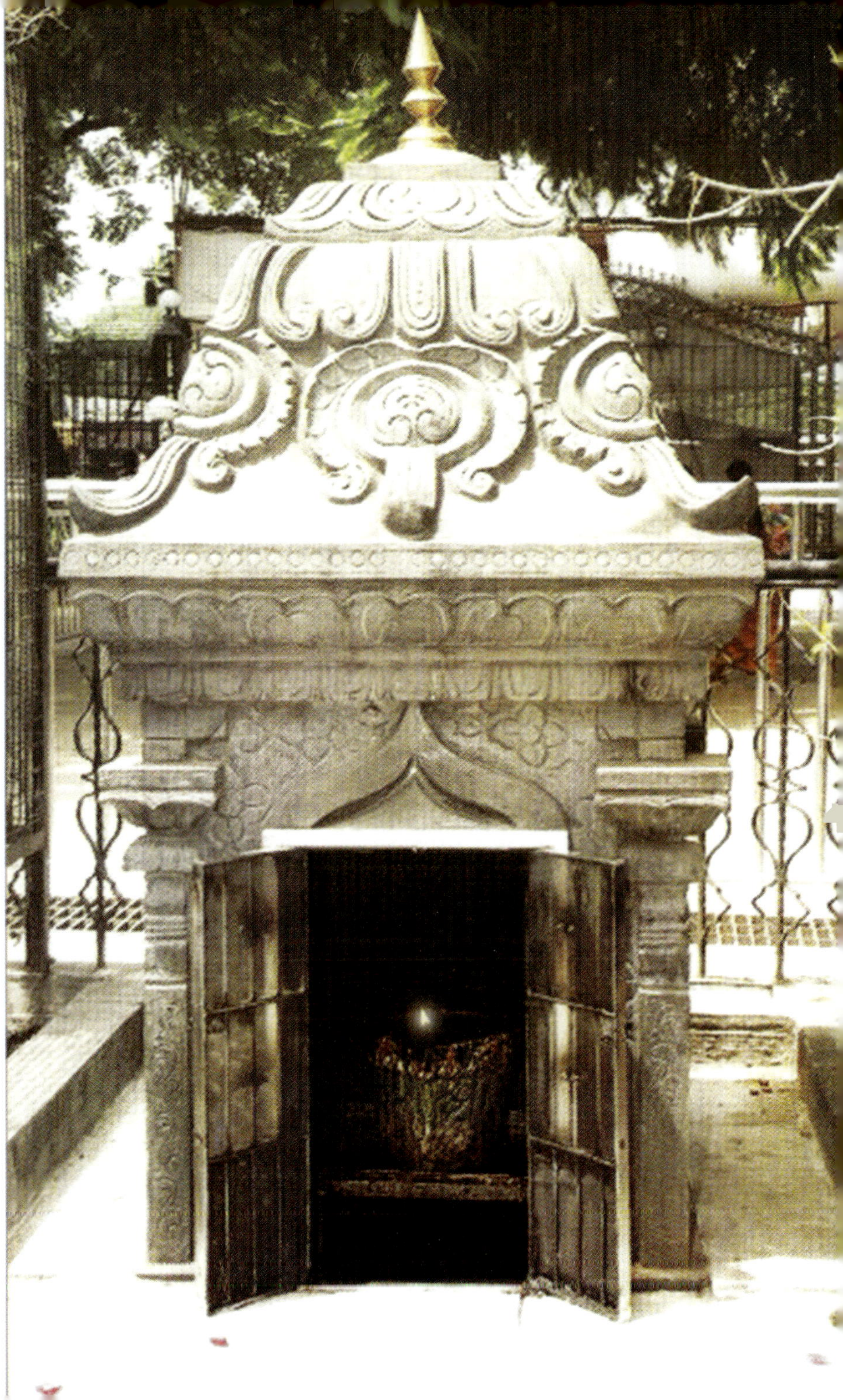

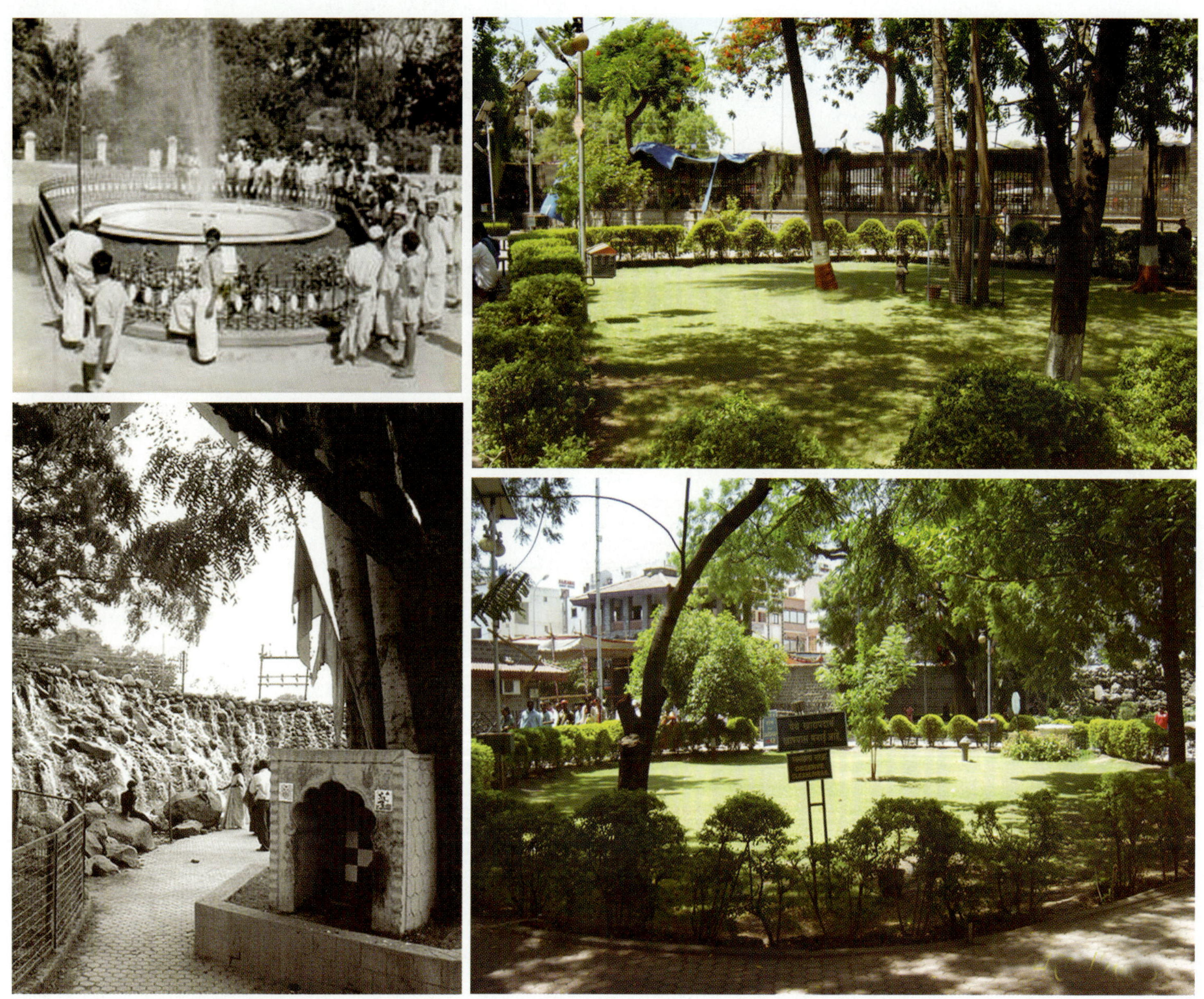

The scenic panorama of Lendi Baugh attracts devotees in droves who click pictures of themselves against the sparkling fountain and amidst the lush green lawns.

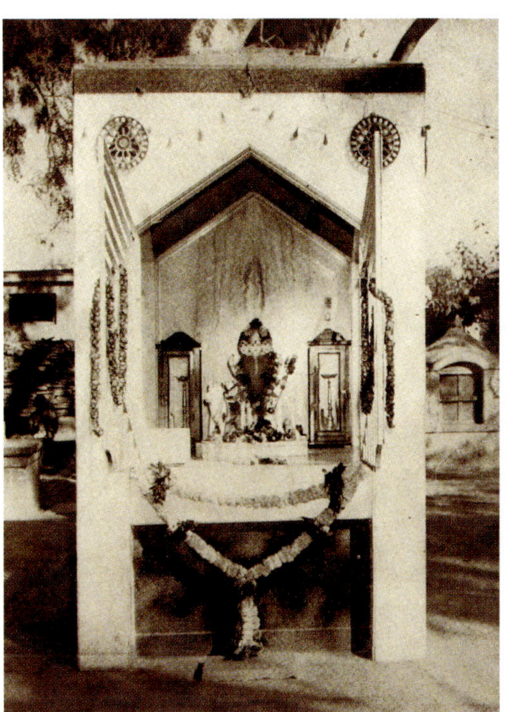

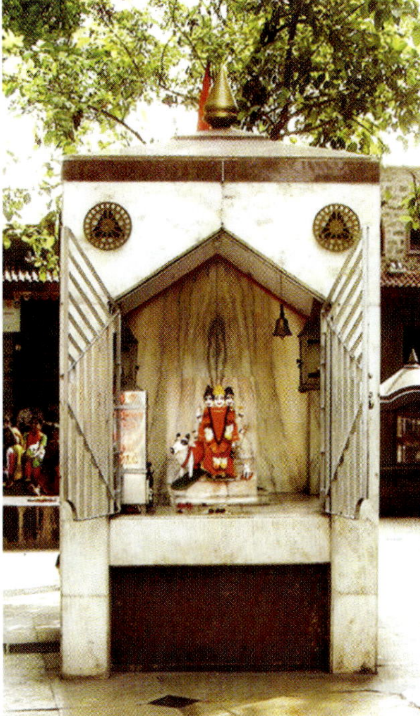

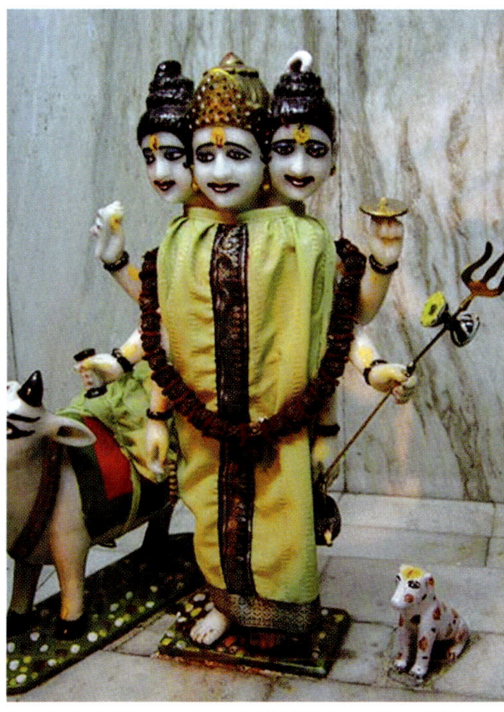

The temple devoted to *Lord Dattatreya*, the three faced idol of *Lord Dattatreya*, depicting *Brahma, Vishnu* and *Mahesh*. *(1975 & 2011)*

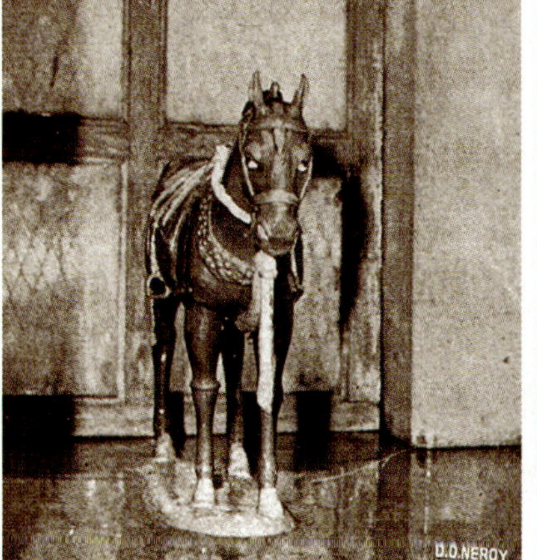

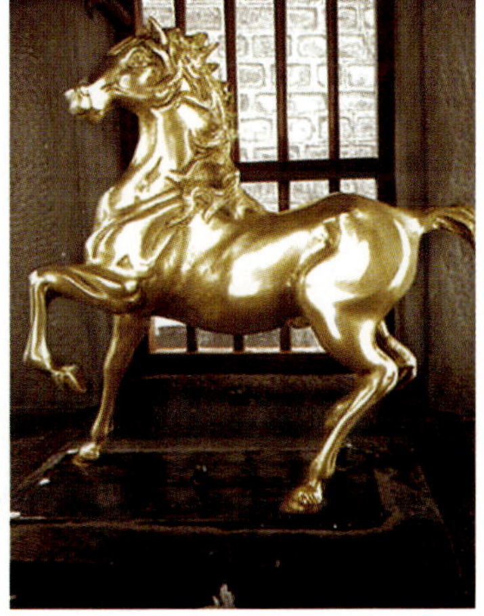

Shyama Karan's new statue carved out of metal which replaced the earlier wooden idol.

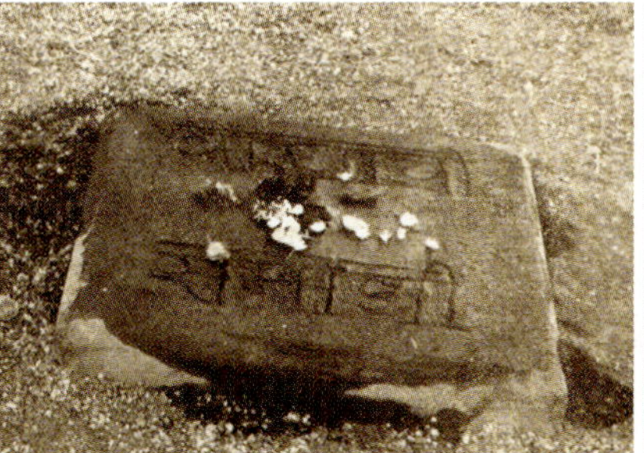

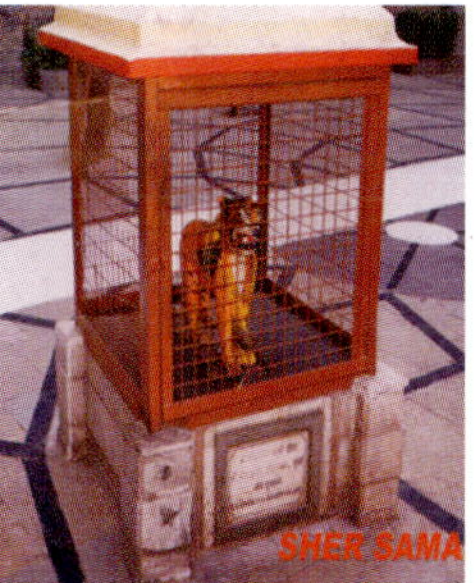

The original Samadhi of the ailing tiger who laid down his life in Baba's presence. A statue for the departed soul has been erected at this spot, in front of Mahadev temple, near Shanti Niwas. A statue of the same stands erect near Baba's stone at Dwarkamai.

SHRI SAI BABA SANSTHAN MUSEUM, SHIRDI

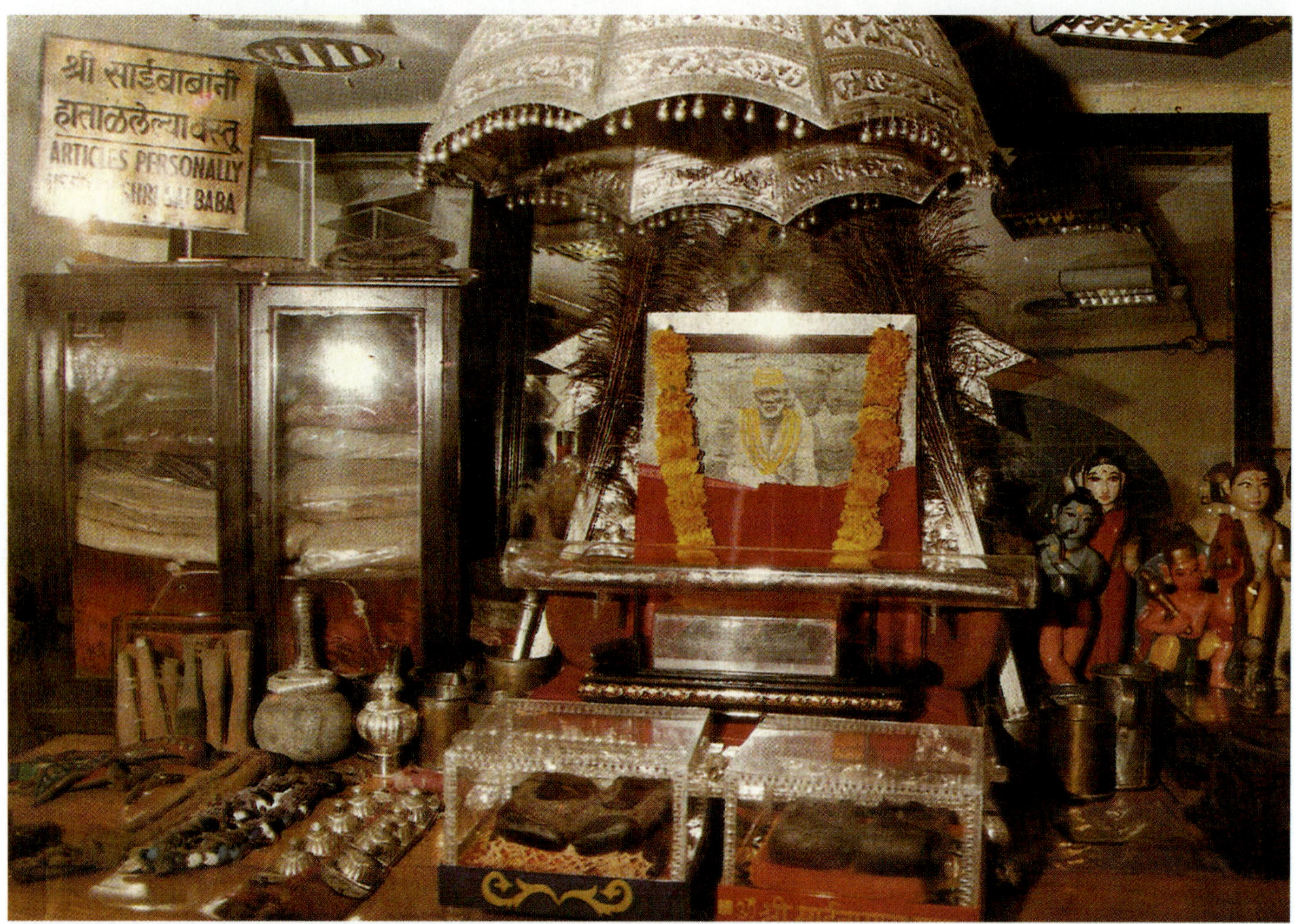

Artifacts related to Baba placed together in different arrangements. The pictures show the following articles-pillow *(takkia)*, gaddi, makhmal garuda nishan, pitambar, padukas, kafni, cloth, satka, tumrales, original photo of Baba, body-brushing stone used while bathing, chillum, Shyama Sunder mala, ankle ring, cloth for tail, statues of Lord Ram, Lakshman and Devi Sita, Hanuman, and Lord Krishna, water mug with silver cover neck, silver photo frame, silver throne, old silver umbrella, one-rupee silver coin mala.

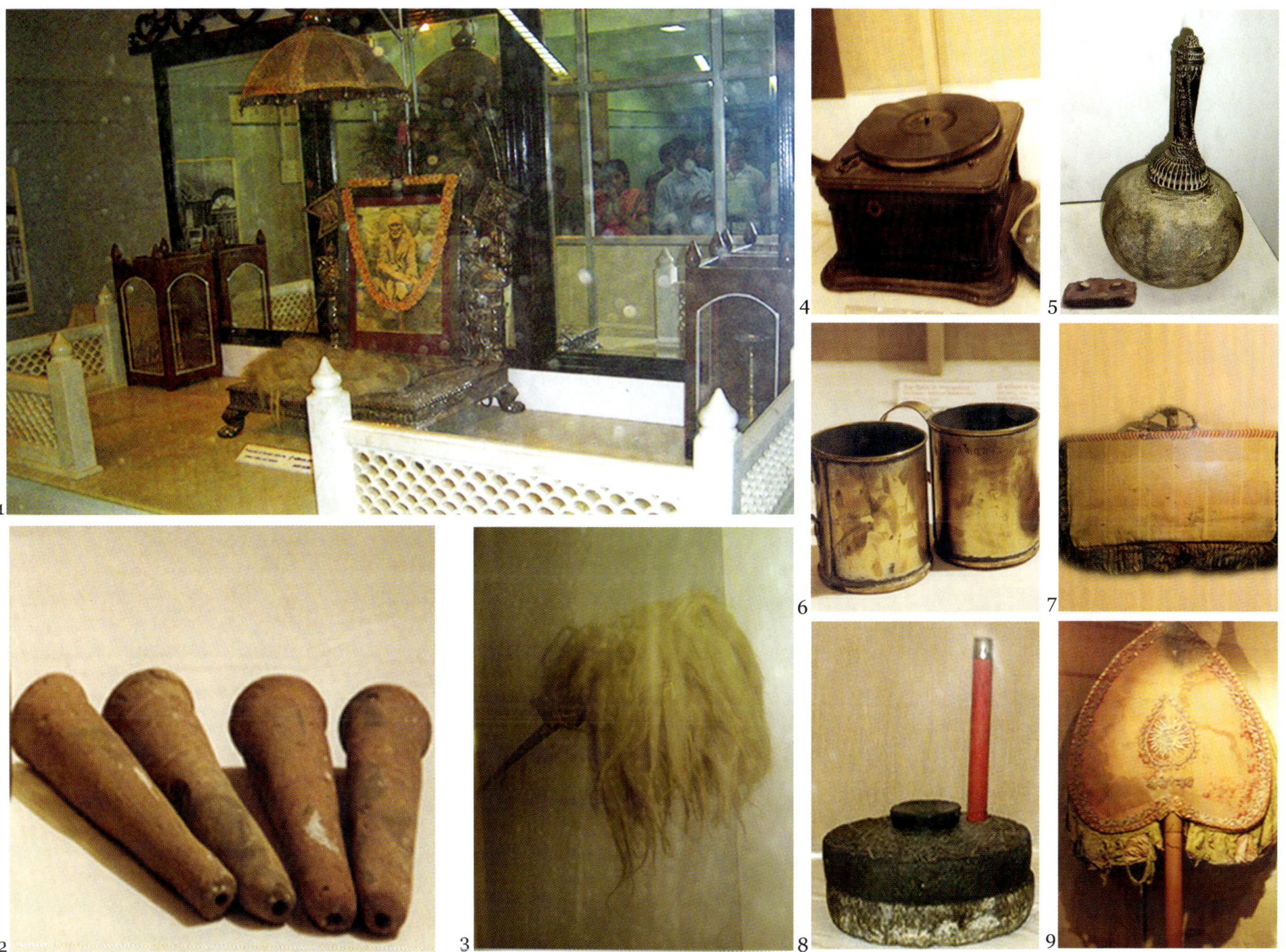

1. A replica of Samadhi as it were in 1920, 2. Chillums, 3. A whisk broom, 4. Gramophone, 5. Baba's water pitcher with a silver cover and body-brushing stone 6. Brass Tumblers, 7. An old time fan with a handle 8. Grindmill 9. A spade shaped ornate pennant atop a staff.

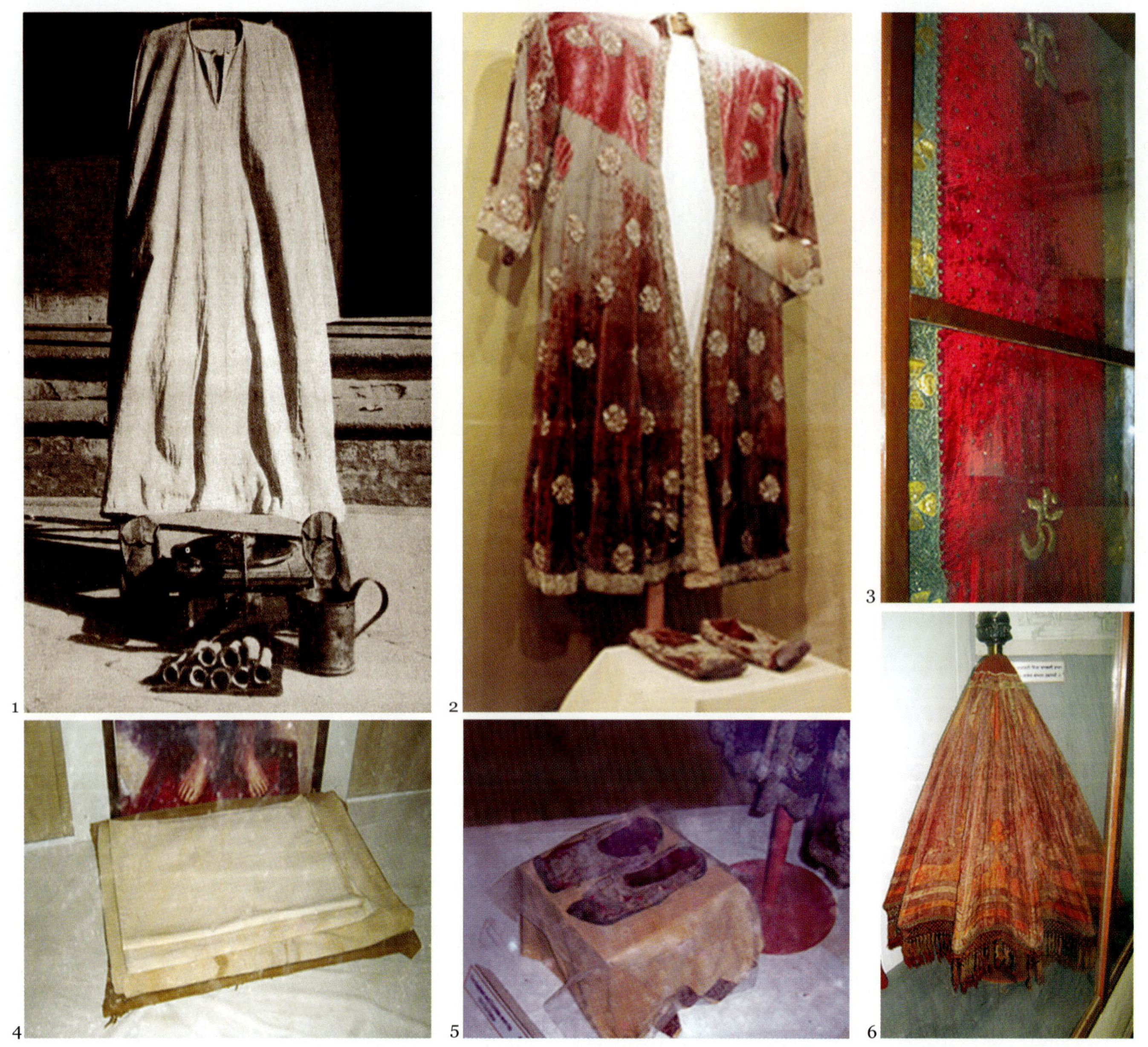

1. Baba's Kafni, Chillum & Brass Tumblers, 2. Baba's velvet coat, 3. A velvet crimson shawl with a green border, 4. Manjar pat cloth, 5. Padukas, 6. A decorative umbrella with exquisite brocade work.

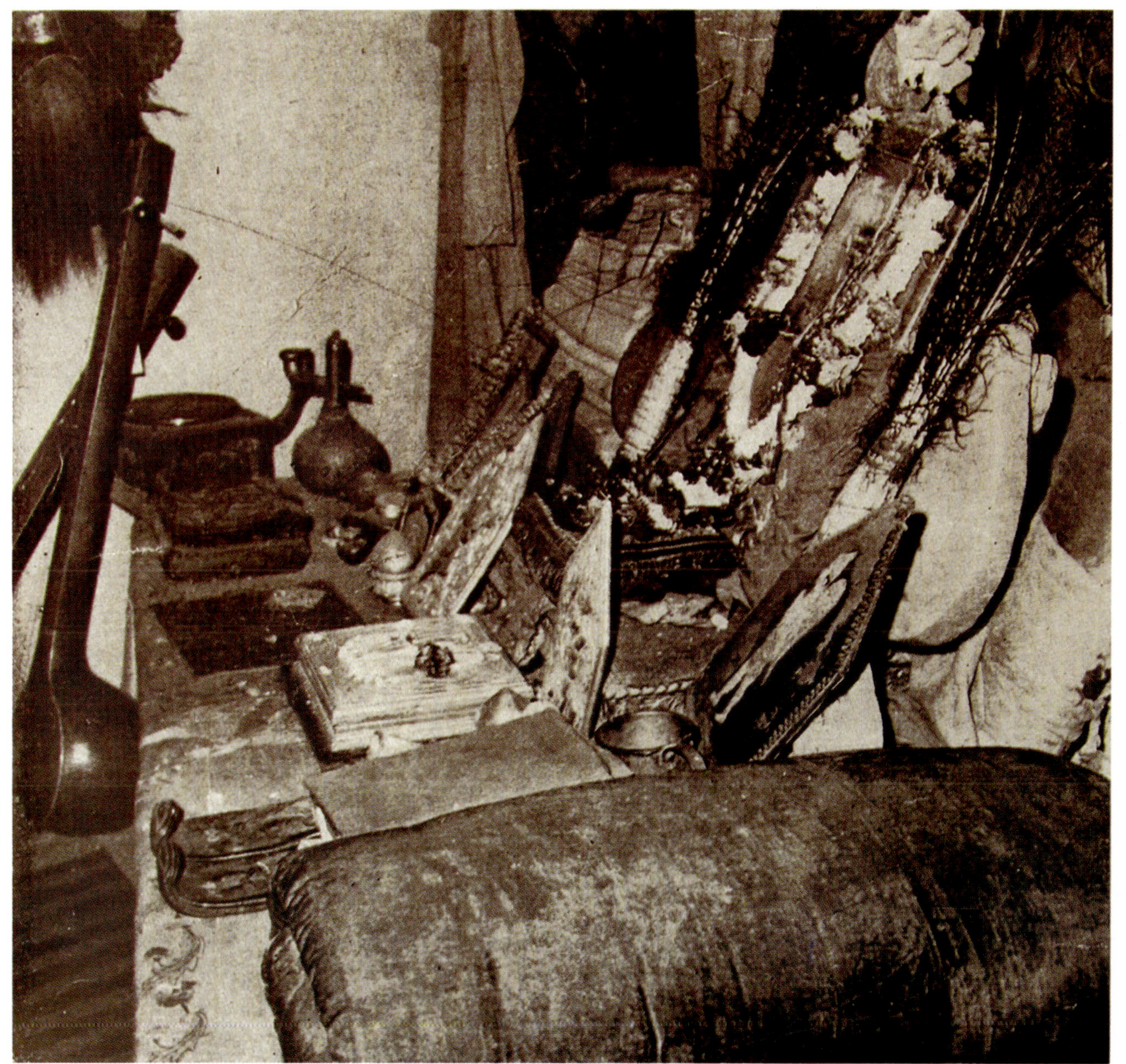

These articles were earlier on display in a showcase inside the Samadhi Mandir.

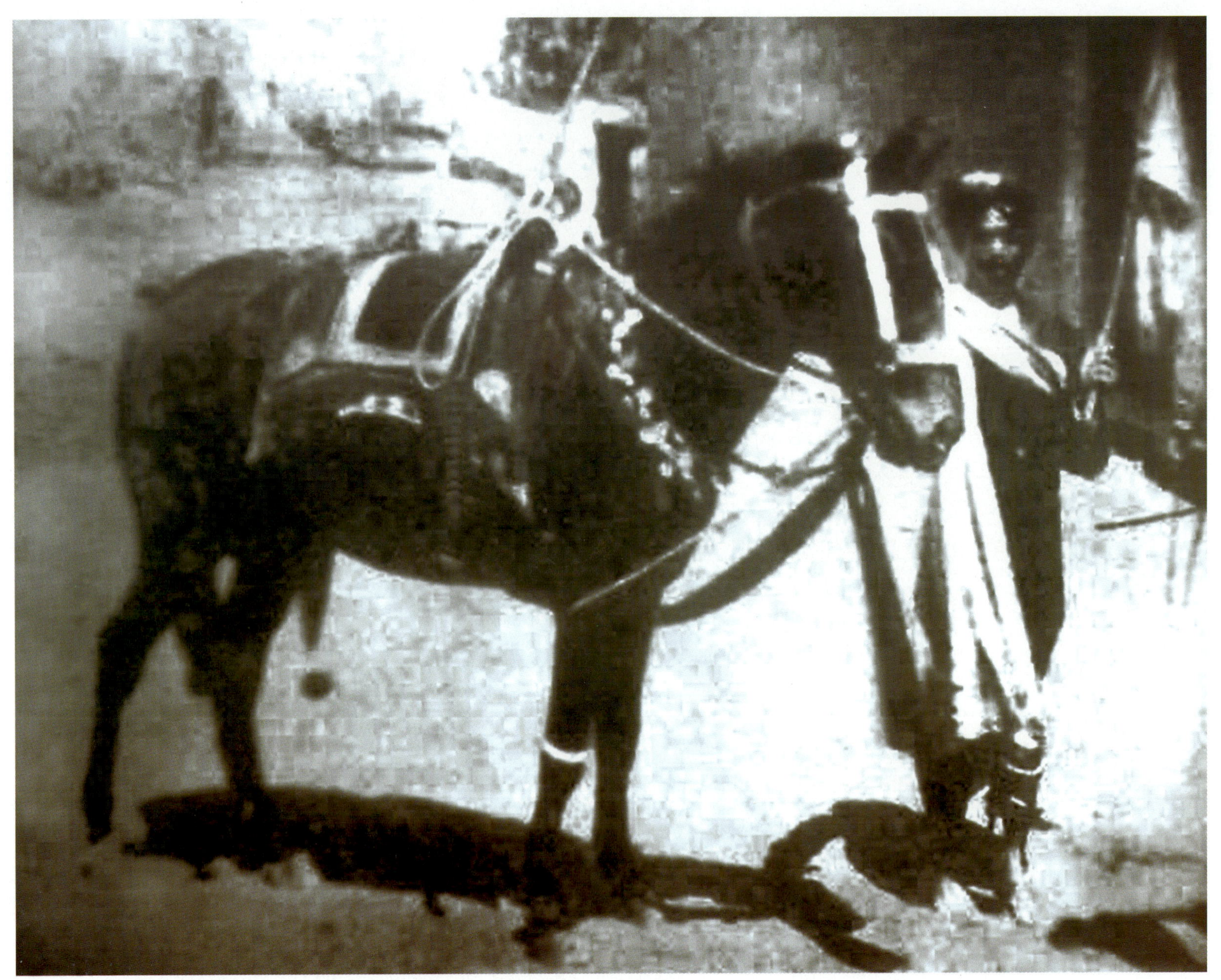

Shyama Sunder horse being held by its trainer Khajgiwala.The black horse was adorned everyday.

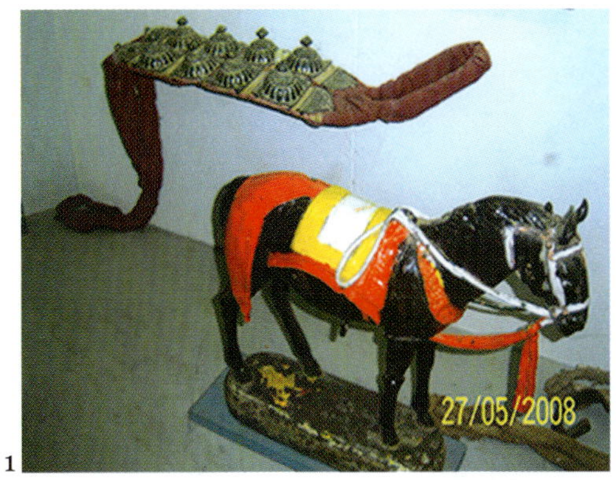

1

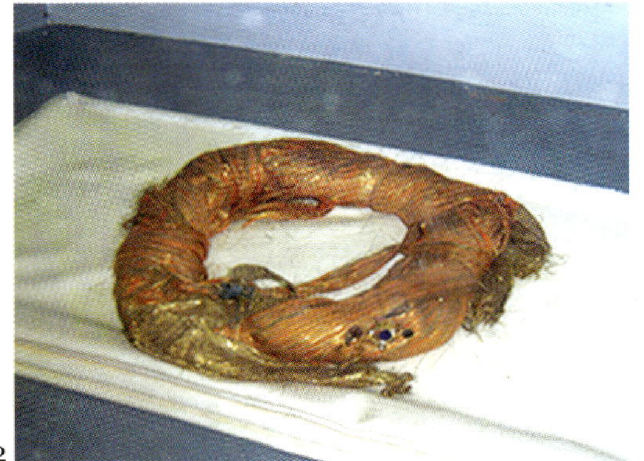
2

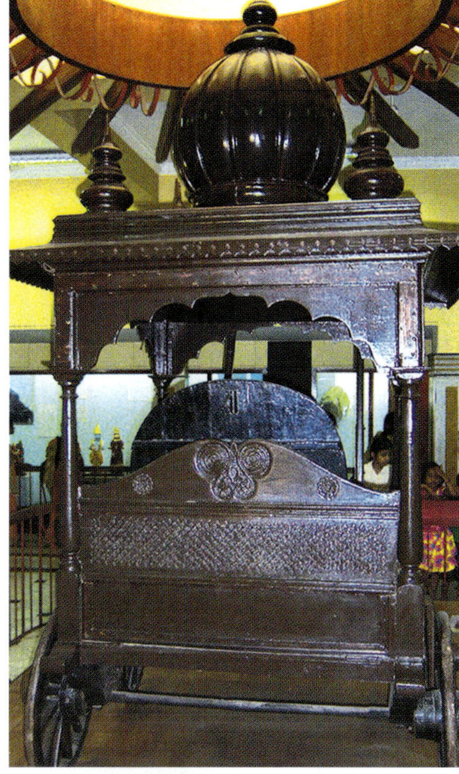
5

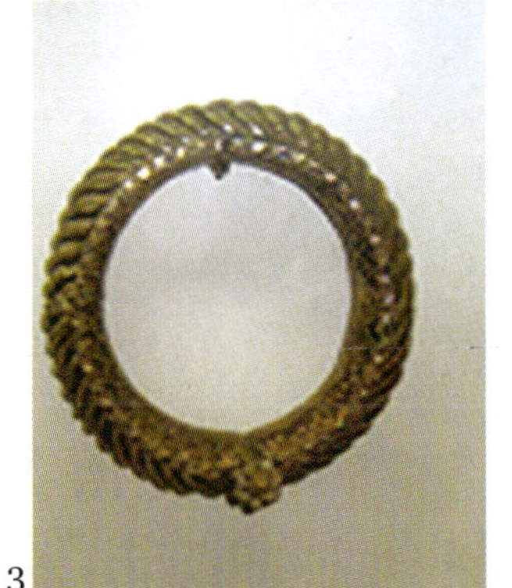
3

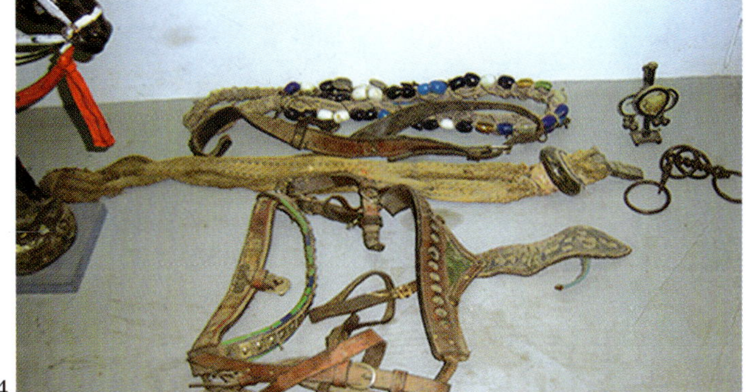
4

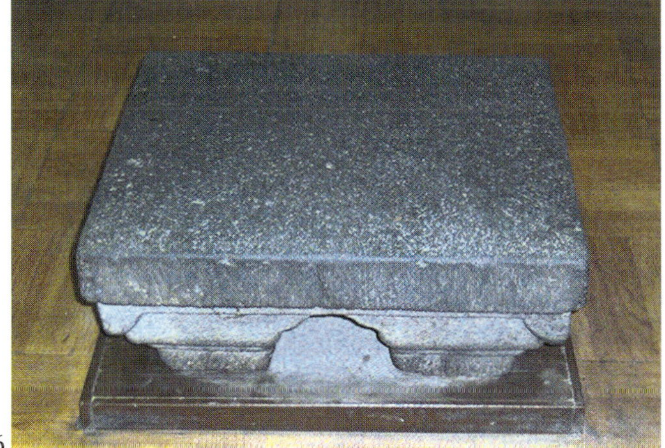
6

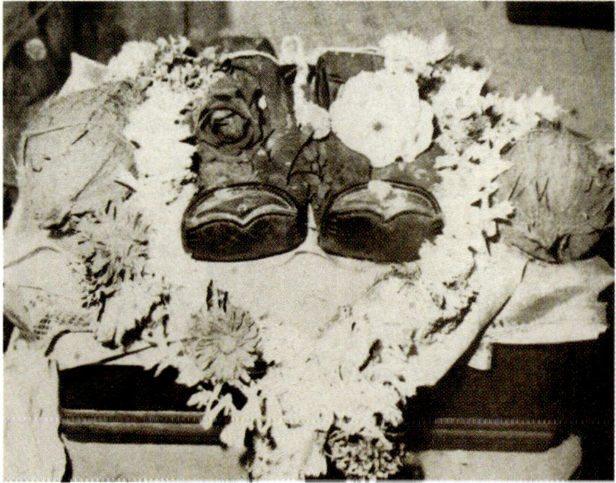
7

(1,2,3,4) Shyama Sunder mala, ankle ring, cloth for tail
5. This chariot (rath) was gifted to Baba by His devotees from Indore. He never sat on it. It was first taken out on Guru Purnima in a procession in 1918, when Baba allowed His photograph to be carried around in it.
6. Baba's bathing seat.
7. Baba's Paduka

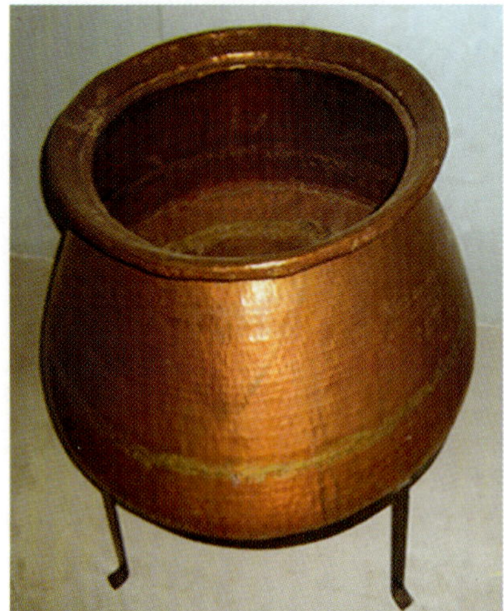
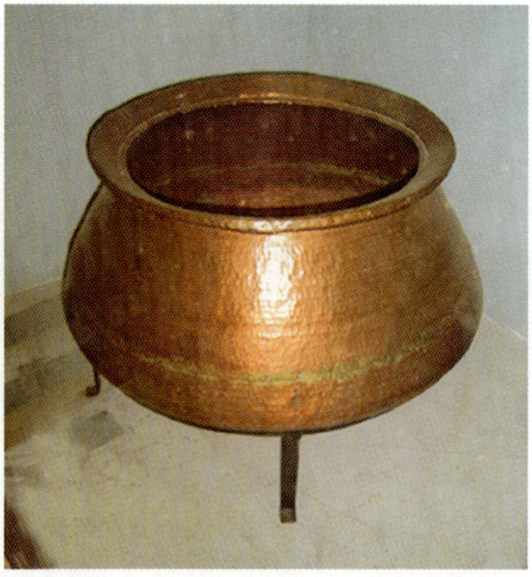

Baba used the two handls to prepare food for his devotees. The smaller catered to around 50 people.

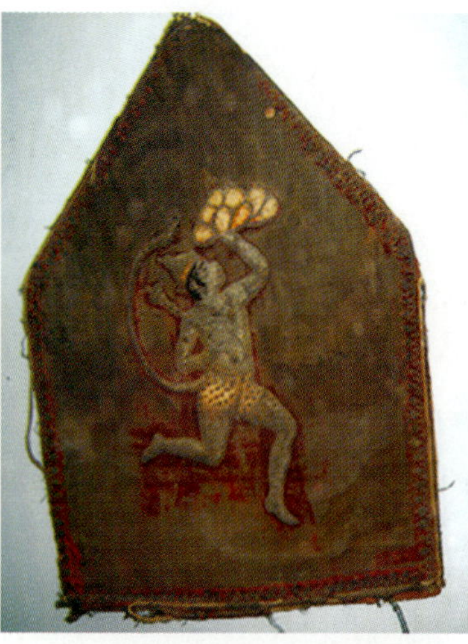
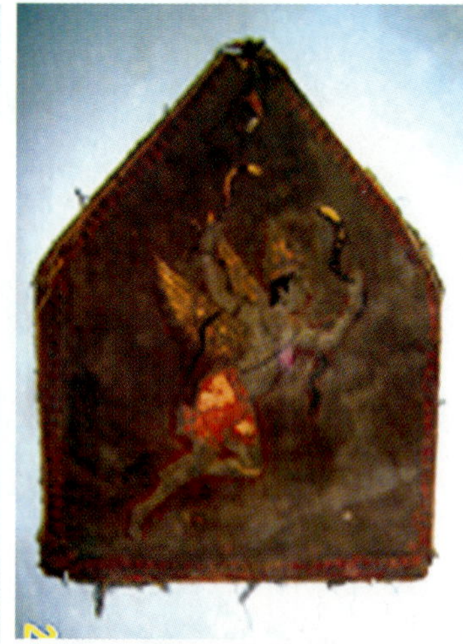

Hanuman marked nishan (Mukmul Abdairi)
Garuda-marked nishan.

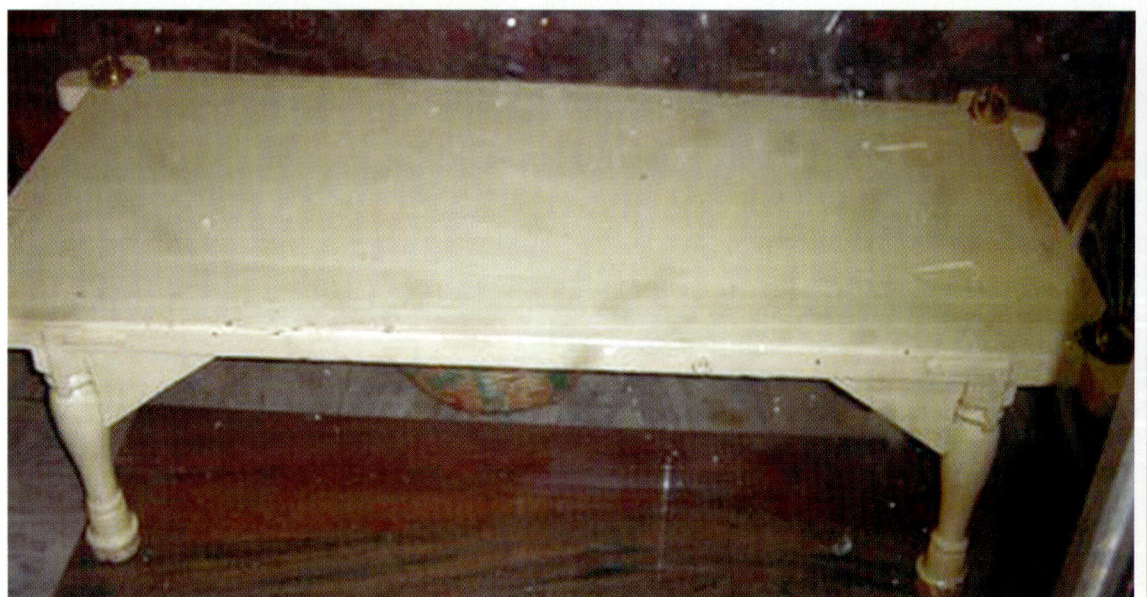

Baba's Bed on which His body was kept for 36 hours after He took Mahasamadhi. Lakshman Mama performed ritualistic Kakad aarti, while Baba's body was lying on this bed.

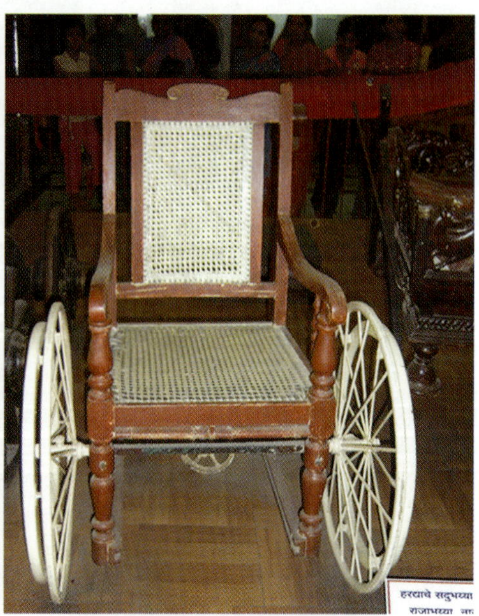

Wheel Chair gifted to Baba, but never used by Him.

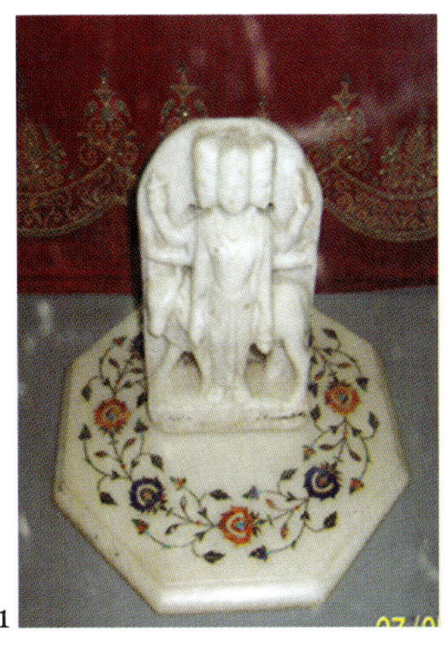
1

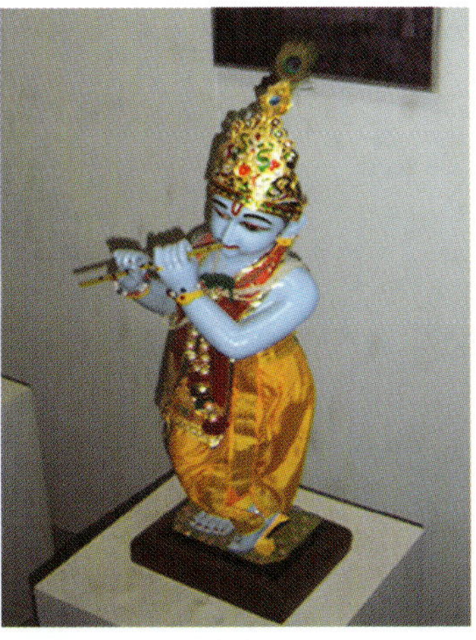
2

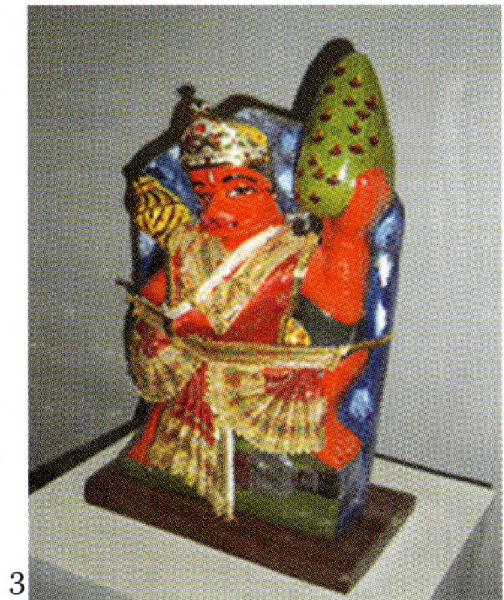
3

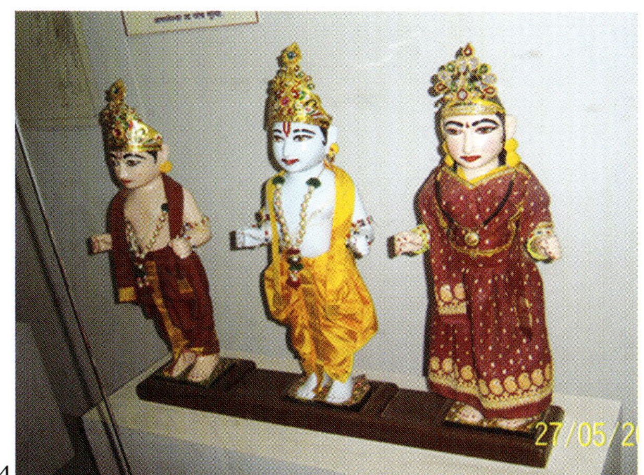
4

1. Statue of Dattatreya
2. Statue of Shri Krishna
3. Statue of Shri Hanuman
4. Statue of Shri Ram, Sita, Lakshman
5. Palki (Palanquin)
   It was donated by Saddu Bhaiya, Chotu Bhaiya Narayan Bhaiya and Raja Bhaiya of Harda.

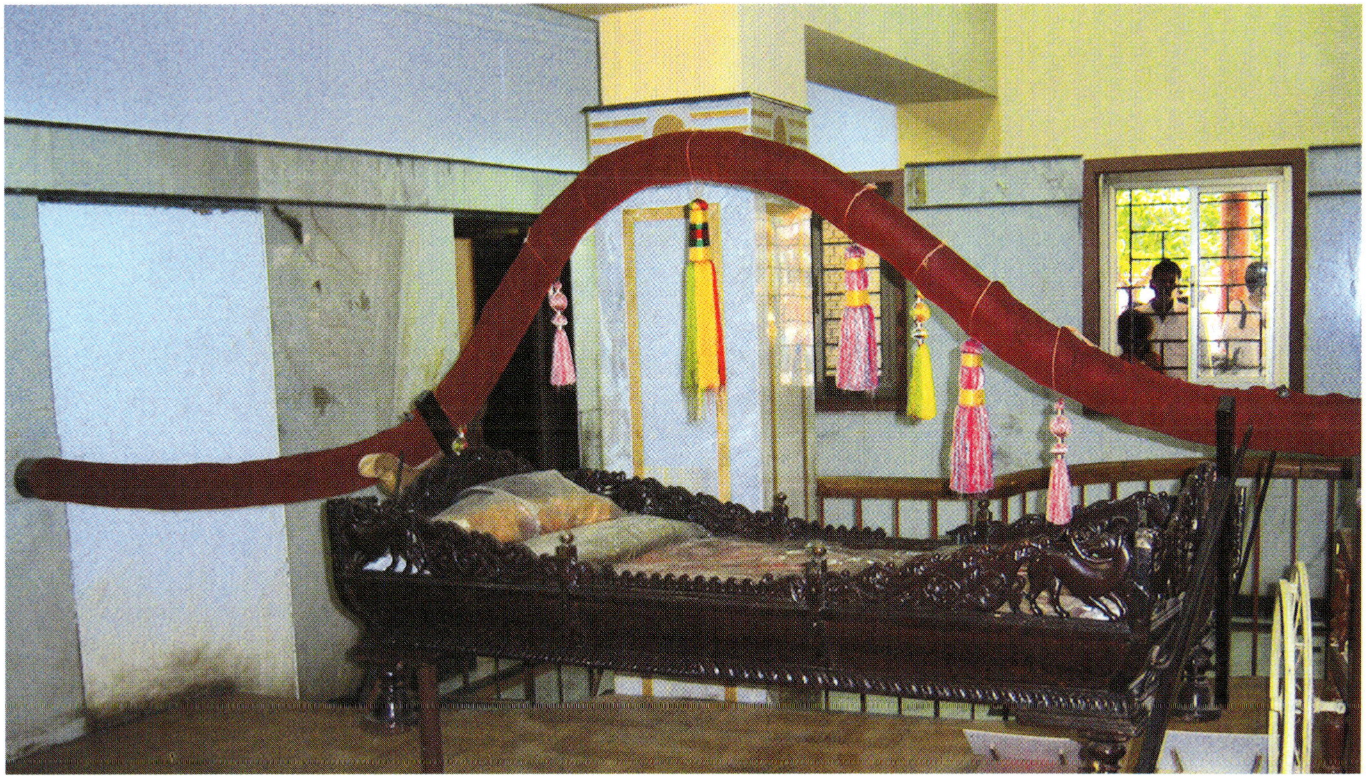

5

DEVOTEES

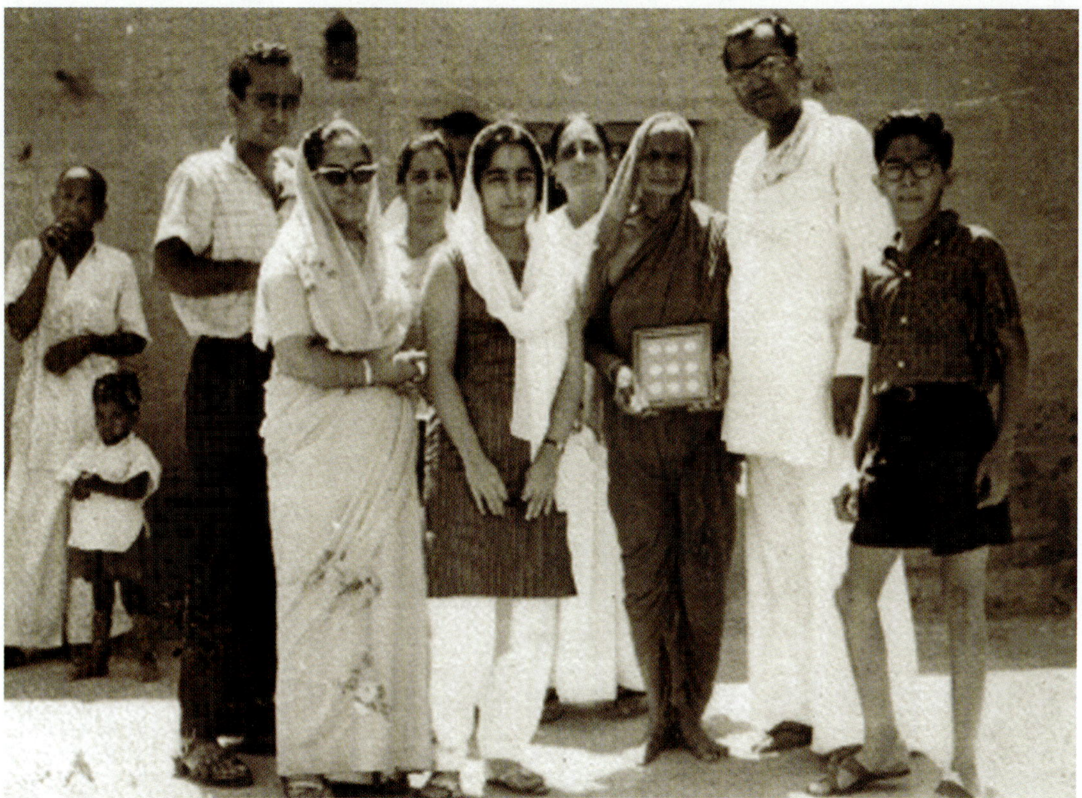

Lakshmibai showing the coins within a frame, with some devotees

Lakshmibai Shinde was one of the chosen ones among the legions of Baba's devotees. She diligently served food to Baba, making sure to cook keeping Baba's preferences in mind. Her simple meals comprised of *Bhakri* (flat bread made out of Jowar, a coarse grain) and vegetables that were inclusive of onion as Baba was partial to onion. She was in attendance when Baba departed from the confines of His mortal frame. Before breathing His last, Baba bequeathed nine coins to her. He first handed five and then added four more. The nine coins are said to represent the nine qualities of a devotee as specified in Hindu scriptures. The coins are symbolic of the nine ways of devotion (bhakti) that a devotee can indulge in. The coins are also viewed as a final offering or donation that Baba gave to a beloved devotee before embarking upon a cross-border celestial journey to heaven. Lakshmibai passed away peacefully on 2nd June 1963.

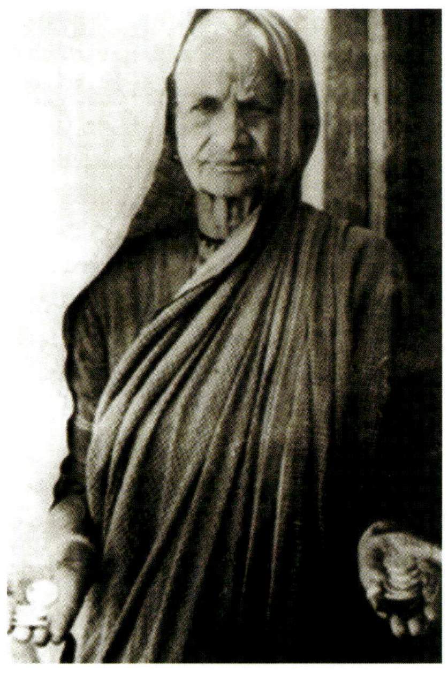
Lakshmibai *(1962)*

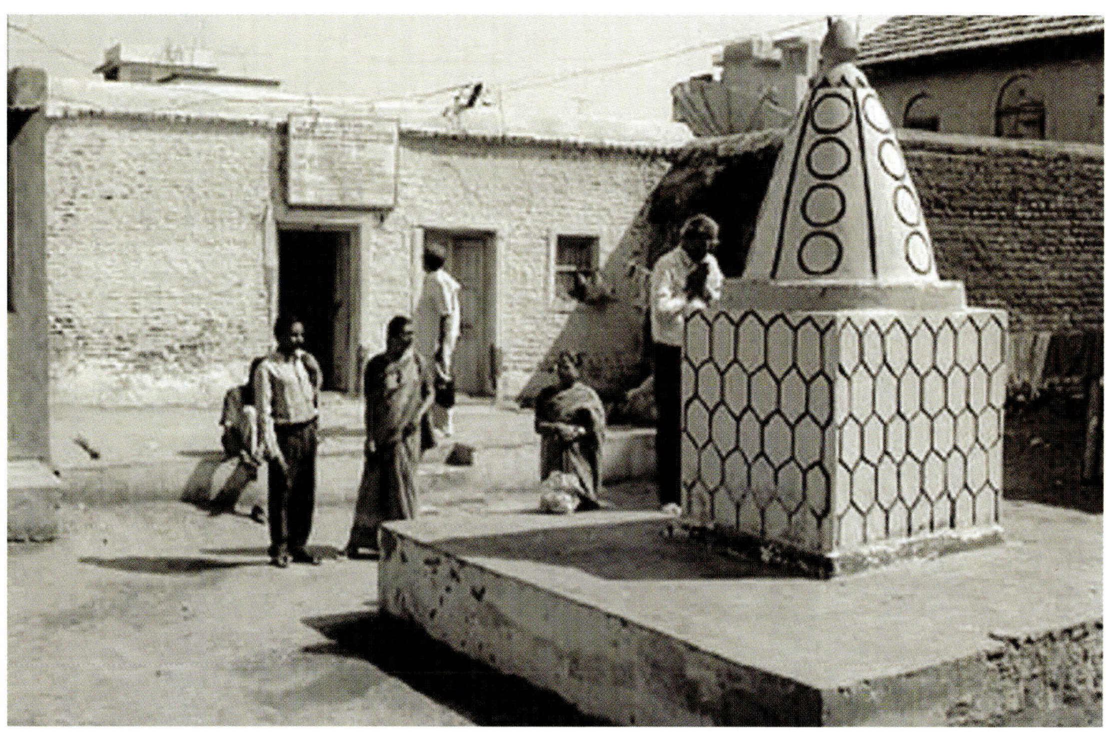
Lakshmibai's house and Samadhi in Shirdi, which has now been demolished

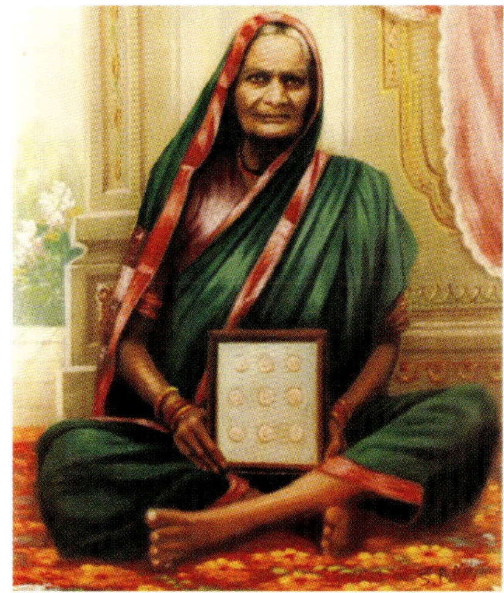
Lakshmibai *(1962)*

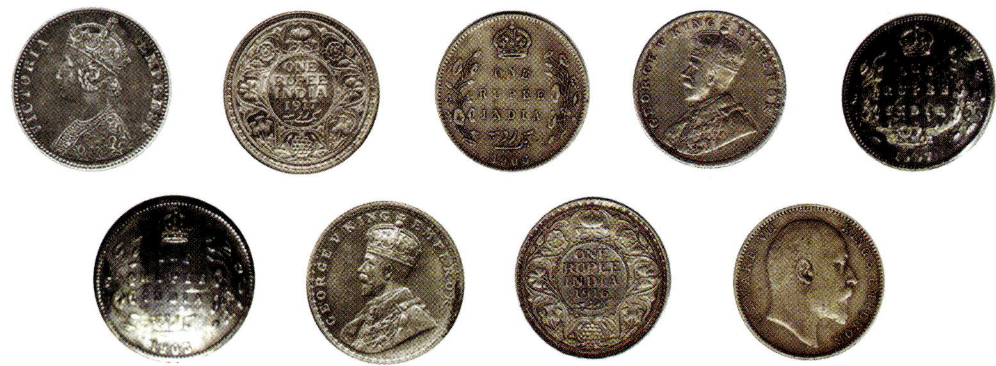

*These coins are replica of the original coins given to Lakshmibai

The Nine divine coins signify the Nine-Fold Path of devotions: 1) Shravana (Listening), 2) Kirtana (Devotional Music), 3) Smarana (Remembering), 4) Pada Seva (Resorting to the Feet), 5) Archana (Worship), 6) Namaskara (Making Obeisance), 7) Dasyta (Service), 8) Sakhyatva (Friendliness), 9) Atmanivedana (Surrender of the self)

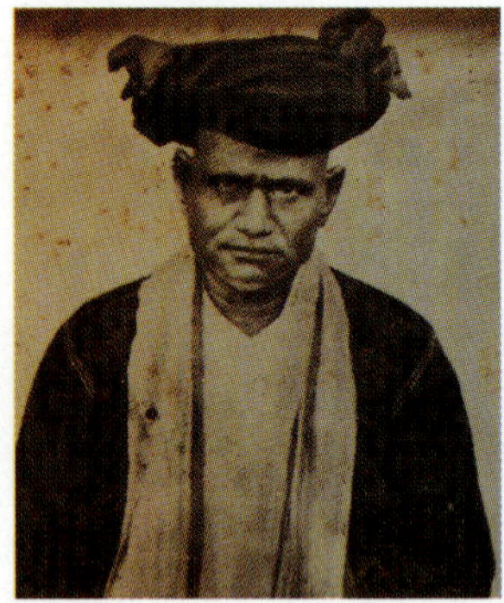
Shri Ganpat Rao Kote Patil

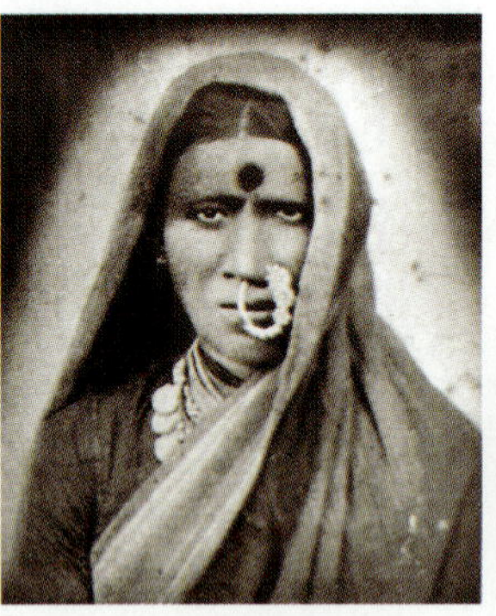
Smt. Baijabai Patil Kote (Baija Maa)

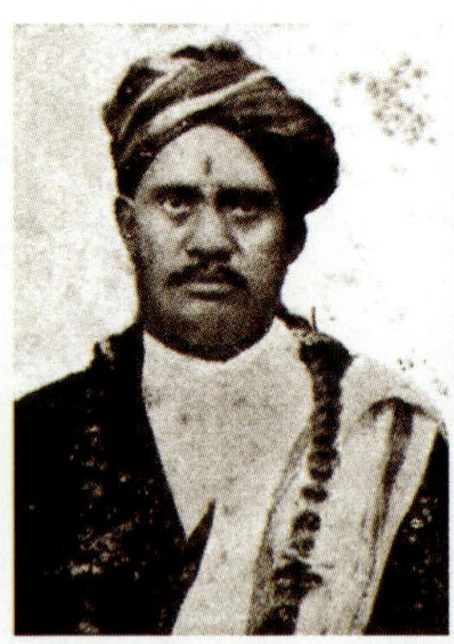
Shri Tatyaji Ganpat Rao Kote Patil *(young)*

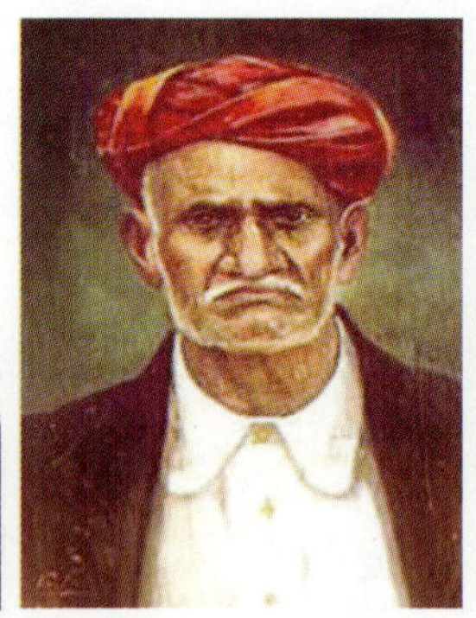
Shri Tatyaji Ganpat Rao Kote Patil *(old)*

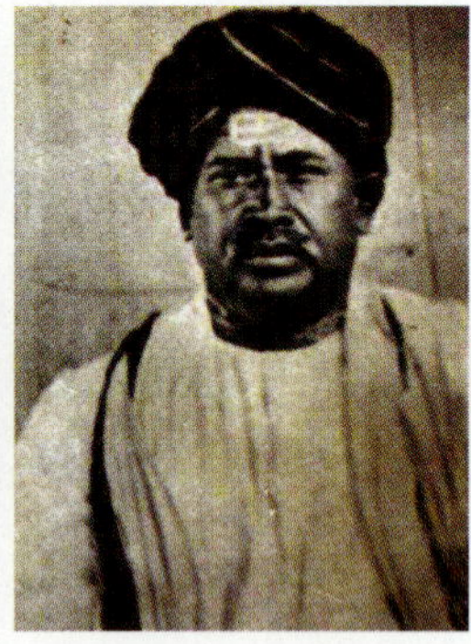
Shri Bayaji Appa Kote Patil

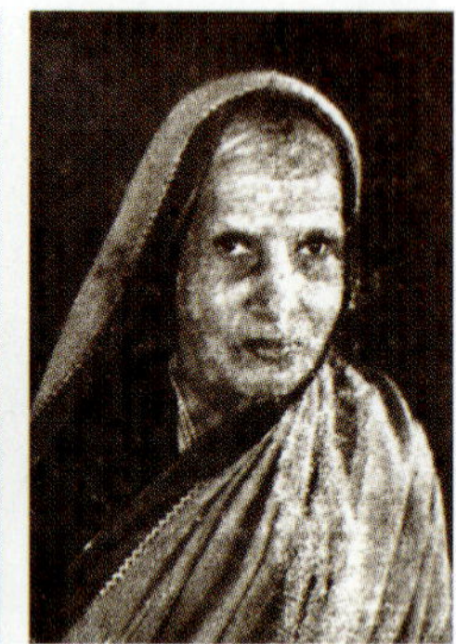
Smt. Rambha Bai Tatya Kote Patil

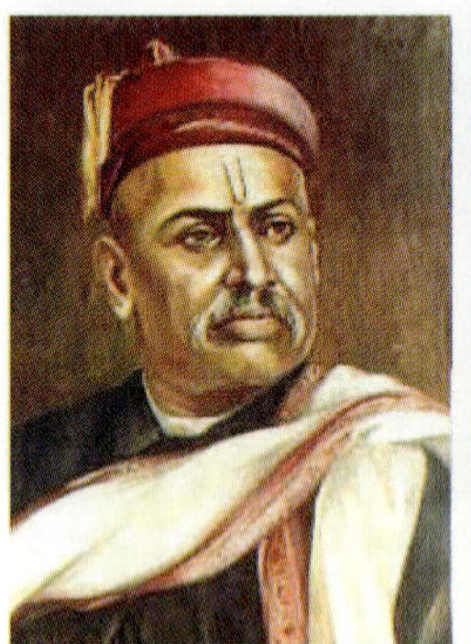
Shri Nanasaheb Chandorkar

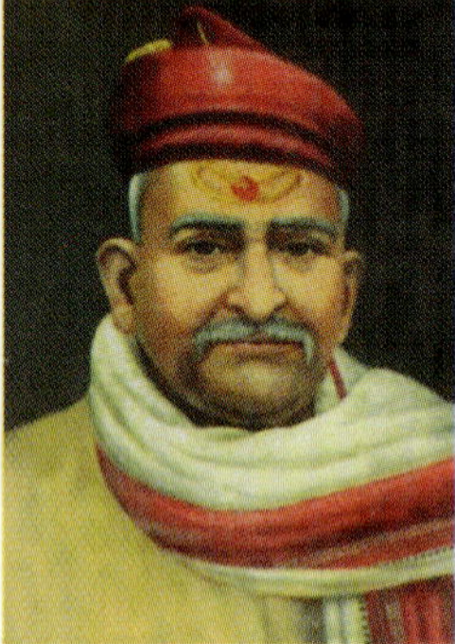
Shri Hari Sitaram Dixit

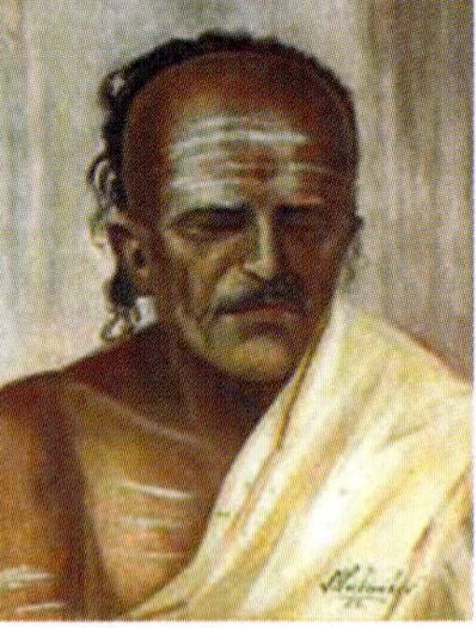
Shri Mahalsapati Sonar

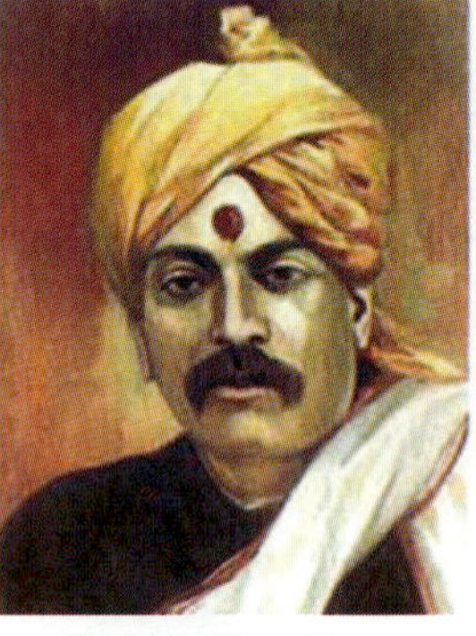
Shri Madhav Rao Deshpande *(Shama)*

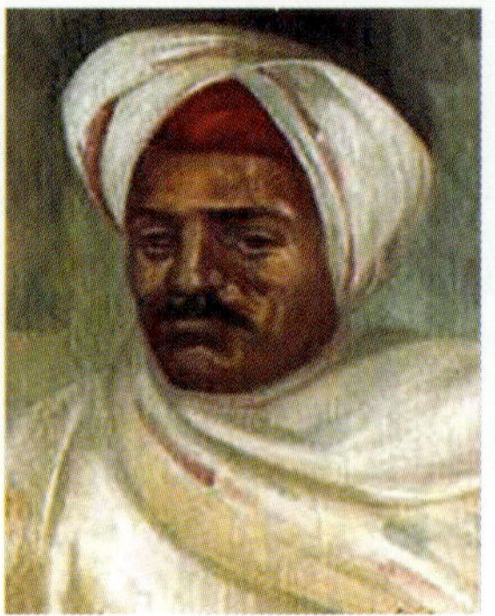
Shri Bhagoji Shinde

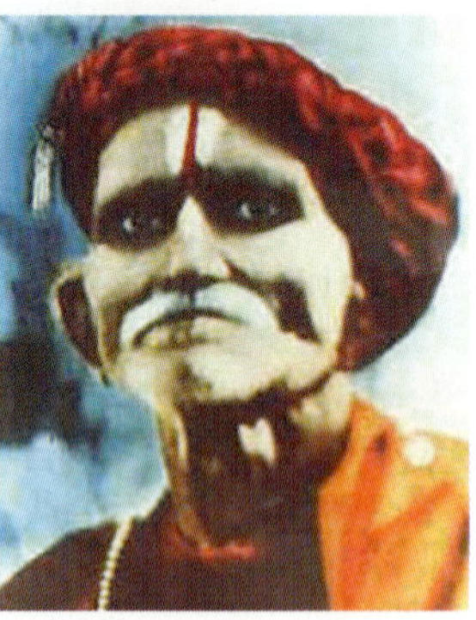
Shri Kashiram Bala Shimpi

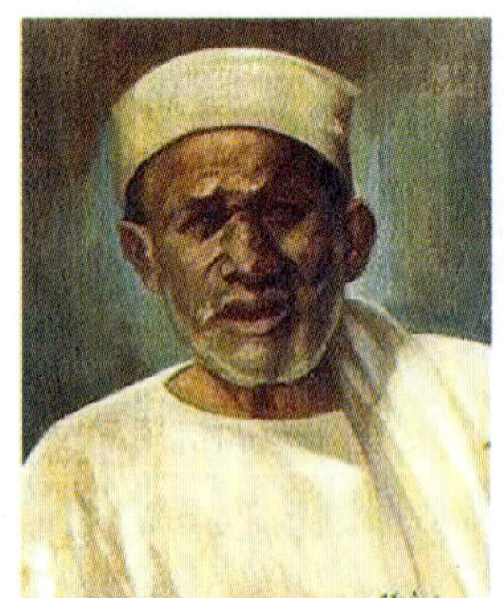
Shri Bhau Maharaj Kumbhar

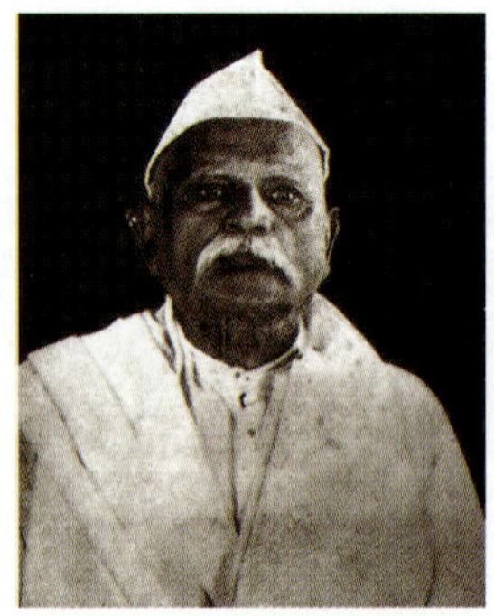
Shri Ramchandra Dadji Kote Patil

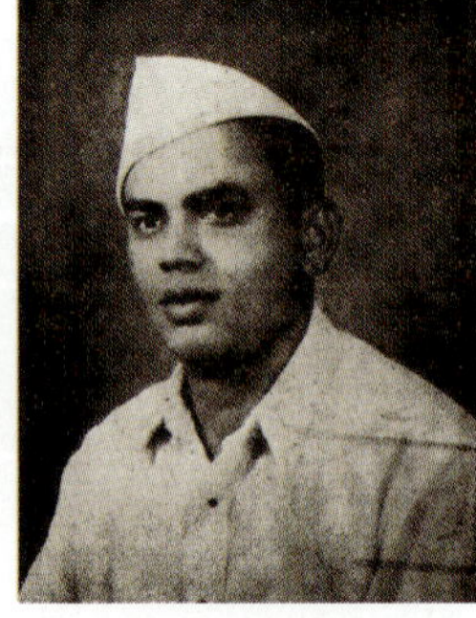
Shri Haribhau Triambaka Rao Shelke Patil

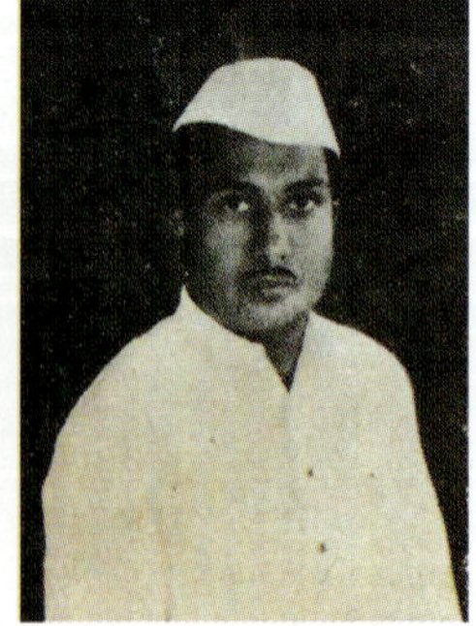
Shri Baji Rao Tatya Kote Patil

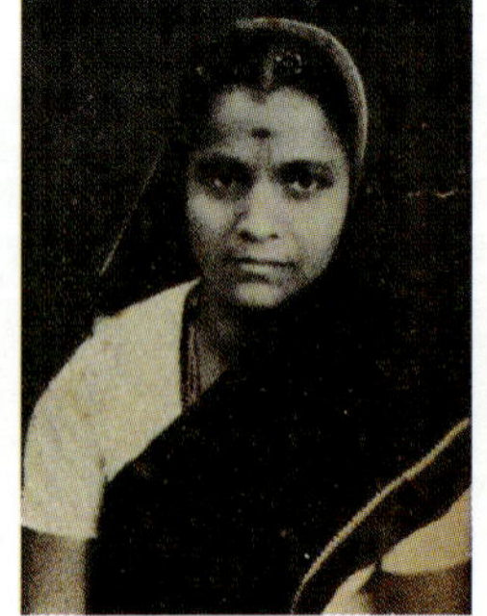
Smt. Mankarni Bai Kote Patil

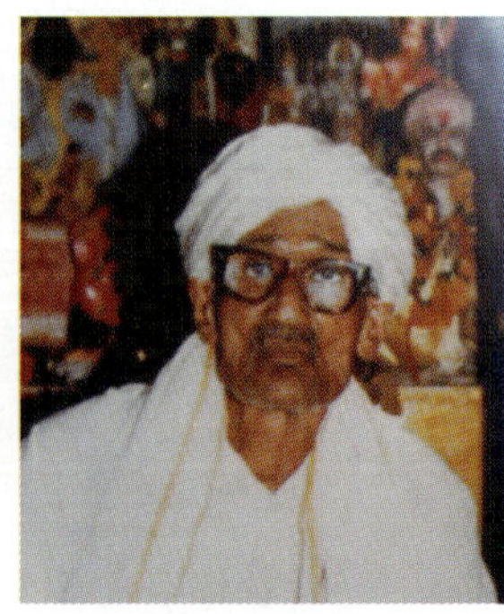
Shri Bapaji Lakshman Rattanparkhi

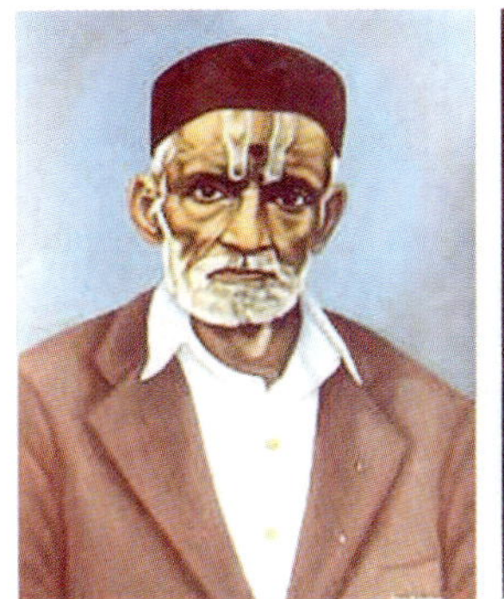
Shri Madhavrao Aadkar

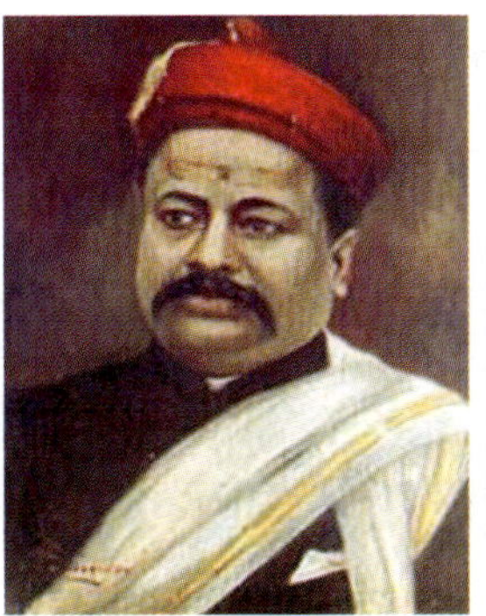
Shri Gopal Mukund Butti

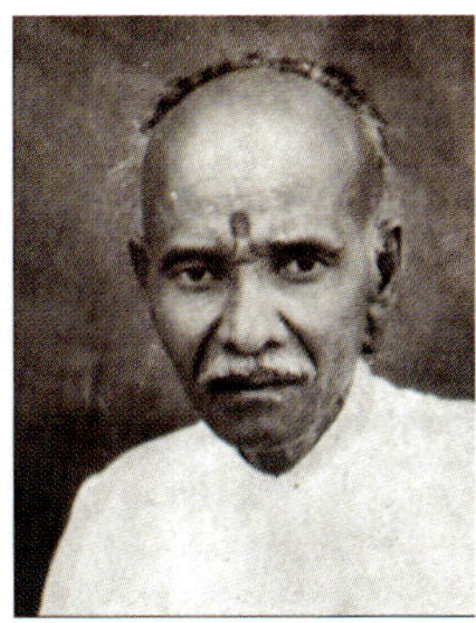
Shri Sagun Meru Naik

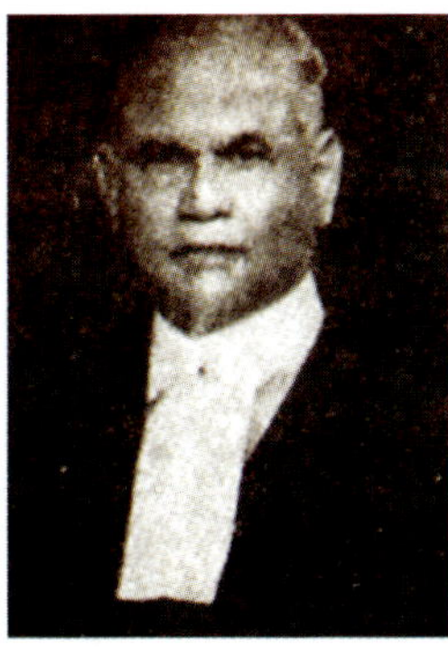
Shri Moreshwar Pradhan

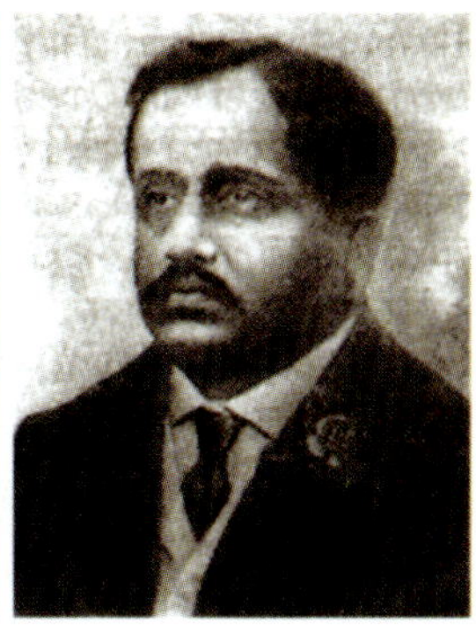
Shri Laxman K. Nulkar

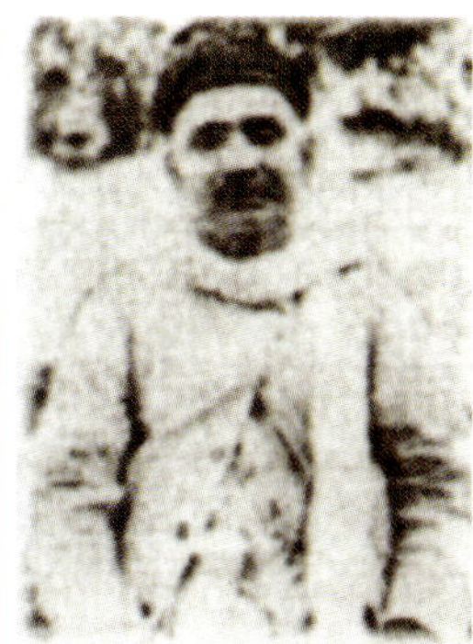
Shri Raghuvir Purandre

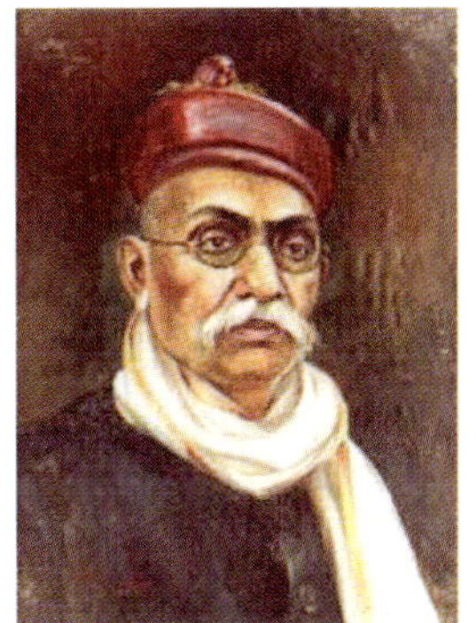
Shri Govind R. Dabholkar *(Hemadpant)*

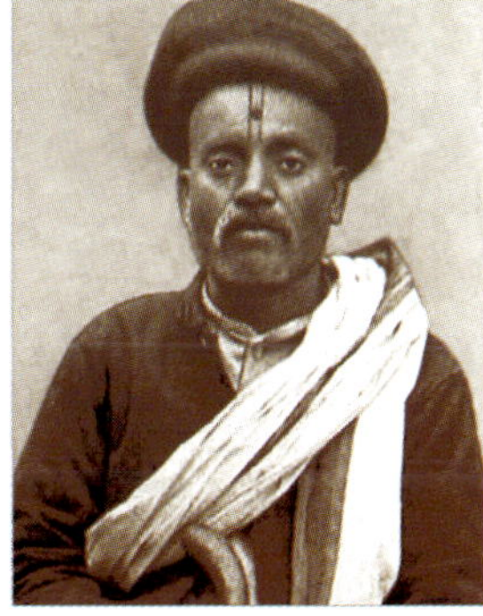
Shri Nanasaheb Nimonkar

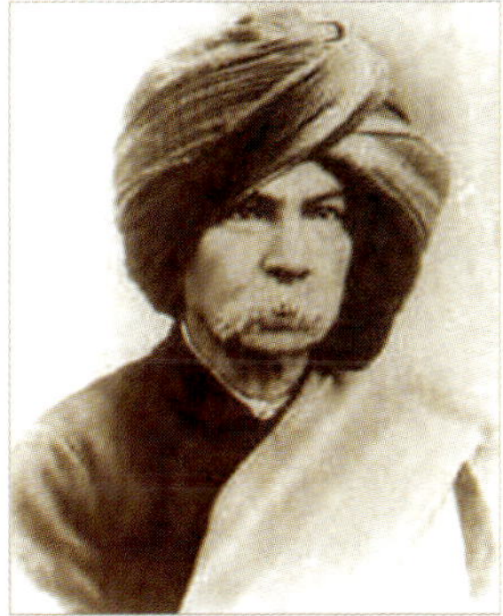
Shri Ganesh Shrikrishna Khaparde

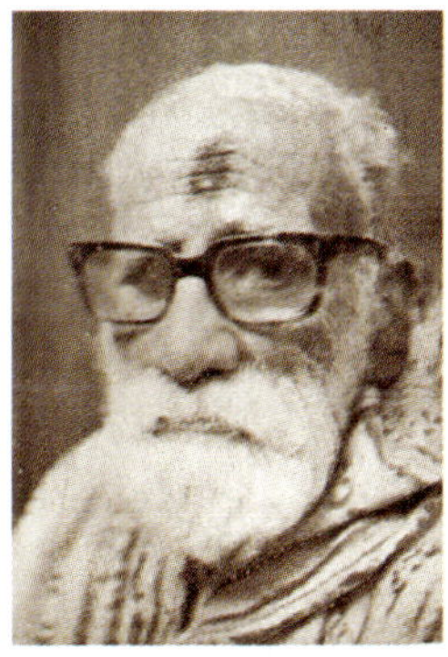
Shri Martand Mahlsapati Sonar

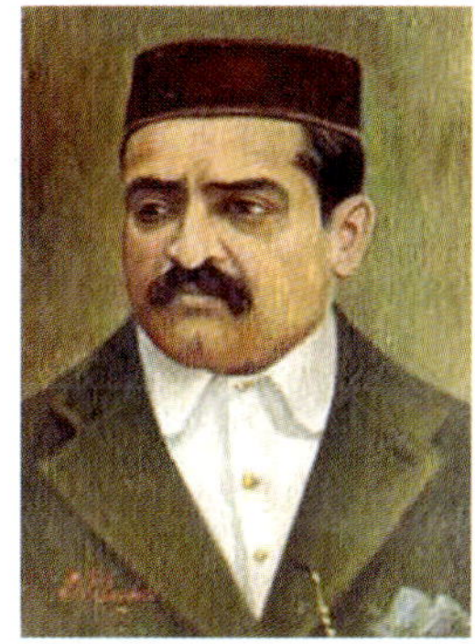
Shri Bala Saheb Bhate

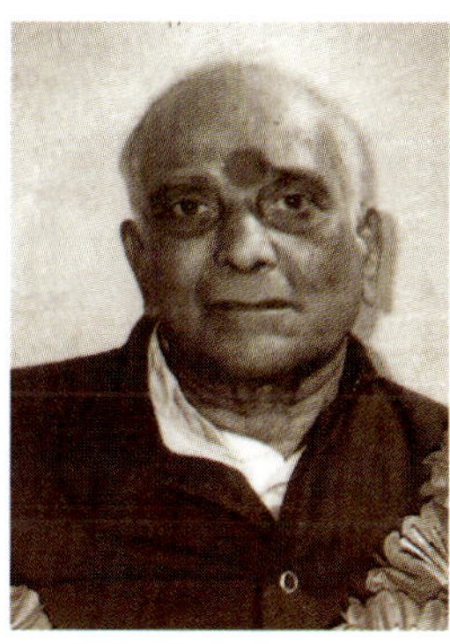
Dr. Keshav Bhagawant Gavankar

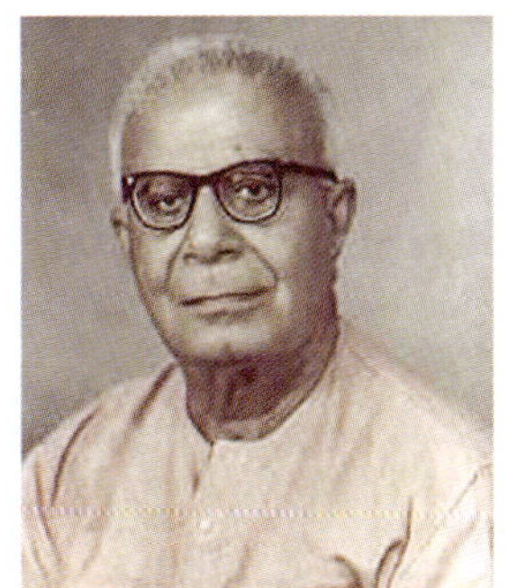
Shri Megha Shyam Rege

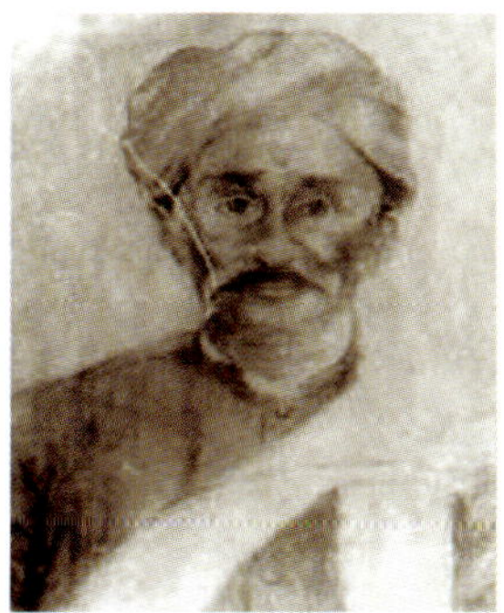
Shri Damodar Ghanshyam Babre

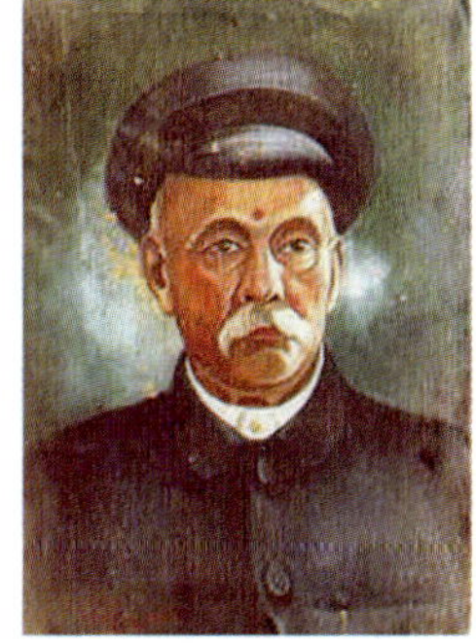
Shri Shamrao Ramchander Jaikar

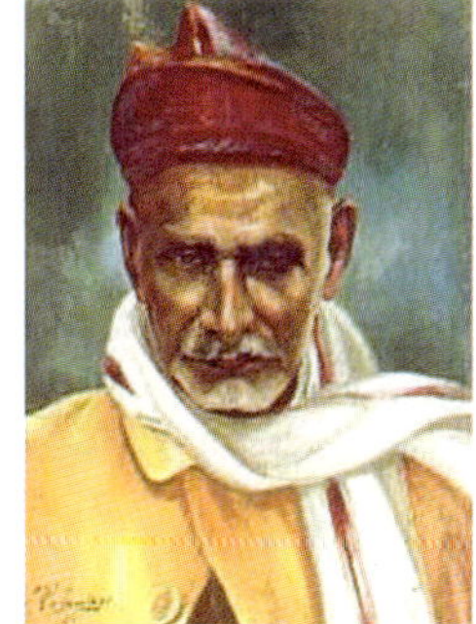
Shri Raghuvir Purandre

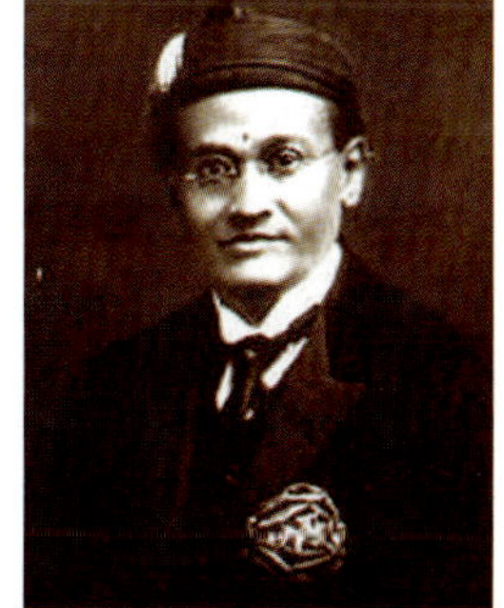
Shri Balasaheb Mirikar

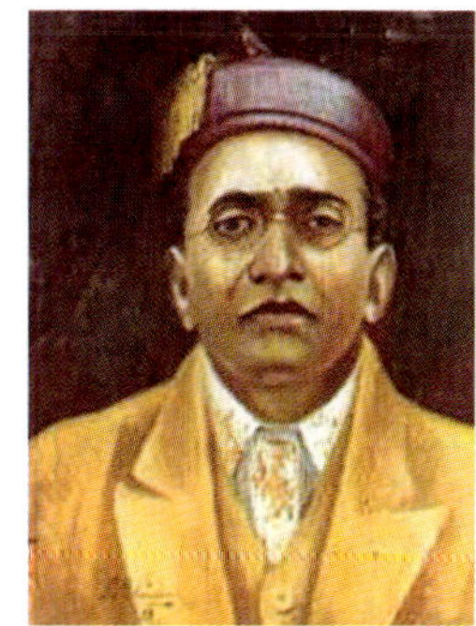
Shri Bhan Saheb Dhumal

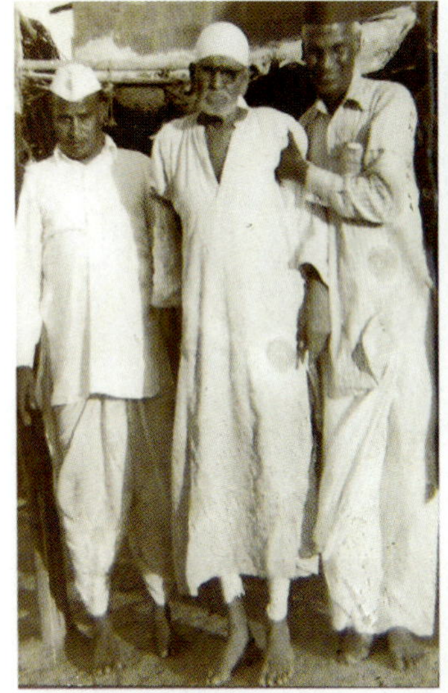

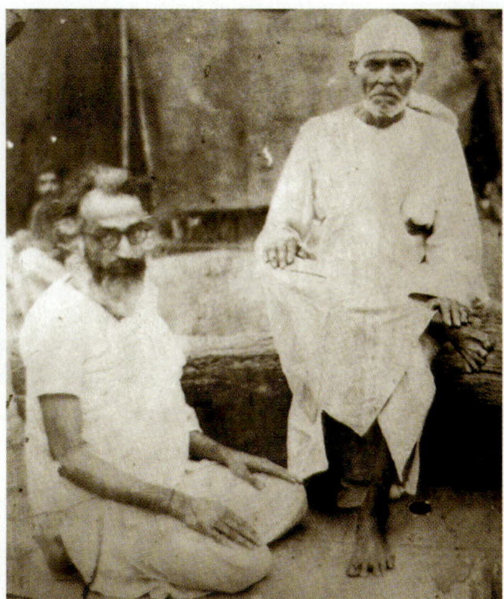

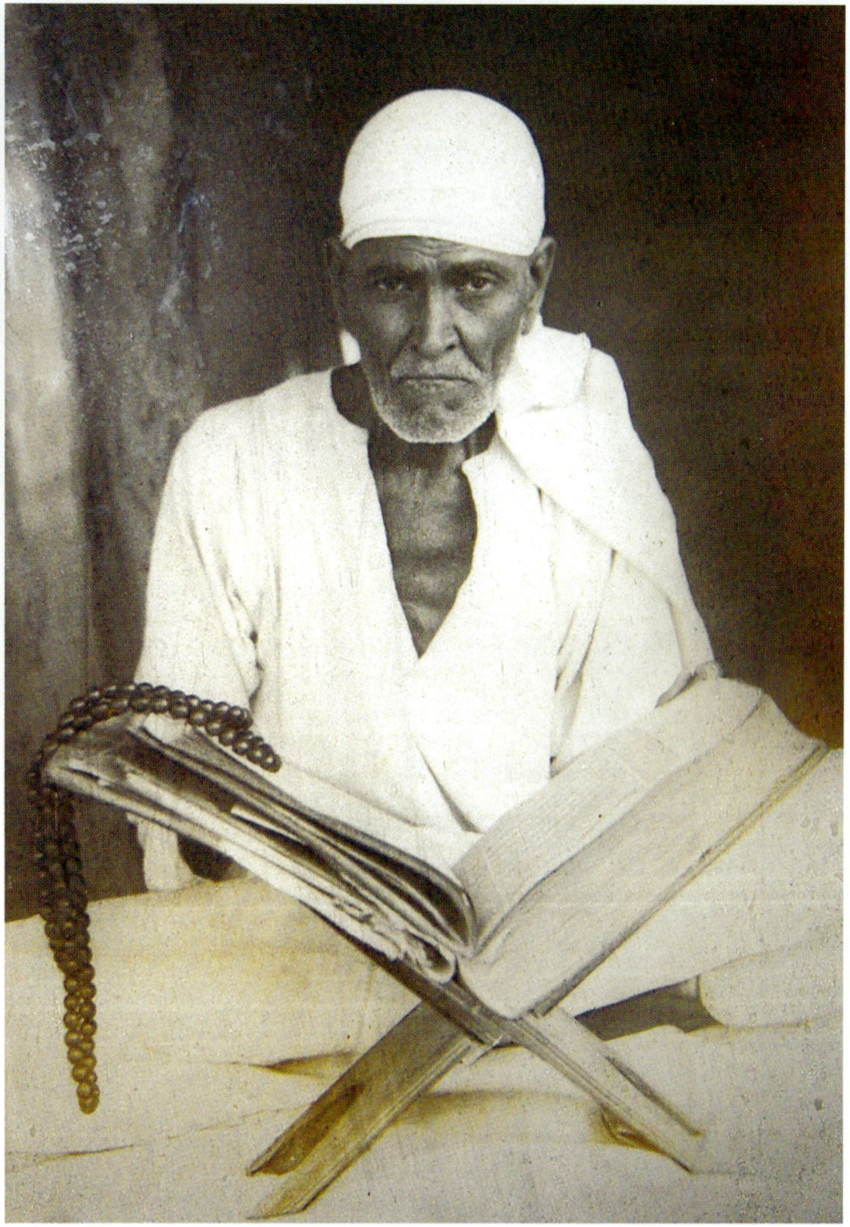

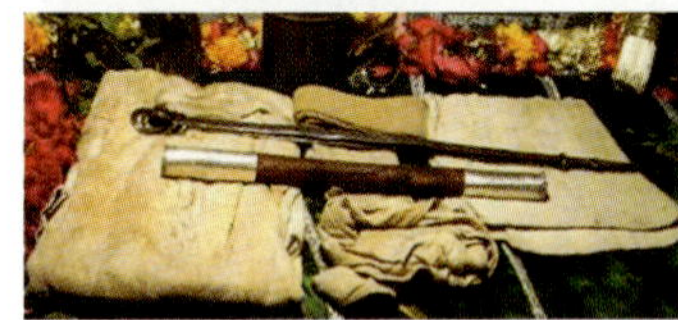

Baba's *Satka, Chimta* and *Kafni* now at Abdul Baba's cottage.

Haji Abdul Baba

Haji Abdul shared a unique bond with Baba. Completely immersed in Baba's worship, he religiously wrote down Baba's words and read them daily. After Baba's Mahasamadhi, he continued to devote his energies for the maintenance of the shrine.

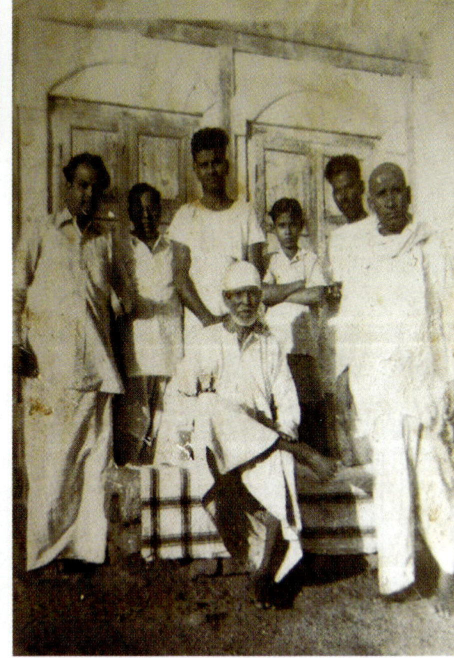

Abdul Baba with devotees

Haji Abdul Baba reading the Holy Quran.

Abdul Baba during his daily attendance at Baba's Samadhi in Samadhi Mandir. →

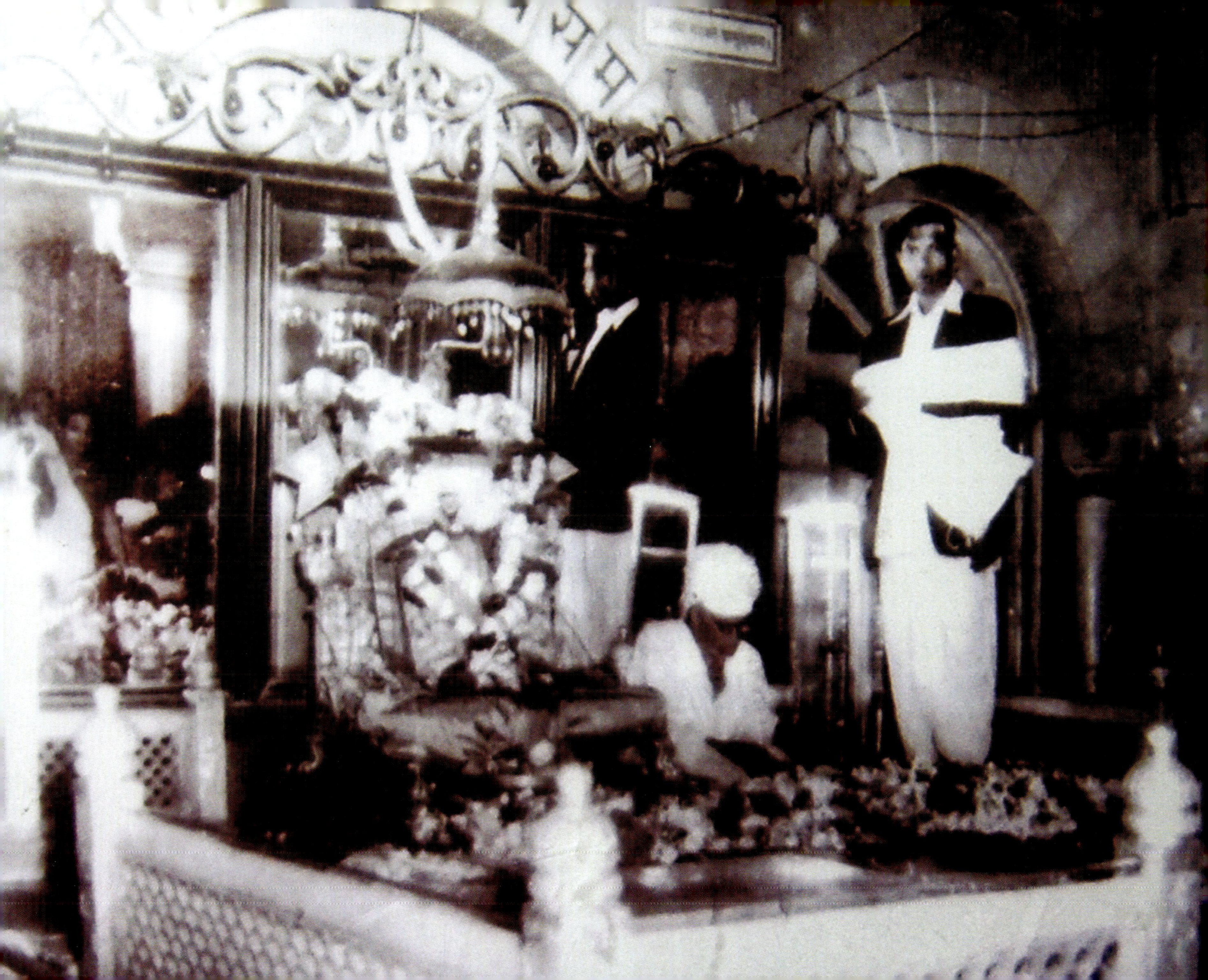

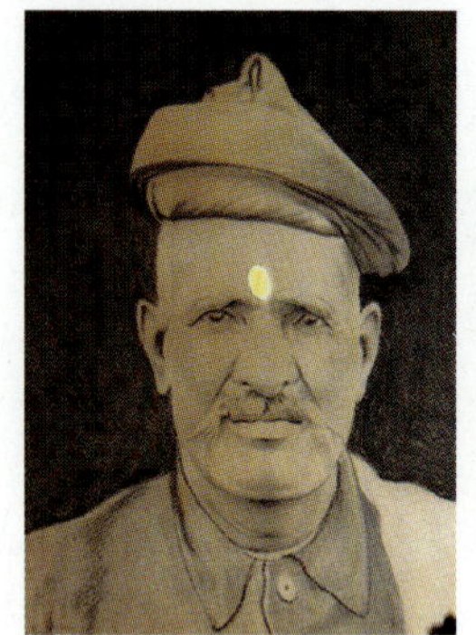
Shri Khushal Chand Sand (Rahata)

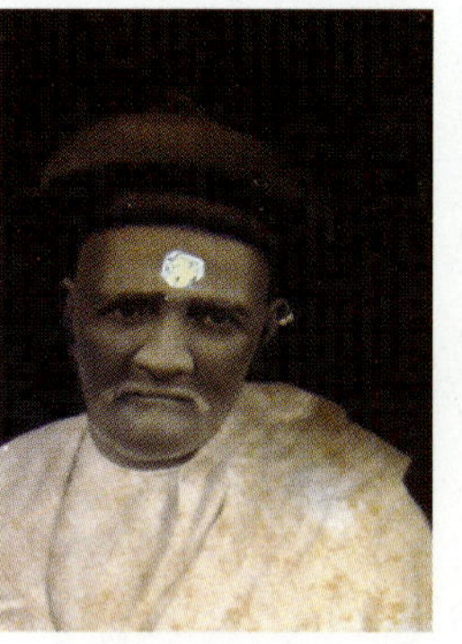
Shri Chandra Bhan Sand (Rahata)

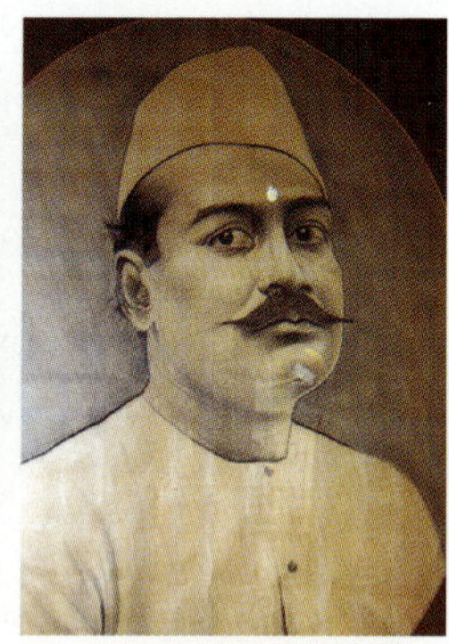
Shri Amolak Sand (Rahata)

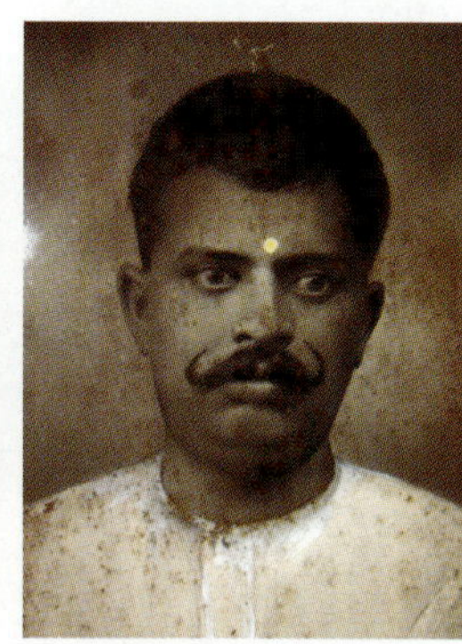
Shri Daulat Ram Sand (Rahata)

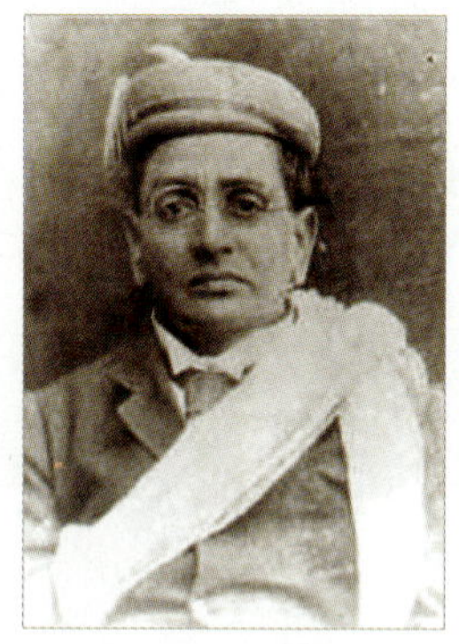
Shri Laxman Ganesh Mahajani

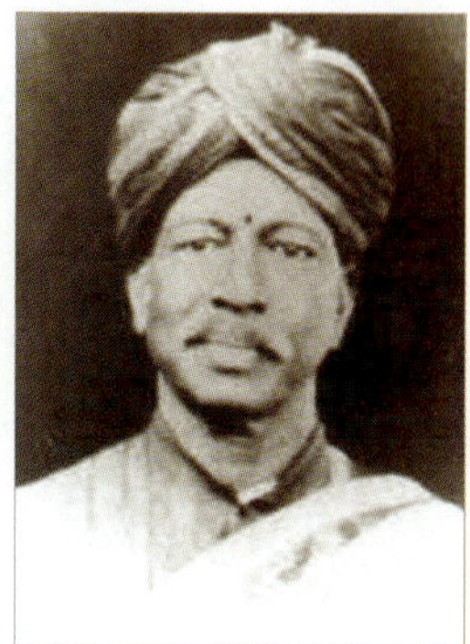
Dr. Pillay

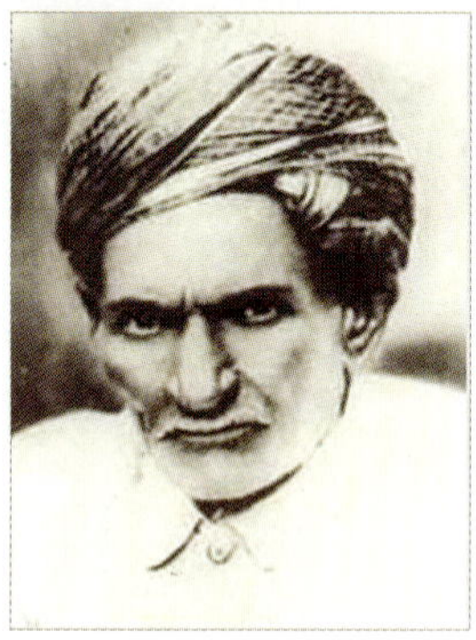
Shri Laxman Govind Mungi

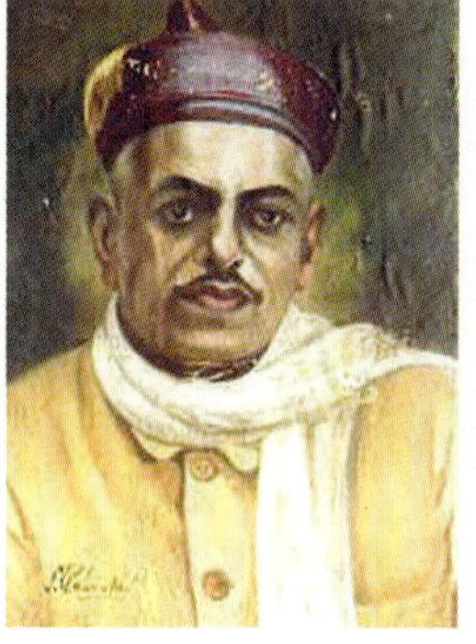
Shri Yashwant Galwankar

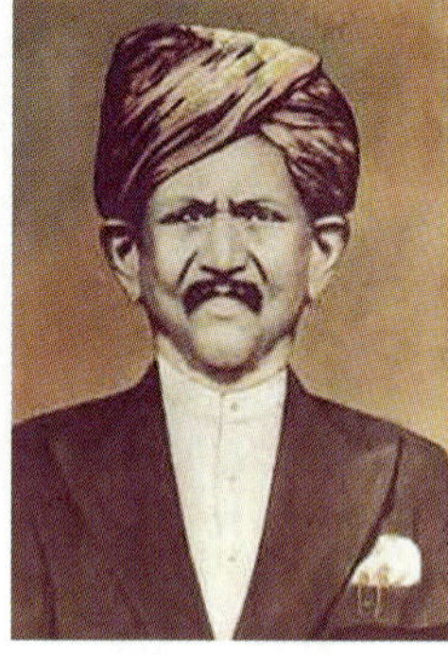
Shri Y. R. Sukher

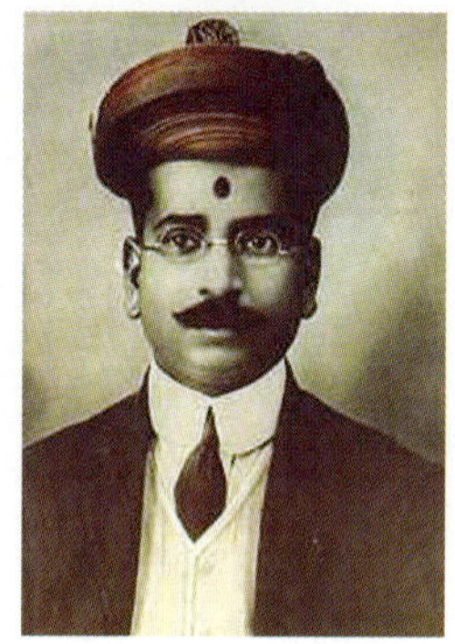
Shri Sundarrao Navalkar

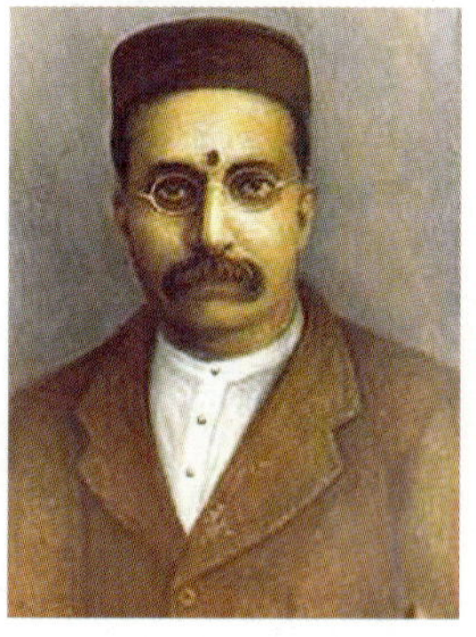
Shri Sadubhaiya Naik

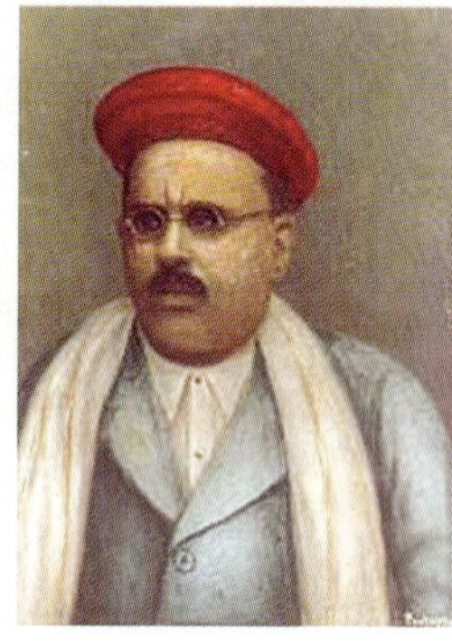
Shri Rajubhaiya Naik

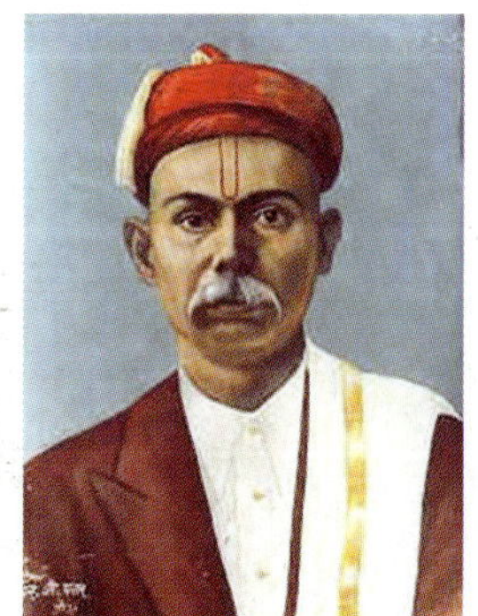
Shri Mahadeo Waman Sapatnekar

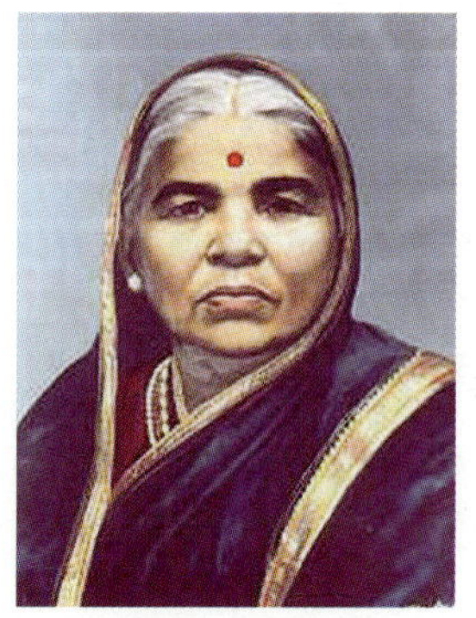
Smt. Parvatibai Sapatnekar

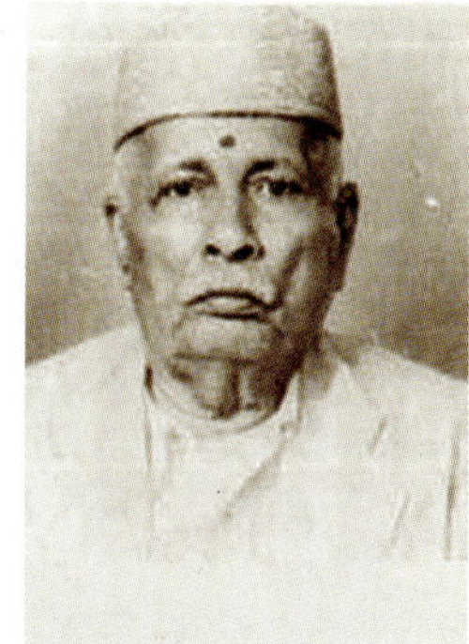
Shri Atmaram Kulkarni

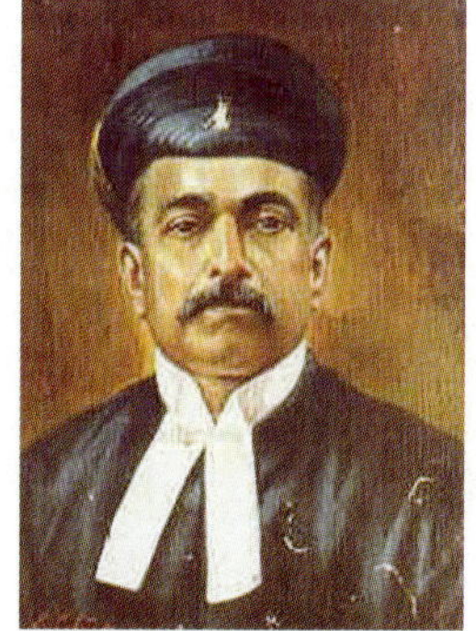
Shri Ramakrishna Shrikrishna Nawalkar

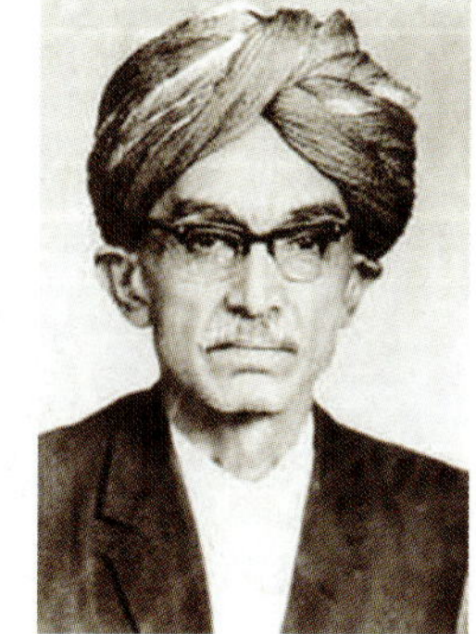
Shri Trimbak Damodar Rasane (son of Damu Anna)

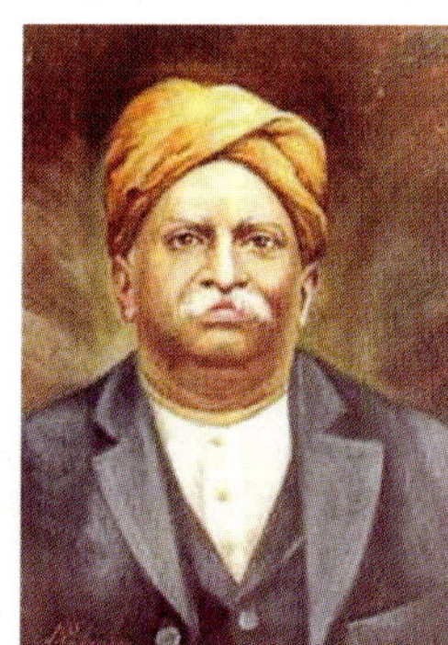
Shri Balasaheb Deo

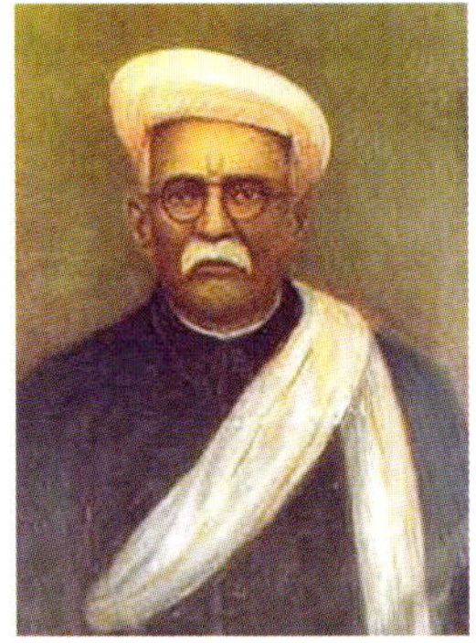

Shri Chotubhaiya Parulkar

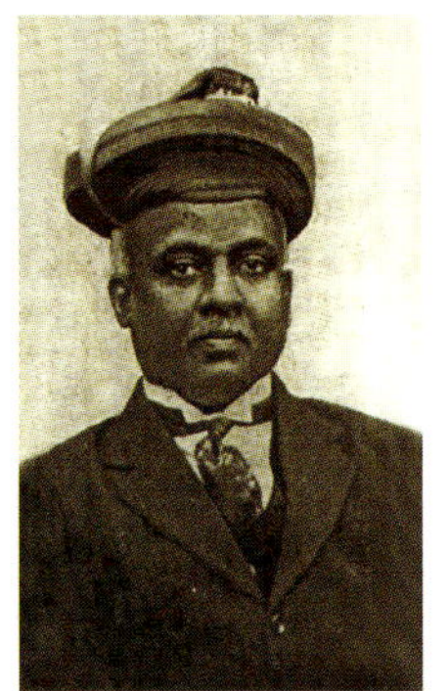

Shri Balakrishnanath Durandar

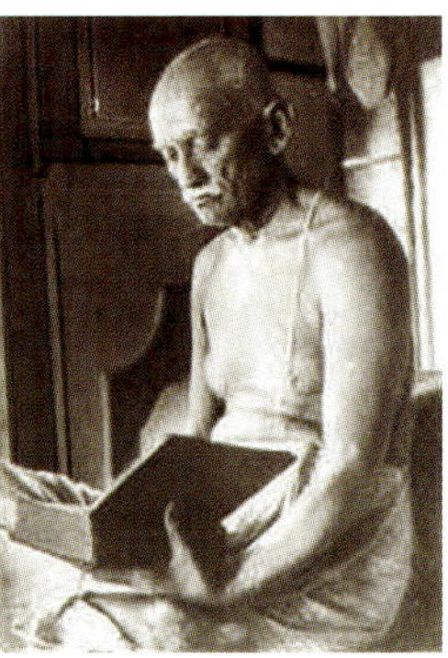

Shri P.R. Awasthi

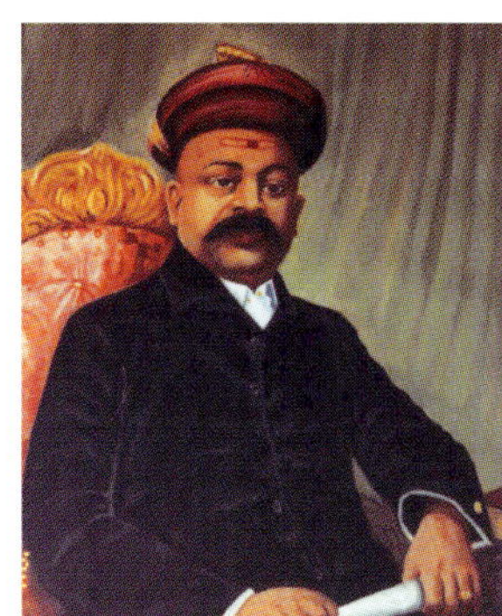

Shri Harish Chandra R Pithale

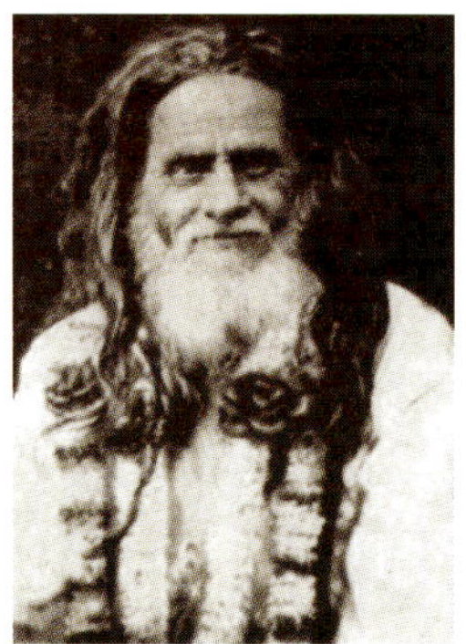

Shri Kusha Bhave

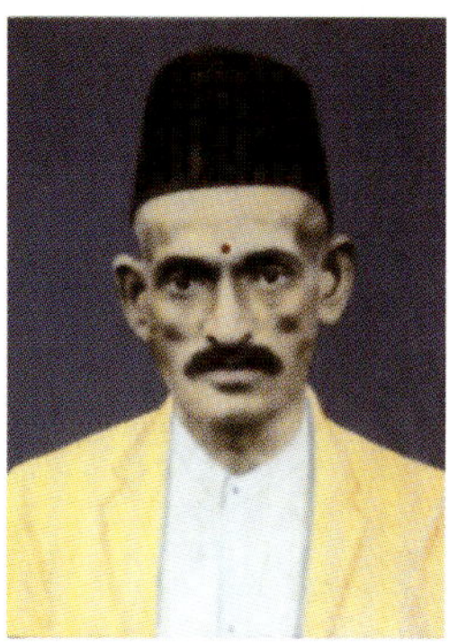

Shri Prahalad Mule Shastri

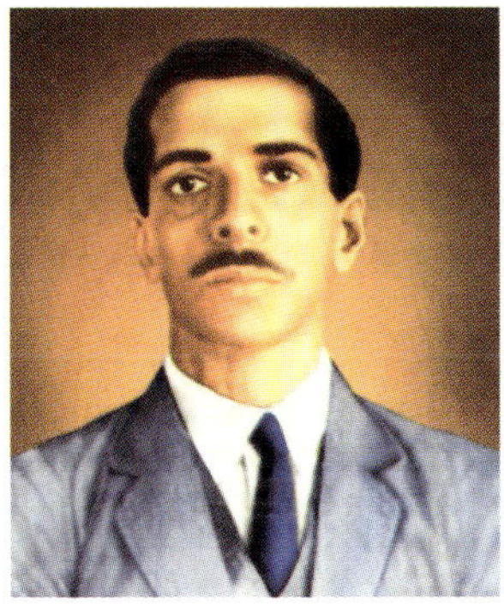

Shri Jyotinder R Tarkhad

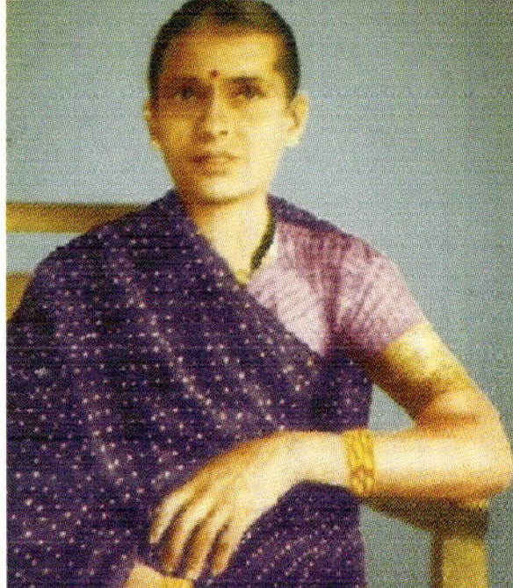

Smt. Sita Bai Tarkhad

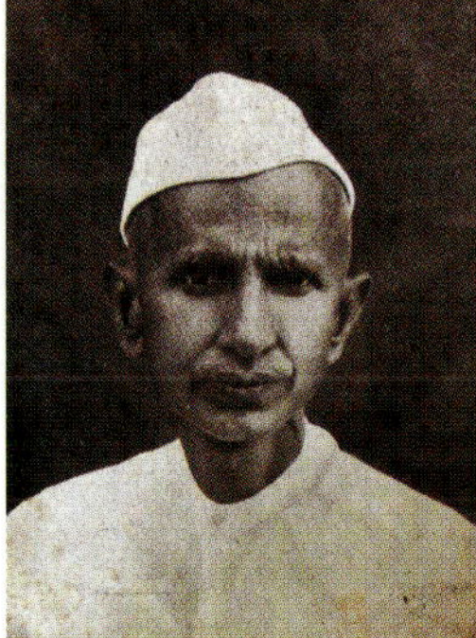

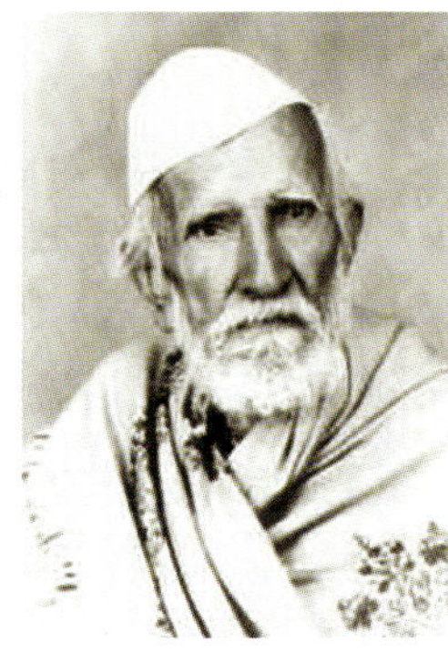

Shri Dattatreya Damodar Rasane (young & old)

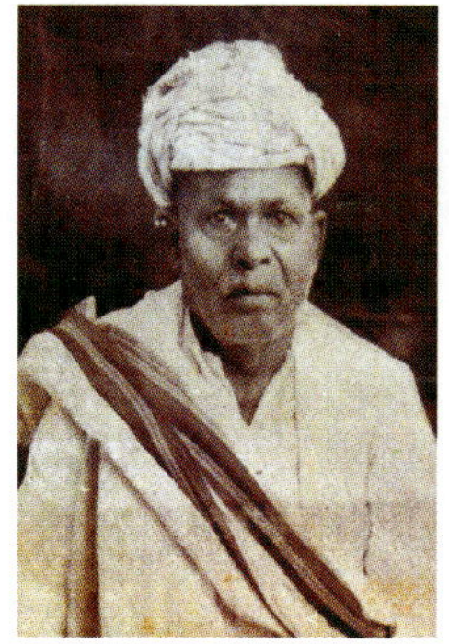

Shri Balaji Bapuji Jagtap

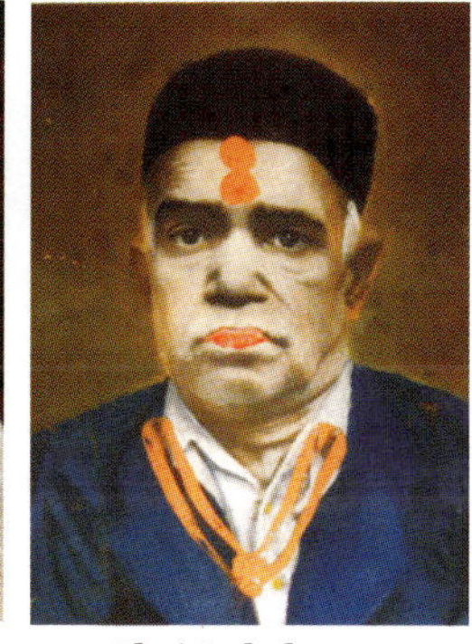

Shri Lakshman Kacheshwar Jakhari (Nanu Mama Pujari)

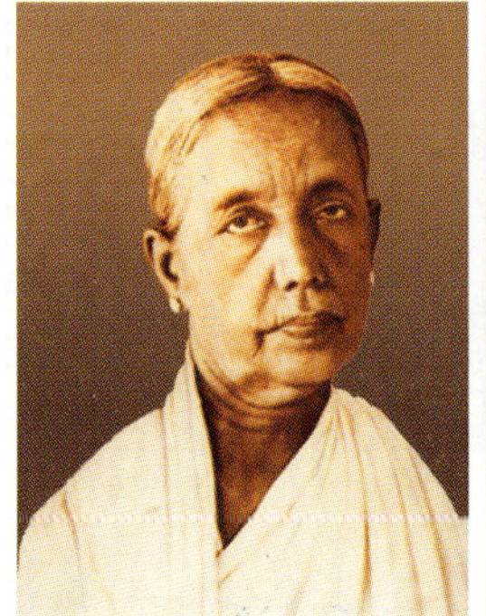

Smt. Savitri Bai Tendulkar

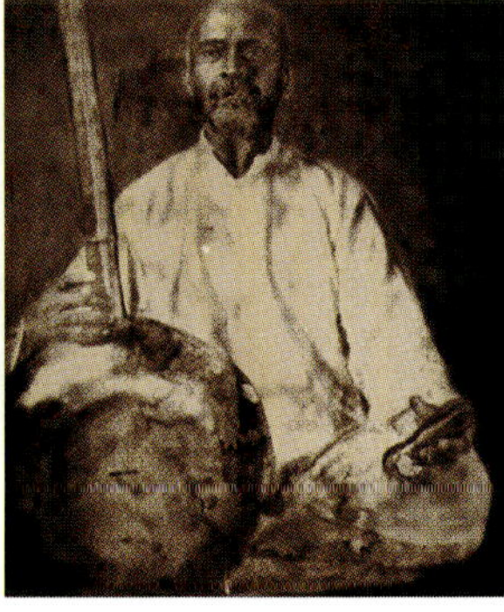

Shri Raghunath Tendulkar

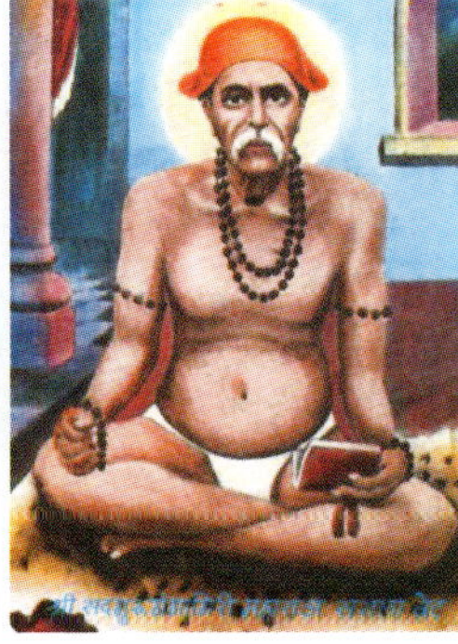

Shri Gangagir Bua

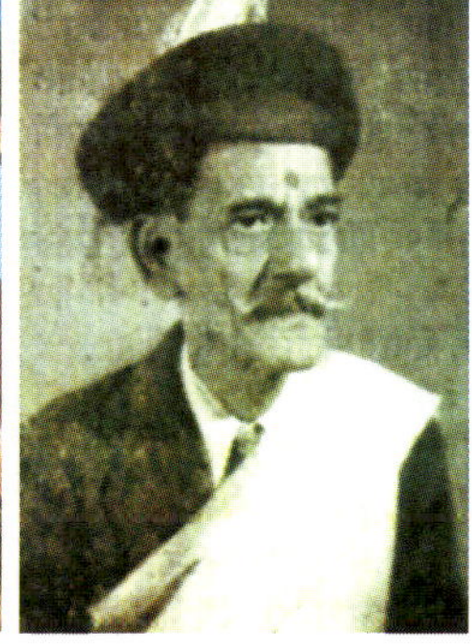

Shri Gorakshkar

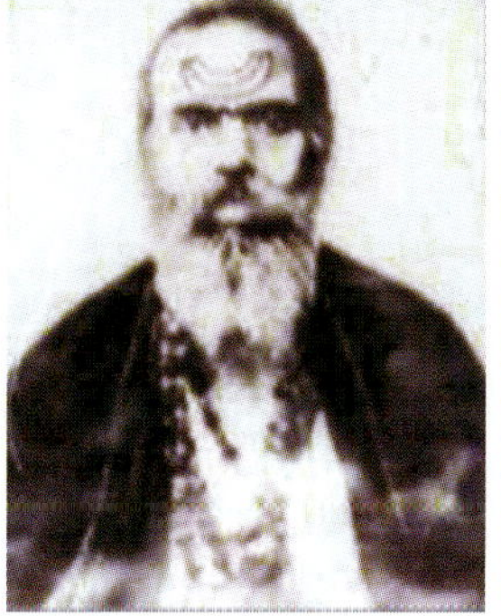

Shri K G Bhishma

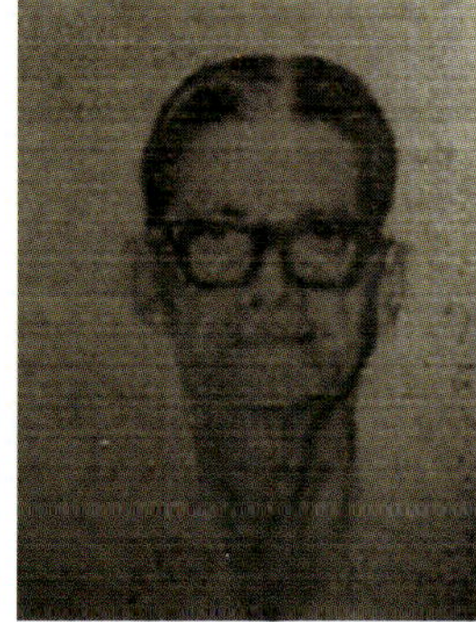

Shri Vitthal Yashwant Deshpande

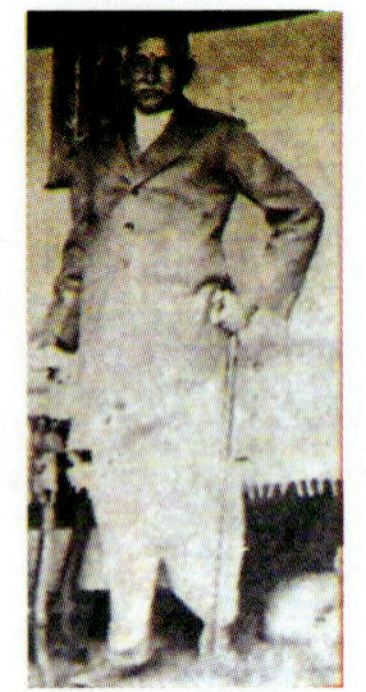

Shri Shantaram Balwant Nachane

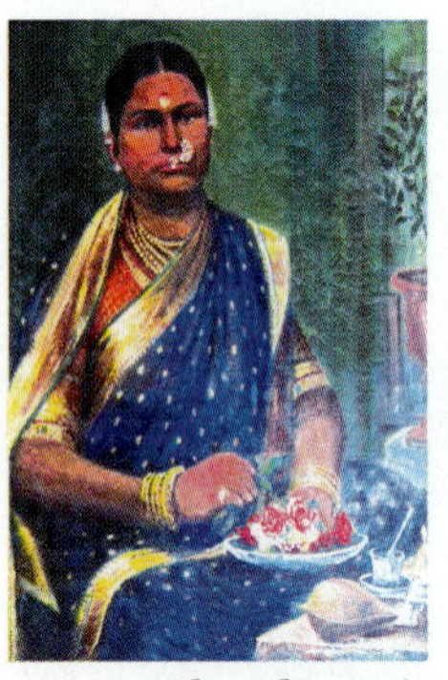

Smt. Chandra Bai Ramchander Borkar

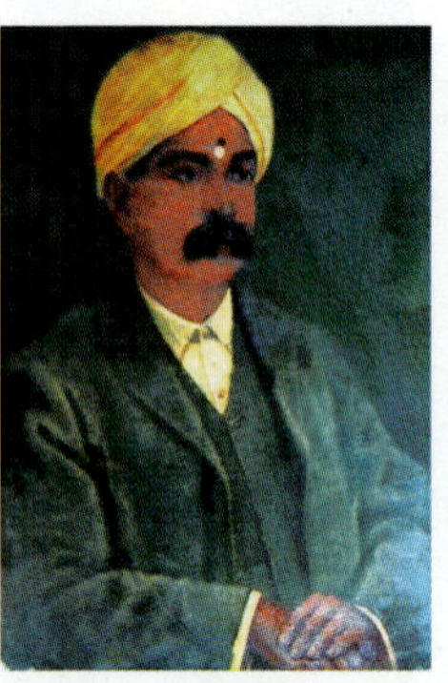

Shri Ramchander Soyroba Borkar

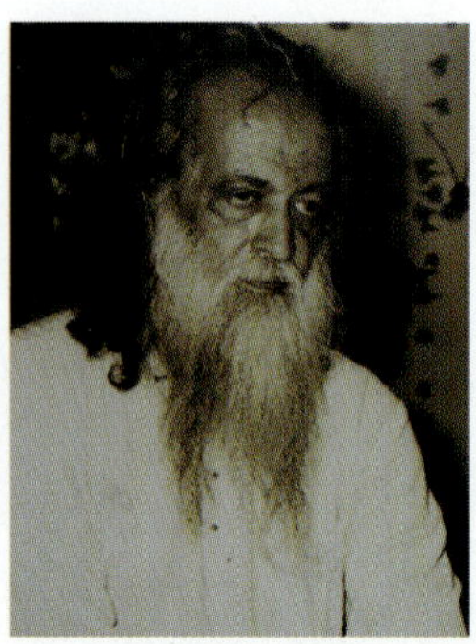

Shri Dev Baba Walawalkar

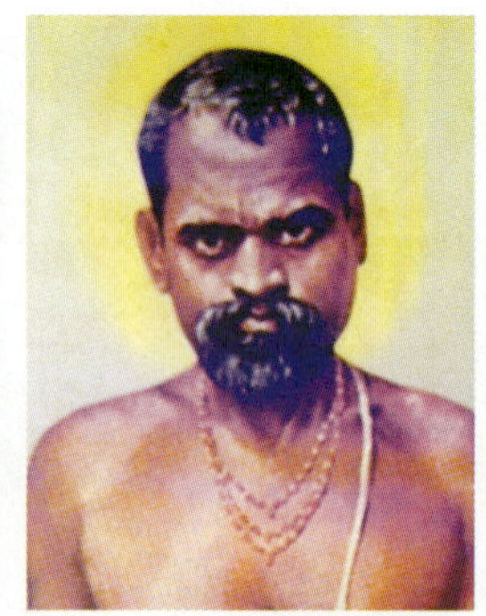

Shri Ram Maruti Maharaj

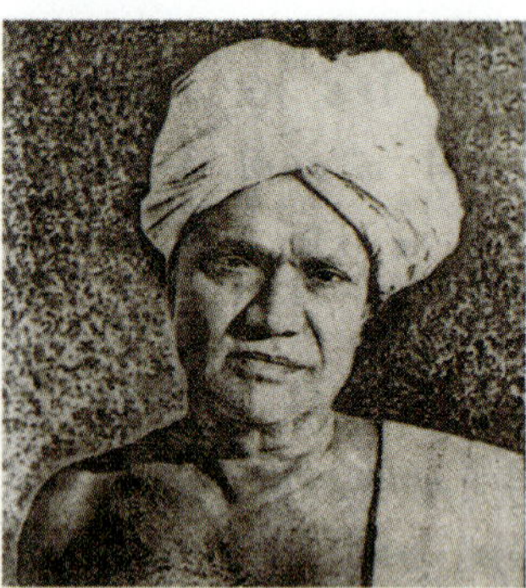

Shri Motta

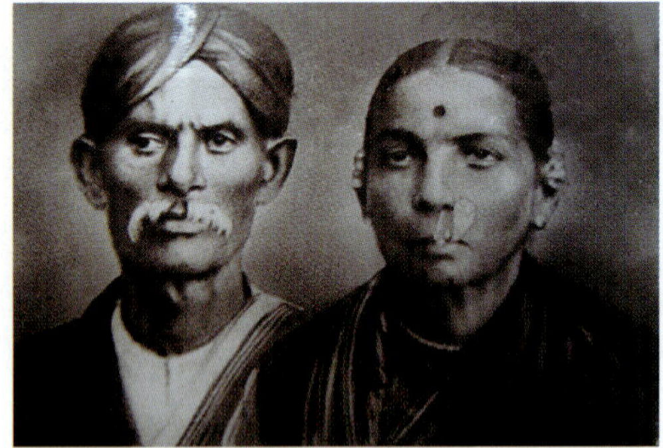

Shri Vishnu Balwant Pithale

Smt. Radhabai Vishnu Pithale

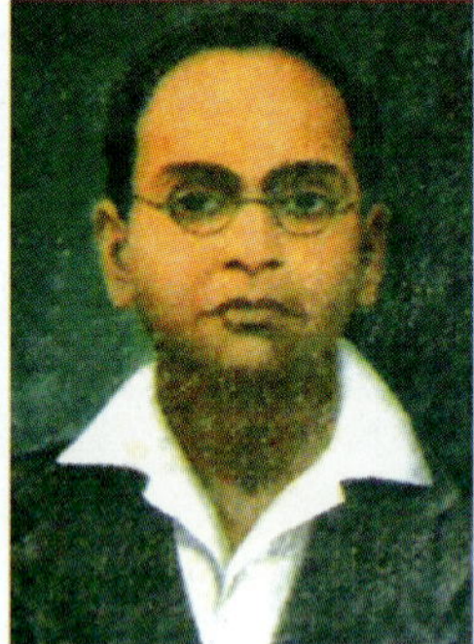

Shri Ram Krishna Dixit (Bapu)

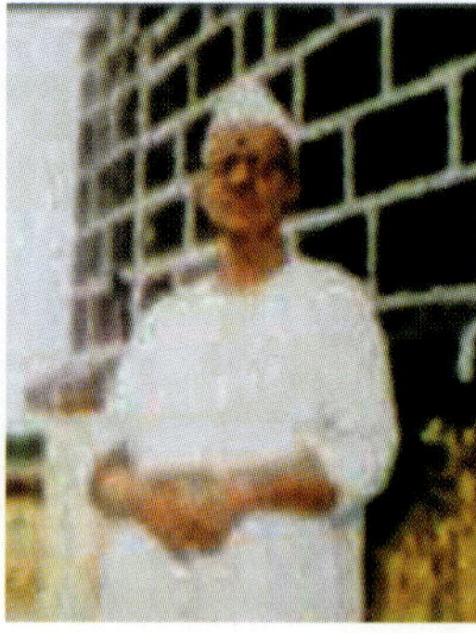

Shri Ramchandra Atma Ram Tarkhad (Baba Saheb)

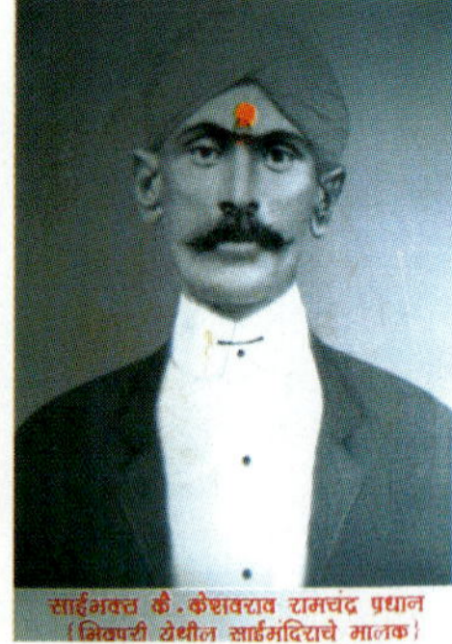

Shri Keshavrao Ramchandra Pradhan

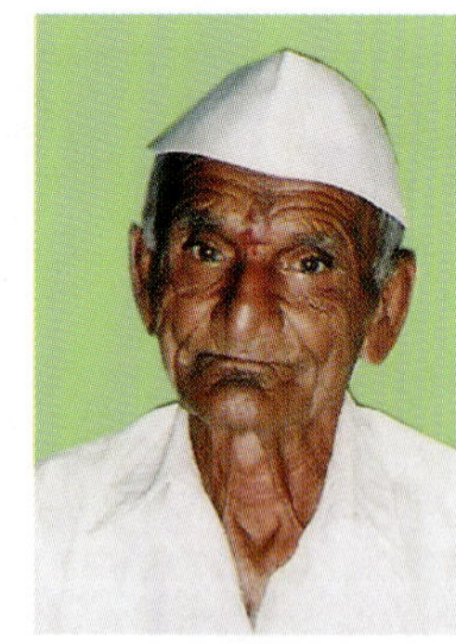

Shri Dattatray Deshpande Nimonkar

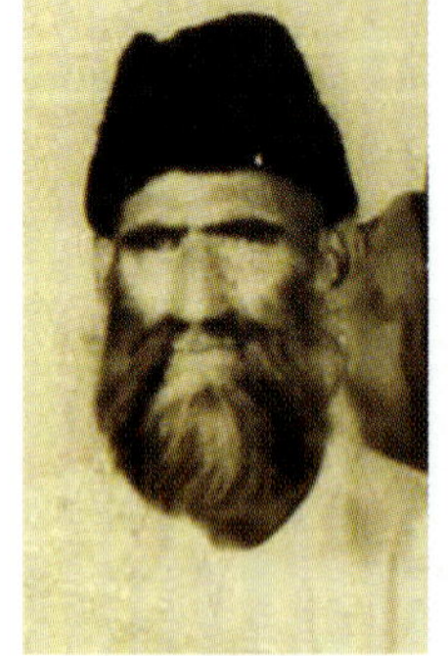

Shri Abduljaan Pathan

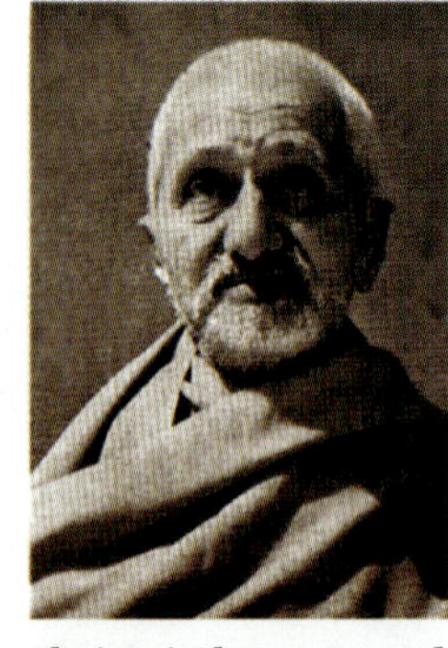

Shri Sai Sharananand (Vaman Pran Govind Patel)

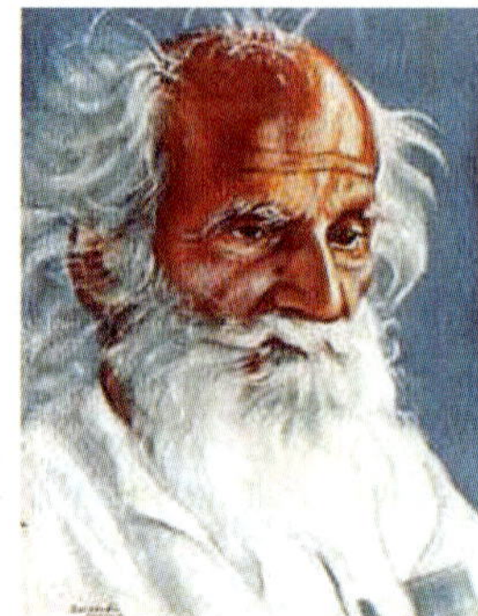

Shri Narasimha Swami

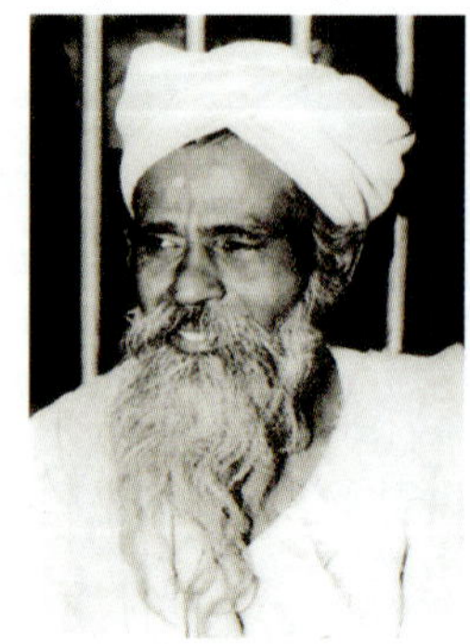

Shri Shivneshan Swami

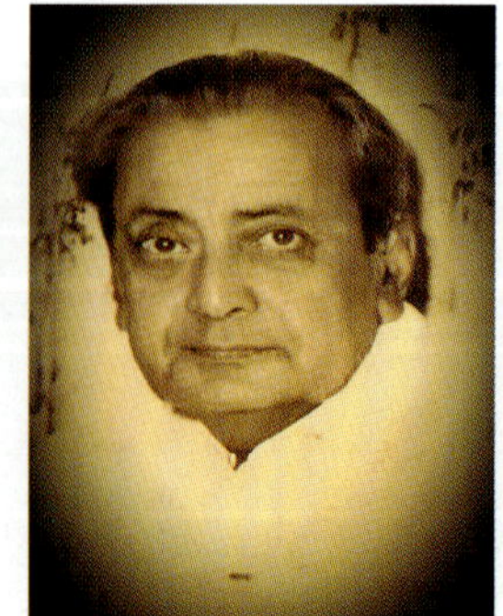

Shri D.D. Neroy

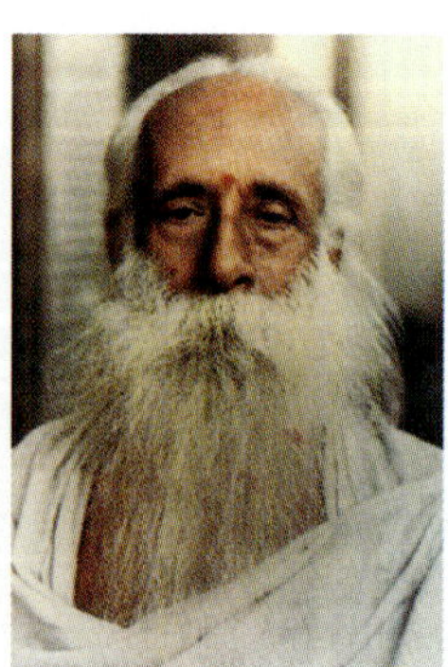

Shri Radhakrishna Swami

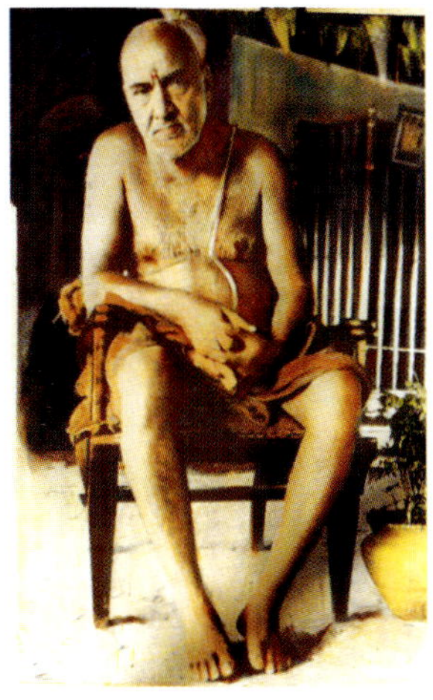
Shri Upasani Maharaj

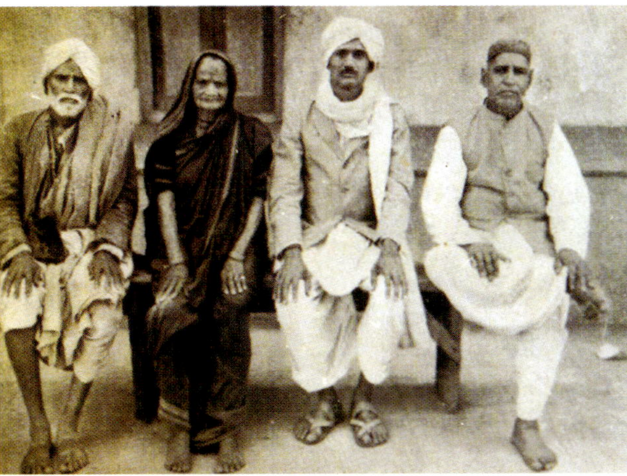
l to r - Shri Martand Mahalsapati Sonar, Smt. Lakshmi Bai Shinde, Shri Bapaji Lakshman Ratanparkhi, Shri Balaji Pillaji Gurav

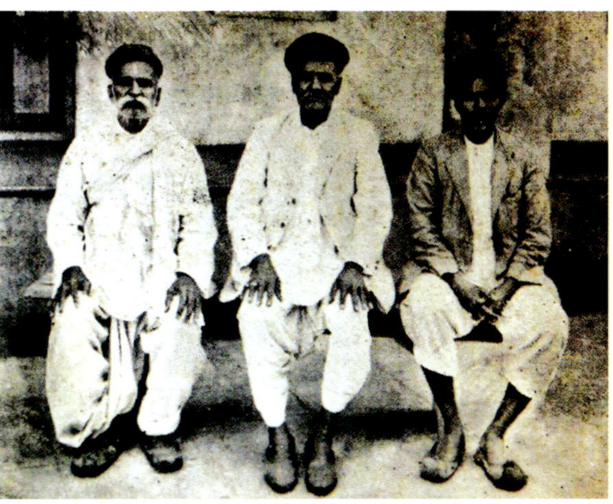
Shri Vamanrao Mankoji Gondkar, Shri Thamaji Bhimaji Shelke, Shri Nivritti Hanumant Gondkar (Shirdi)

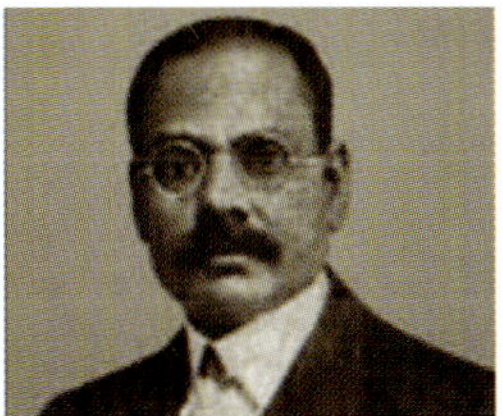
Prof. G G Narke

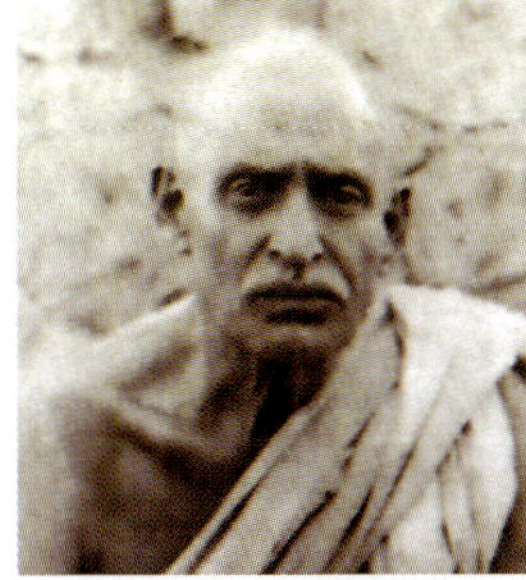
Shri Bapu Saheb Jog

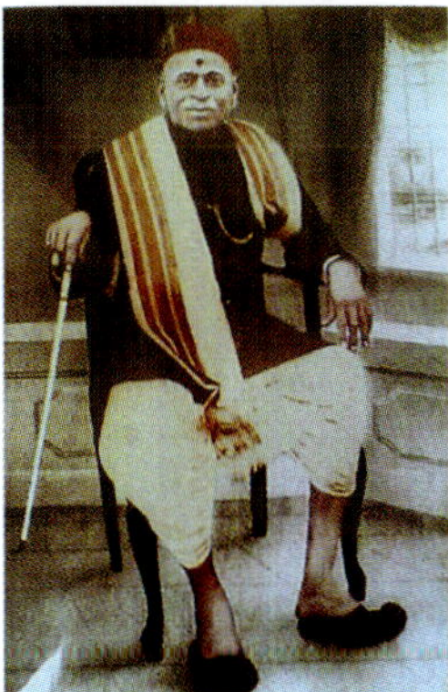
Shri Nandram Marwadi Sanklecha

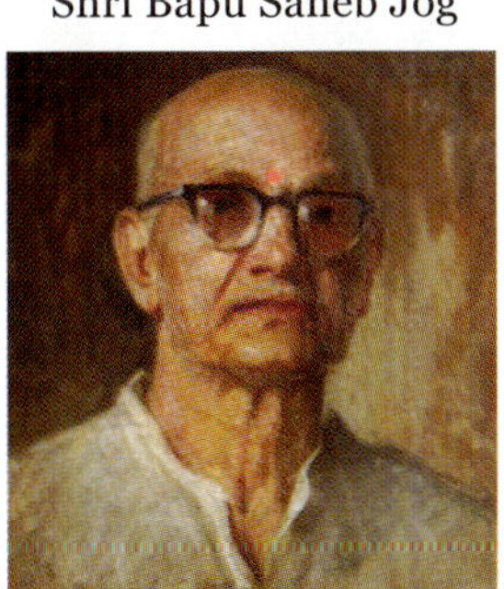
Shri Balaji Vasant Rao Talim *(Sculptor)*

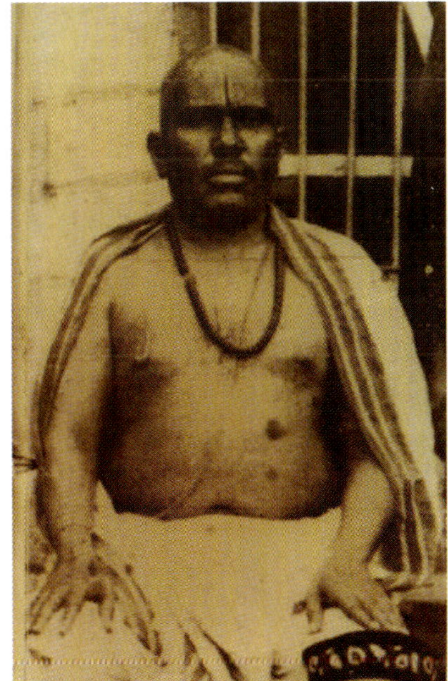

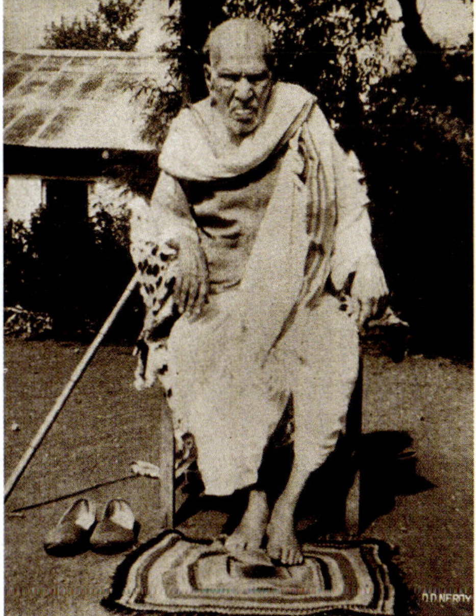

Das Ganu Maharaj (Young & Old)- A former police constable, Das Ganu spent his life singing paens to Baba. He devoted his time on earth in spreading Baba's glory among the ignorant masses. His soulful hymns drew Sai bhaktas in hordes to Shirdi.

REVERED SAINTS

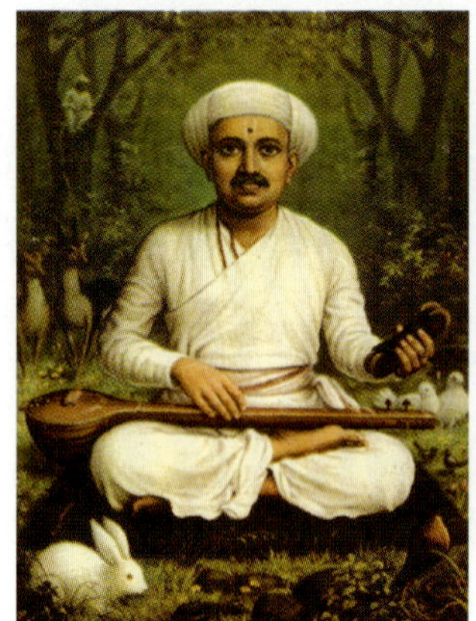

Saint Tukaram
(1608-1645)

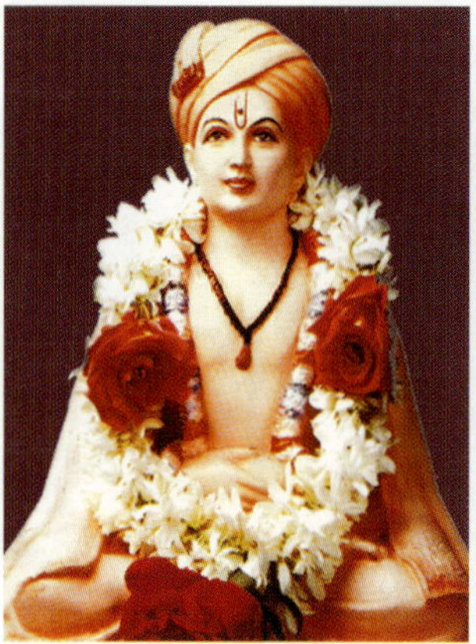

Saint Gyaneshwar
(1275-1296)

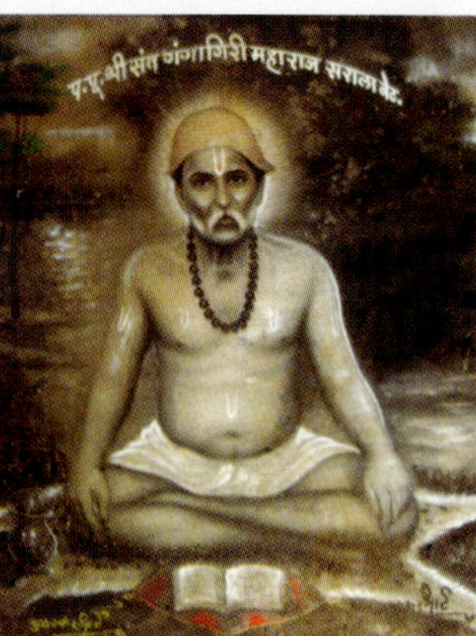

Saint Gangagiri Maharaj

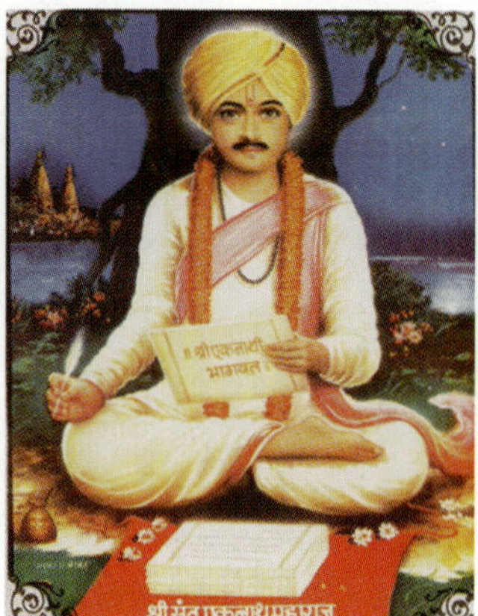

Saint Eknath
(1533-1599)

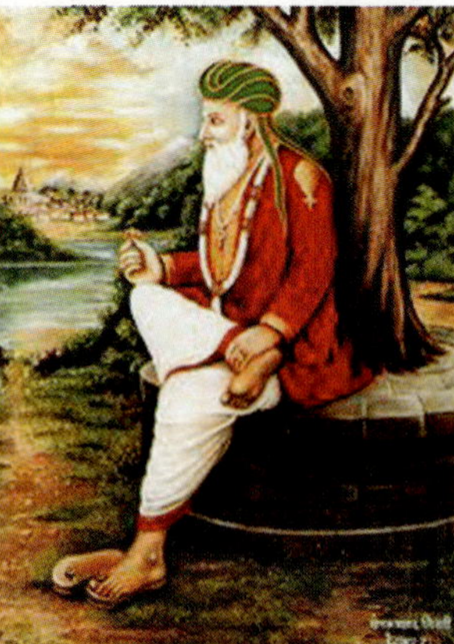

Manik Prabhu
(1817-1865)

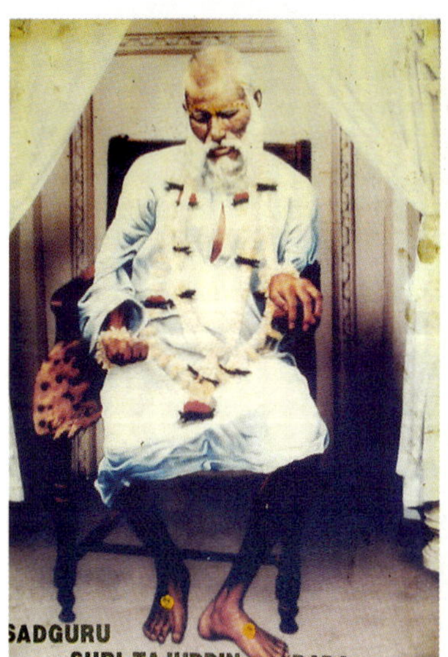

Shri Tajuddin Baba
(1861-1925)

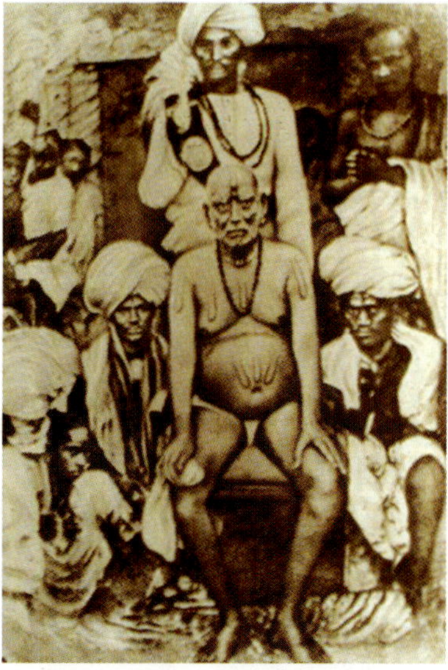

Swami Samarth Akkalkot Maharaj
(Samadhi 1878)

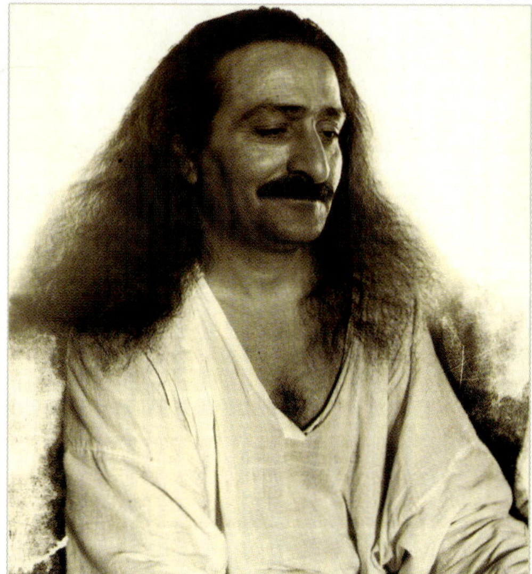

Mehar Baba
(1894-1969)

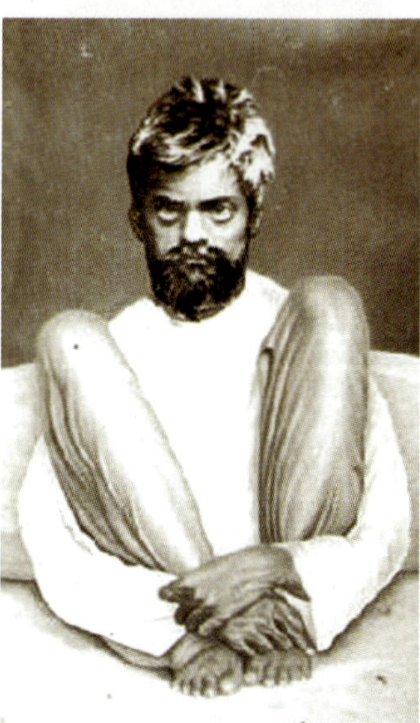

Shankar Maharaj

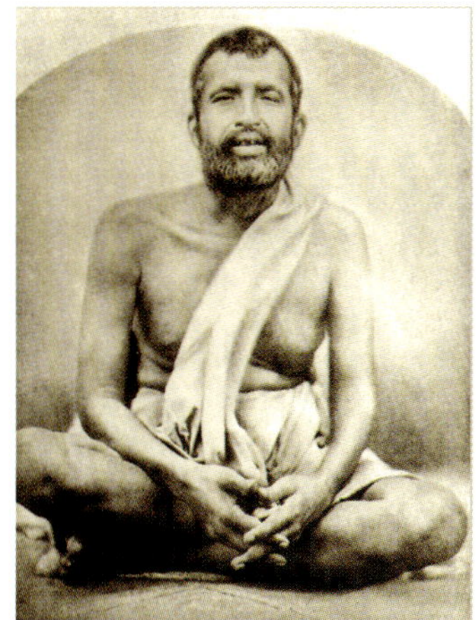
Shri Ramakrishna Paramhans
(1836-1886)

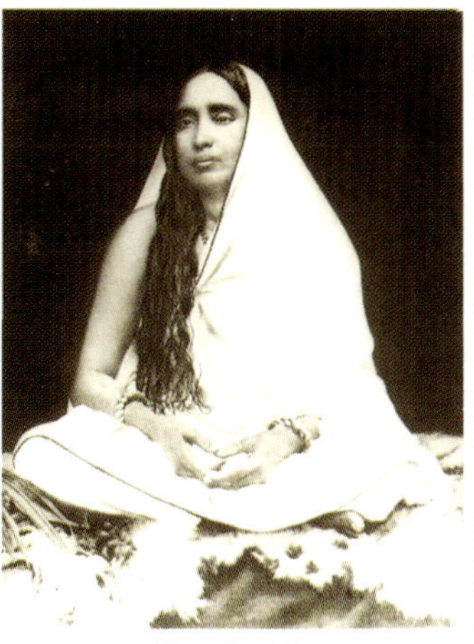
Sharda Maa
(1853-1920)

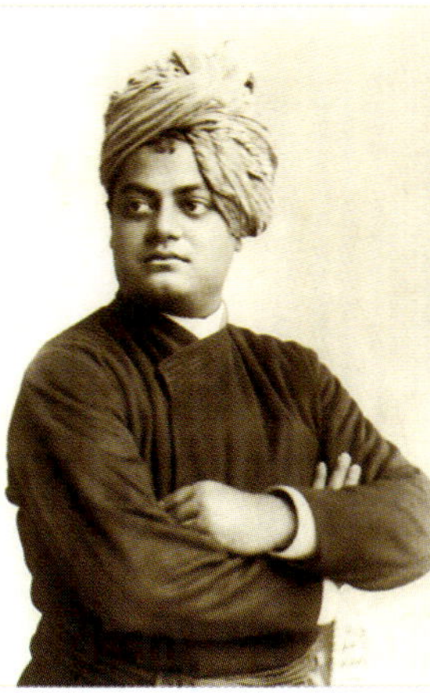
Swami Vivekanand
(1863-1902)

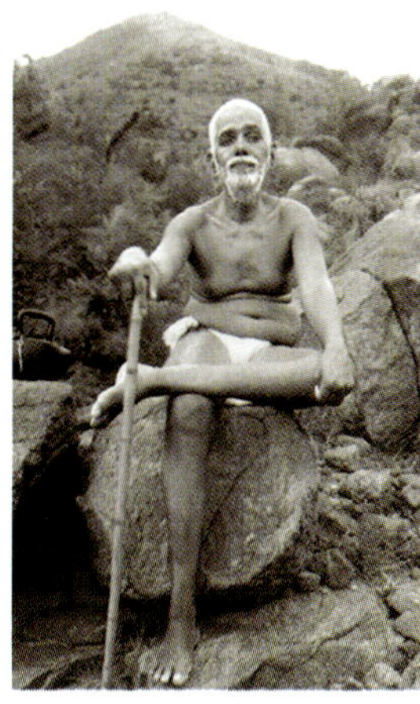
Raman Maharishi
(1879-1950)

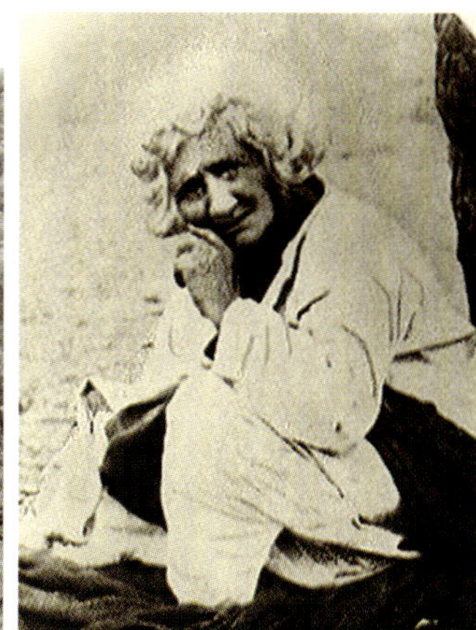
Hazrat Baba Jaan
(1806-1931)

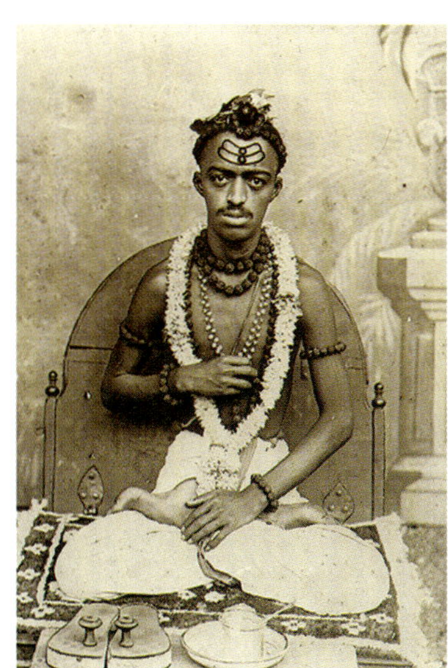
Narayan Maharaj
(1885-1945)

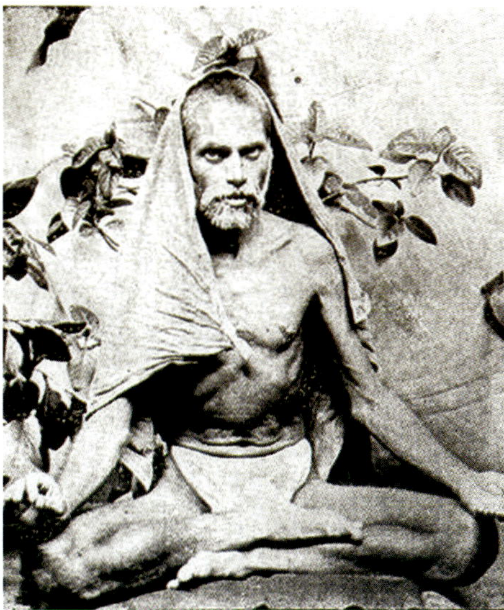
Vasudevanand Saraswati (Tembe Swami)
(1854-1914)

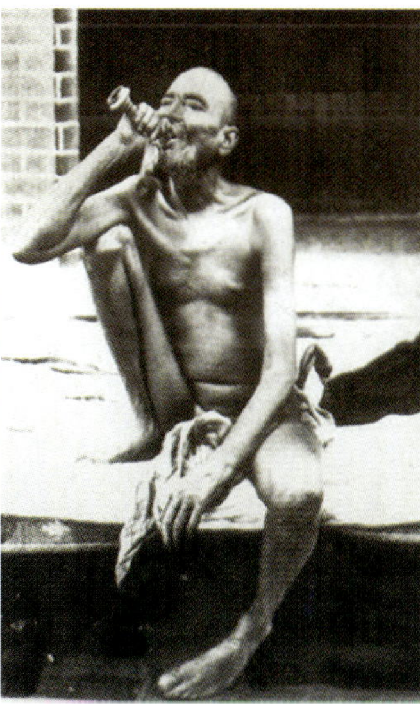
Saint Gajanan Maharaj
(Samadhi 1910)

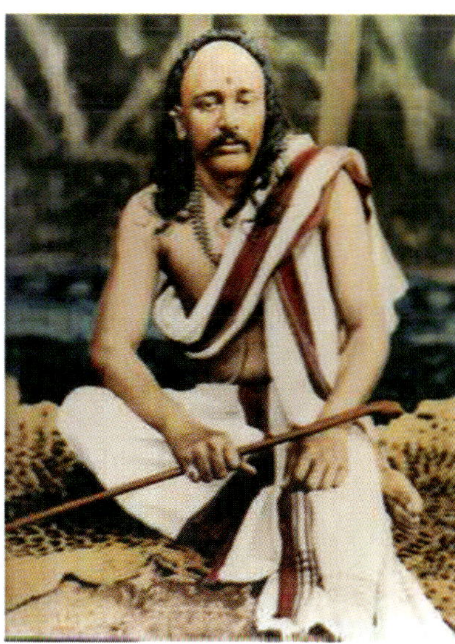
Bale Kundri Maharaj
(Birth 1855)

ORIGINAL PHOTOGRAPHS

Sai Nath's first Photograph

This is Baba's first ever photograph. The credit goes to Shri Kanshiram Shimpi who managed to get Baba's approval for getting clicked by a photographer after a great deal of cajoling. Titled 'Baba in a pensive mood', the photograph shows Baba gazing solemnly, with His right elbow resting on His right knee.

Opposite page: Invisible Baba

This photograph was taken by a devotee named Gopal Dinkar Joshi in 1912. Joshi wanted to take a photograph of Baba. He kept his camera mounted and ready before Baba returned from Lendi Baugh. Before doing this, he asked Baba for permission to take His photograph. Baba said, "I don't want a photograph of mine, but you can certainly take a photograph of the devotees accompanying me." Upon Baba's return from Lendi Baugh, Joshi seized the opportunity and took a photograph of Baba. Shama saw this and told Baba that Joshi had taken His photograph. Again Baba said the same thing, "I don't need any photograph of mine. What am I to do?" Joshi got the photograph printed, and to his utter surprise, Baba is not visible in it. The umbrella, Bhagoji Shinde and other devotees are clearly visible, but in Baba's place there is a luminous light and only His feet can be seen.

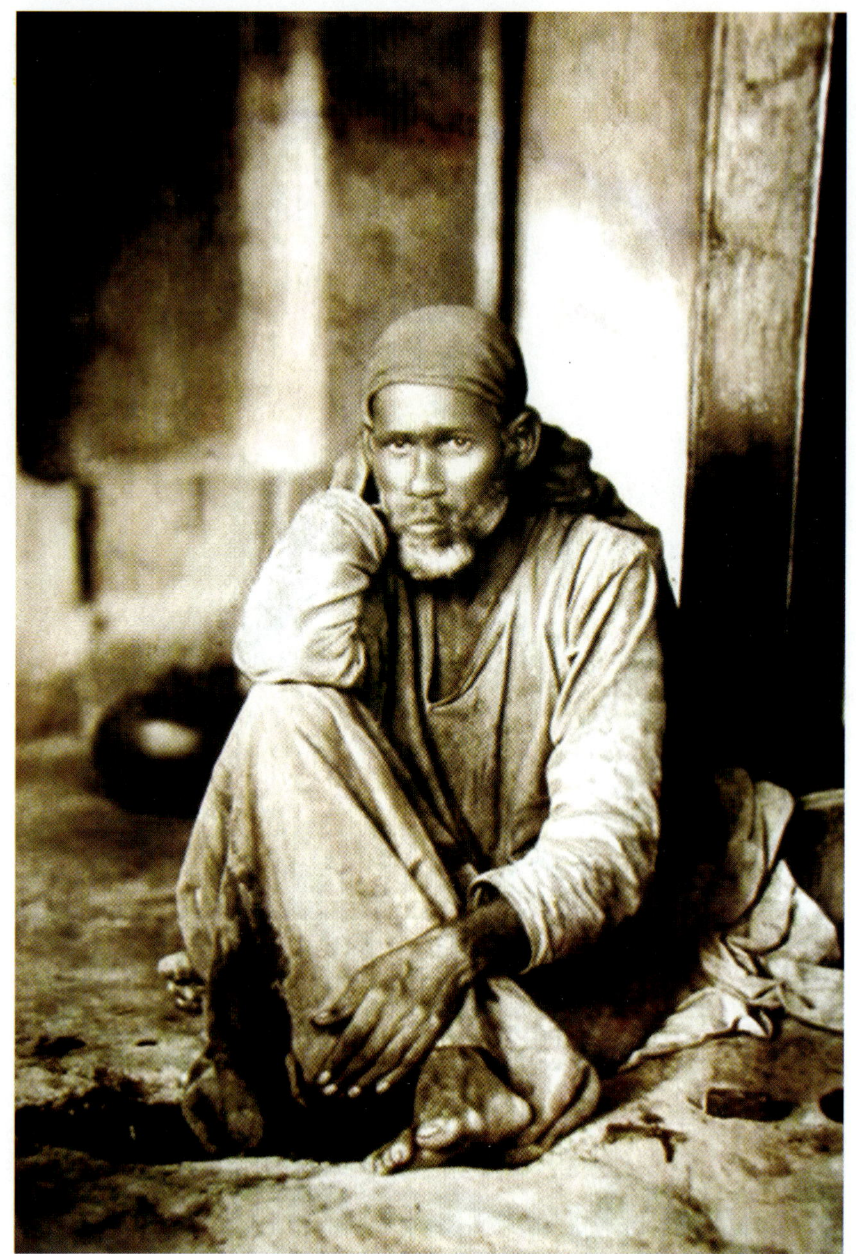

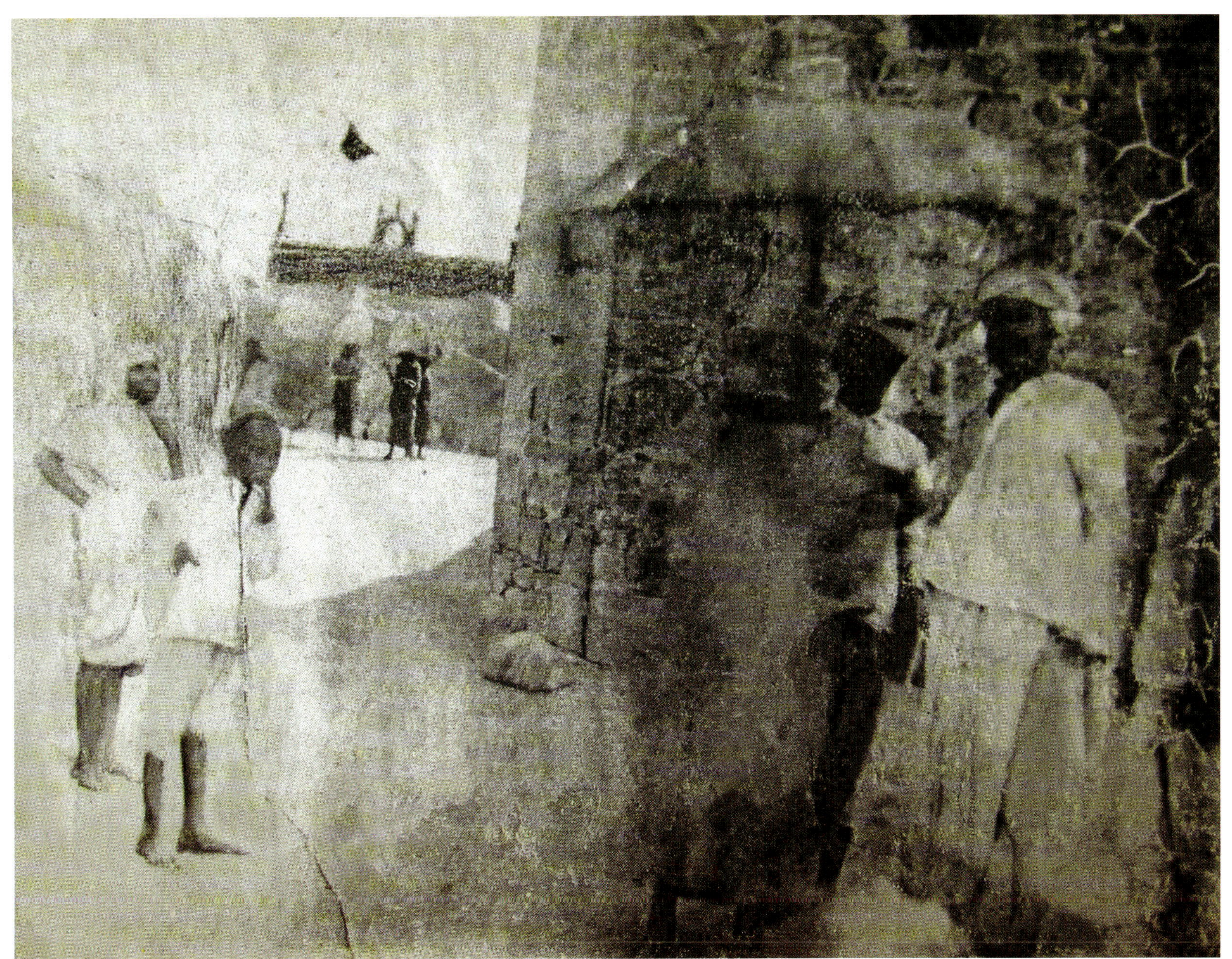

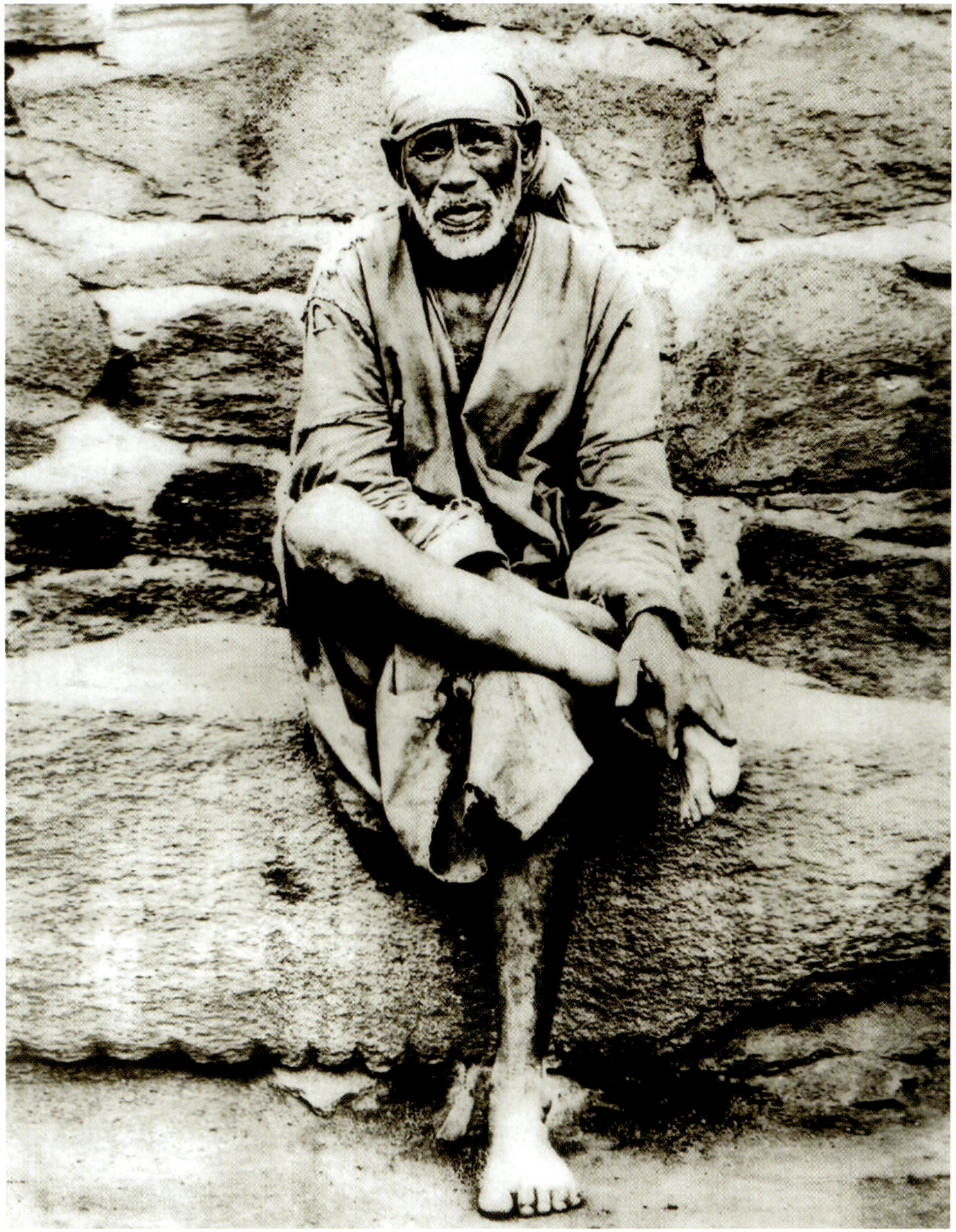

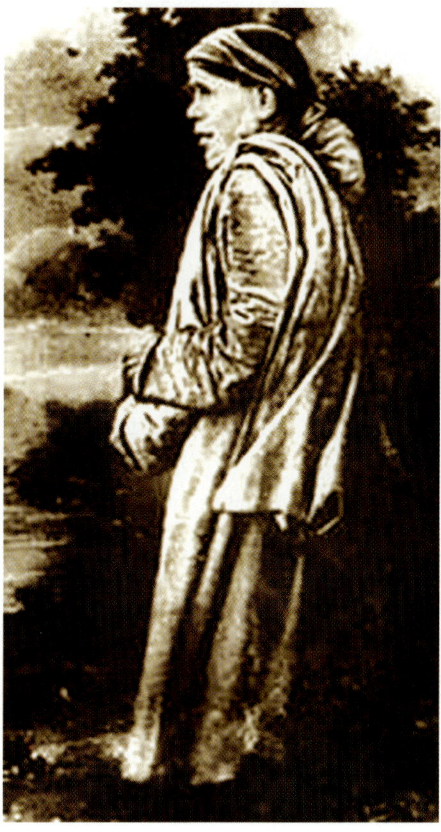

A profile view of Baba on His daily round of seeking bhiksha (alms). On his left shoulder, a cloth is hung, in which he collected the offerings of people.

← Sai Nath sitting on a stone. Photograph by Shri Deshmukh *(1909)*

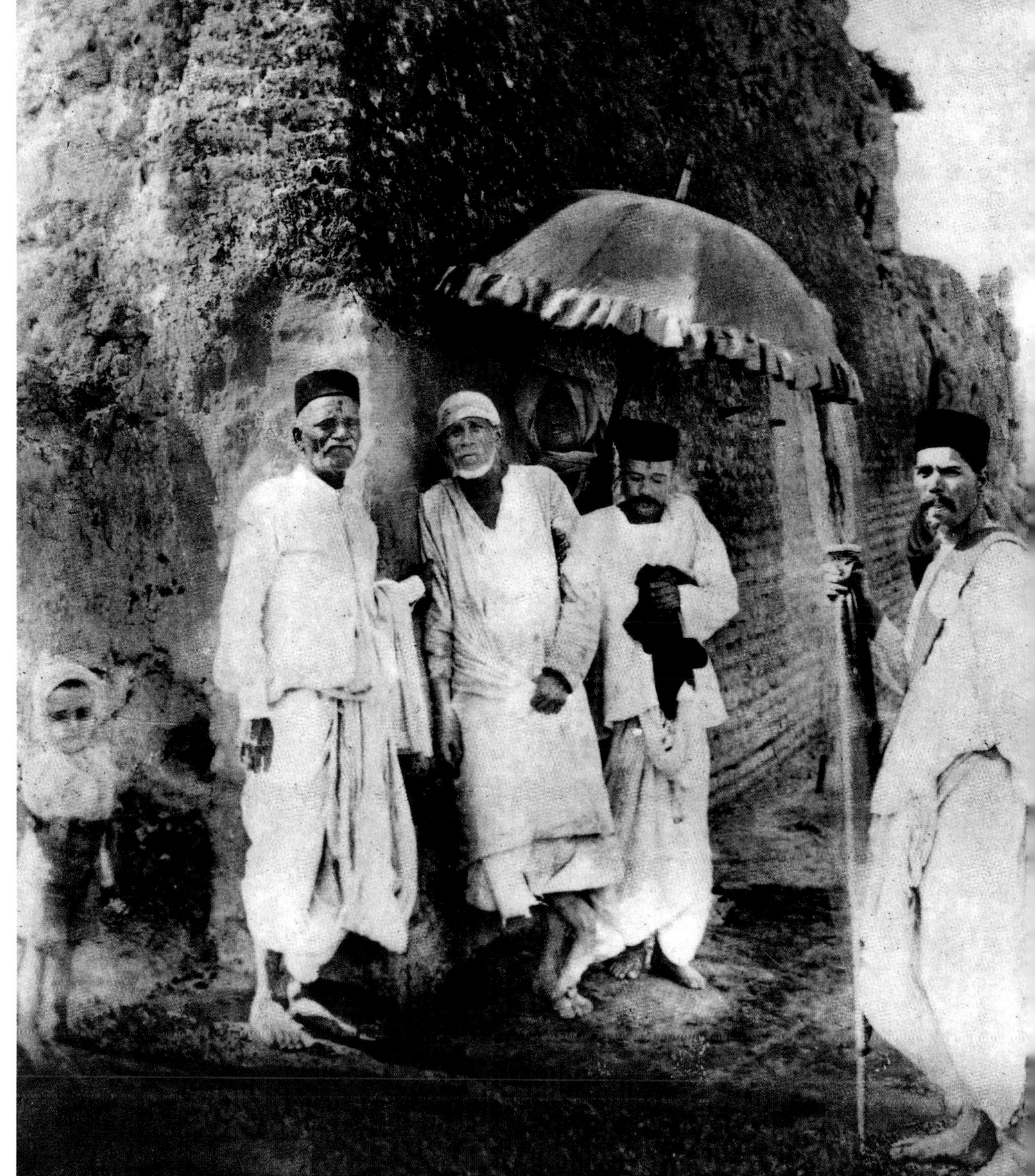

Baba's Umbrella Photo

This is an original photograph of Baba going to Lendi Baugh (1916). Baba is leaning against Balaji Pilaji Gurav's home. Gopalrao M Butti is on the left of Baba, while Nana Sahib Nimonkar is on his right. The little boy standing next to him is his grandson, Gopalrao Nimonkar. Behind Baba an embroidered umbrella is being carried by Bhagoji Shinde.

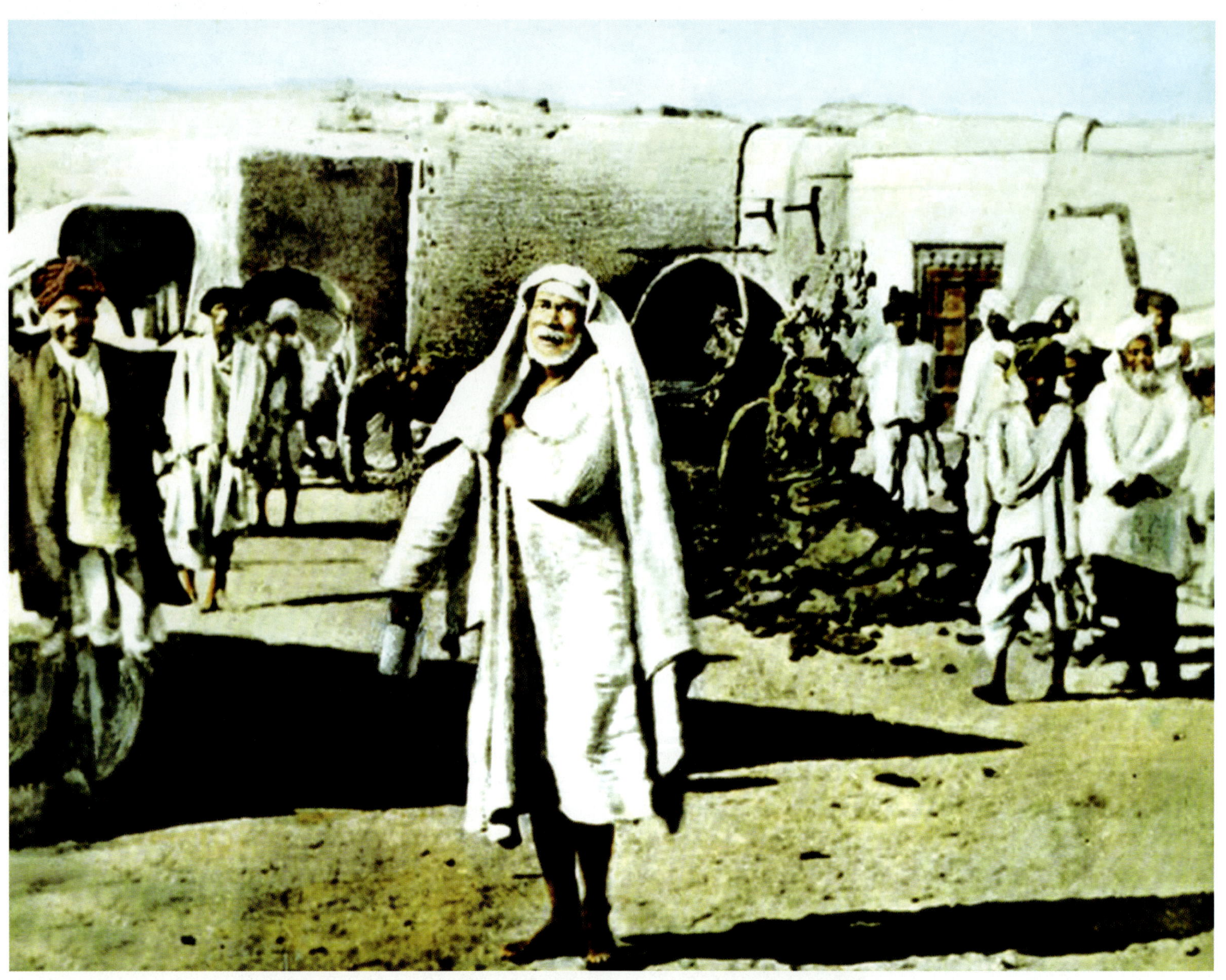

Baba going for Bhiksha- In the background are the temporary shops where villagers would bring their wares for sale. Baba having the tumrale in His hand and a cloth over His head.

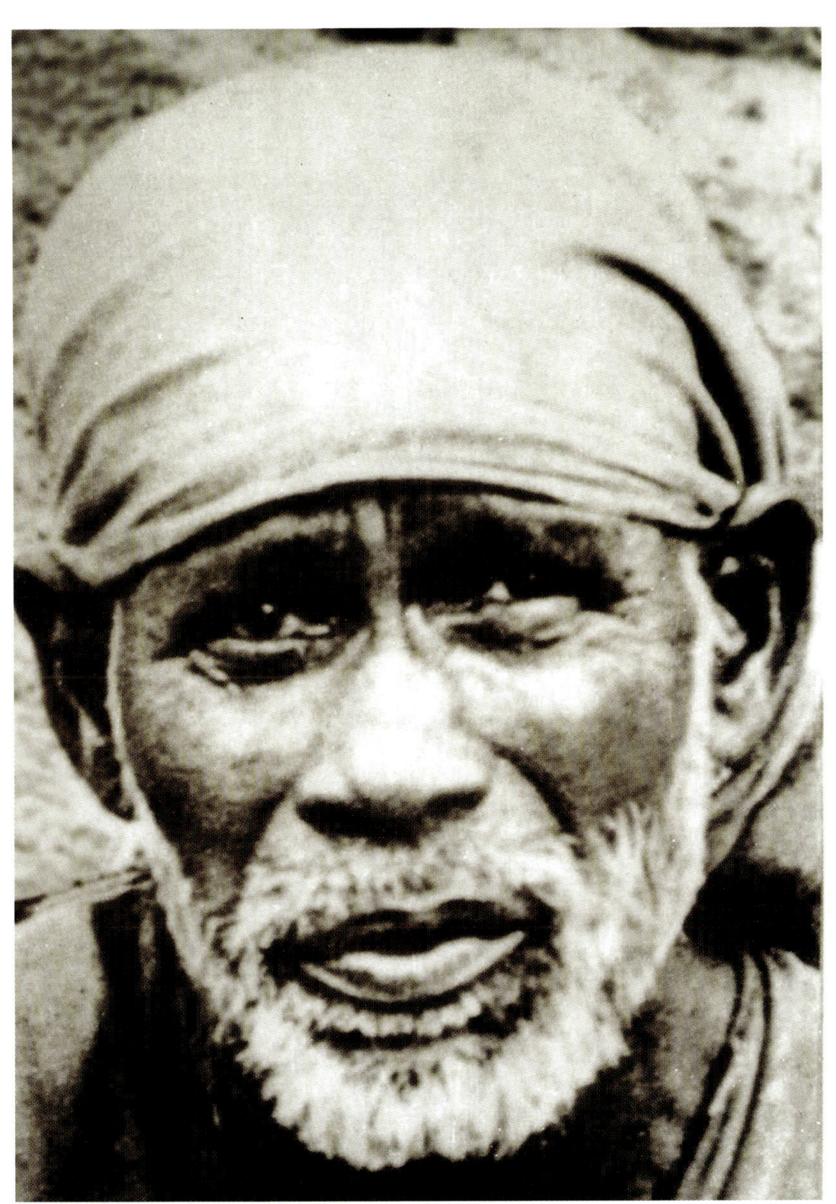

Baba looks straight into our eyes, His eyes full of wisdom and compassion.

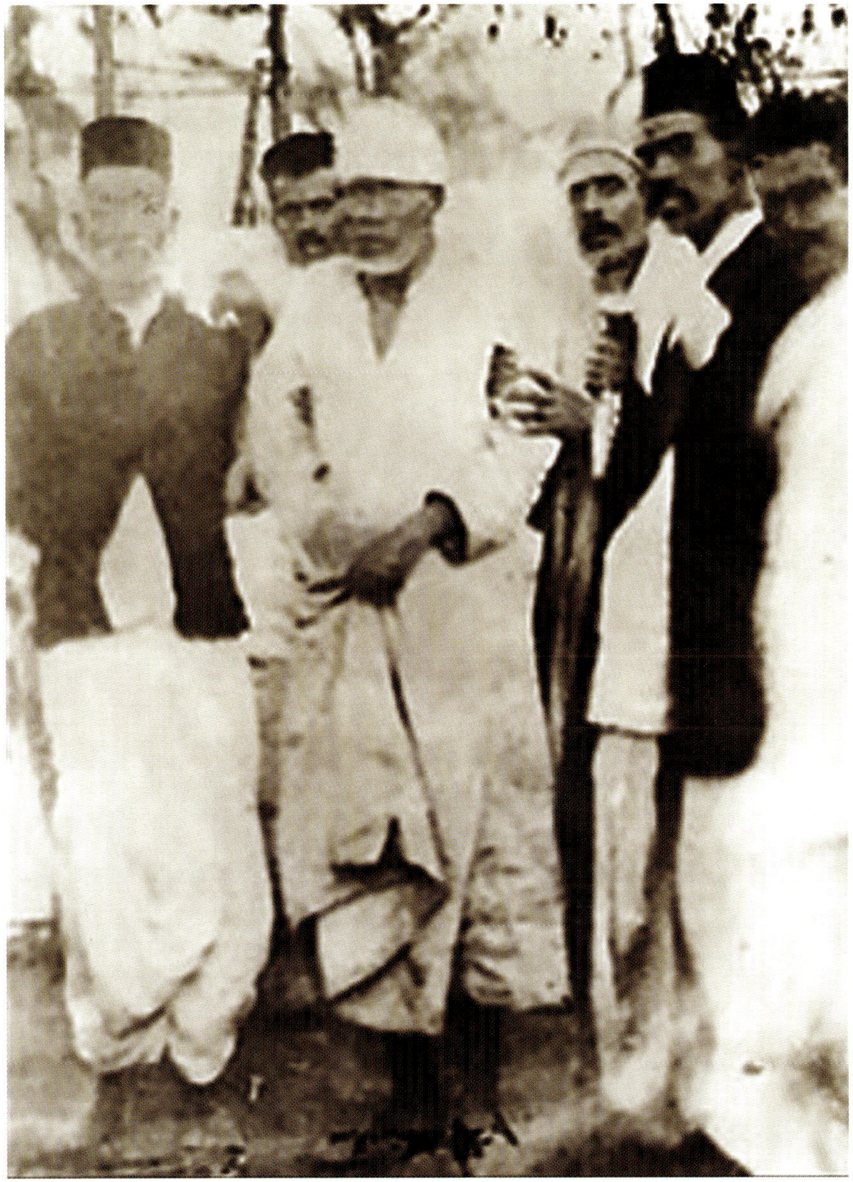

Sai Baba with His devotees. One of them is offering support to Baba.

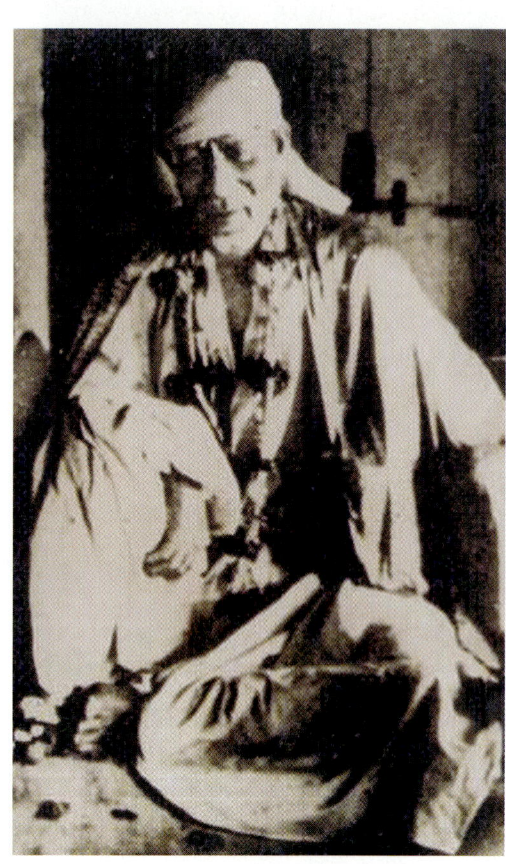

Baba in a smiling mood

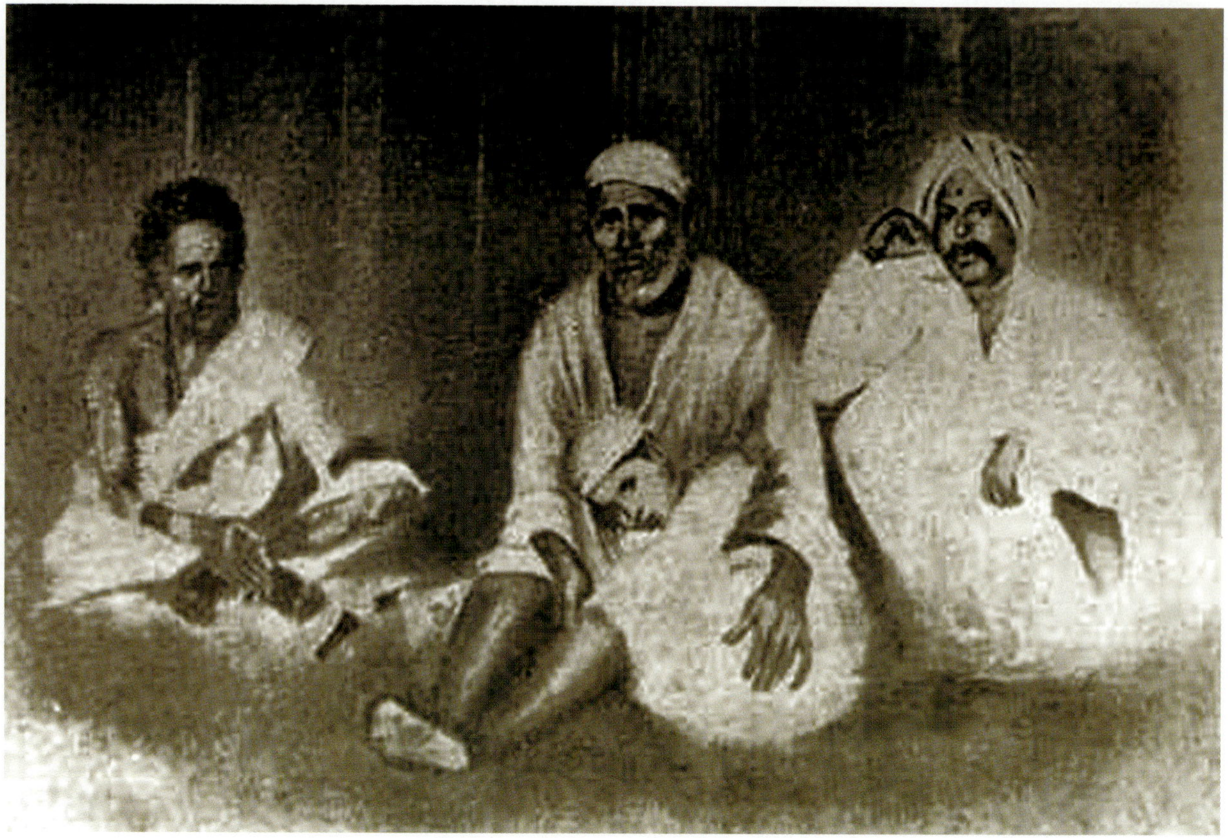

A rarest of the rare photograph showing Baba with two of His soulmates. Shama, His constant companion on His left and Mahalsapati, the Khandoba temple priest on His right. A young Muslim lad is resting on Baba's outstretched legs.

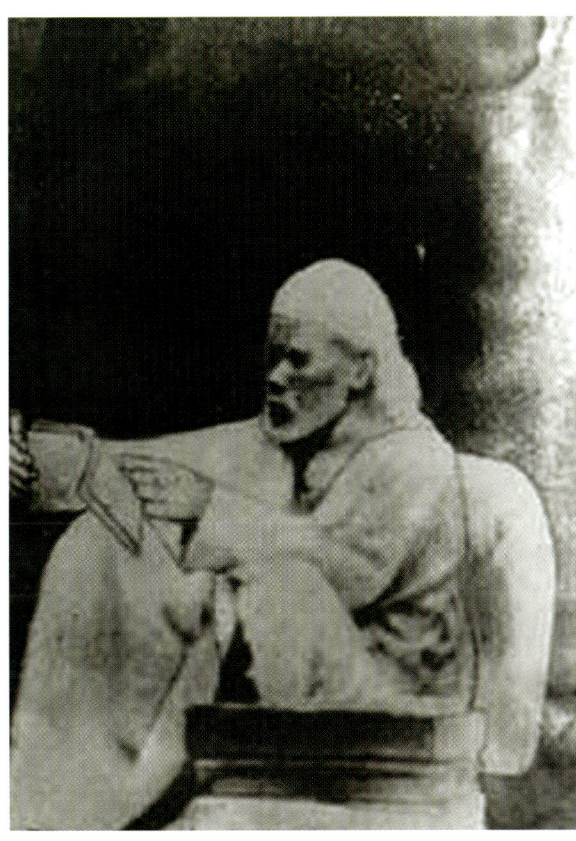

This photograph is from the first edition of the Shri Sai Satcharita, and the original photograph is in Dabholkar's home. The title is 'Baba with Tukaram's Gatha in hand'.

This unusual photograph of Baba sitting in Dwarkamai was taken with Baba's consent by the owner of V.S. Photographers, an ardent devotee of Baba, at the request of Vasudev Sadashiv Joshi of Sholapur. *(1915)*

→

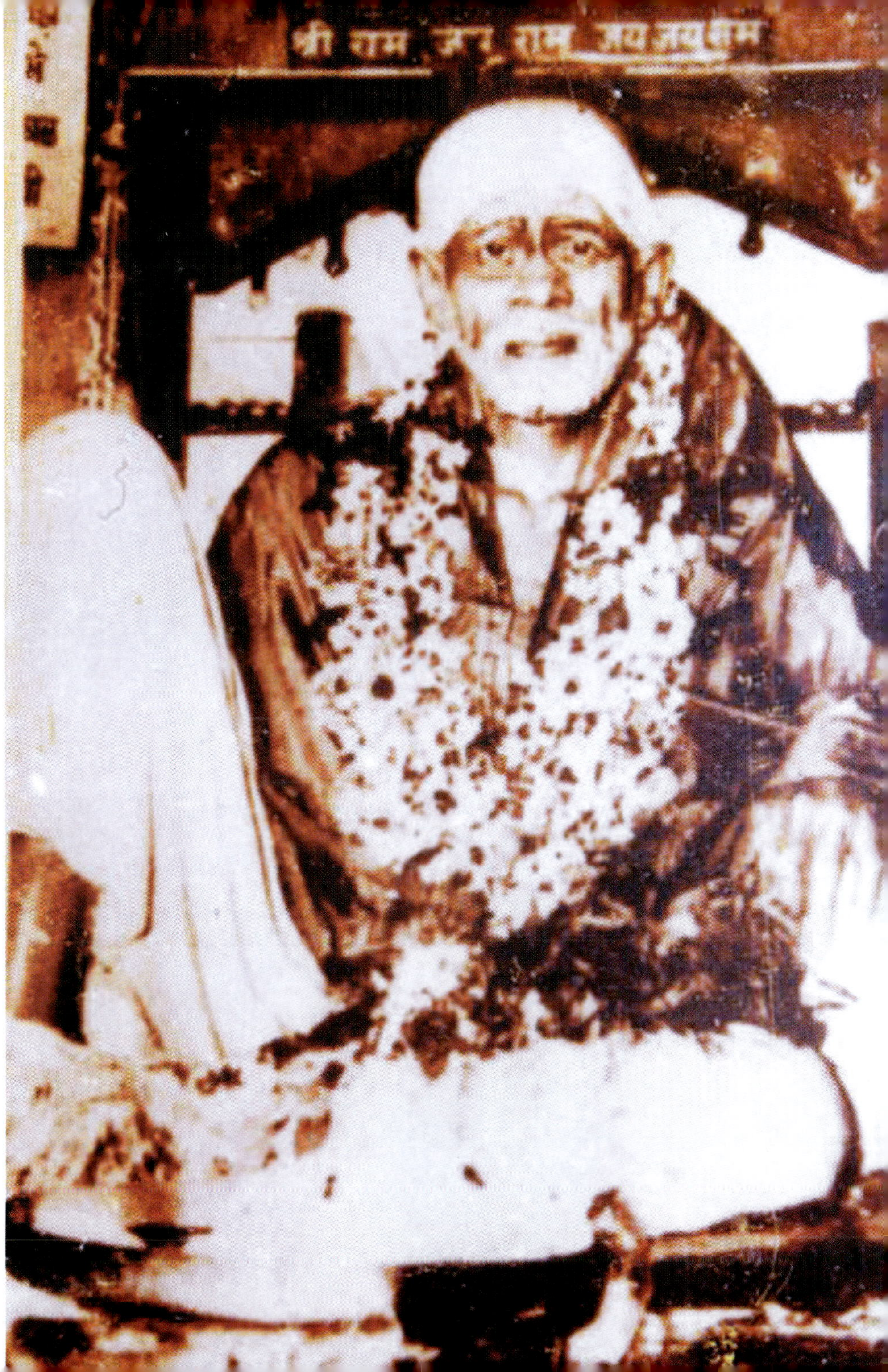

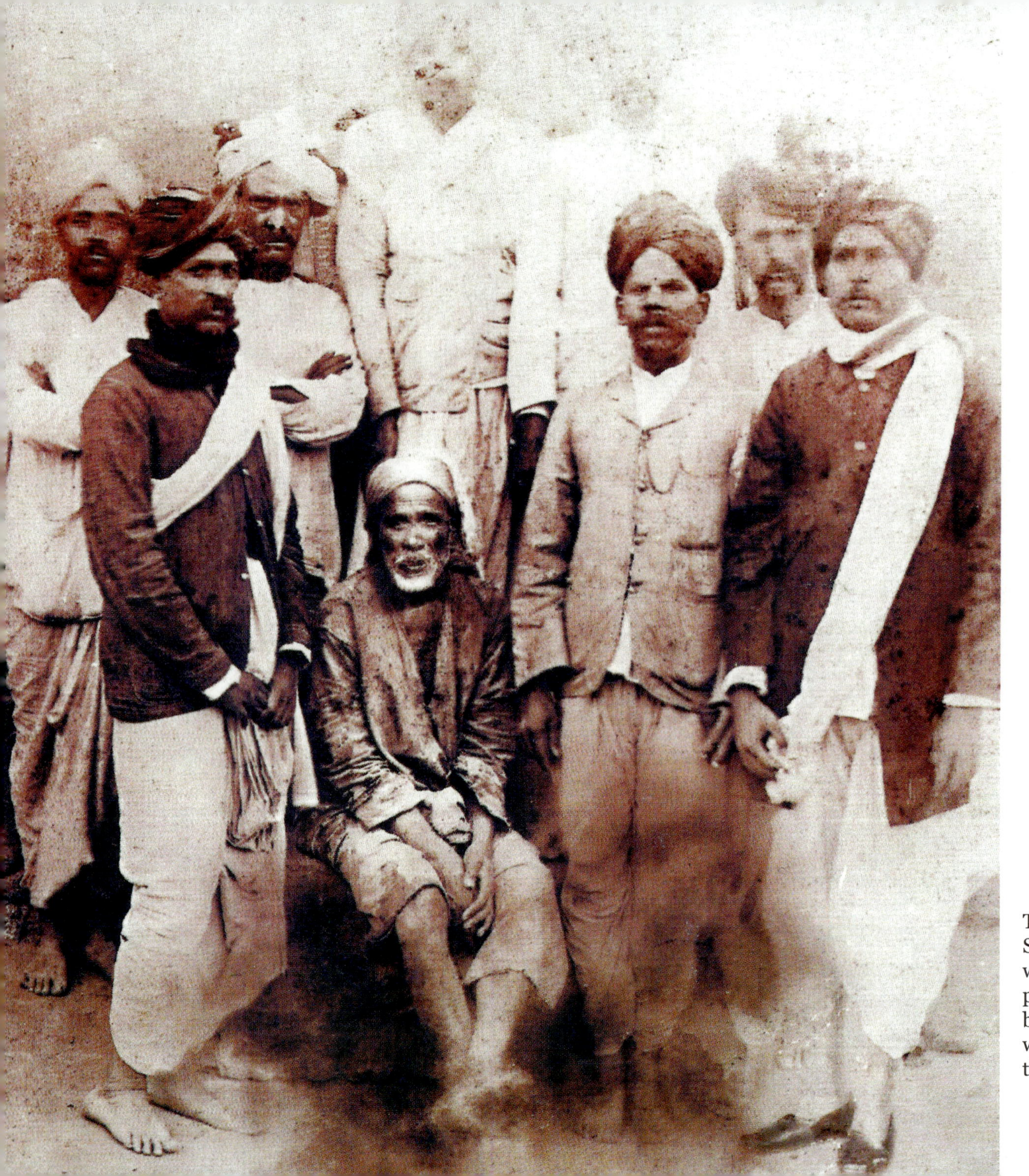

This photograph of Sai Baba was taken by Shri Puppal, a professional photographer who had trained under the British. Baba's posture is relaxed as He sits surrounded by His devotees. Every single person is wearing a typical headgear reflecting their rural background.

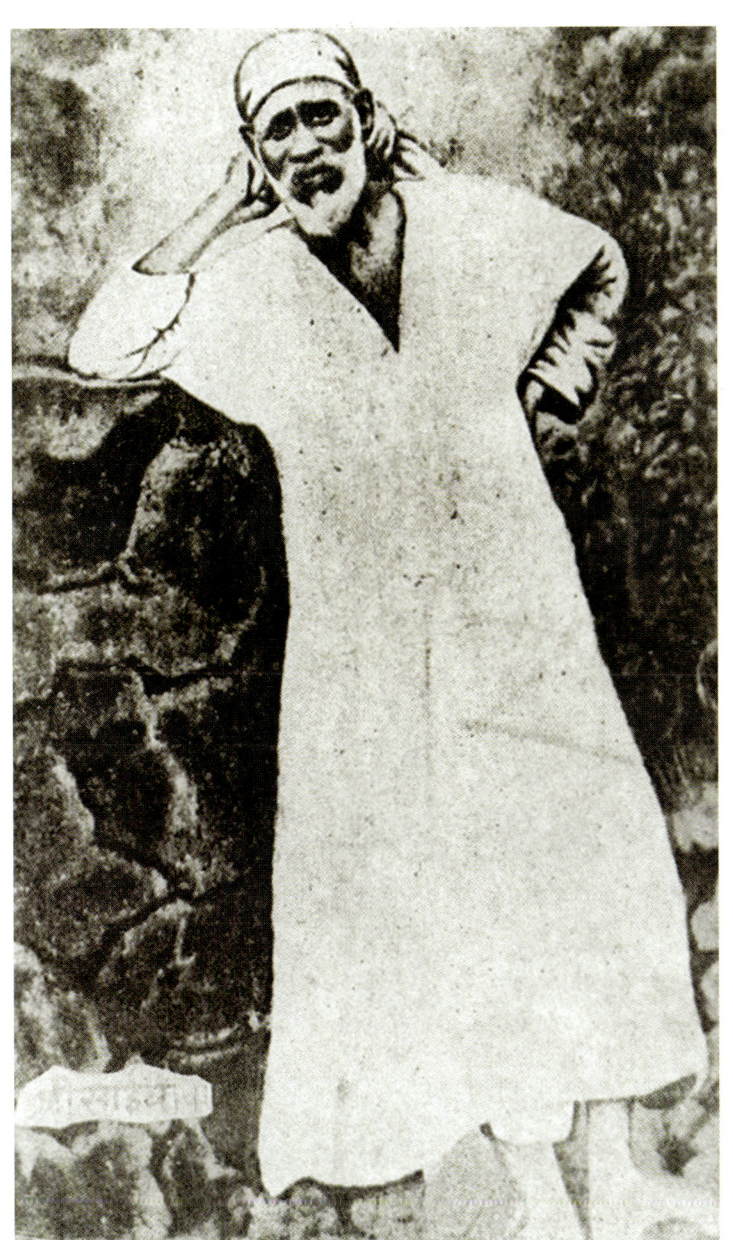

Shri Sai Baba leaning against a wall

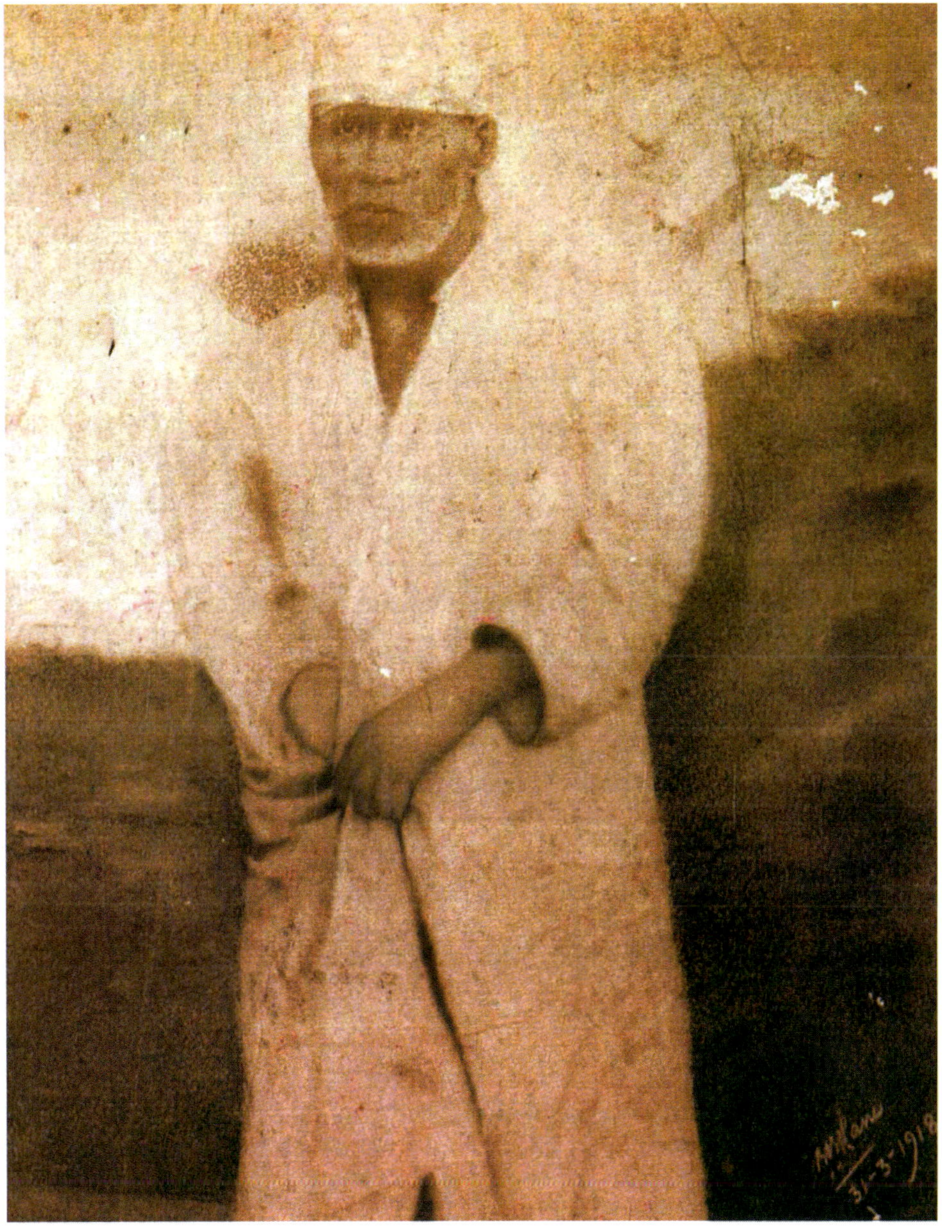

Baba clutching his Kafni. *(March, 1918)*

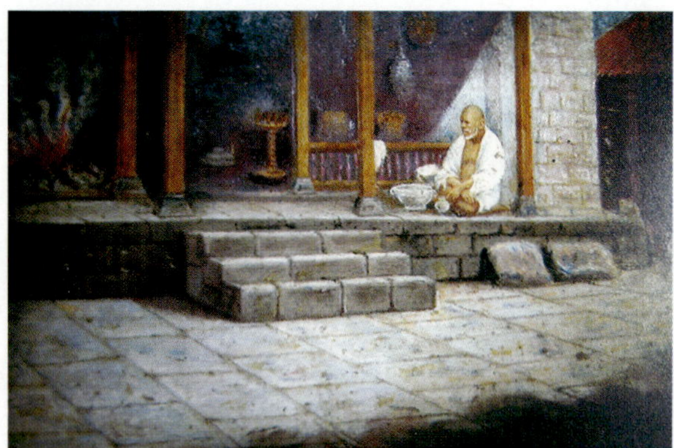

Painting by Shyamrao Ramchandra Jaikar, now at Shri Tarkhad's house (Mumbai).

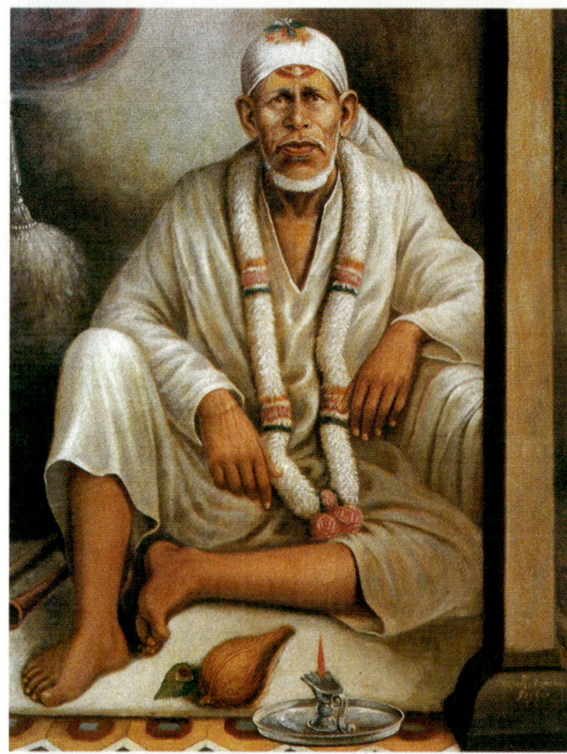

Portrait showing 'Dwarkamai Pose' which now resides in the Museum

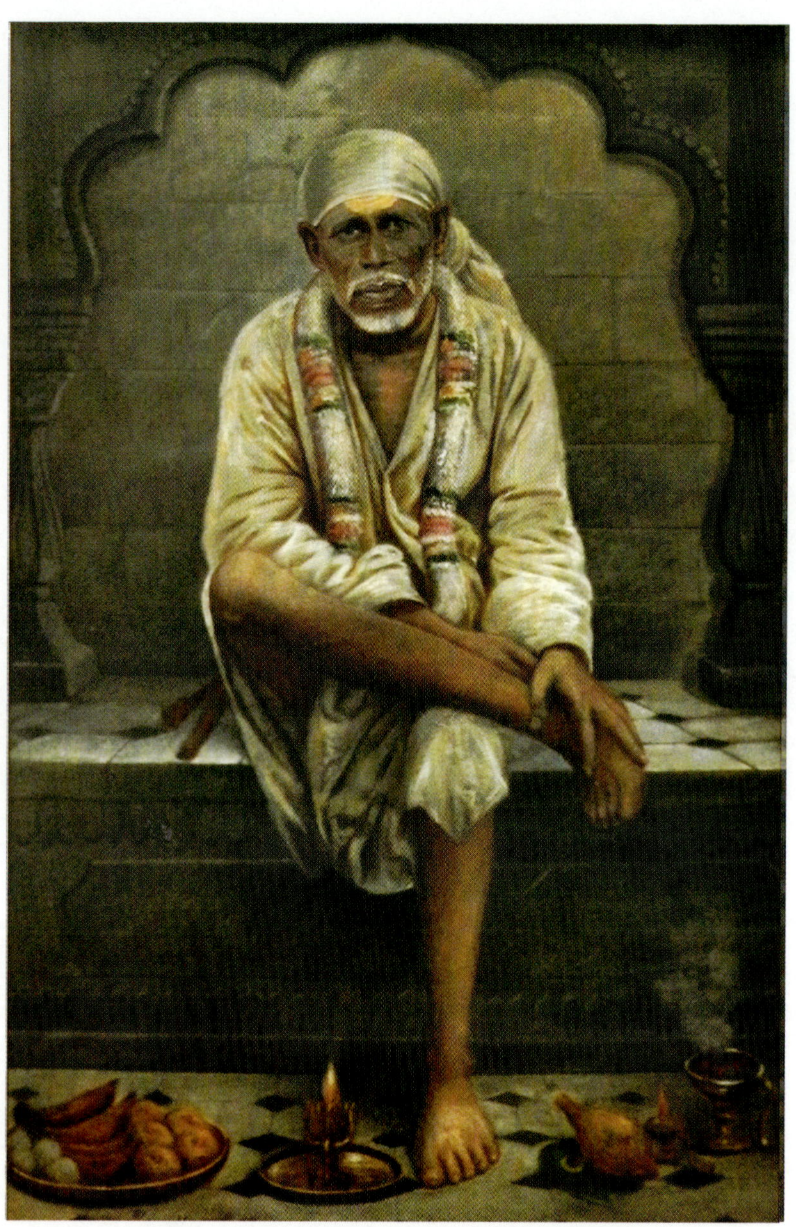

Oil painting of Baba by Artist Shri Vinayek (now at Hemadpant's house in Mumbai)

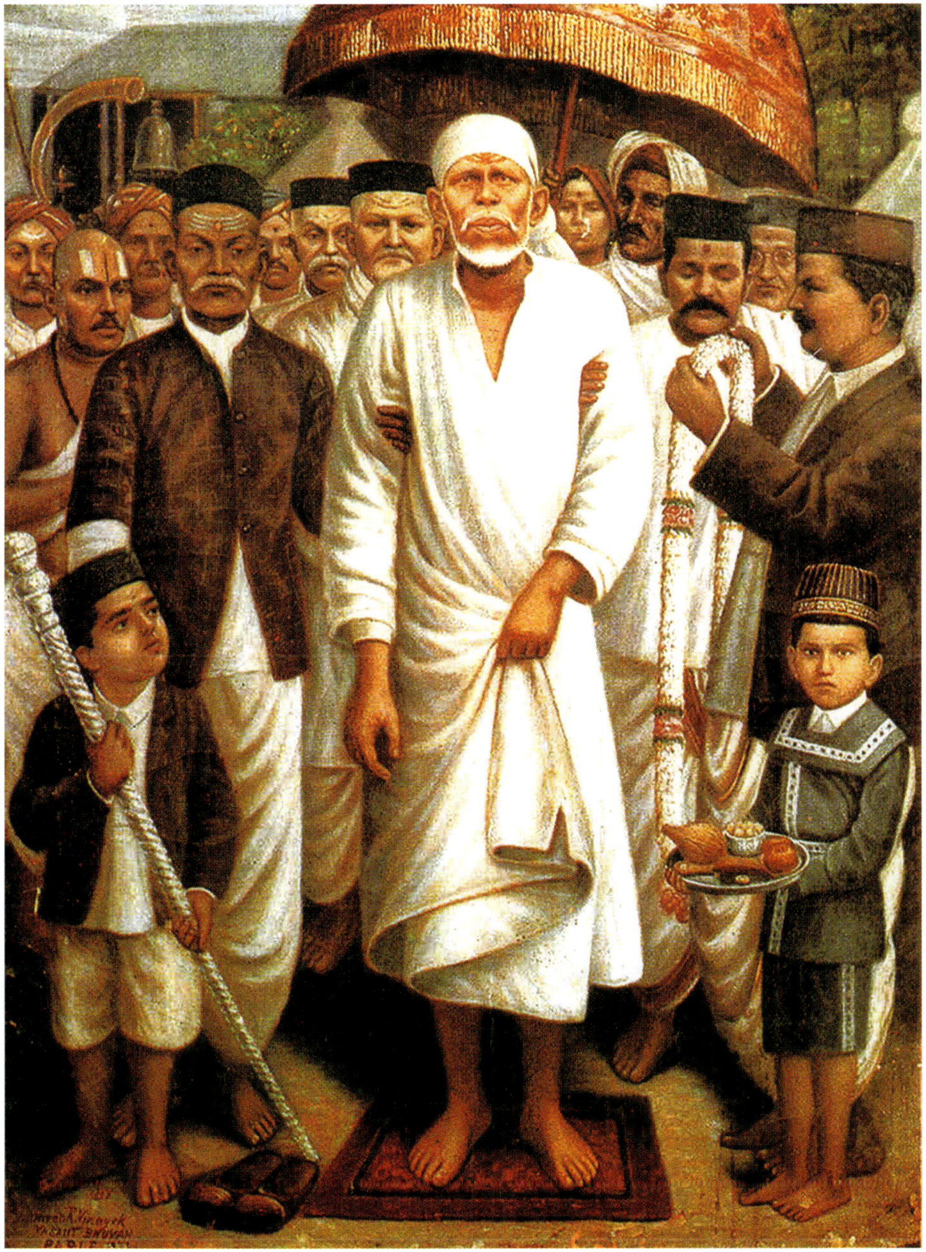

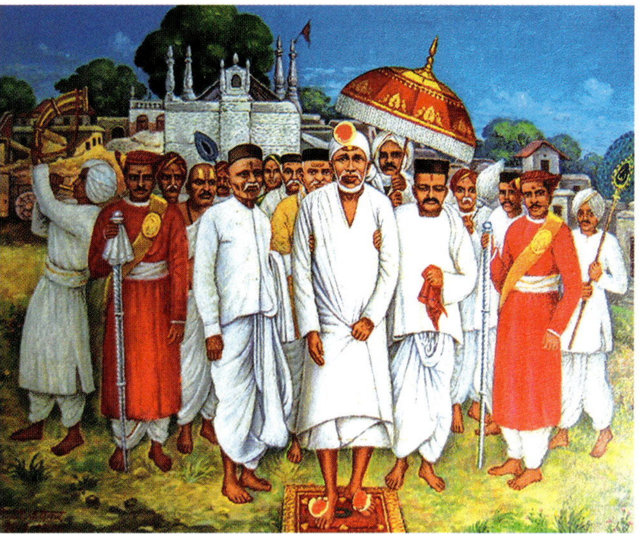

Chavadi procession painting by renowned artist Shyamrao Ramchandra Jaikar, now at Shri Vishnu Balwant Pithale's house in Mumbai.

This awesome painting (by R. Vinayek Vasant Bhuvah) shows Baba going to Chavadi in a procession, accompanied by His ardent followers. Bhagoji Shinde is shown holding an ornate umbrella while Shamrao Jaikar's son, often referred to as Little *(Chhota)* Sainath holds the silver staff. The central figure of Baba is flanked by Nana Sahib Nimonkar on His right and Gopalrao M Butti on His left. Moreshwar Pradhan holds a garland and his son Bapu gazes out, carrying a silver platter laden with offerings.

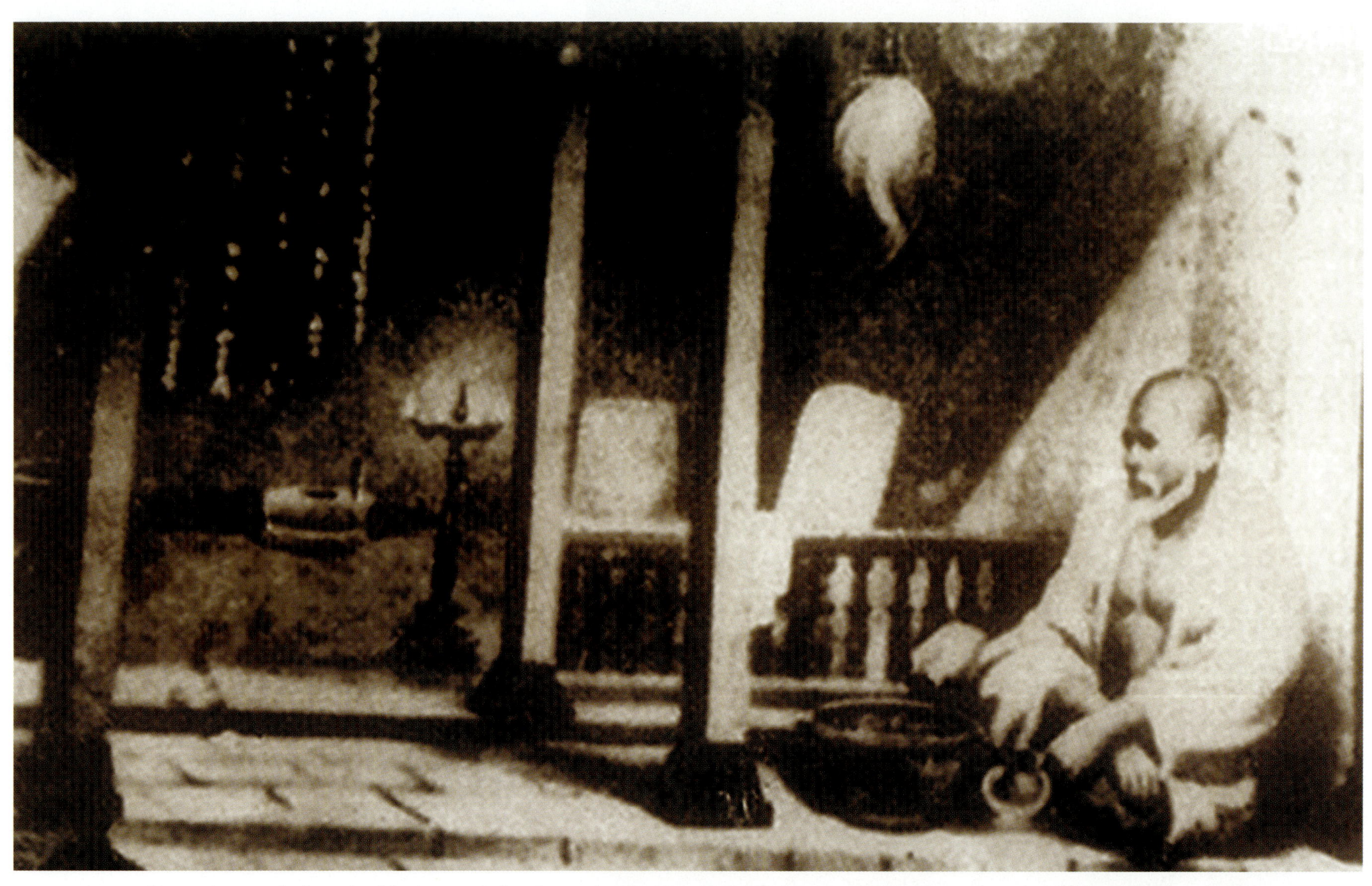

Baba getting ready for His ablutions. His headgear *(patka)* is off and the pot is full of water. This picture shows Baba sitting outside Dwarkamai. The whisk broom hangs suspended from the roof and the grindmill and lamp are inside the balustrade.

The Big Painting of Baba on the Stone

This oil painting of Baba sitting on the stone was made by D.D. Neroy. Neroy was a photographer and artist. He was devoted to Kamu Baba (a saint in Girgaon, Mumbai). After mounting this painting in an ornate frame, he happily offered it to his Guru. Kamu Baba appreciated the painting and the kind gesture, but he refused to accept it. He told Neroy to take it to Shirdi and place it in the Sabhamandap of the Dwarkamai. Neroy said to his Guru, "It took me three years to make this portrait and one-and-a-half months to get it framed. Never mind the expense, now you reject it ! " Kamu Baba calmly said, "It's not a question of rejecting it, but a keen desire that you take it to Shirdi and place it where thousands of devotees will have the benefit of praying to it." Thus, this painting came to be installed in the Sabhamandap of Dwarkamai.

The original wooden frame was embellished by a silver coating and is now stationed in a glass enclosure. Every morning, before Kakad aarti, the portrait is decorated with sandalwood paste and garlanded.

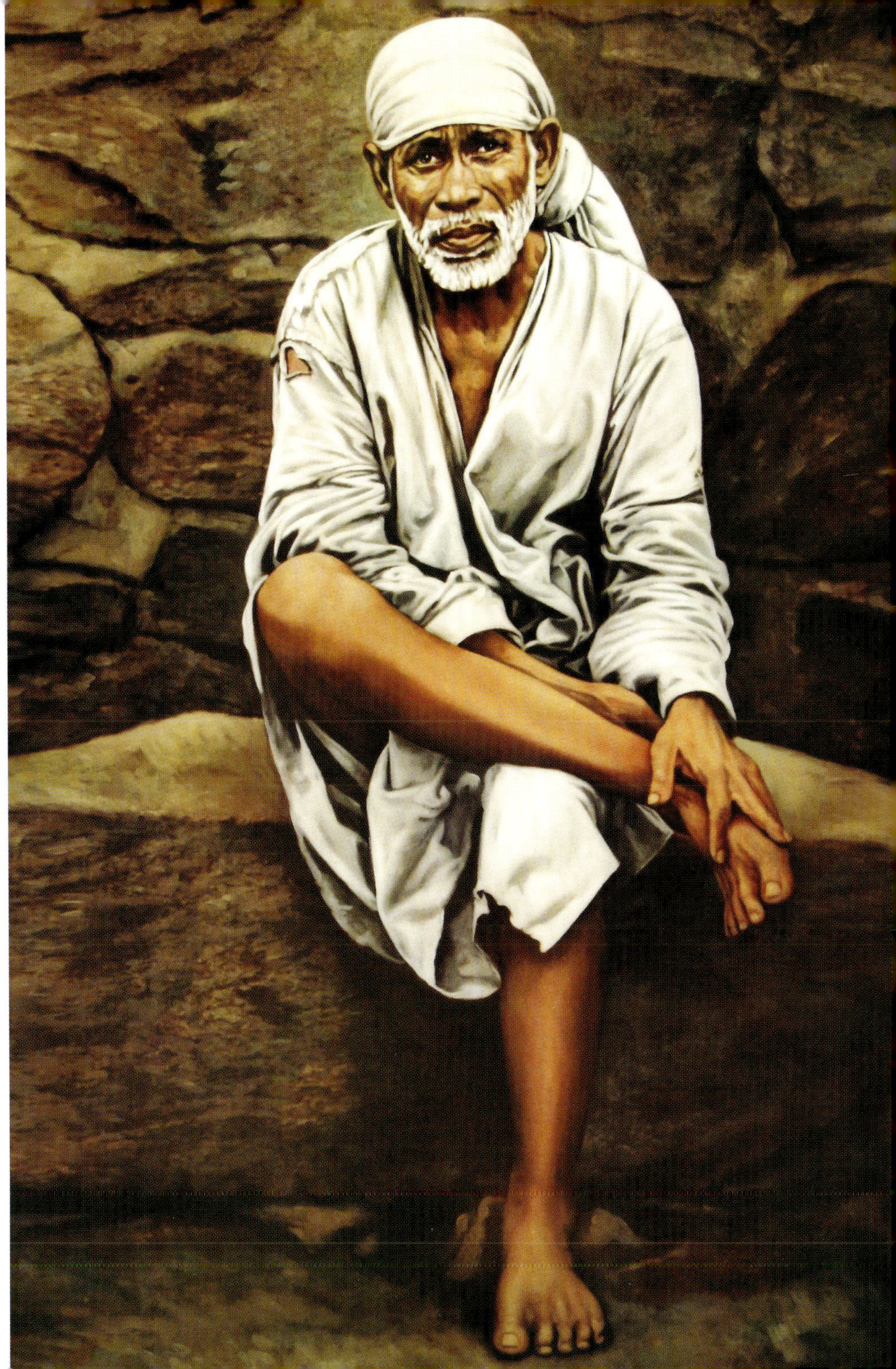

LANDMARKS OF SHIRDI – PRESENT AND PAST

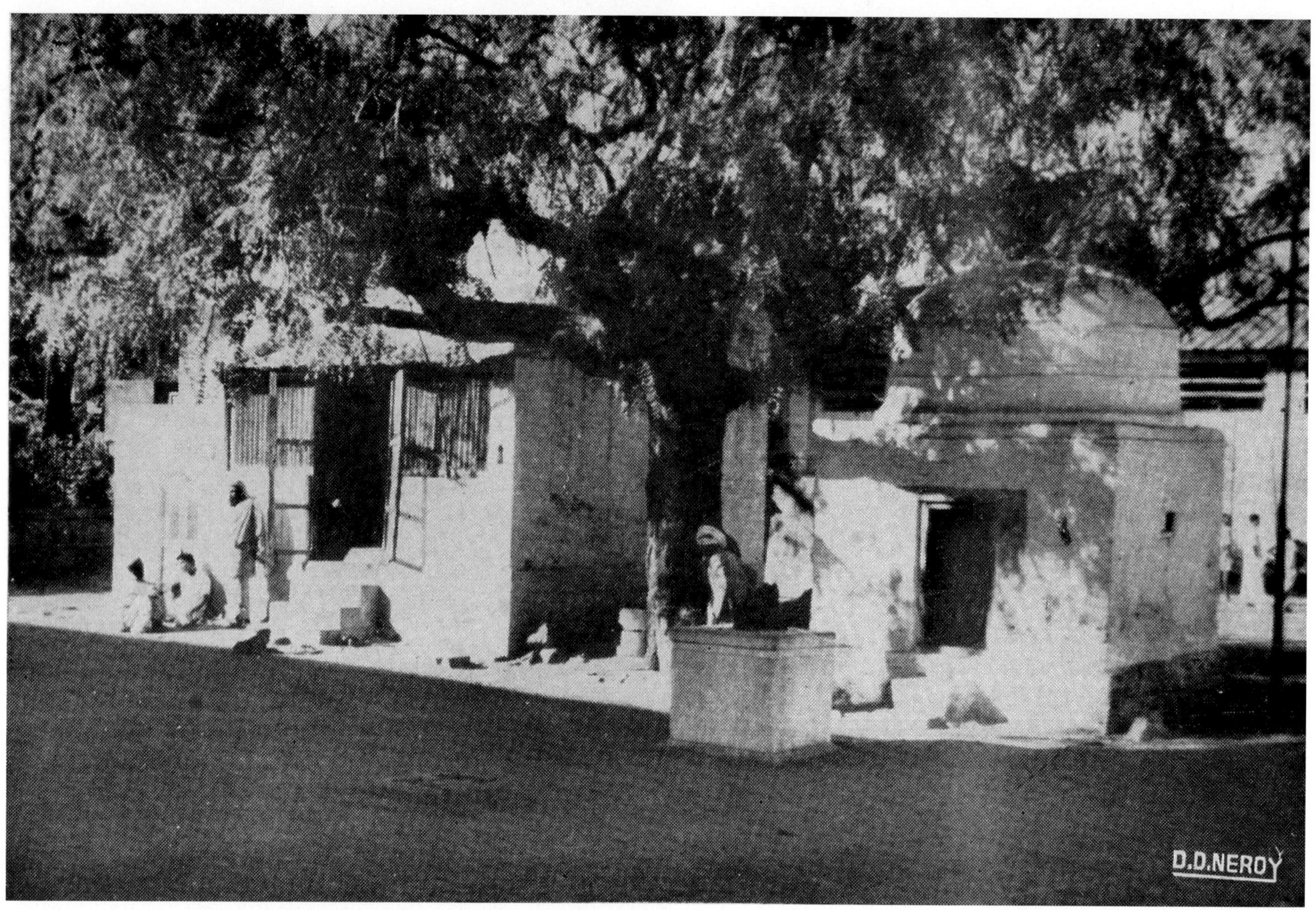

The original trio of temples with their modest paraphernalia- In the middle stands the Shani Temple, flanked by Shiva temple on its left and Ganpati temple on its right *(1972)*

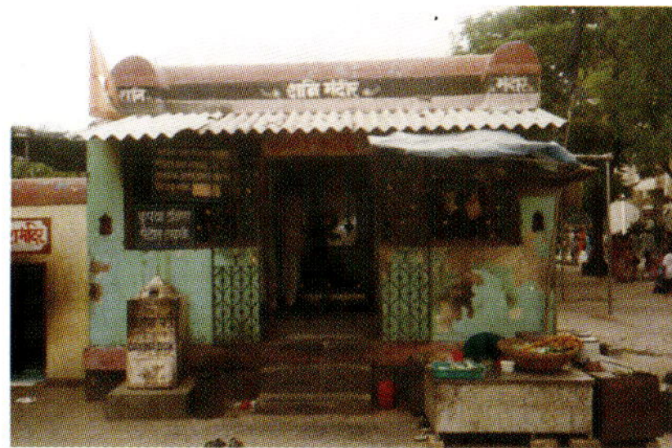

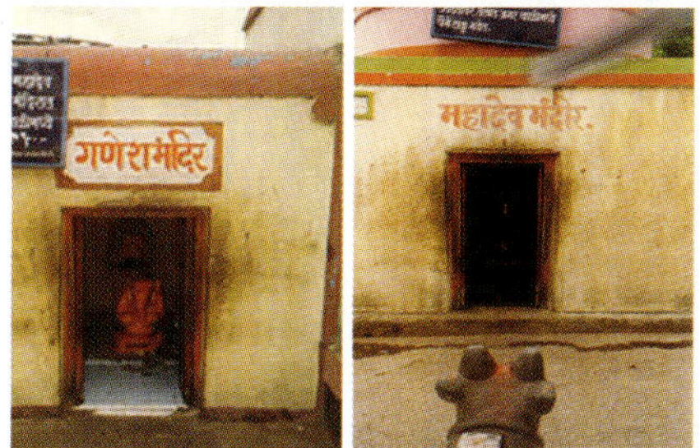

The three temples earlier *(1998)*

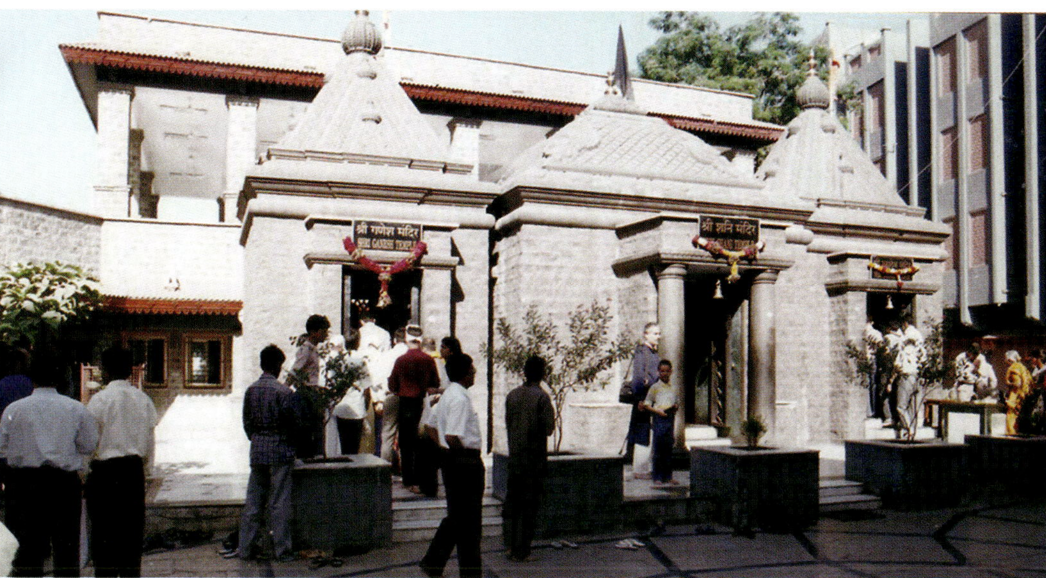

The three temples *(2010)*

The three temples in a close up view; in July 1999, the residing deities of the three temples were moved back into the renovated temples from the Kalash temple, where they were temporarily housed during the temple complex extension plan launched in 1998. Seen below are the individual deities in their splendid ambience.

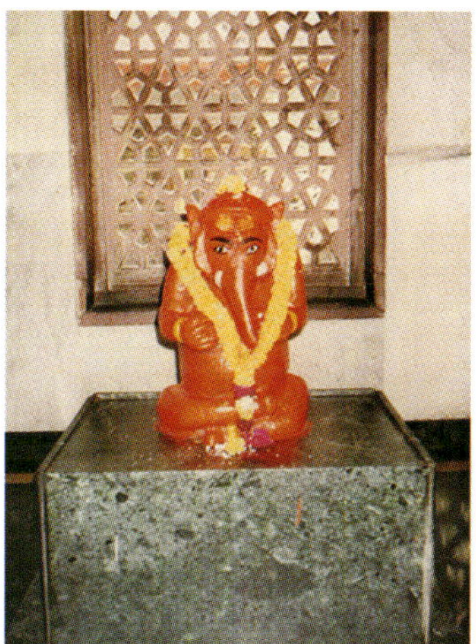

Lord Ganesha

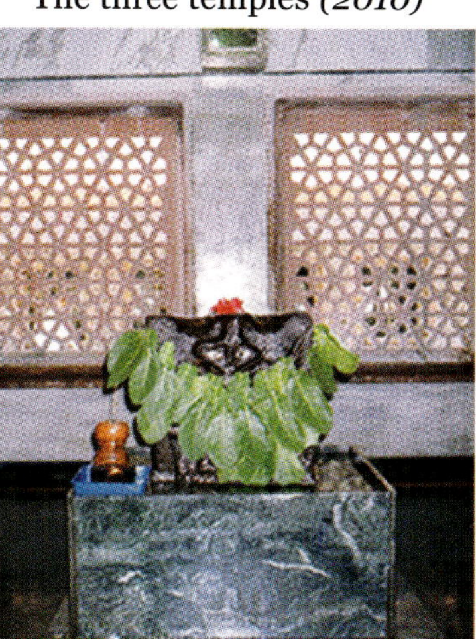

Lord Shani

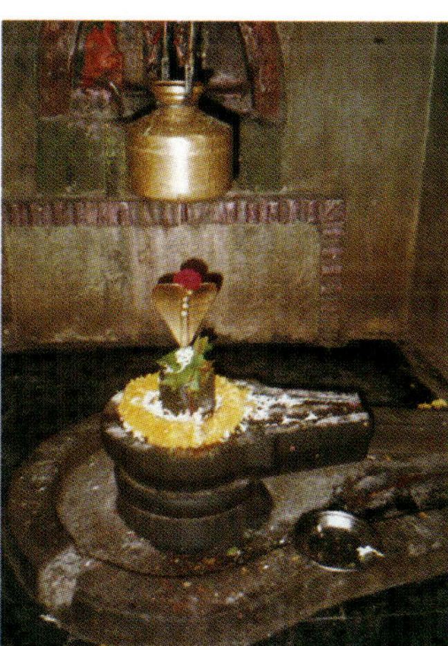

The Shivling

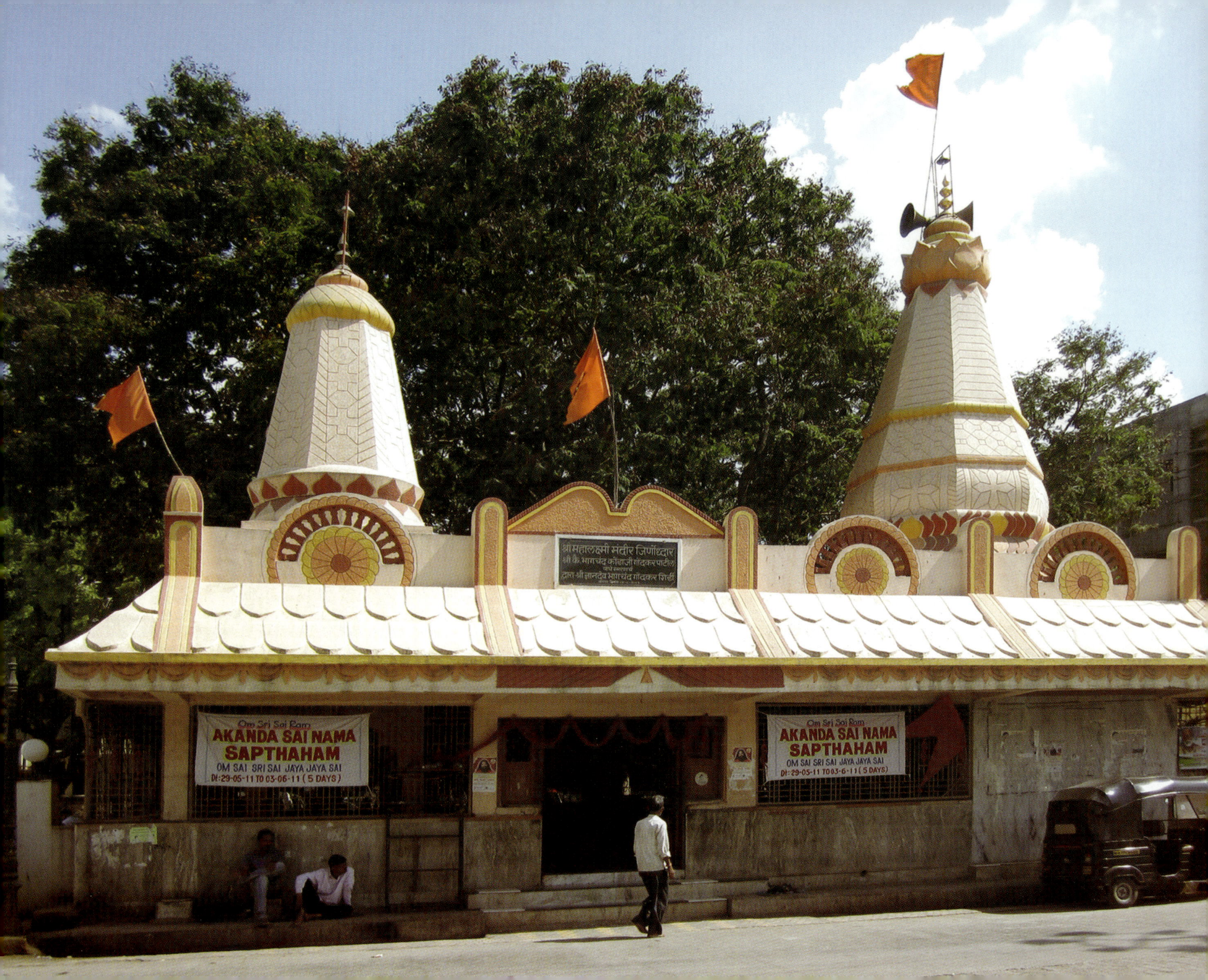

श्री महालक्ष्मी मंदीर जिर्णोद्धार
Om Sri Sai Ram
AKANDA SAI NAMA
SAPTHAHAM
OM SAI SRI SAI JAYA JAYA SAI
DI:29-05-11 TO 03-06-11 (5 DAYS)
Om Sri Sai Ram
AKANDA SAI NAMA
SAPTHAHAM
OM SAI SRI SAI JAYA JAYA SAI
DI:29-05-11 TO 03-6-11 (5 DAYS)

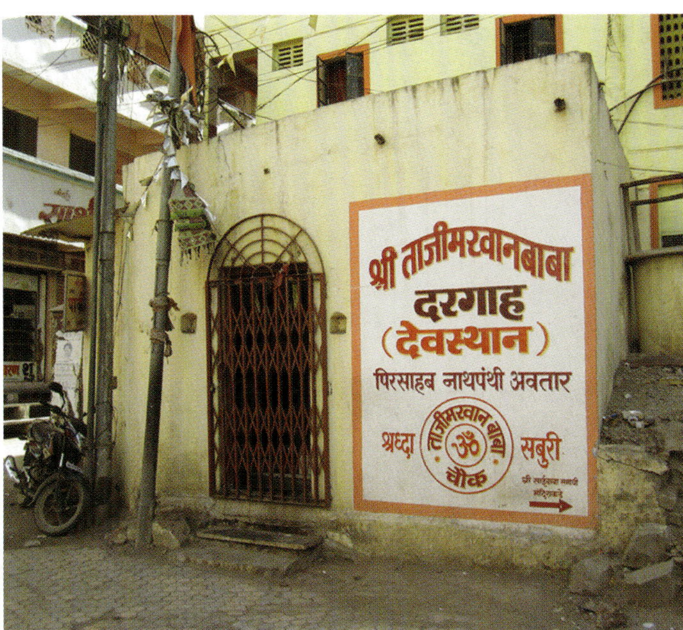

Tajimkhan Baba dargah. *(2011)*

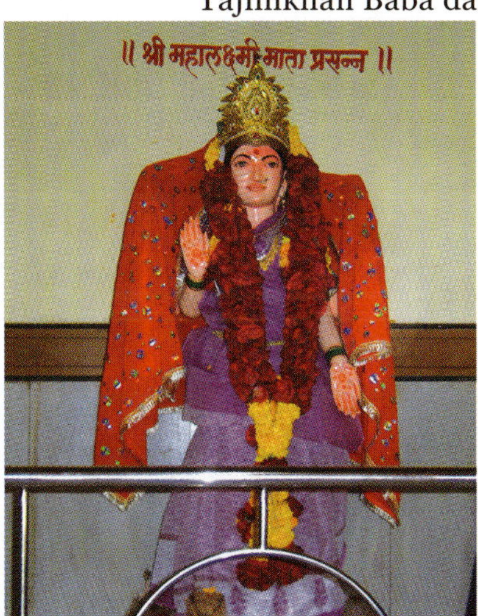

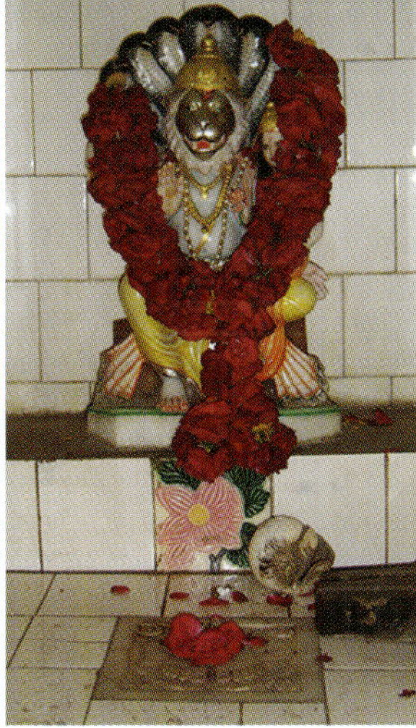

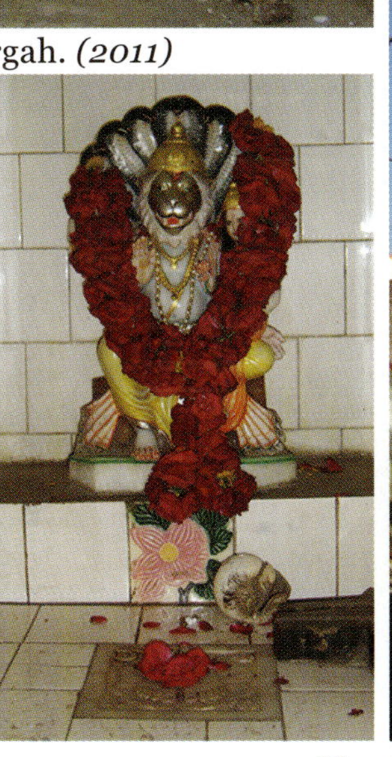

Mahalakshmi temple (Inside view)

Narsingh temple Inside and outside *(2011)*

The old Ashtalakshmi Temple stands in splendid glory on Pimpalwadi Road in Shirdi.The temple, renovated in 2001 now houses many idols other than the original idol of Ashtalakshmi. People come here from far to seek succour for their physical ailments. *(2011)*

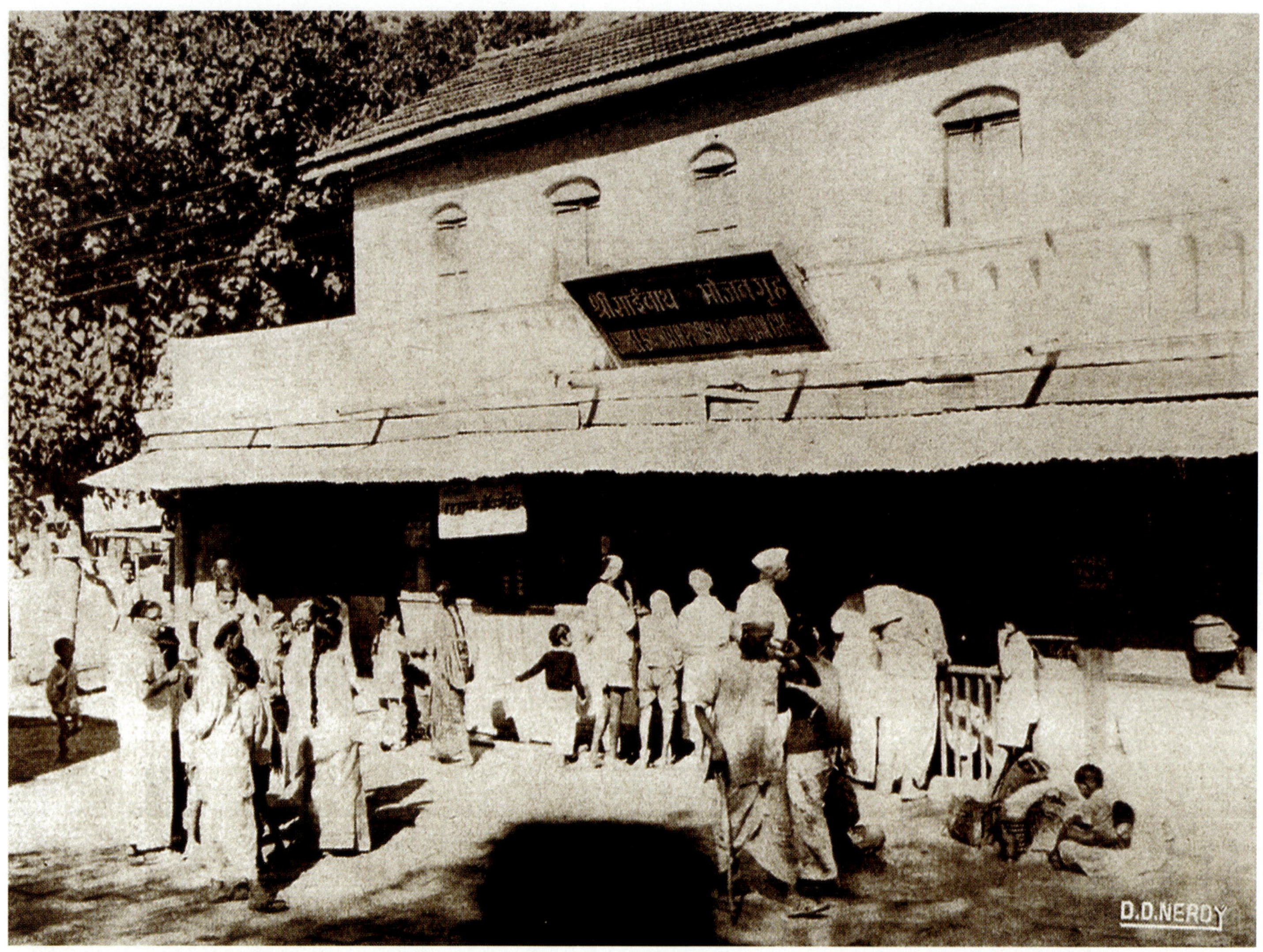

The original Dixit Wada- Intoxicated by his passionate devotion to Baba, Hari Sita Ram Dixit, a wealthy solicitor from Mumbai, shifted base to Shirdi. He and his brother got permission from Baba to build a residence for Baba's devotees in Shirdi, and they dedicated it for public use on Ram Navami in 1911. The Wada was a double storey building where devotees stayed on ground floor and Dixit prayed and studied scriptures on top floor. In the 1950s the Sansthan used the hall on the ground floor as canteen and the adjacent rooms as reading rooms. Dixit Wada now houses a Museum and top floor rooms serve as record rooms.

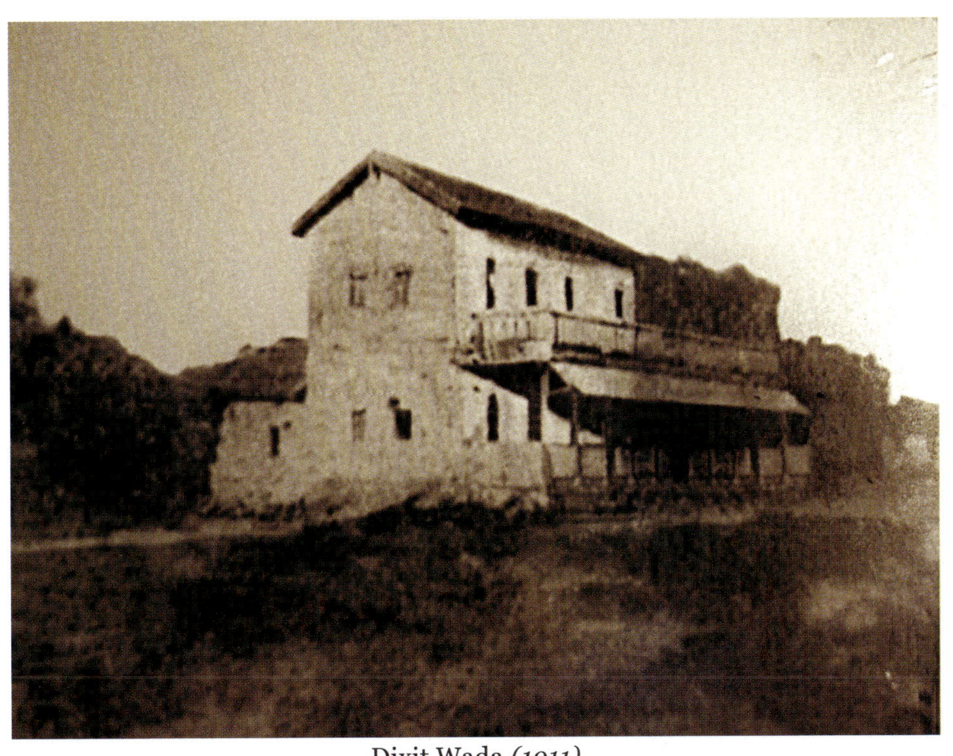

Dixit Wada *(1911)*

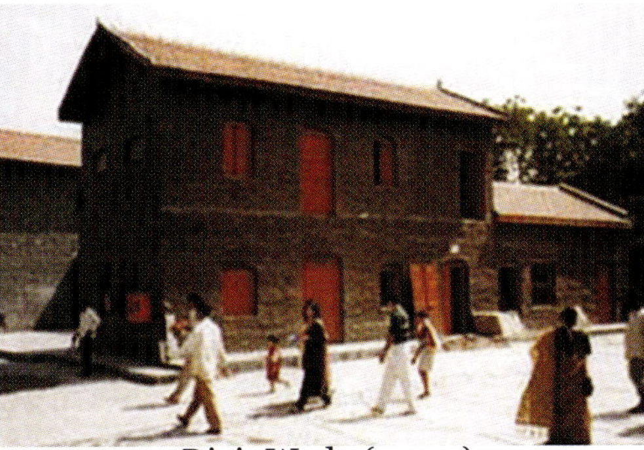

Dixit Wada *(2000)*

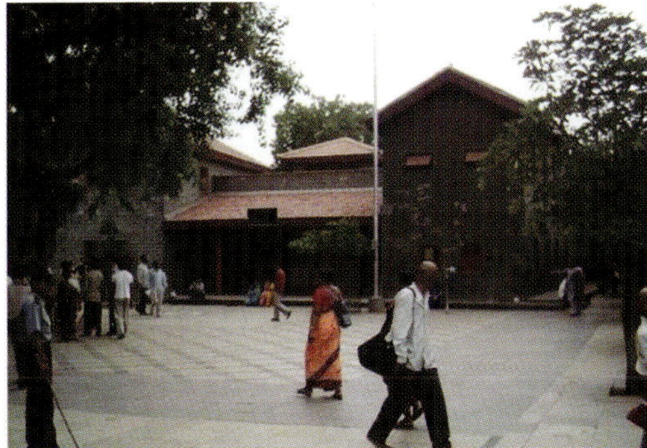

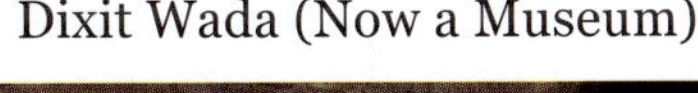

Dixit Wada (Now a Museum)

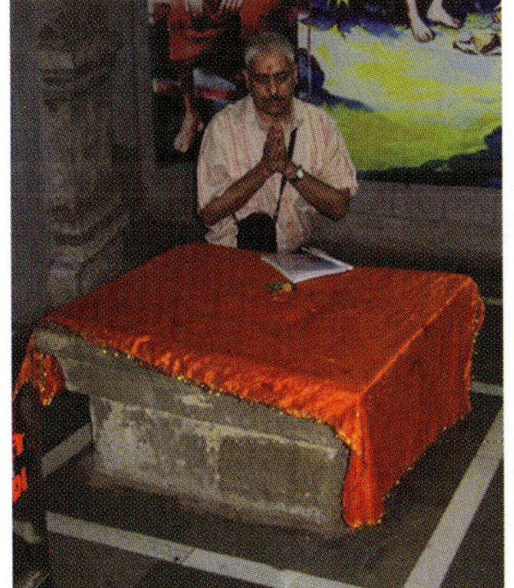

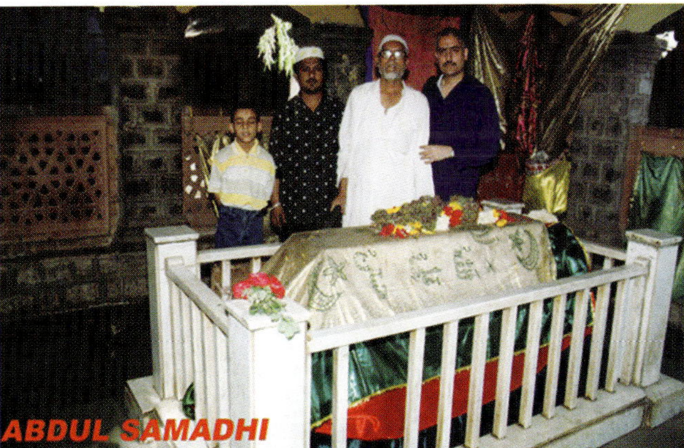

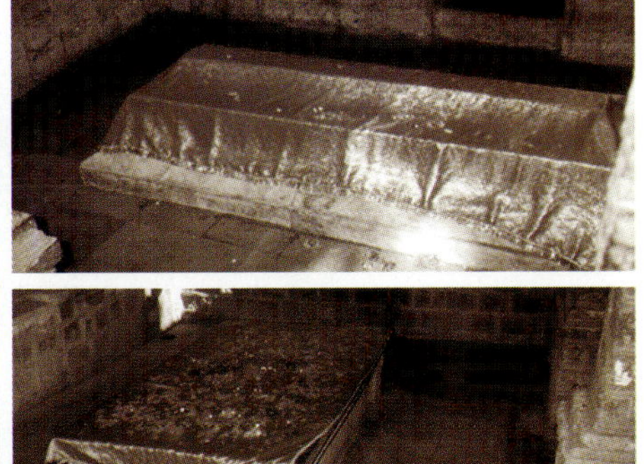

The author kneeling before Tatya Kote Patil's Samadhi, the man whose deadly afflictions Baba took upon himself; author standing with his son Raunak at Abdul Baba's Samadhi, the Samadhi of Nanawali (on top) and Bhau Maharaj Kumbhar's Samadhi *(1998)*.

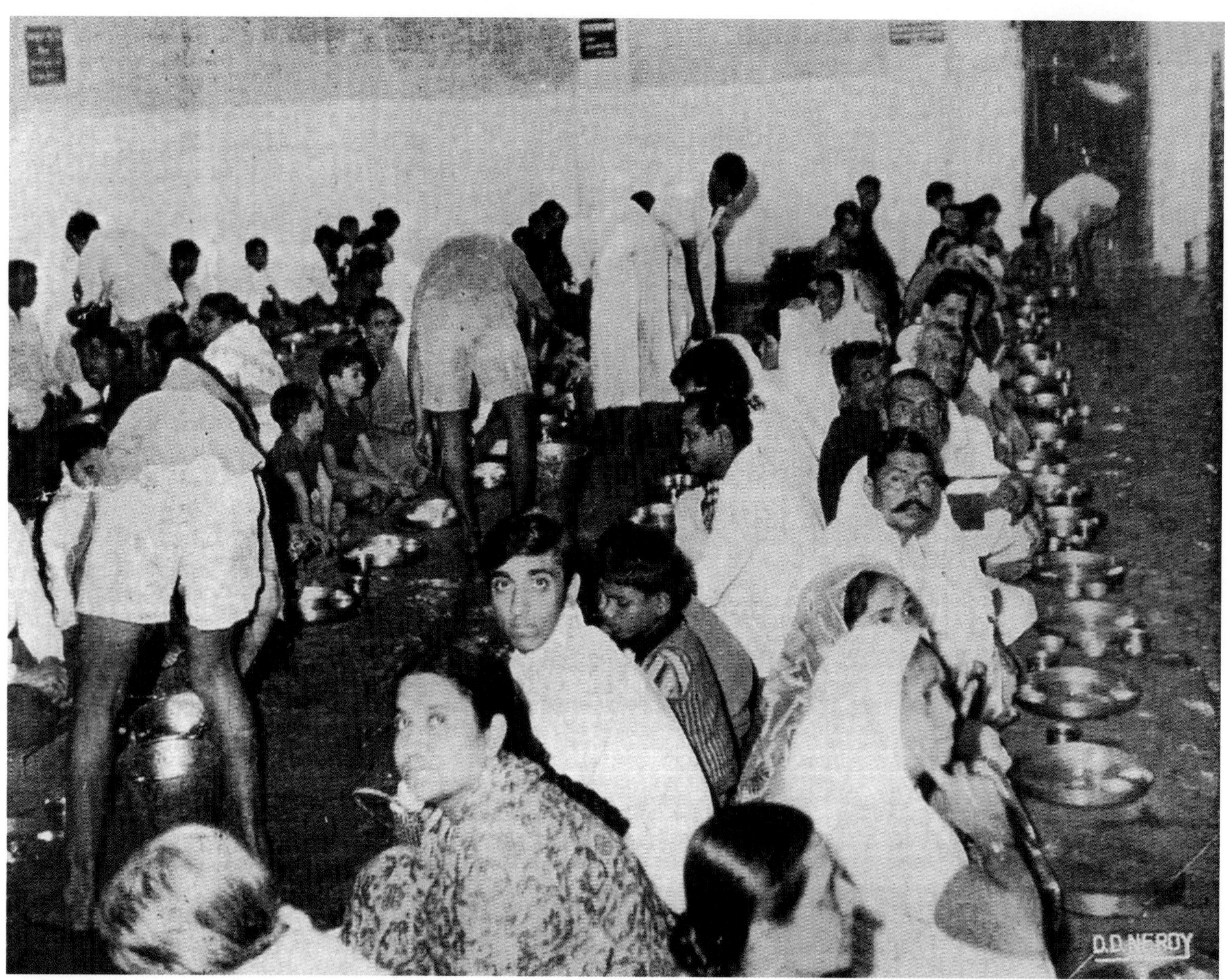

Devotees having Sai's Prasad in Prasadalya of Shirdi *(1972)*

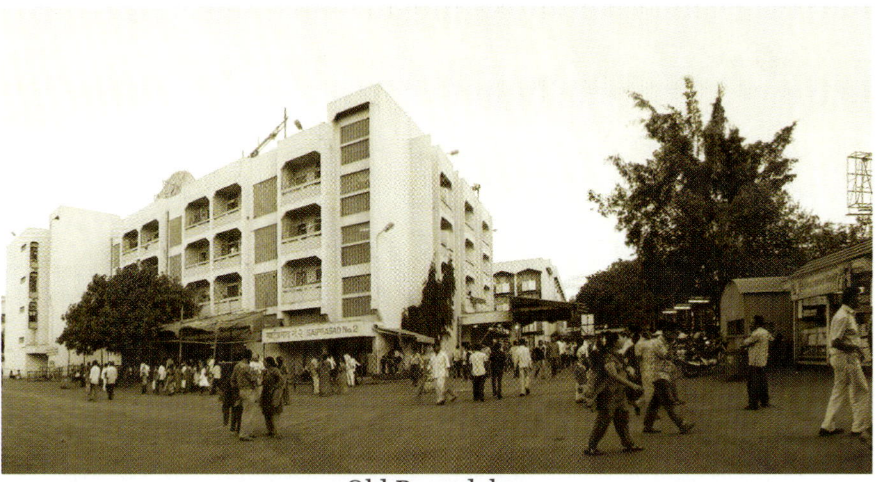

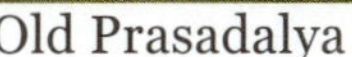

Old Prasadalya

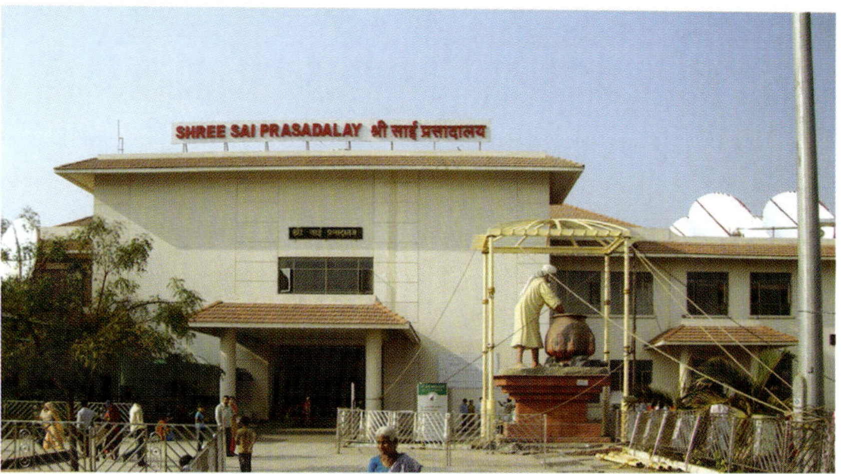

New Shri Sai Prasadalya *(2011)*

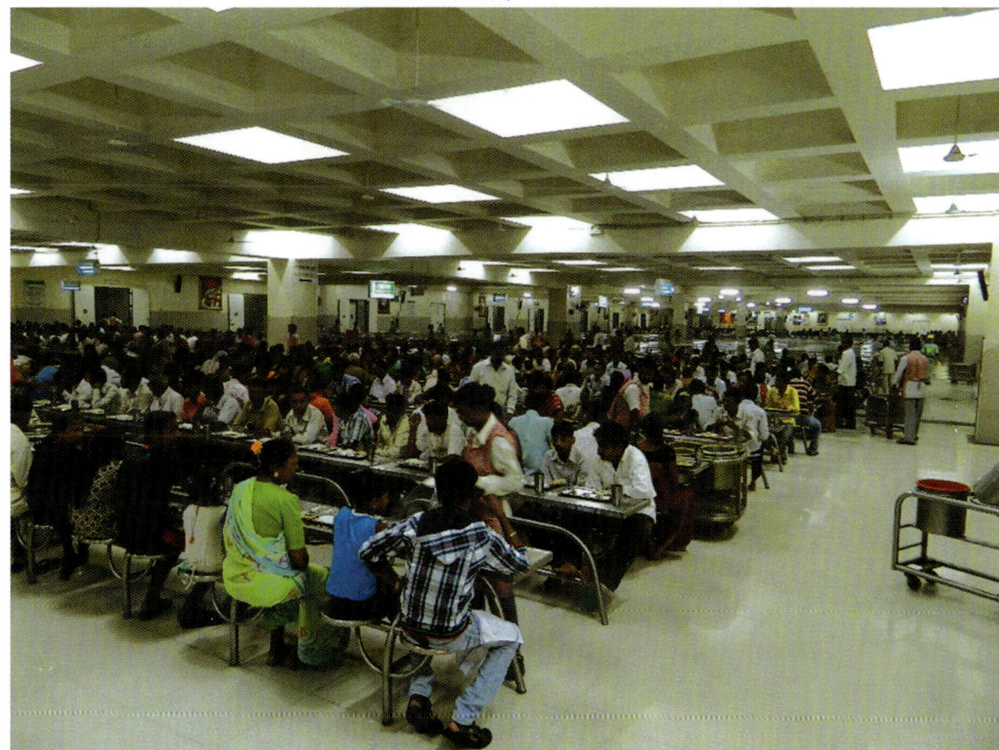

More than 5000 devotees can have their meal at once in the new Prasadalya. *(2011)*

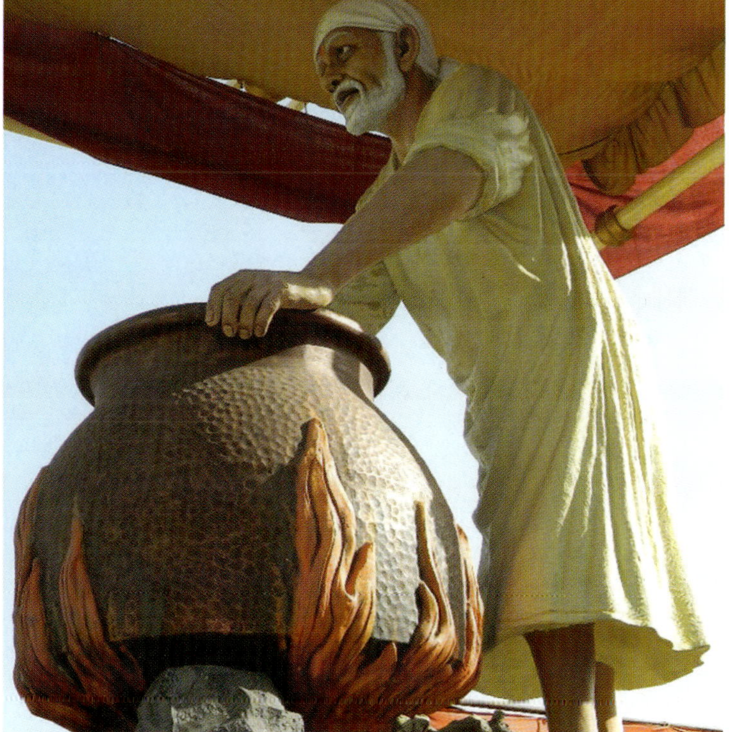

Shri Sai Baba's statue outside the new Prasadalya.
The pose conveys the intent. *(2011)*

HOUSES OF BABA'S CLOSE ASSOCIATES

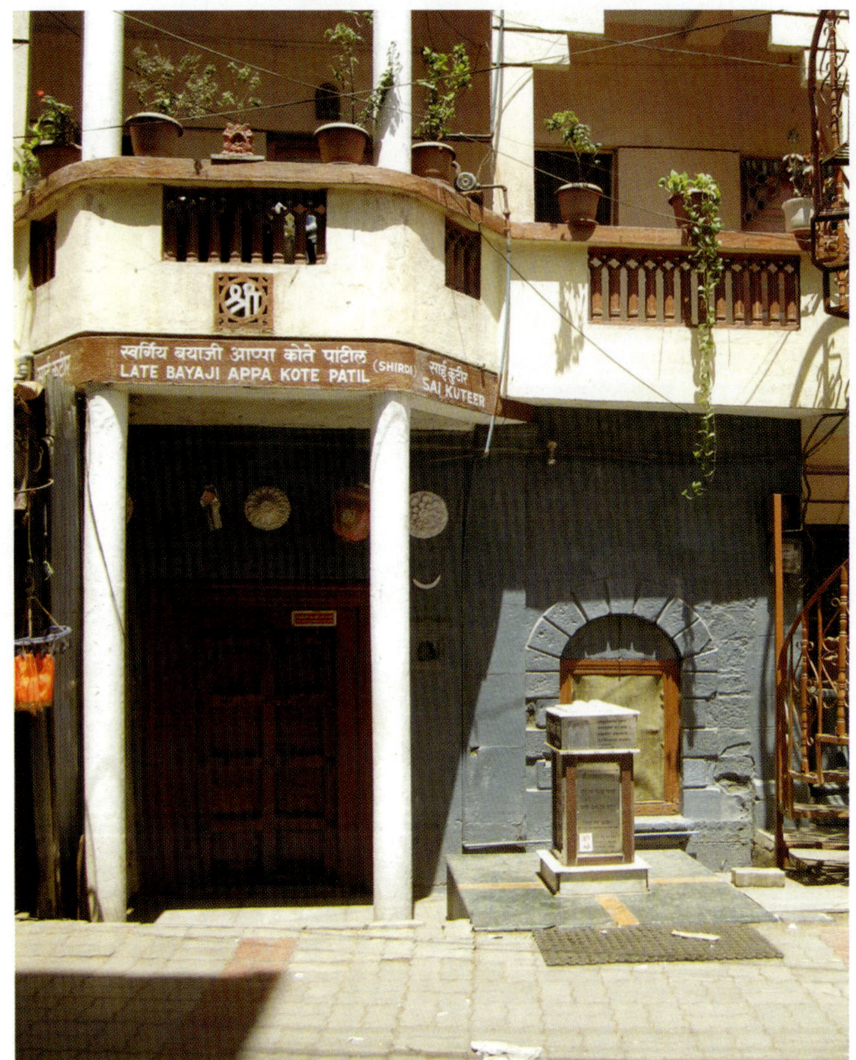

Bayaji Appa Kote Patil's House.

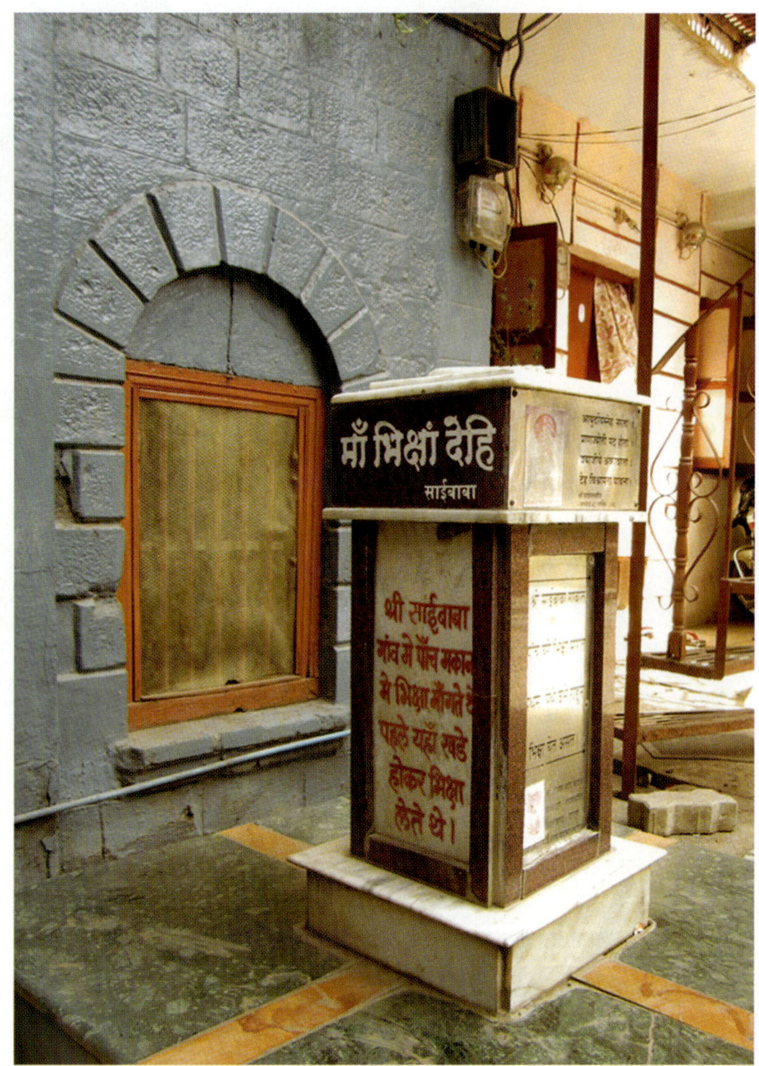

The place where Baba stood and asked for alms.

The house where Baba stood and asked for alms. Patil grew from infancy to adulthood under Baba's watchful eyes. He was present when Baba took Mahasamadhi in 1918.

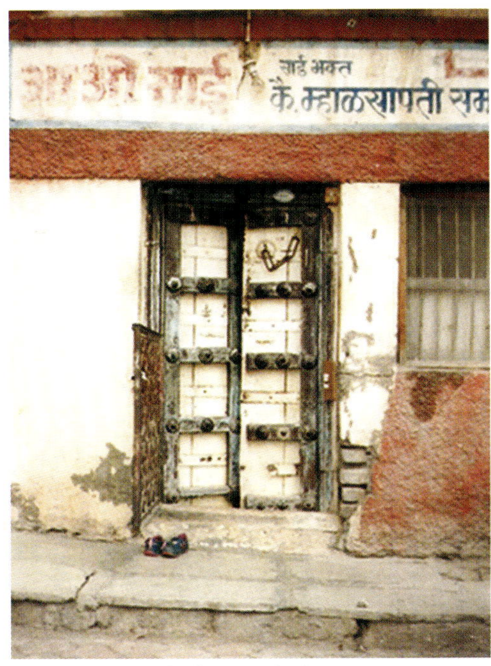

Mahalsapati's house

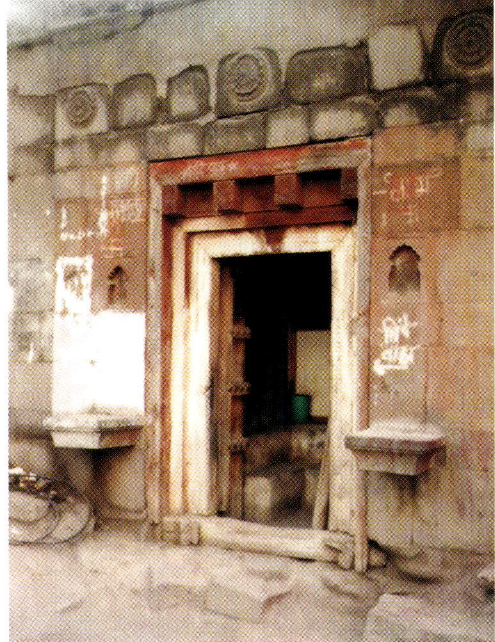

Shinde Wada (Outside)

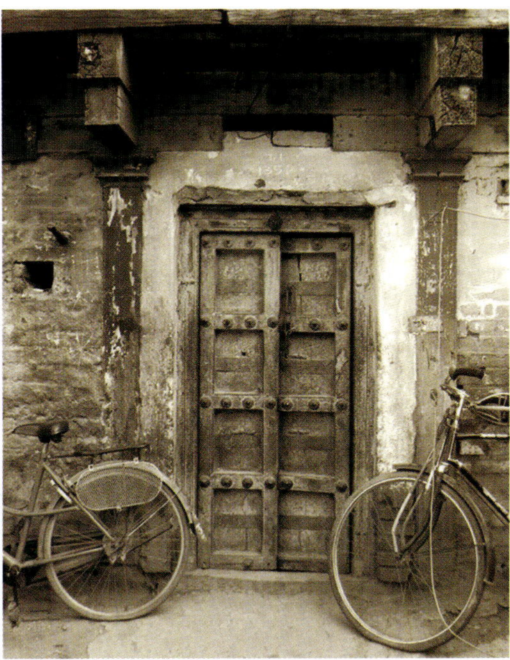

Shinde Wada (inside)

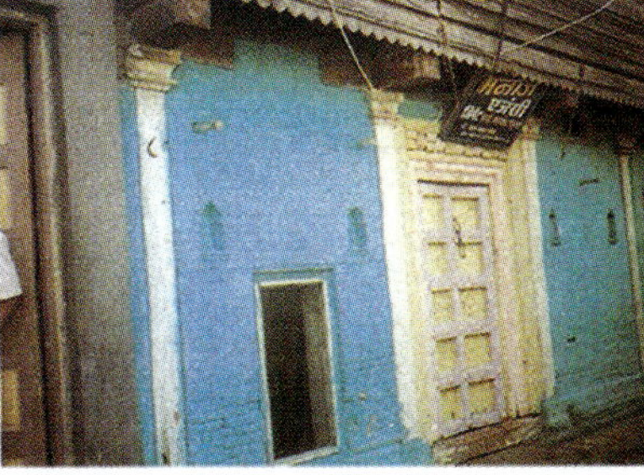

Vamanrao Gondkar's House

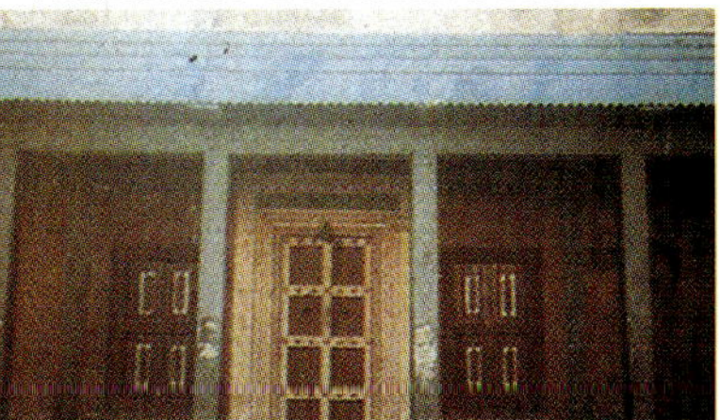

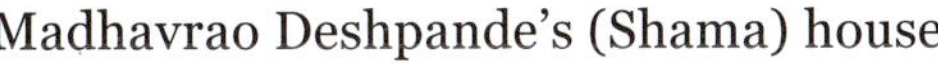

Madhavrao Deshpande's (Shama) house

Nandram Marvadi Sanklecha's housc

Sakharam Patil Shelke's house

NEEMGAON

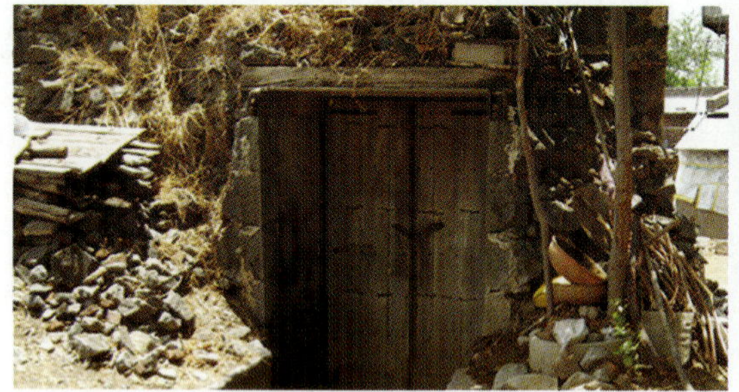

Wooden entrance to inner chambers of the fort which opened miraculously to receive Baba.

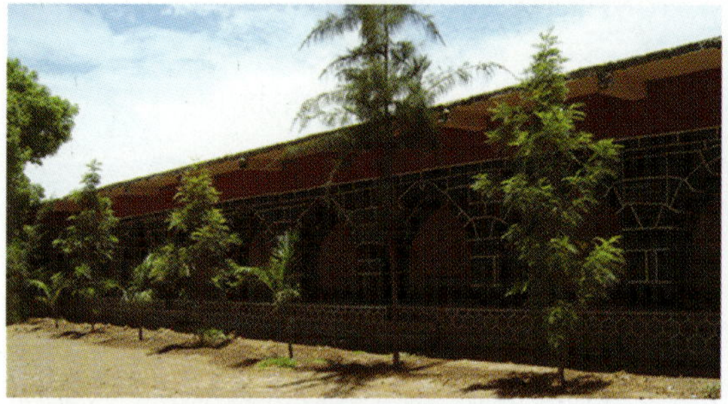

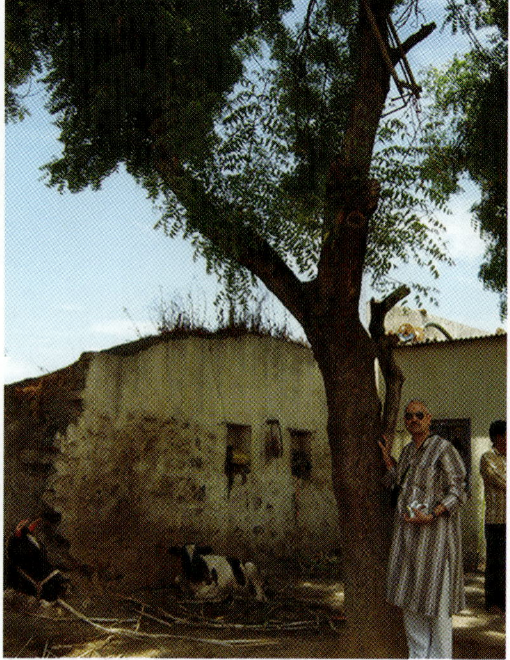

The neem tree which sprouted magically, two decades after Baba's Mahasamadhi.

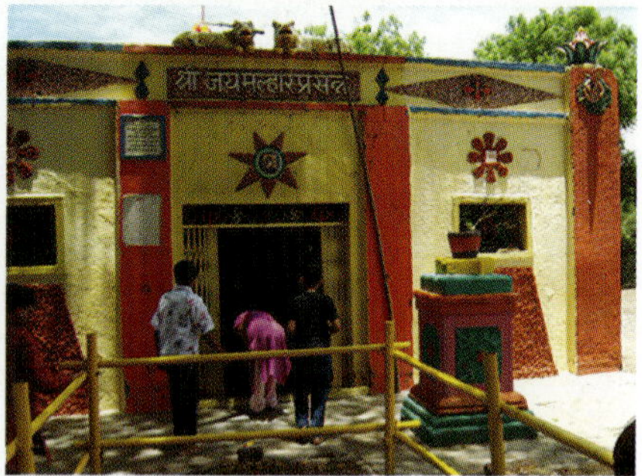

Entrance of Khandoba temple which was graced by Baba's visits.

The verandah/chavadi where Baba walked to and fro is now a garden.

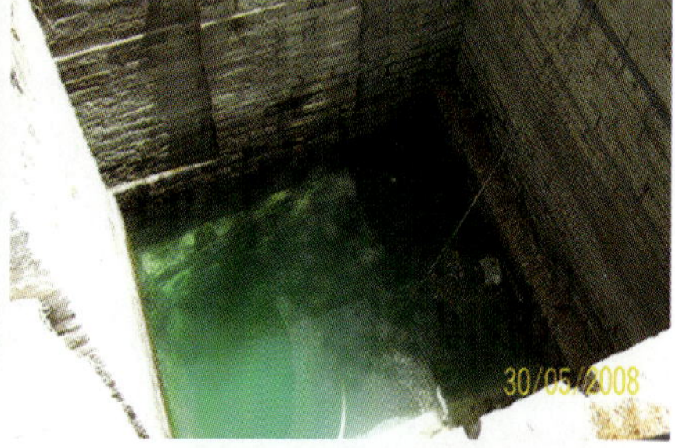

The tank lined by steps, where Baba performed ablutions.

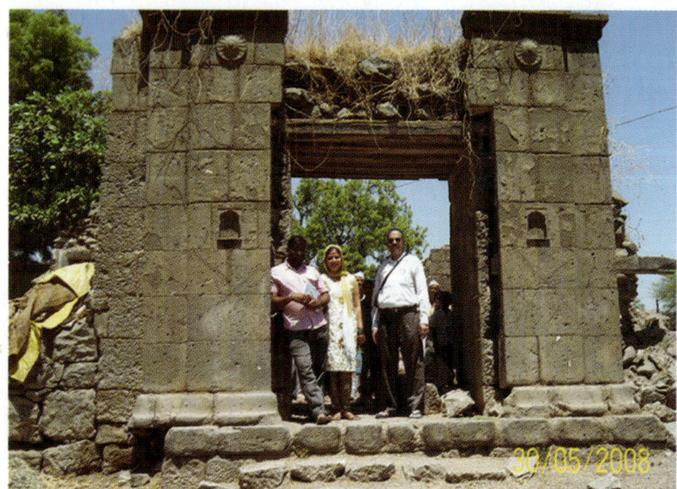

The dilapidated doorway of the fort of Nana Sahib Dengle, a profound devotee of Baba.

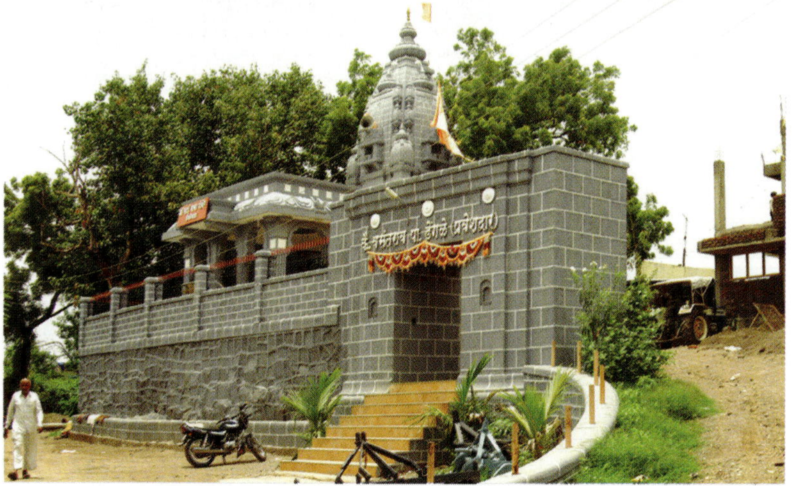

A recently constructed temple commissioned by Dengle's descendents. *(2012)*

The bridge spanning Godavari takes people across from Manmad to Shirdi. In the absence of such a sturdy bridge, a rope ferry was in use around 1884. The low lying replacement bridge often went underwater during 1950's. Devotees reached across the shores of Godavari via boats. They coutinued their journey by tonga (a horse carriage) and were jubilant upon sighting the flags of the Samadhi Mandir from Neemgaon.

The word Godavari is an amalgamation of three words: *go* (earth), *denara* (bestower) and *vari* (the best). The river's banks have reflected the glory of many saintly aura. Eight miles away from the nurturing shores of Godavari, Shirdi nestles cosily in the vicinity of the Ganges of the South.

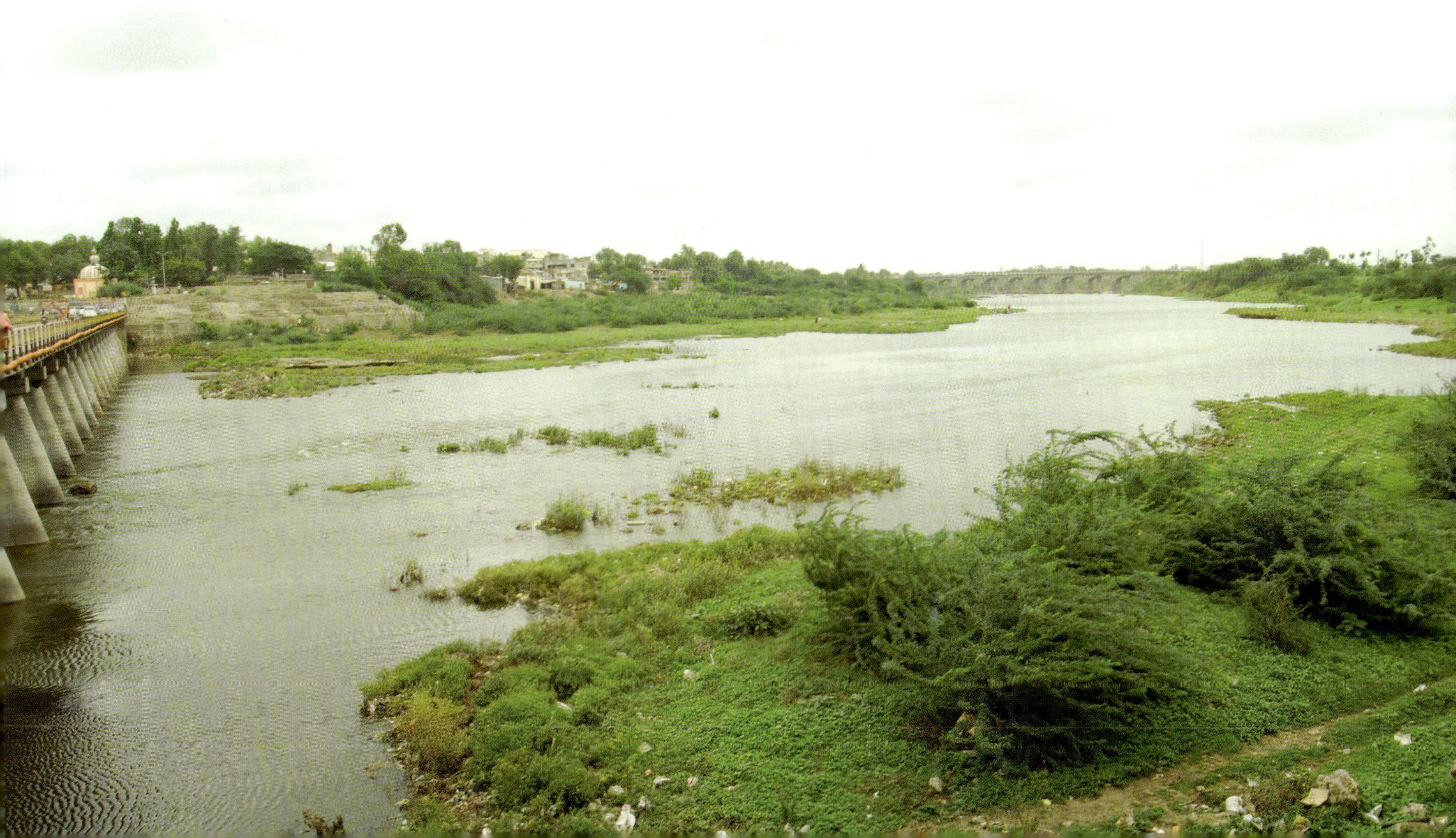

RAHATA

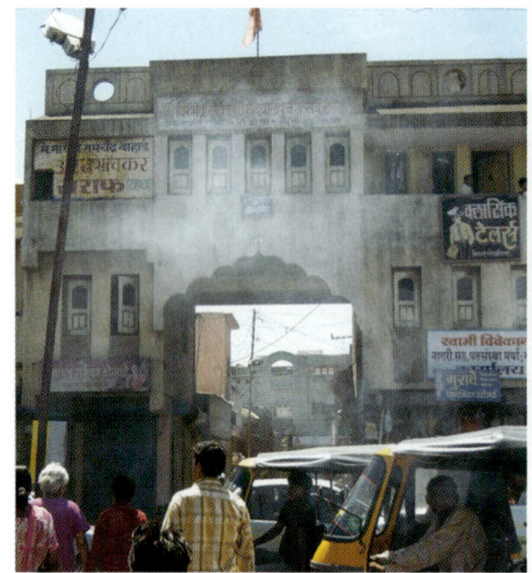

The arched gateway (Vess) to Rahata village where the villagers gathered to receive Baba.

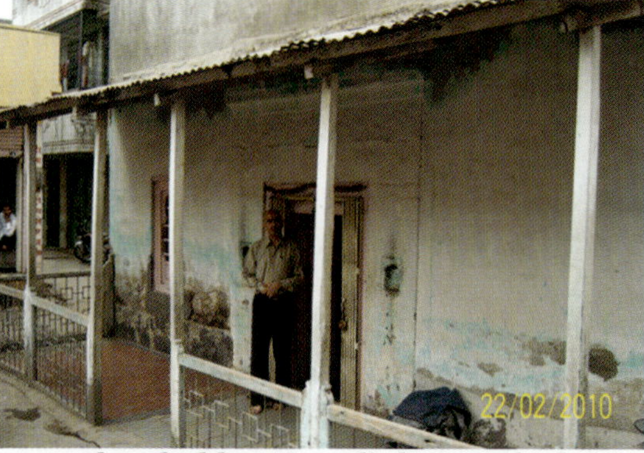

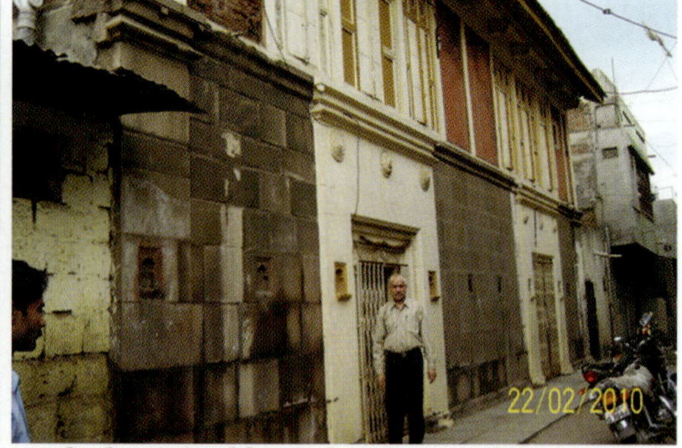

Chandrabhan Saand's house which was regularly visited by Baba. Descendents of Chandrabhan reside in this extension adjoining the blessed room.

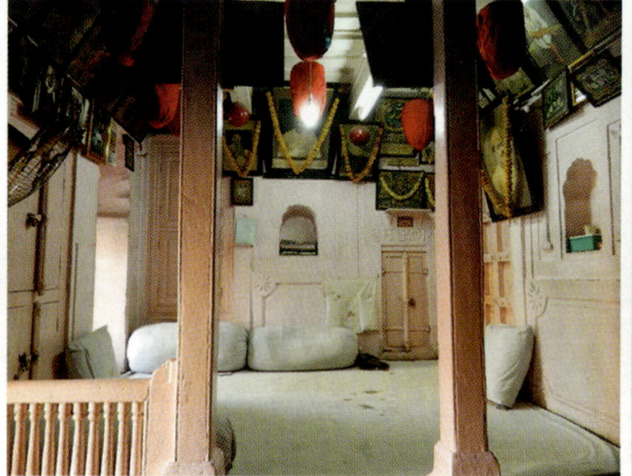

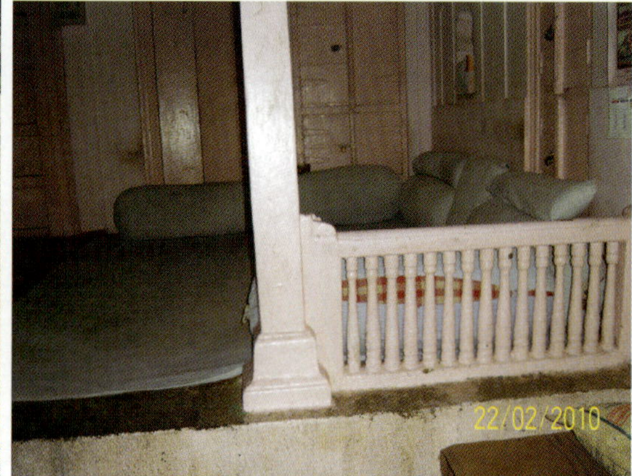

The room blessed by Baba's august presence. The right wing of the same room.

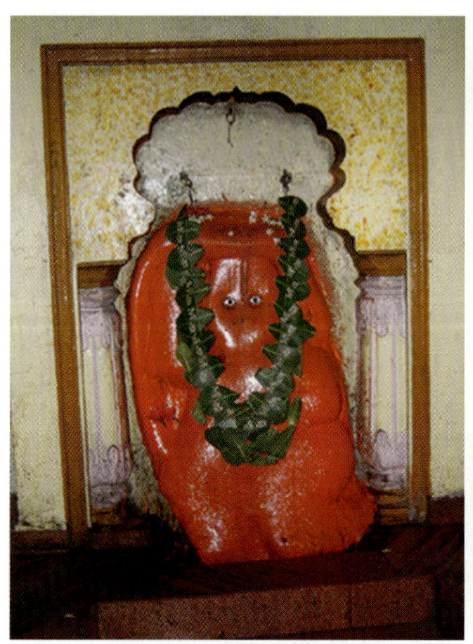

The idol of Lord Maruti.

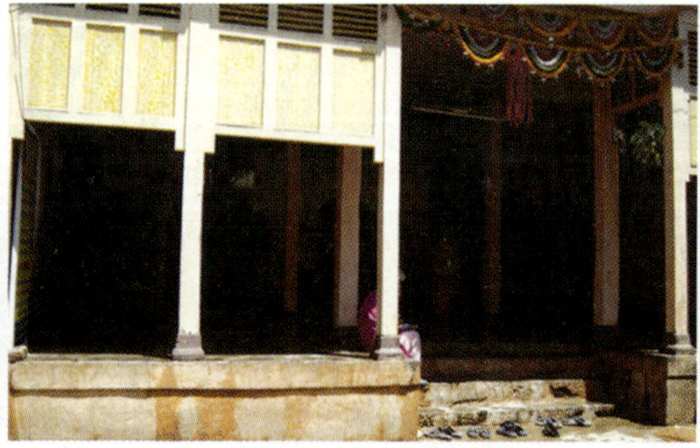

The local Maruti Mandir graced by Baba's stay around 1890.

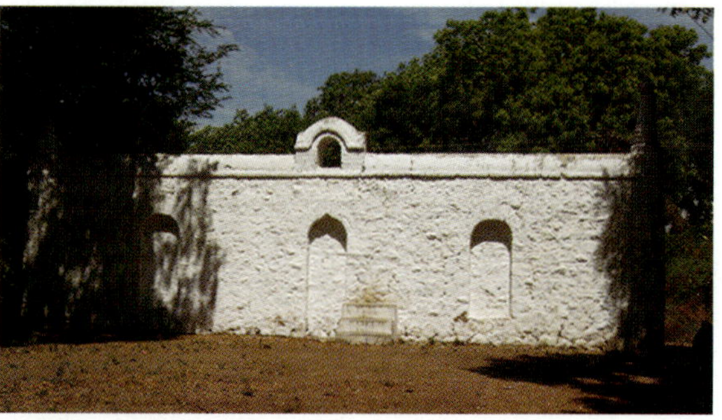

The single walled structure of Idgah where Muslims gather to offer namaz in the open.

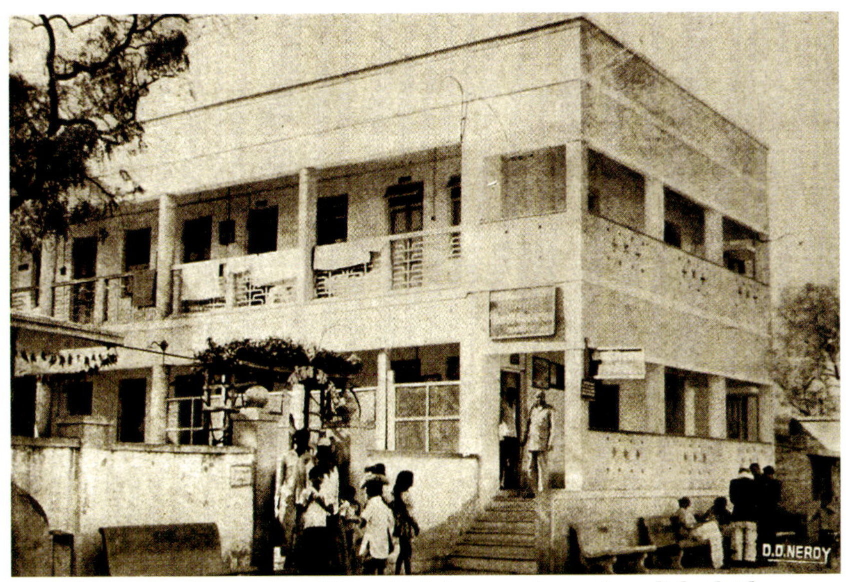

Shirdi Sansthan's enquiry office which has now been demolished. The neem tree spread over the roof of Gurusthan temple can be seen in the left corner.

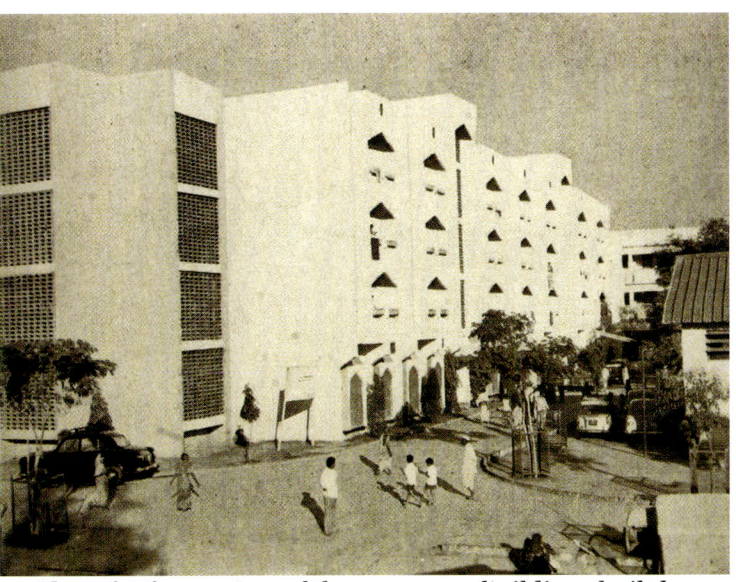

Shanti Niwas- One of the numerous buildings built by Sansthan for accommodating pilgrims

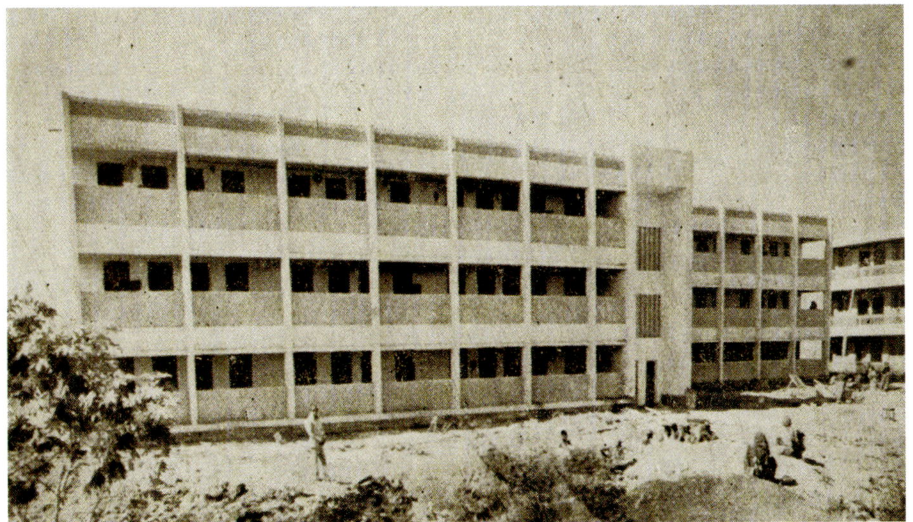

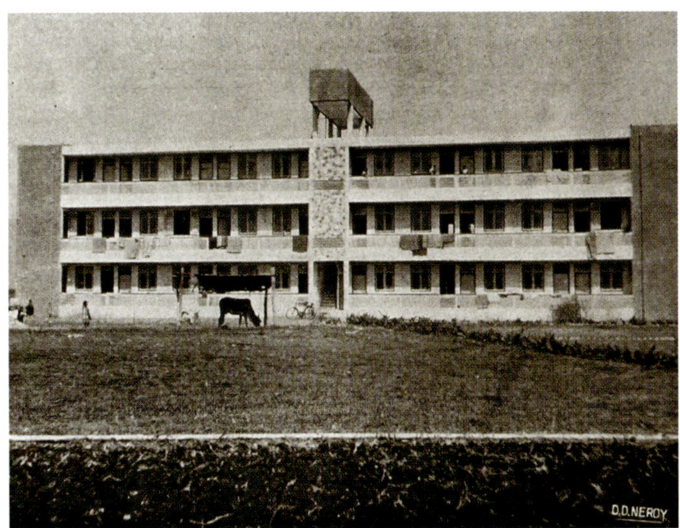

Sai Nagar- A colony of living quarters of staff members of Sansthan. *(1975)*

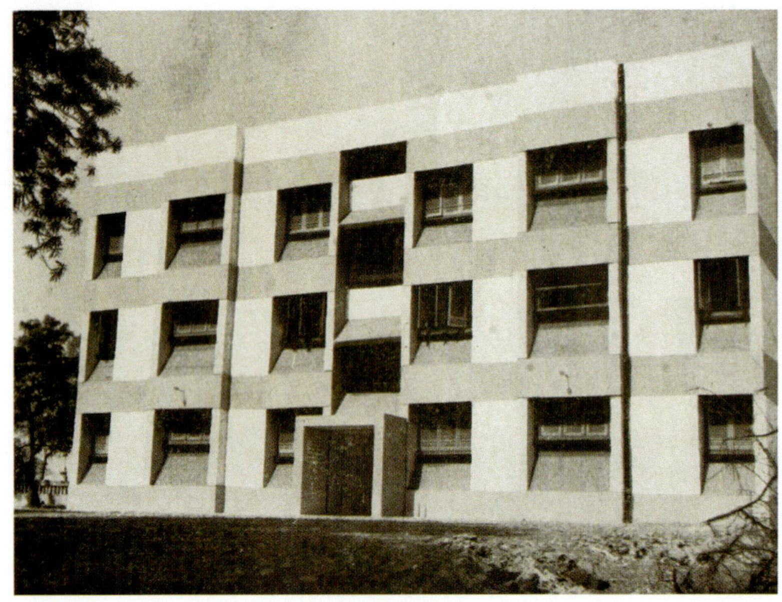

Sai Niwas- A guest house by Sansthan for travellers, near Lendi Baugh. *(1975)*

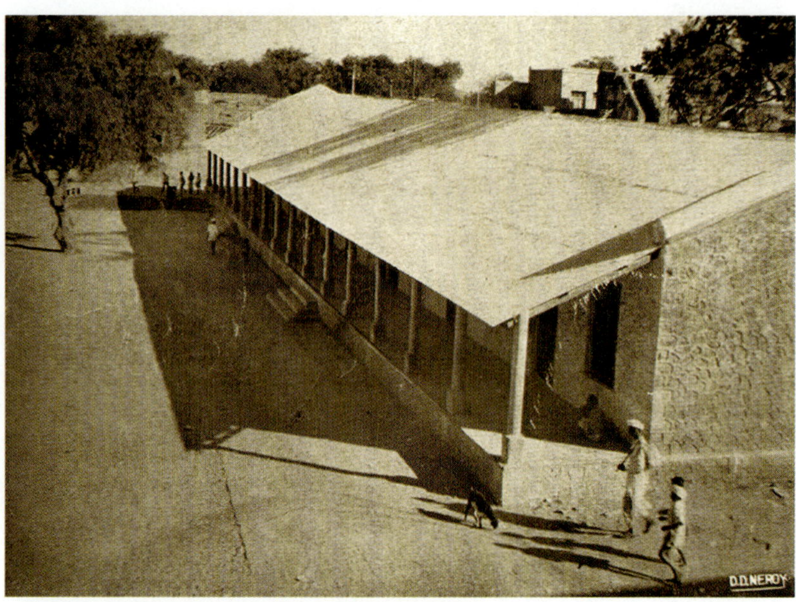

Primary school of Shirdi. This roofed complex was a temple of learning for the masses, dispensing literacy to all classes. *(1974)*

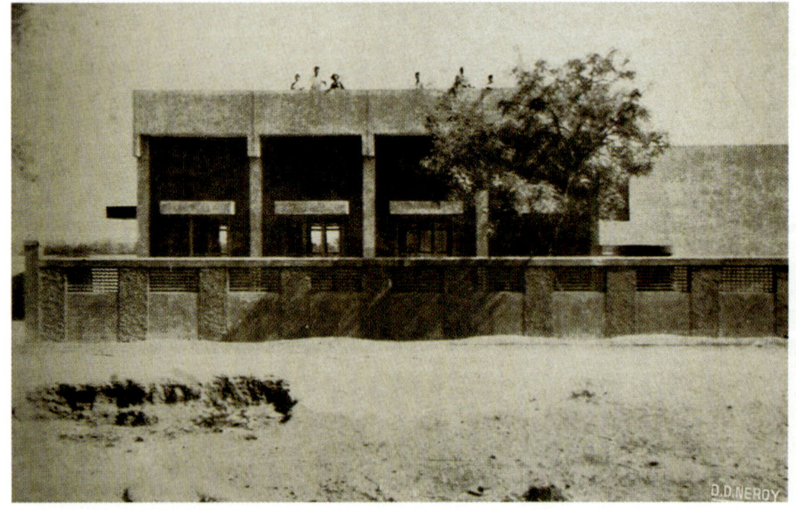

Mangal Karyalaya- A specially constructed building, earmarked for propitious purposes like marriage ceremonies. *(1972)*

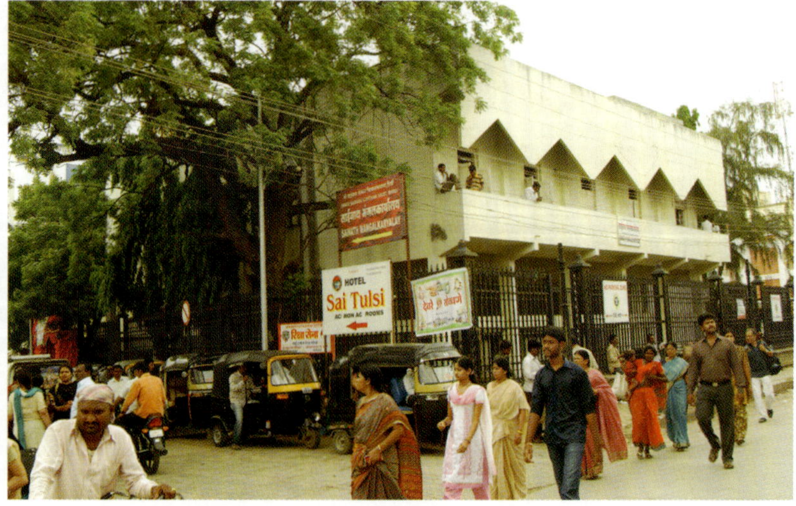

The newly refurbished 'Mangal Karyalaya' continues to serve its purpose. *(2012)*

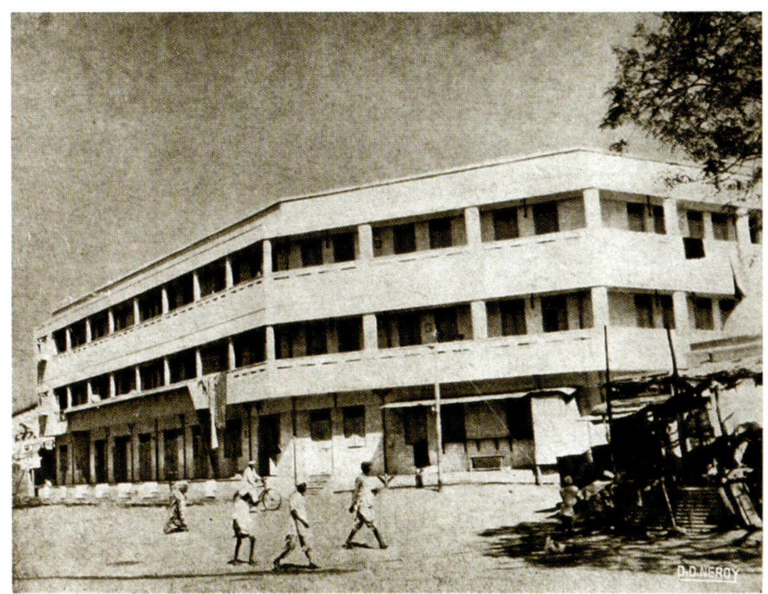

Seva Dham- Accomodation for pilgrims. *(1972)*

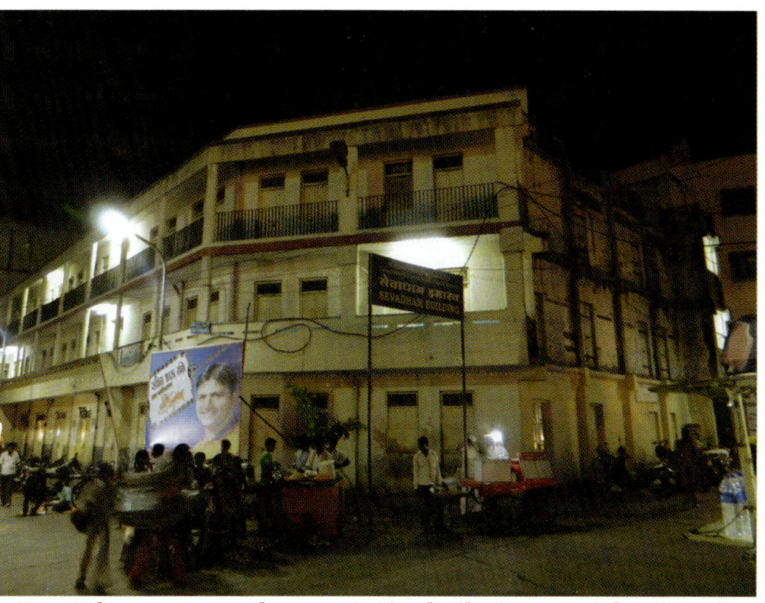

Seva Dham acts as a beacon to tired pilgrims at night. *(2011)*

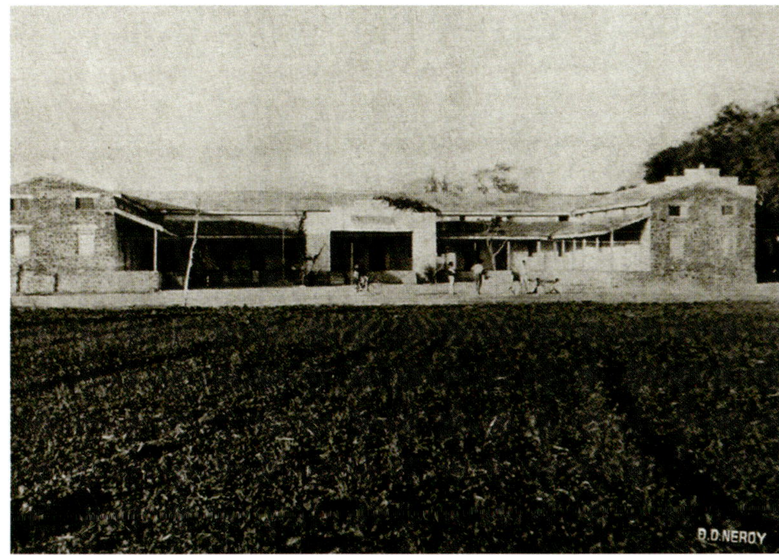

Sai Baba High School- Old Building. *(1975)*

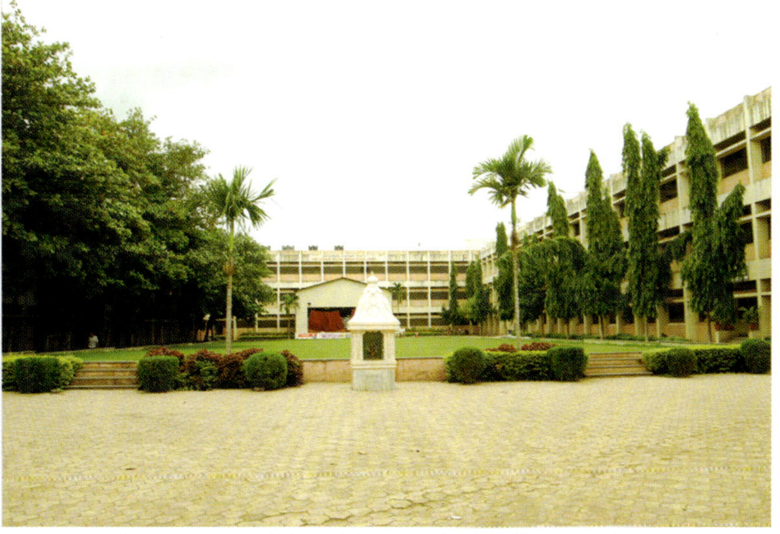

A grander version of the old Sai Baba High School; is now a three storied I.T.I., located in a lush green campus. *(2012)*

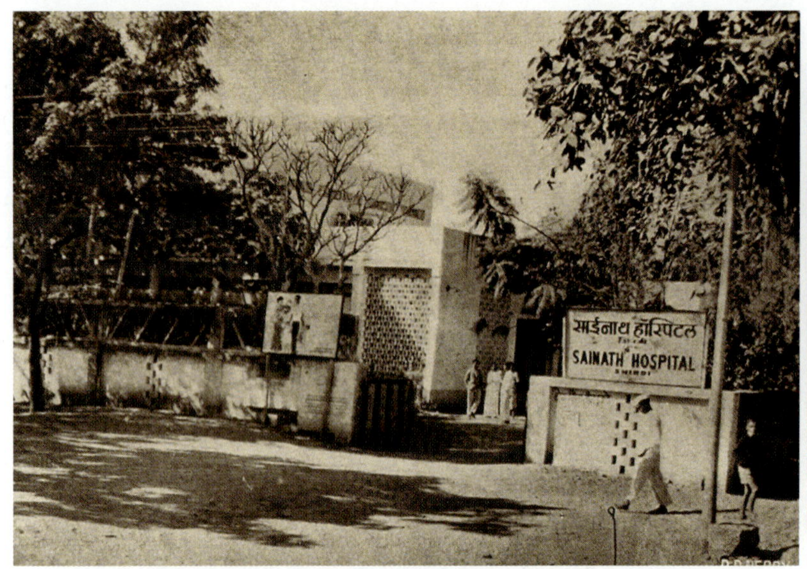

Sai Nath Hospital: Here illnesses are cured through Baba's blessings and of course medicines. (1975)

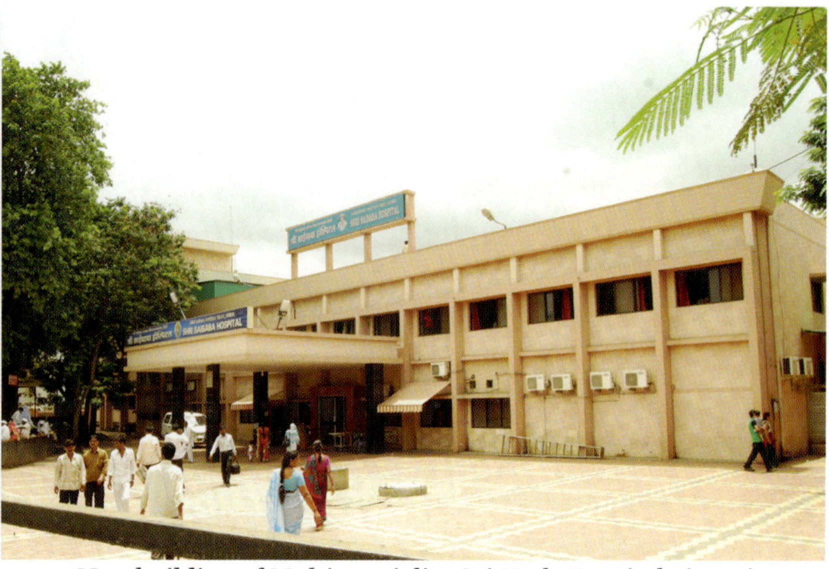

New building of Multi speciality Sai Nath Hospital. *(2012)*

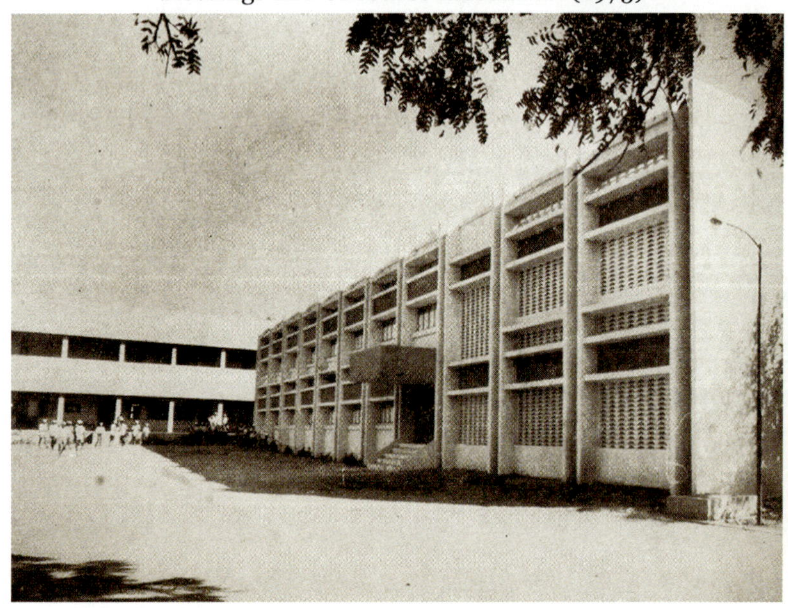

Sansthan Staff in the foreground of the freshly constructed accommodation for pilgrims. *(1973)*

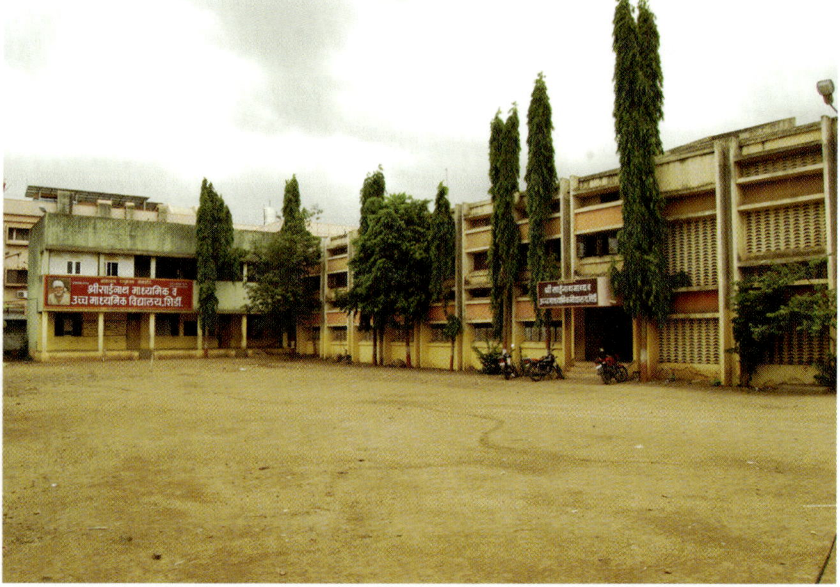

Tree lined avenues of the Shri Sai Nath Secondary School, Shirdi, which was earlier used by the devotees for their stay. *(2012)*

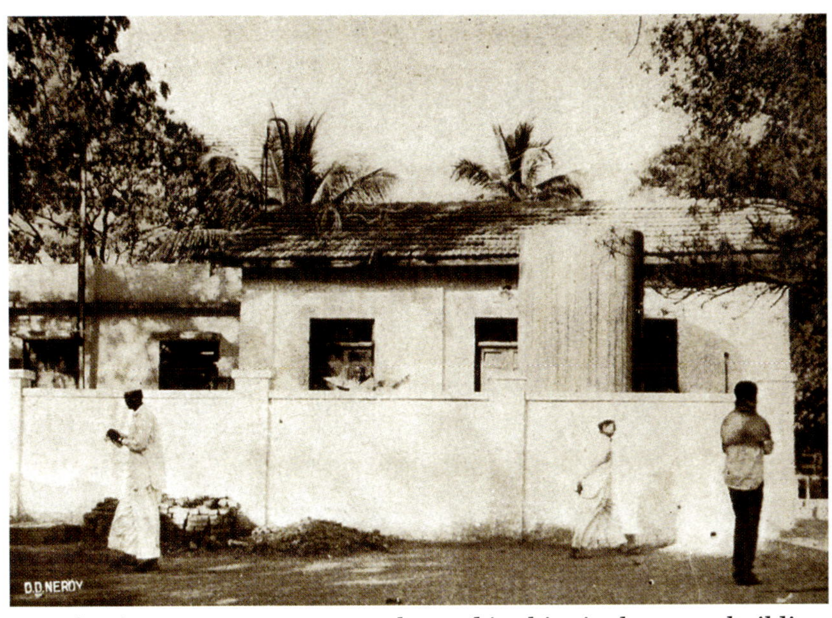

Sansthan's power generator was housed in this single storey building.

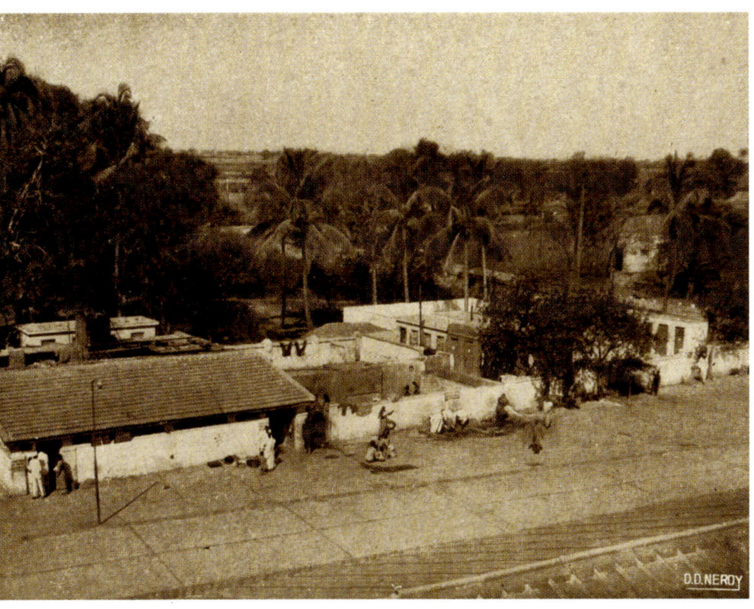

The earlier structures which served as washrooms for travellers. These have now been demolished.

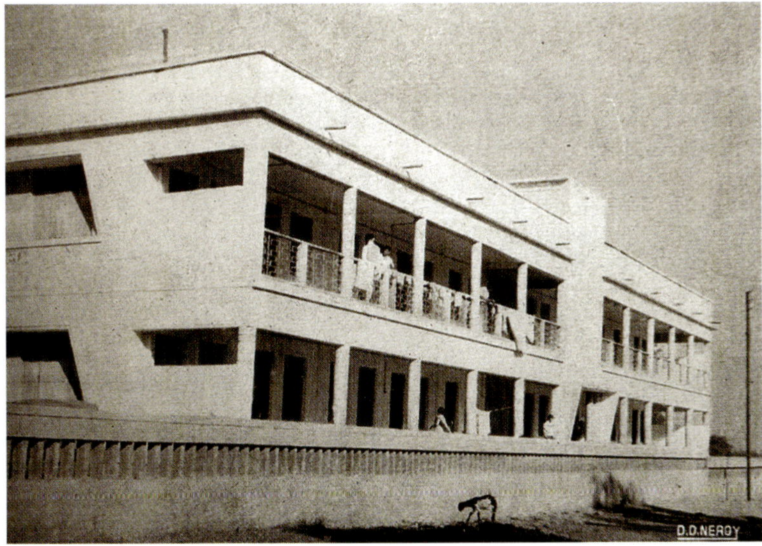

Bhakta Niwas- Accomodation for pilgrims. *(1975)*

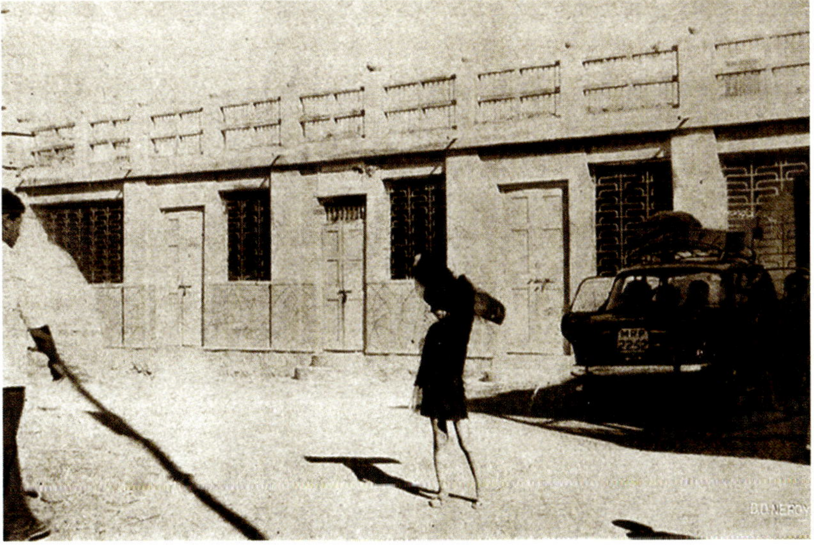

Sai Nath Chhaya- Residential arrangement for invited guests and artists who performed seva. *(1975)*

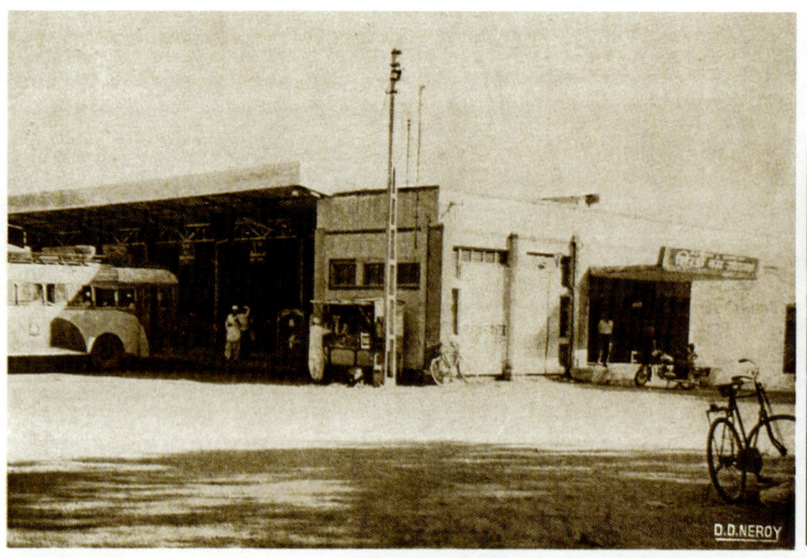

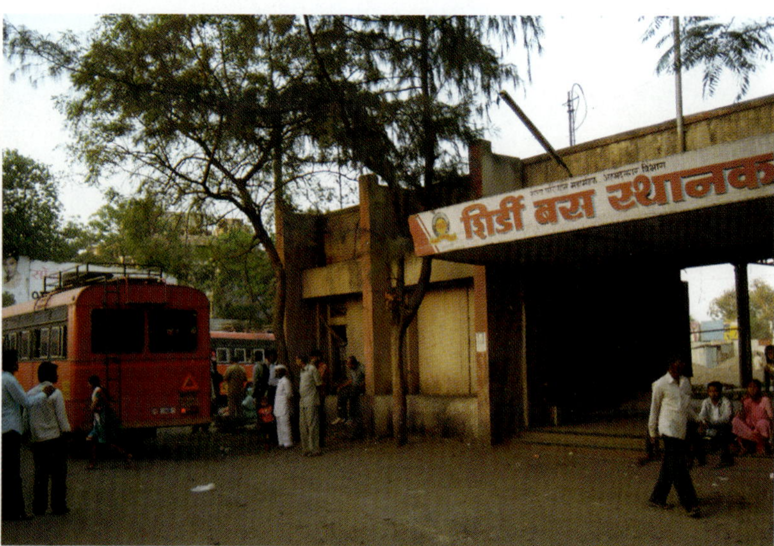

Shirdi Bus Stand- Two images across time: In sepia *(1974)* and in colour. *(2012)*

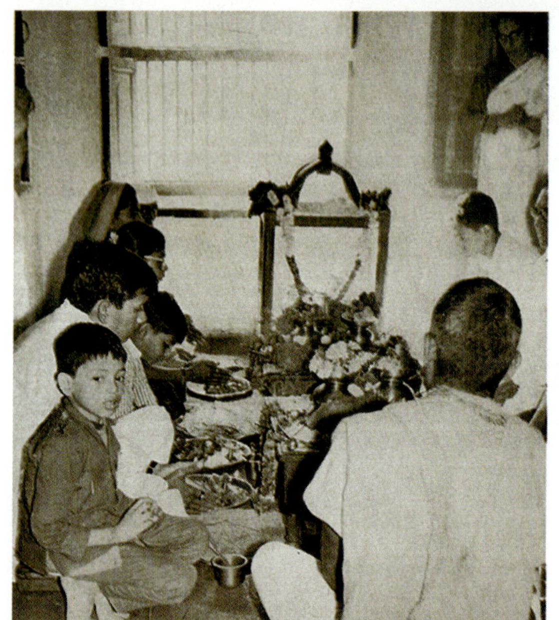

Satya Narayan Puja- Ritual service being performed under the aegis of Sansthan in the temple complex. *(1975)*

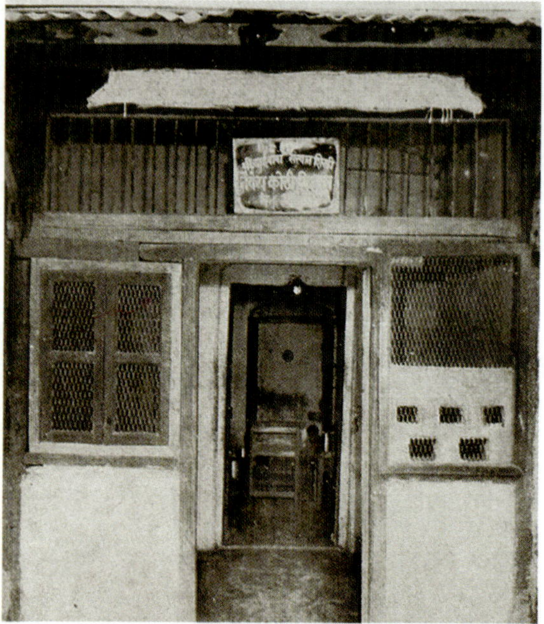

Old Naivedya Kothi (Prasad House) is the place where devotees queued up to get prasad. It has now been demolished. *(1975)*

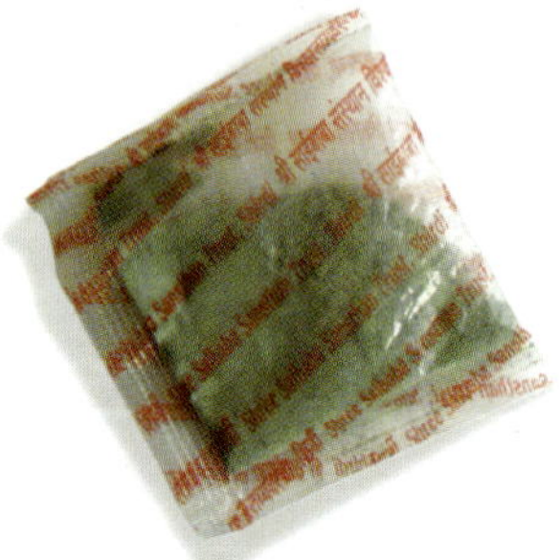

Baba's Vibhuti *(Udi)*

Baba said, "*Worldly life is like this udi and a day will come when, like it, we will also become vibhuti.*" This is the true significance of the udi.

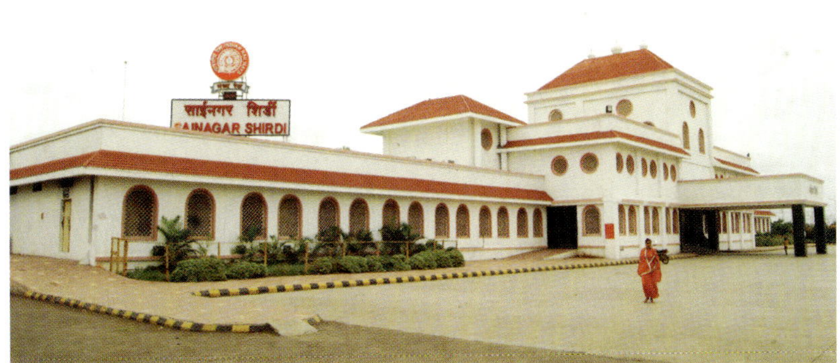

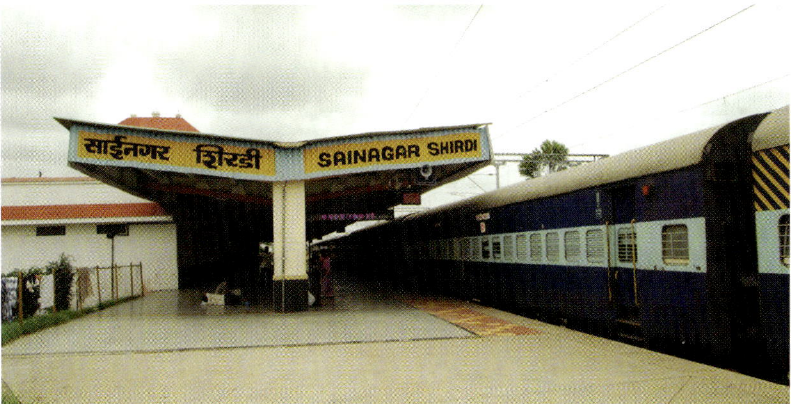

Sai Nagar railway station is among the latest public utility constructed near Shirdi. A train stands ready to depart from the platform. *(2012)*

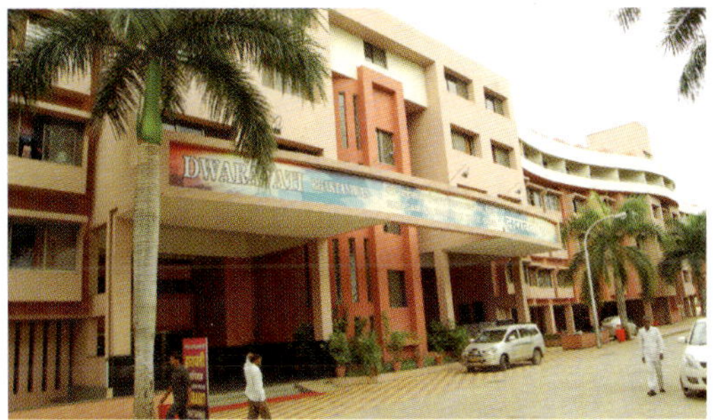

Dwarawati, a new guest complex built for devotees by the Sansthan. *(2012)*

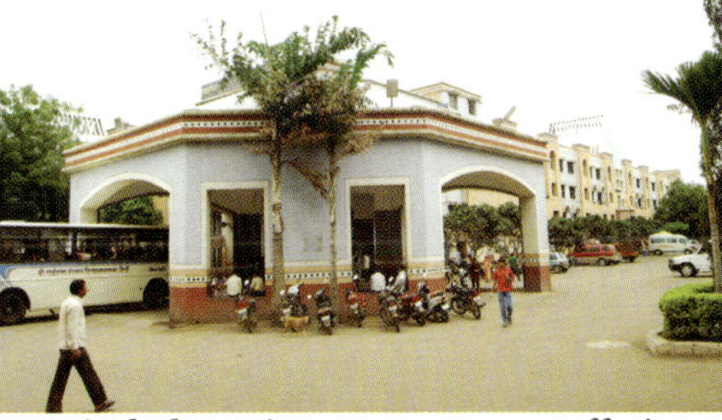

Sai Bhakta Niwas, a 500 room offering from the Sansthan, fully equipped with latest facilities. *(2012)*

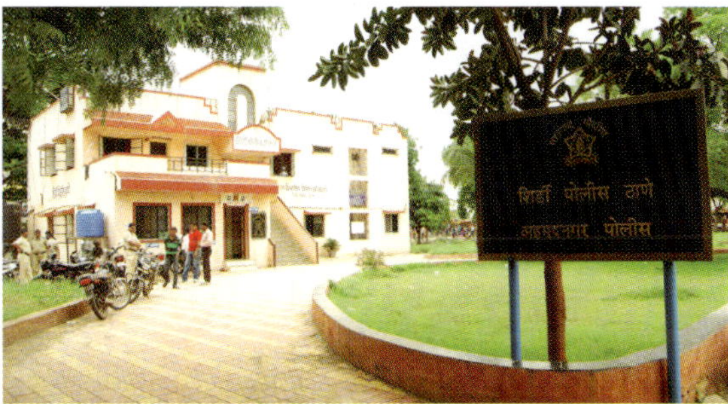

The local police station stands watch over law and order. *(2012)*

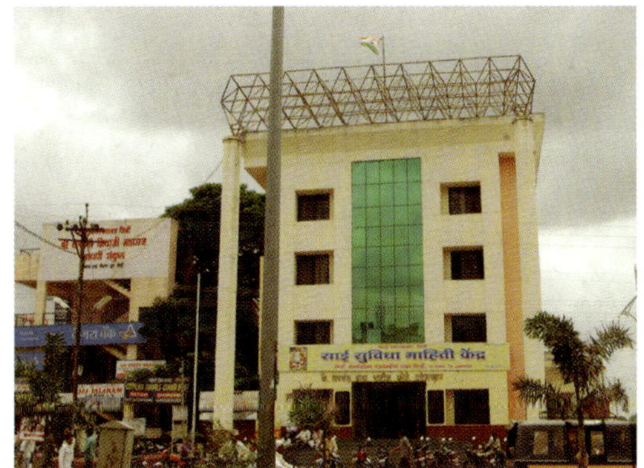

Sai Suvidha Mahiti Kendra

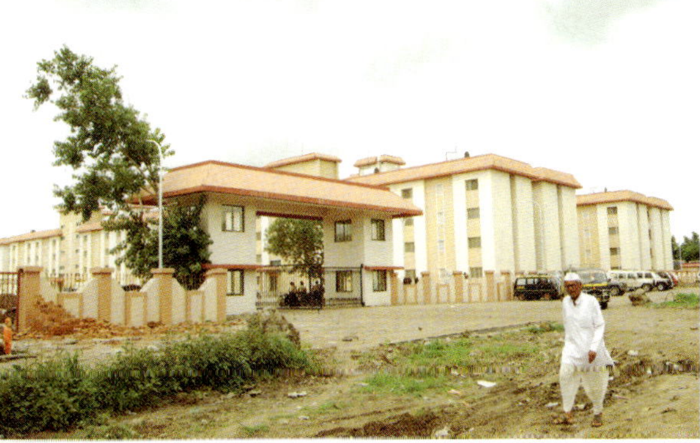

Yet another accomodation for devotees is under construction at Shirdi. *(2012)*

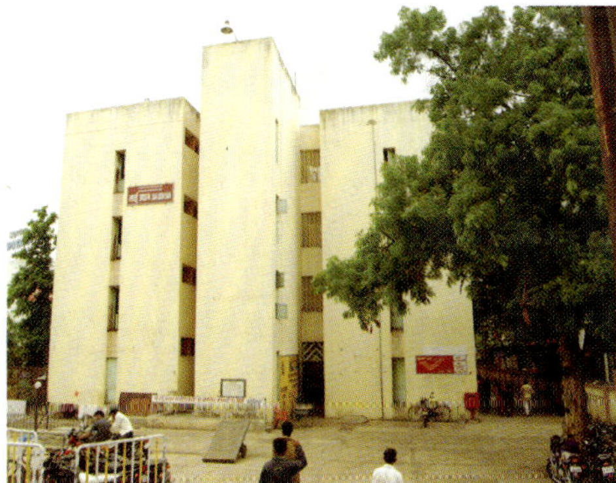

Sai Udhyan, an older complex for devotees stands tall at Pimpalwadi Road. *(2012)*

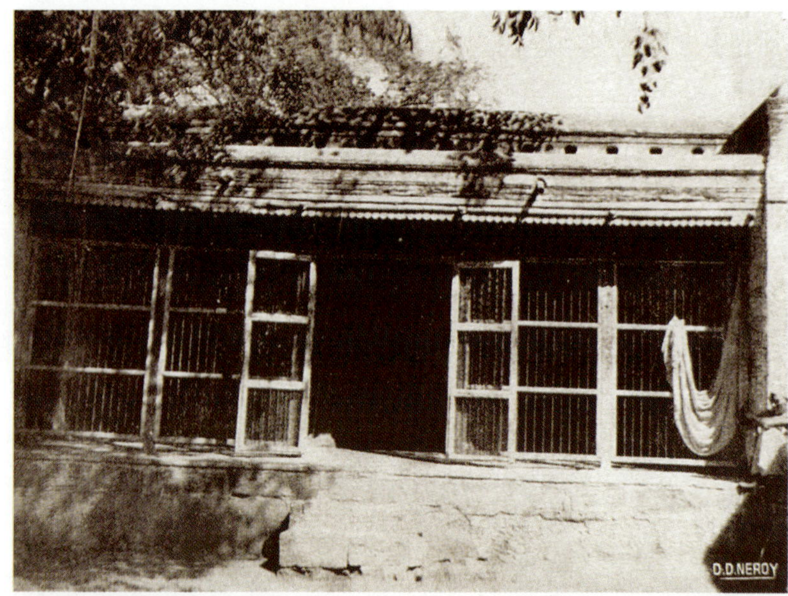

Dakshinmukhi Hanuman Mandir *(1970)*

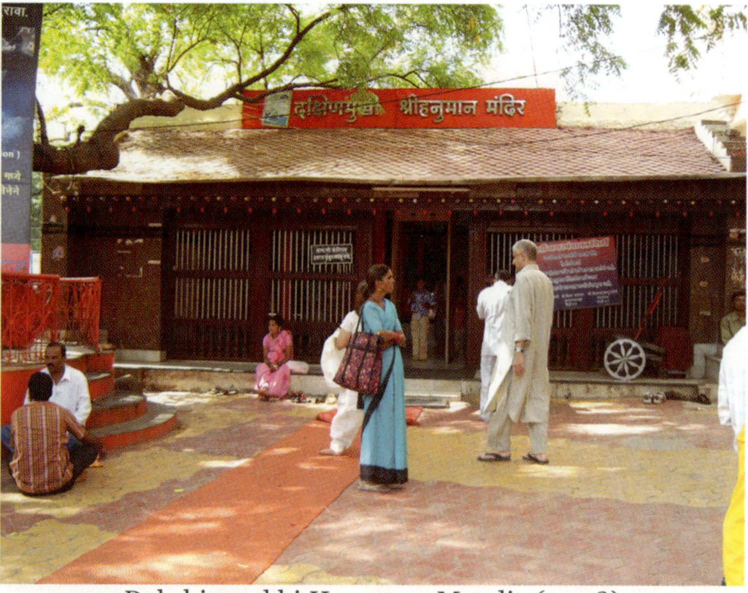

Dakshinmukhi Hanuman Mandir *(2008)*

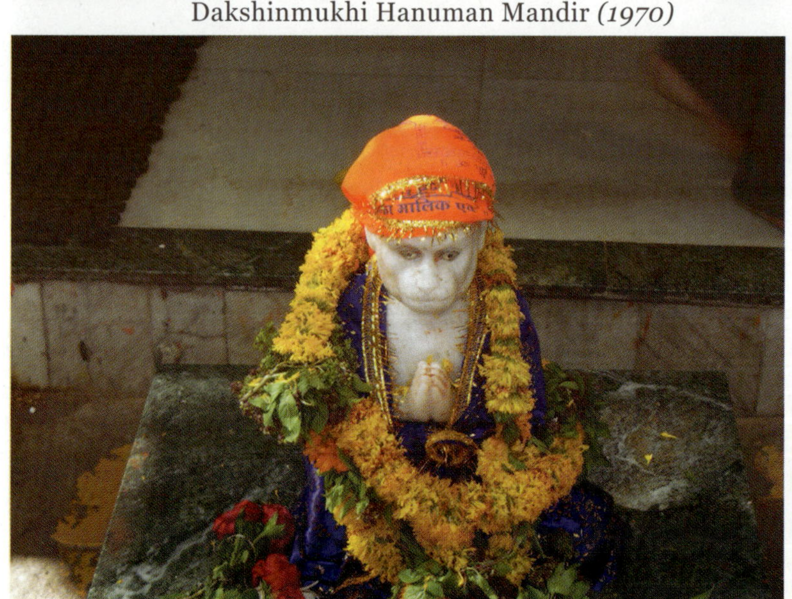

Idol of Maruti (Lord Hanuman)

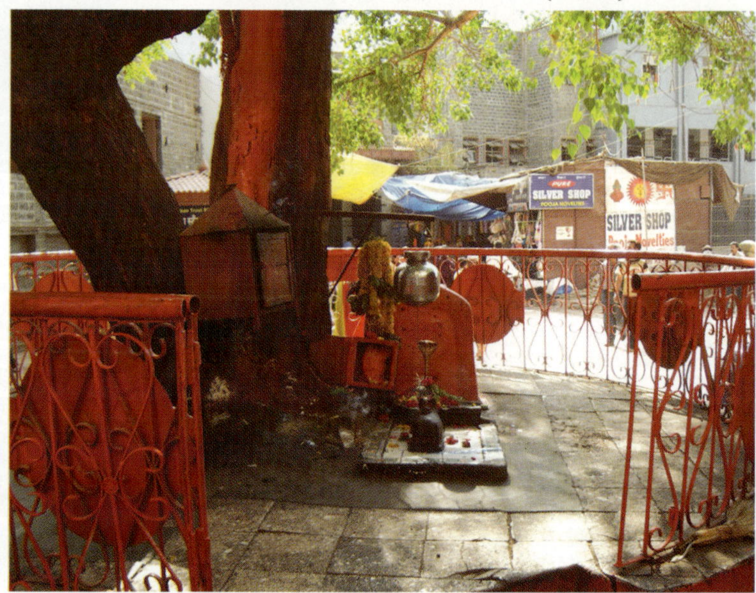

Shivling and *Nandi* out side Dakshinmukhi Hanuman Mandir installed by Shri Narsimha Swami

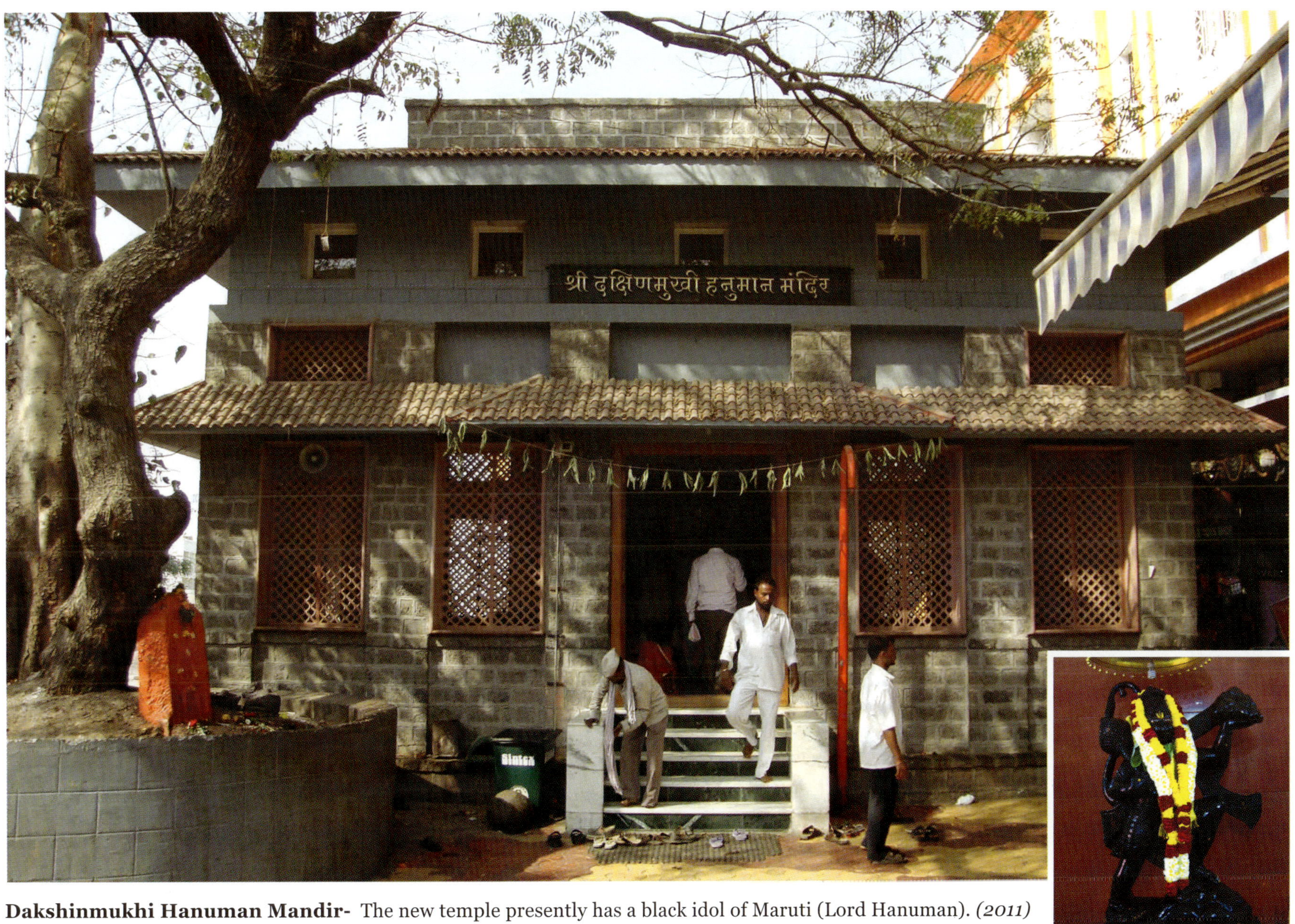

Dakshinmukhi Hanuman Mandir- The new temple presently has a black idol of Maruti (Lord Hanuman). *(2011)*

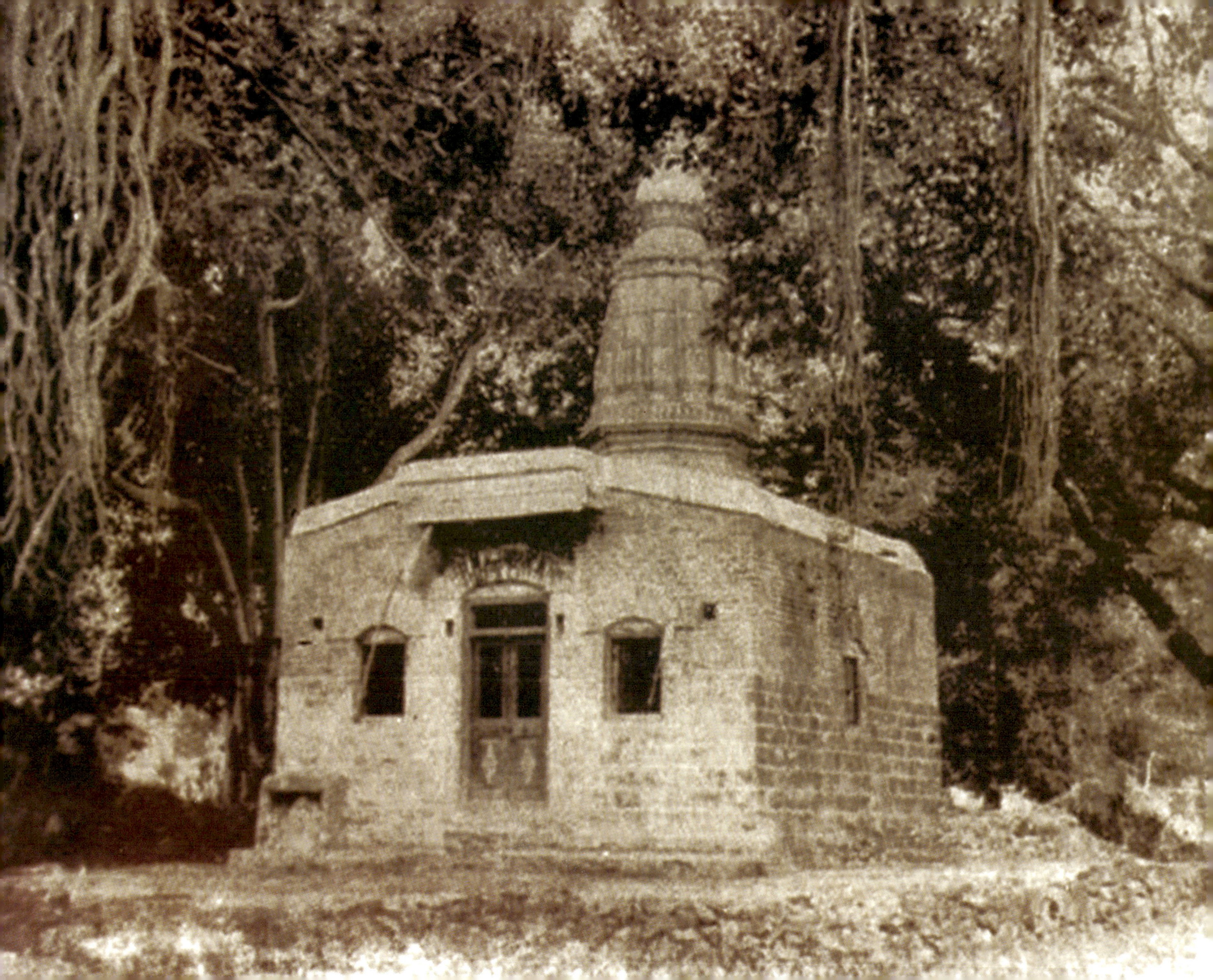

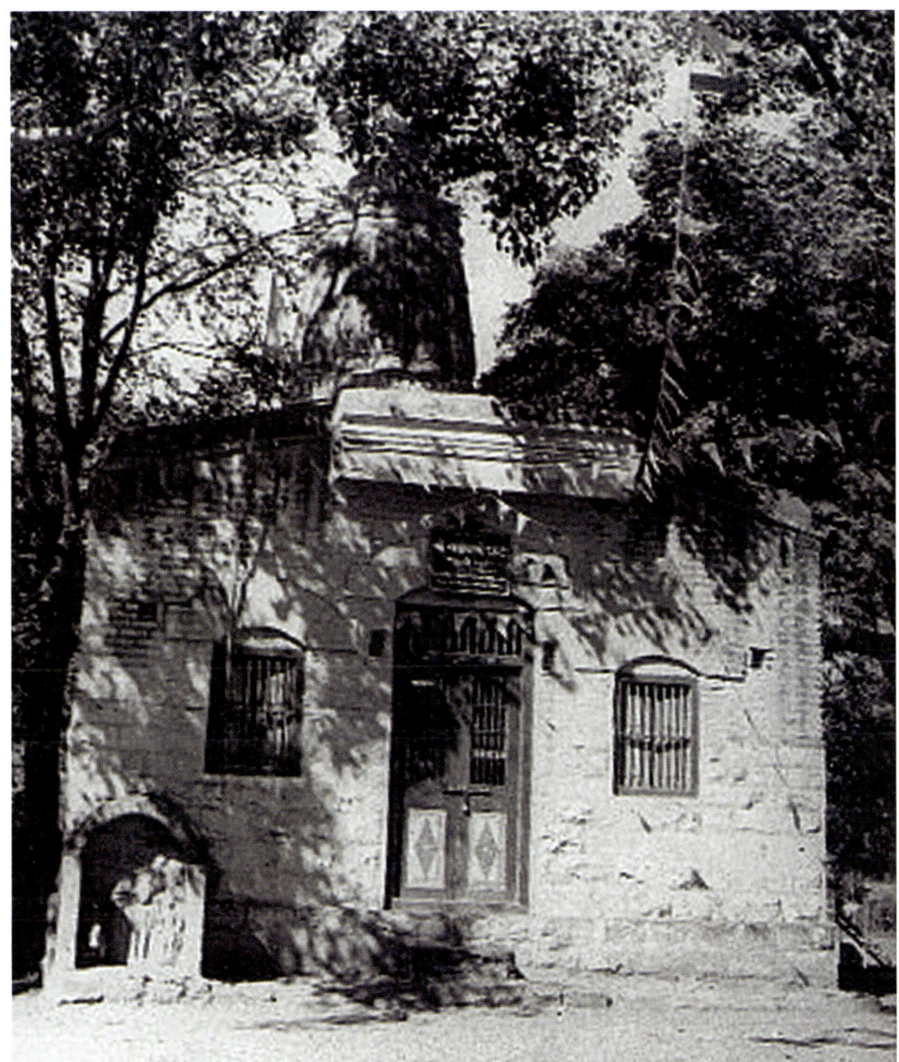

Khandoba Temple as in *(1965)*

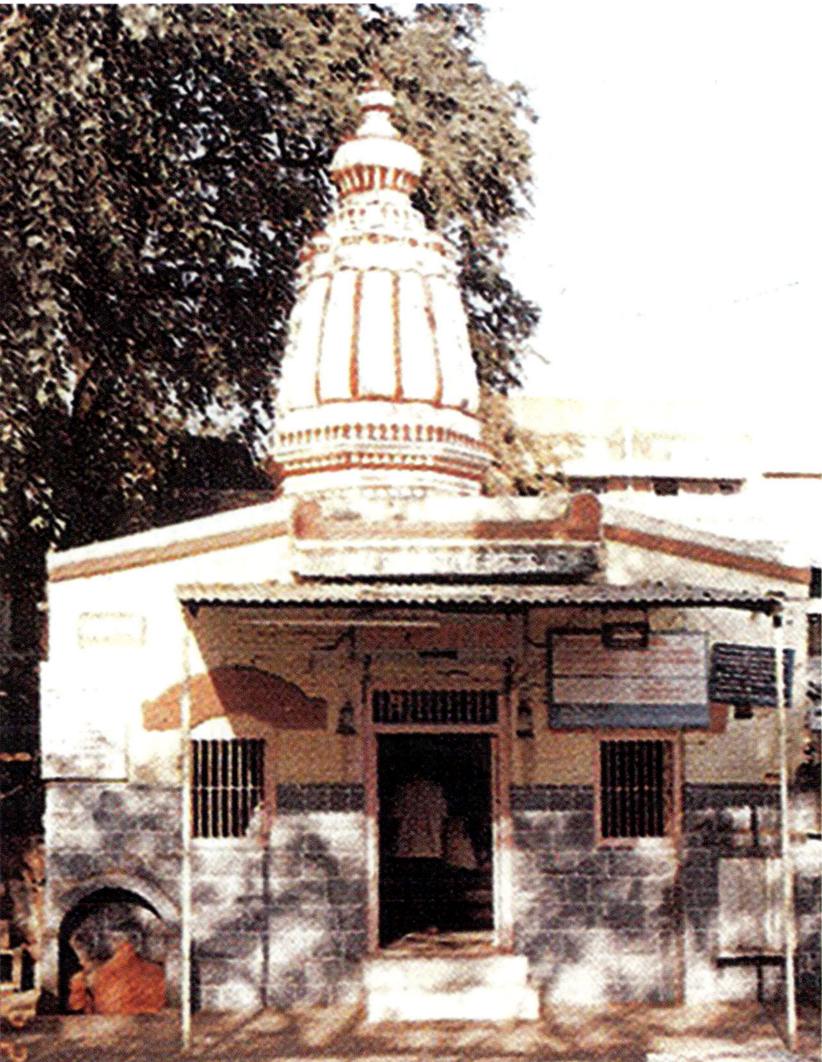

Khandoba Temple *(2010)*

The Khandoba temple is a 500 year old structure dedicated to Lord Khandoba. It is at this venerable site that the resident priest Mahalsapati welcomed the young mendicant who had arrived in Shirdi with a marriage party. "Aao Saijee Maharaj" was the welcome phrase which got attached to Baba and to this date, he is referred to as Sai Nath Maharaj. The temple is 15ft long and 15ft wide. In the centre is a stone idol of Khandoba flanked by the idols of his wife Mhalsa on the left and Banai on the right They are believed to be incarnations of Shiva, Parvati and Ganga respectively.

← Khandoba Mandir in 1920's

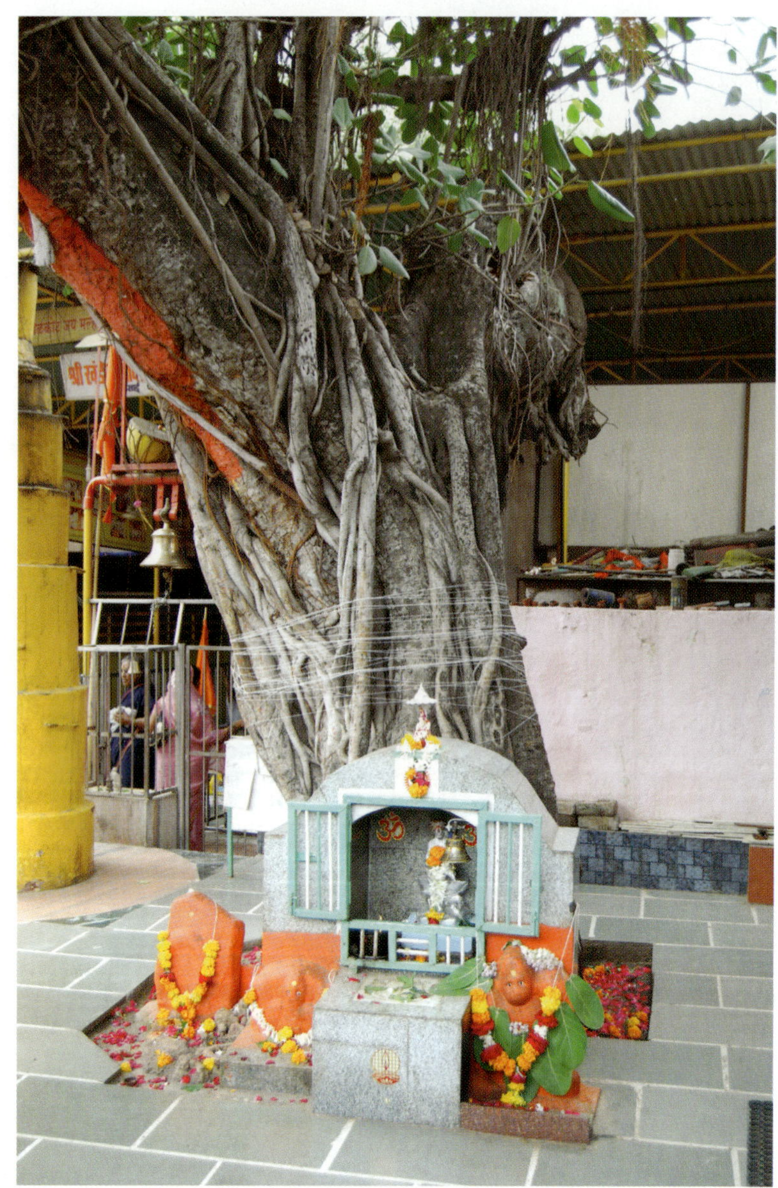

Banyan Tree outside Temple *(2008)*

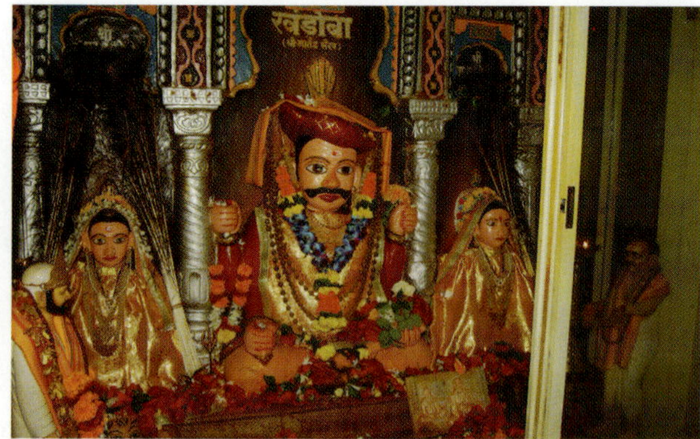

Lord Khandoba *(2006)*

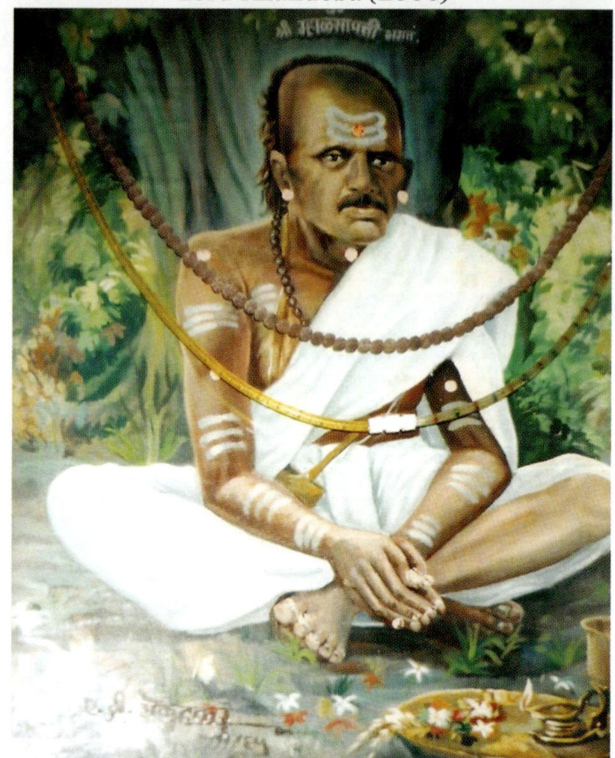

Mahalsapati's painting inside the temple by A. G. Shekadkar *(1965)*

FESTIVALS CELEBRATED IN SHIRDI

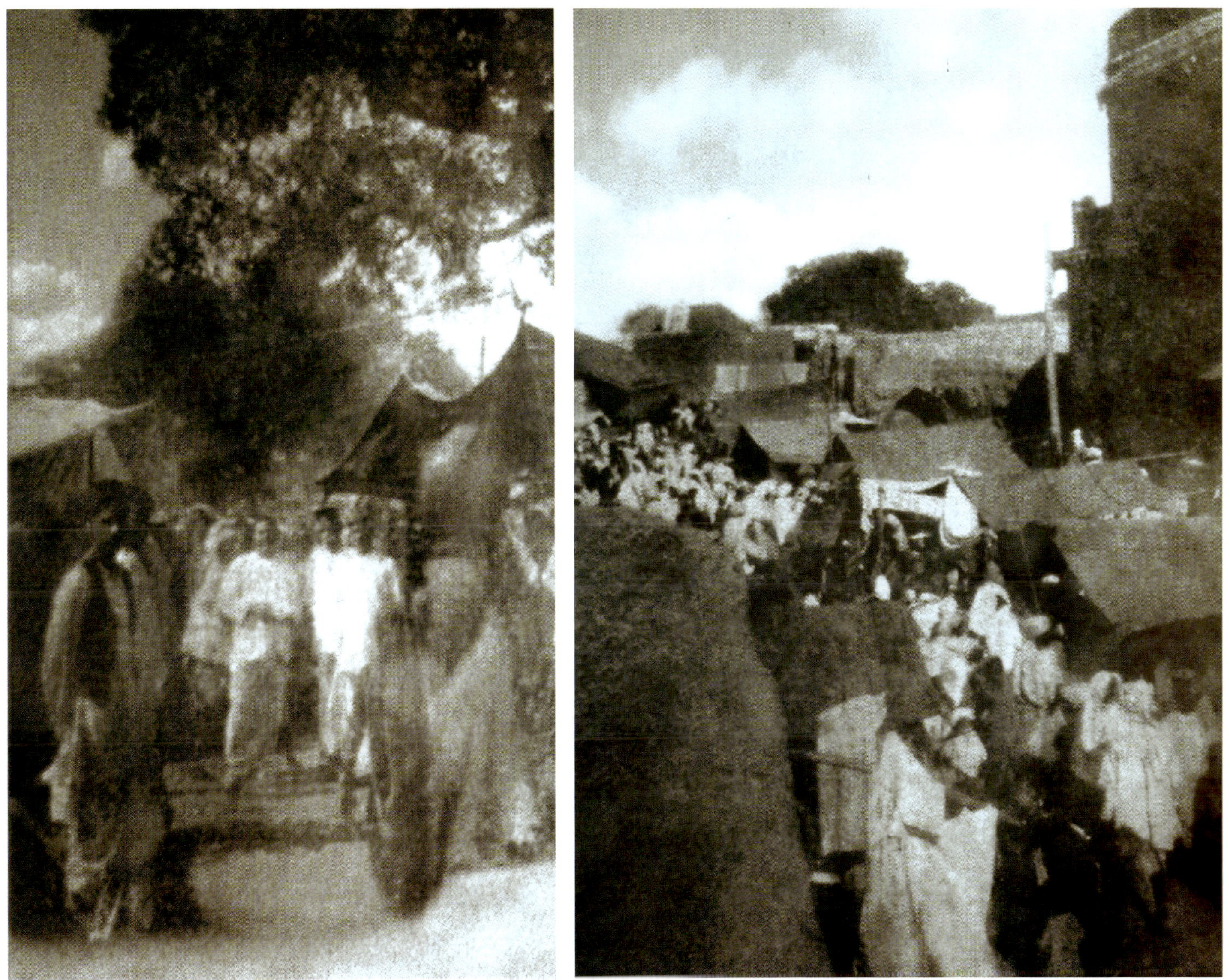

Trade and commerce picked up during Ram Navami and other festivals. People flocked at the tented bazaars that sprung up around these times. *(1940)*

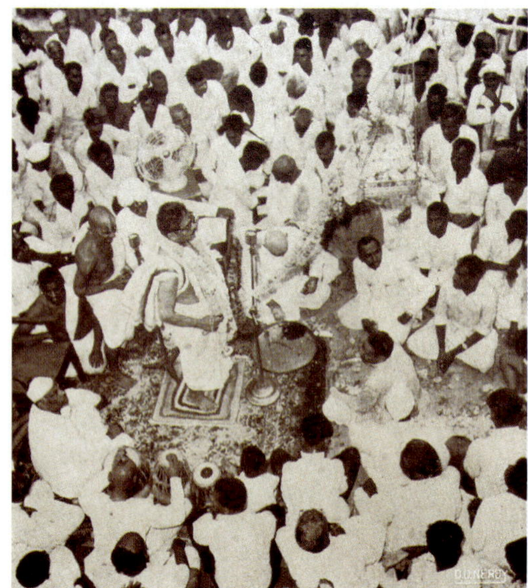

Lord Rama's cradle being pulled with a flower covered string.

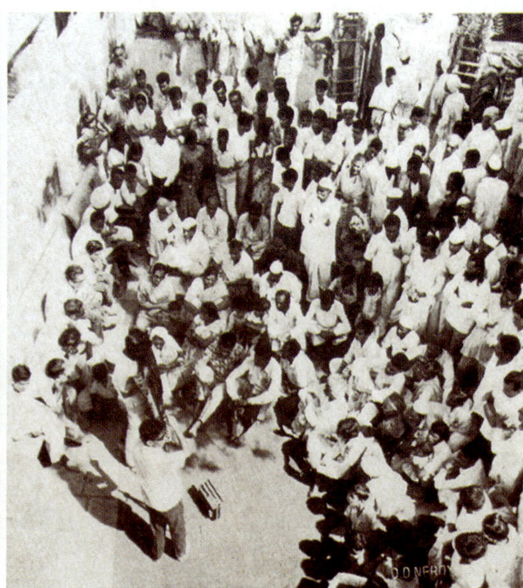

Clothes offered to Baba are auctioned off by Sansthan. The devotees feel gratified to possess these clothes which have hugged Baba's idol. *(1975)*

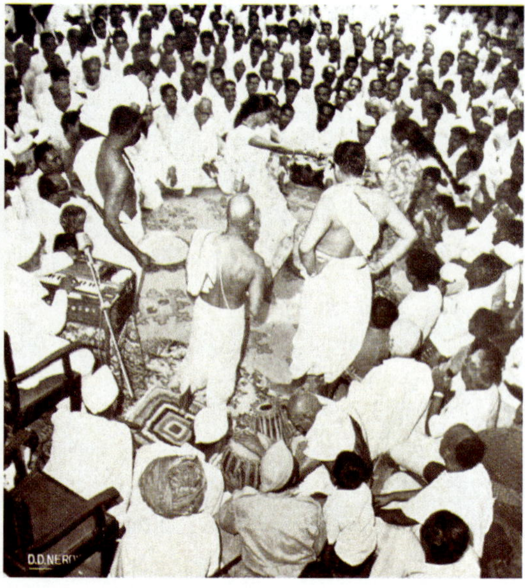

The sport of *'Gopis' – Fugadi*

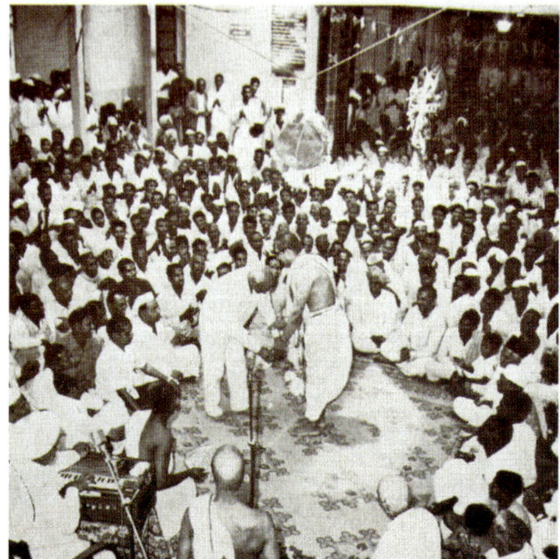

The sport of *'Gopals' – Fugadi (1975)*

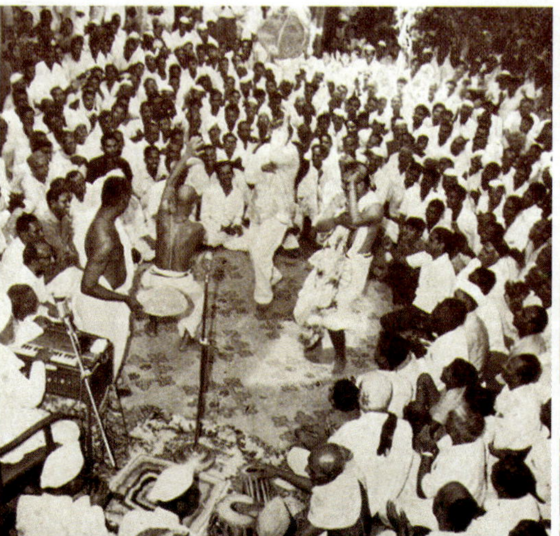

The sport of *'Gopals' – Haath Kohni*

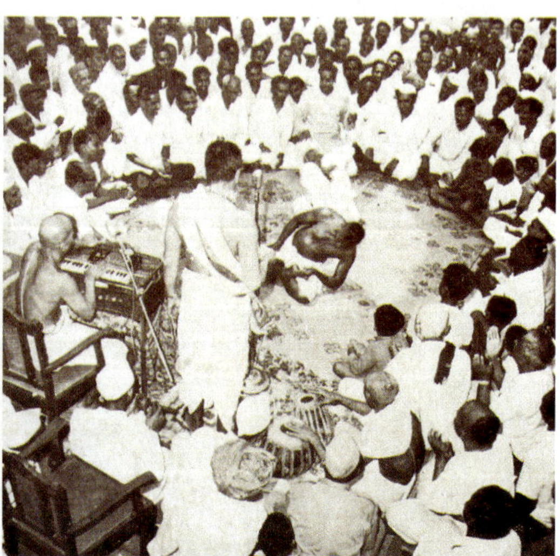

The sport of *'Gopals' – Ranghoda (1975)*

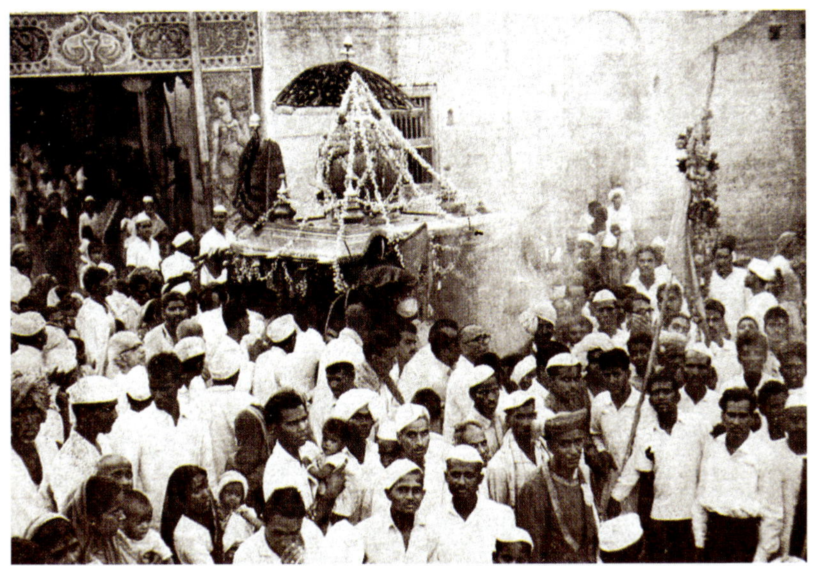

Baba's chariot being towed during Ram Navami

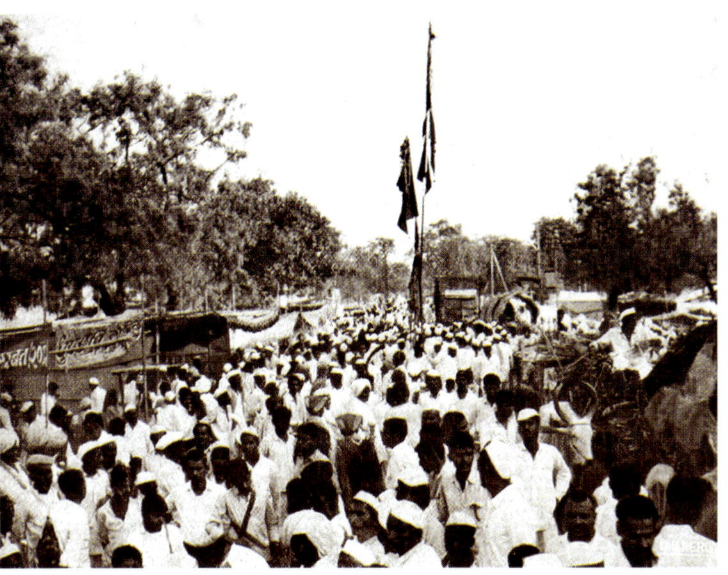

Flag Procession during Ram Navami (1975) *(Chaitra Maas)*

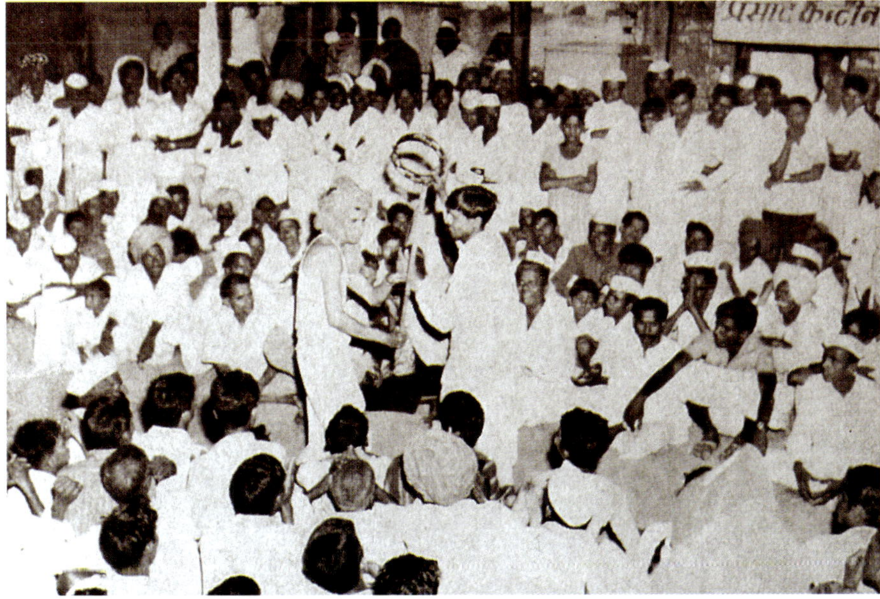

Cultural programmes, *bhajans* and *bharood*.

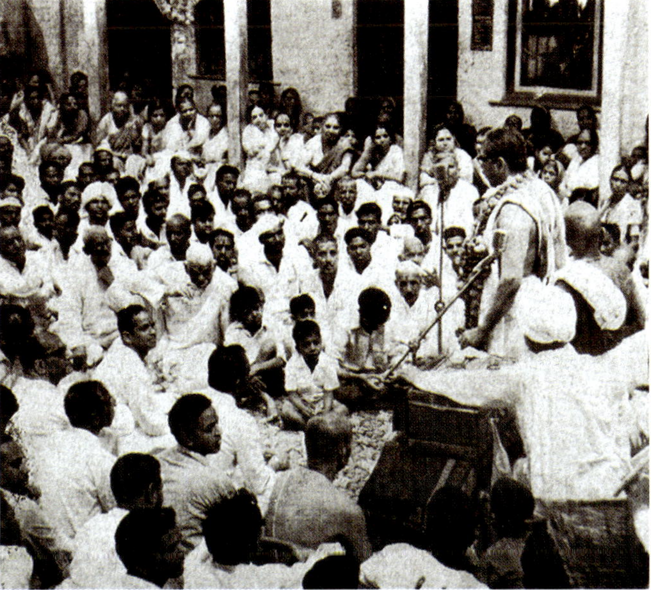

A captivated audience at a Ram Navami *Kirtan*

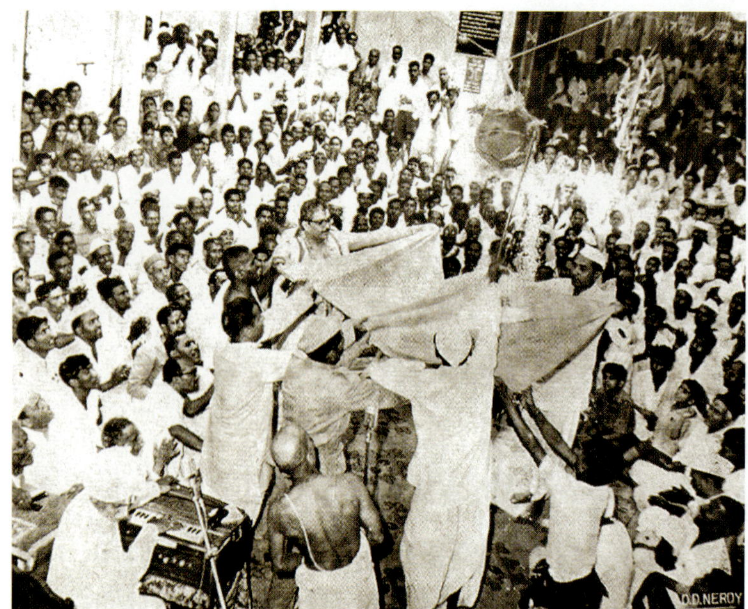

Dahi handi- a cloth spread under the curd filled pot

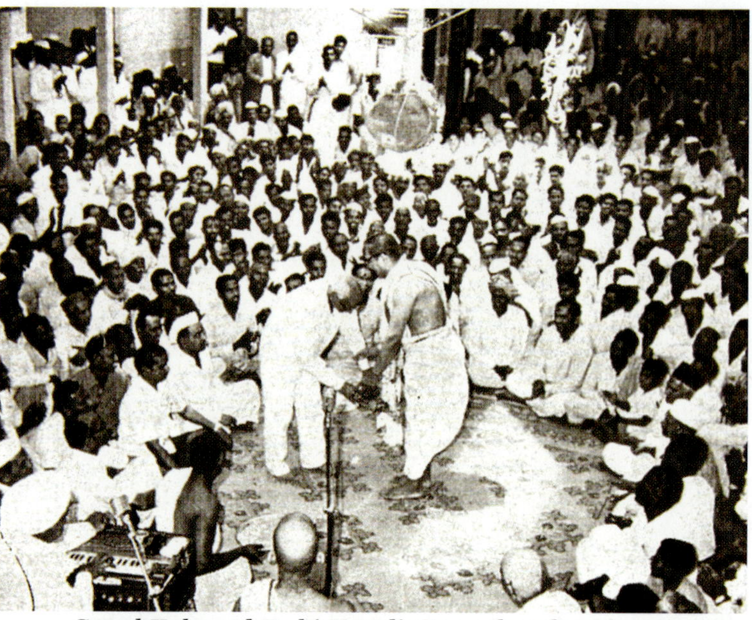

Gopal Kala and *Dahi Handi*, *Seemolanghan (1975)*

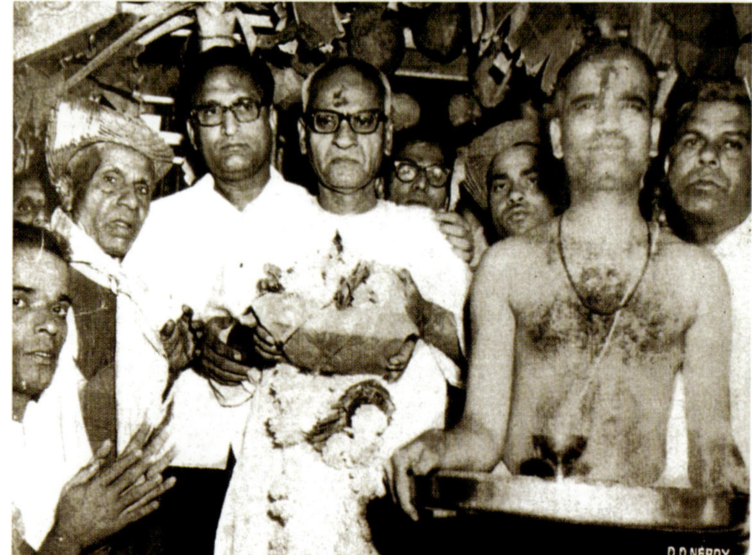

Baba's *Pothi (Shri Sai Satcharitra)* taken out during Ram Navami procession

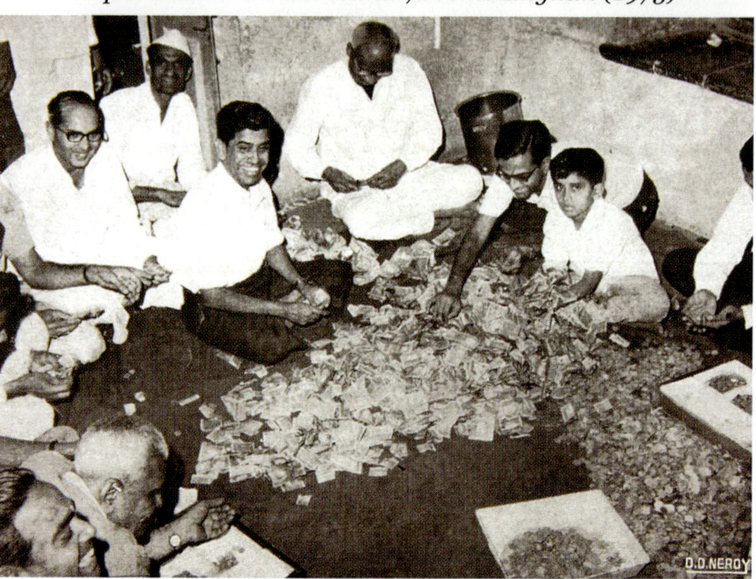

A donation counting exercise in progress

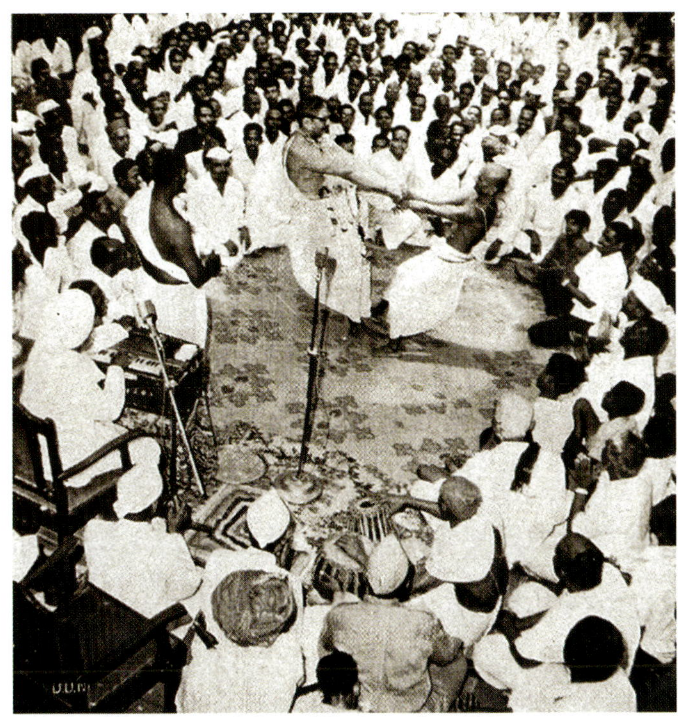

The sport of *fugadi* being played by men

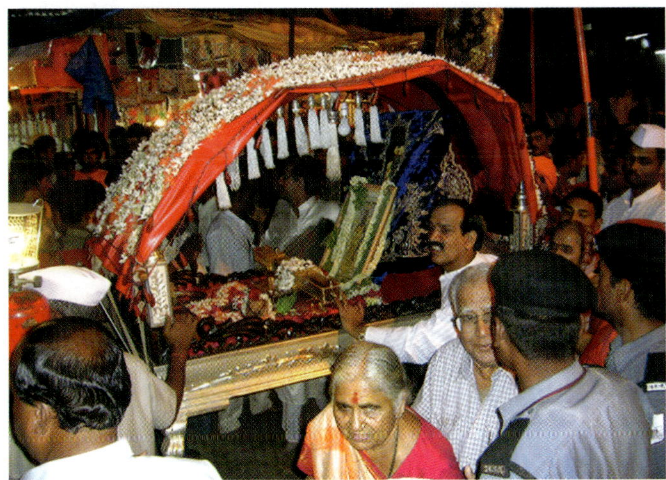

Palki procession (*2011*)

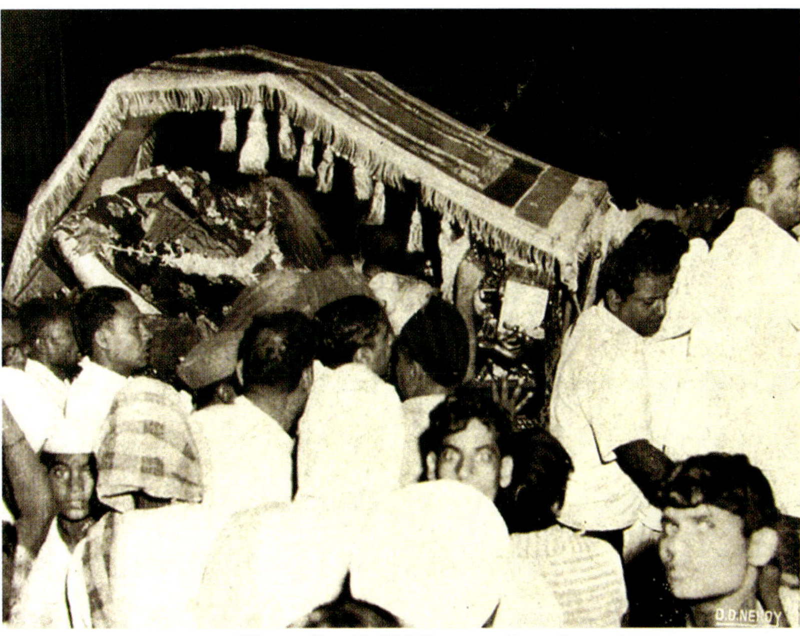

Thursday Palki Procession *(1975)*

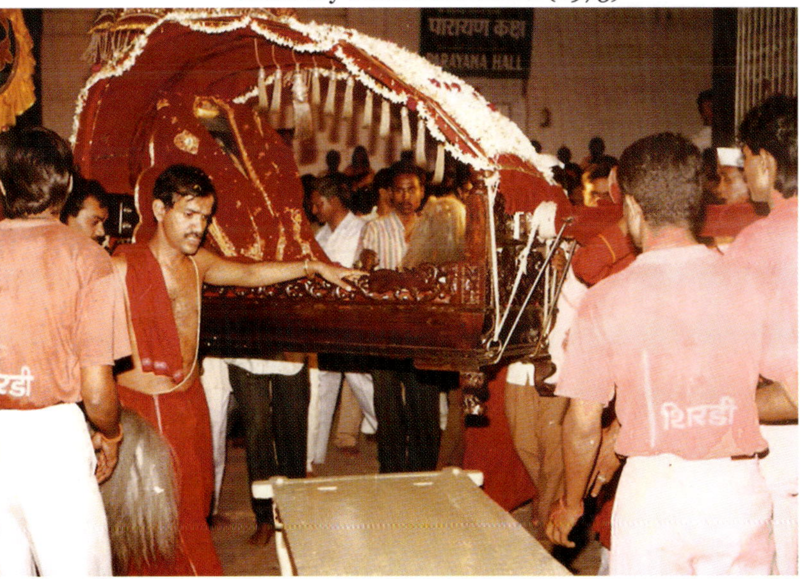

Palki procession on yet another Thursday (*2000*)

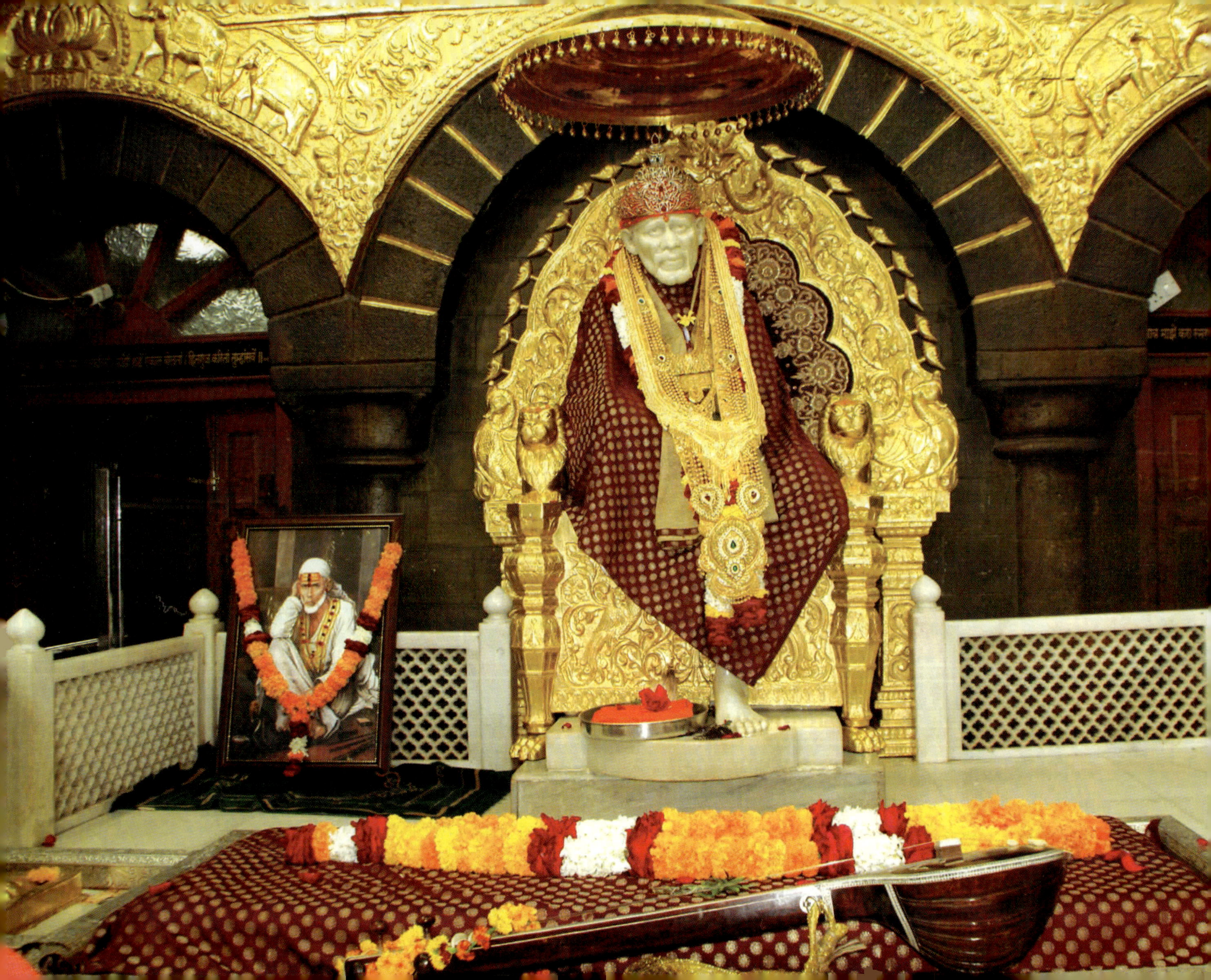

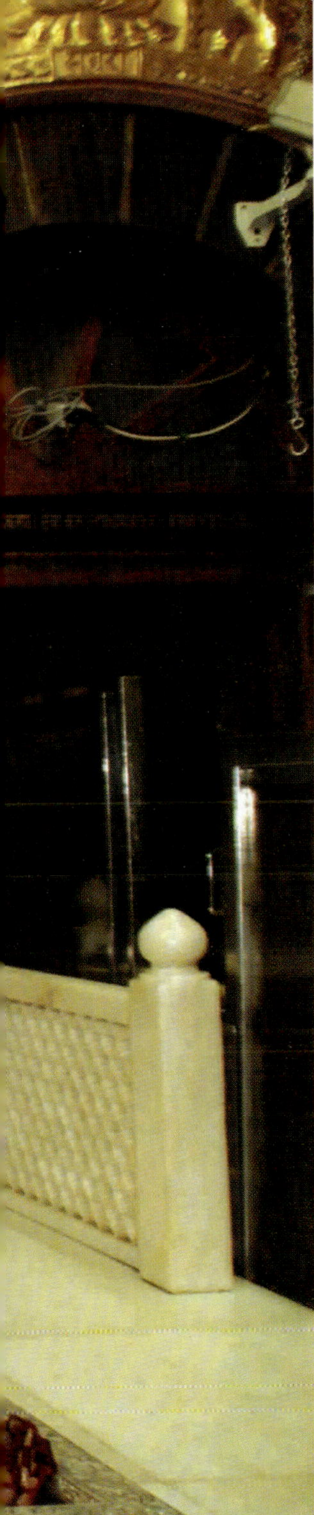

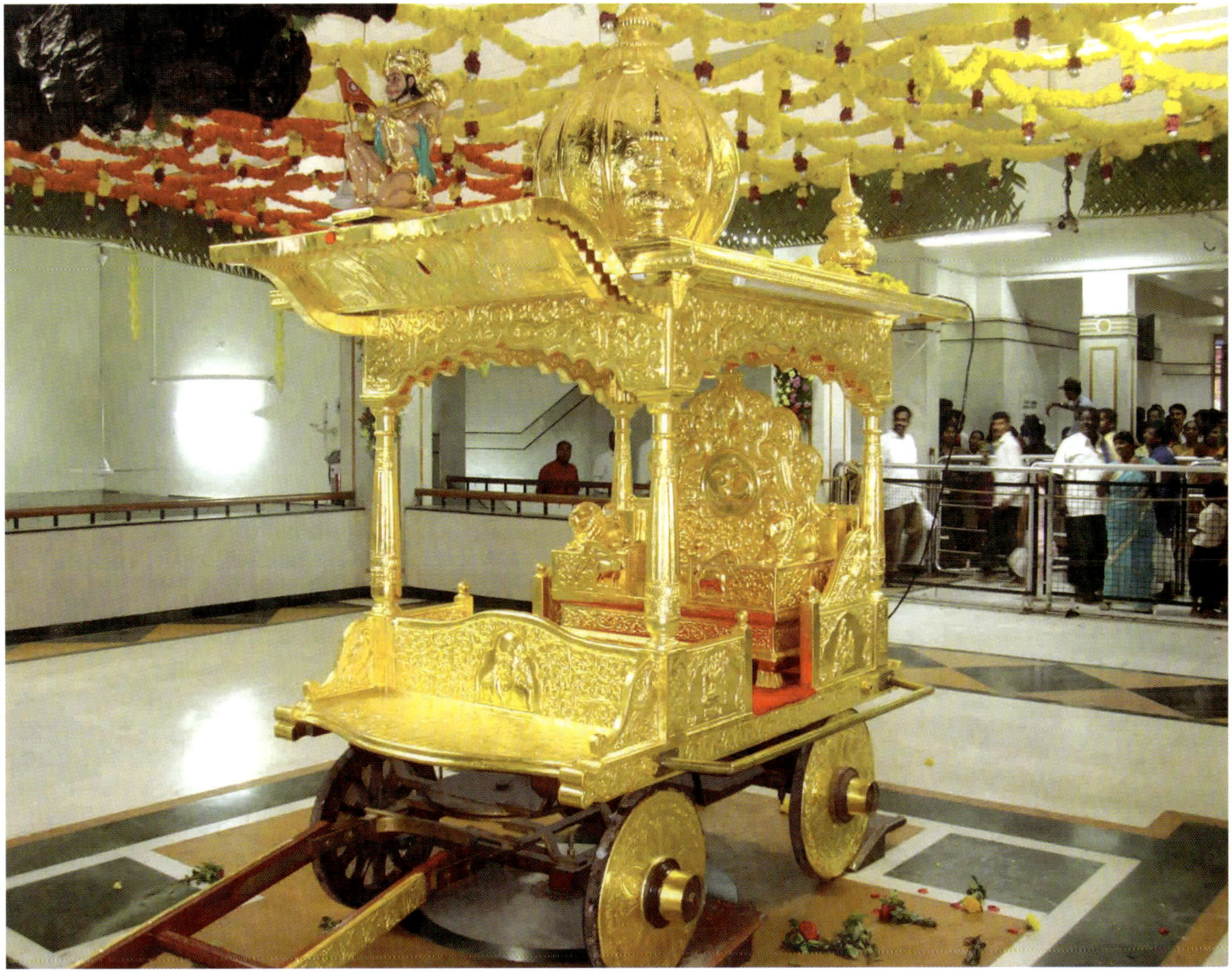

"The Golden Chariot" is a symbolic tribute from the Sansthan and finds a place in the premises of Samadhi Mandir. *(2011)*

← An Indian string musical instrument *Veena* is placed besides the Samadhi on the occasion of Ramnavami. *(2010)*

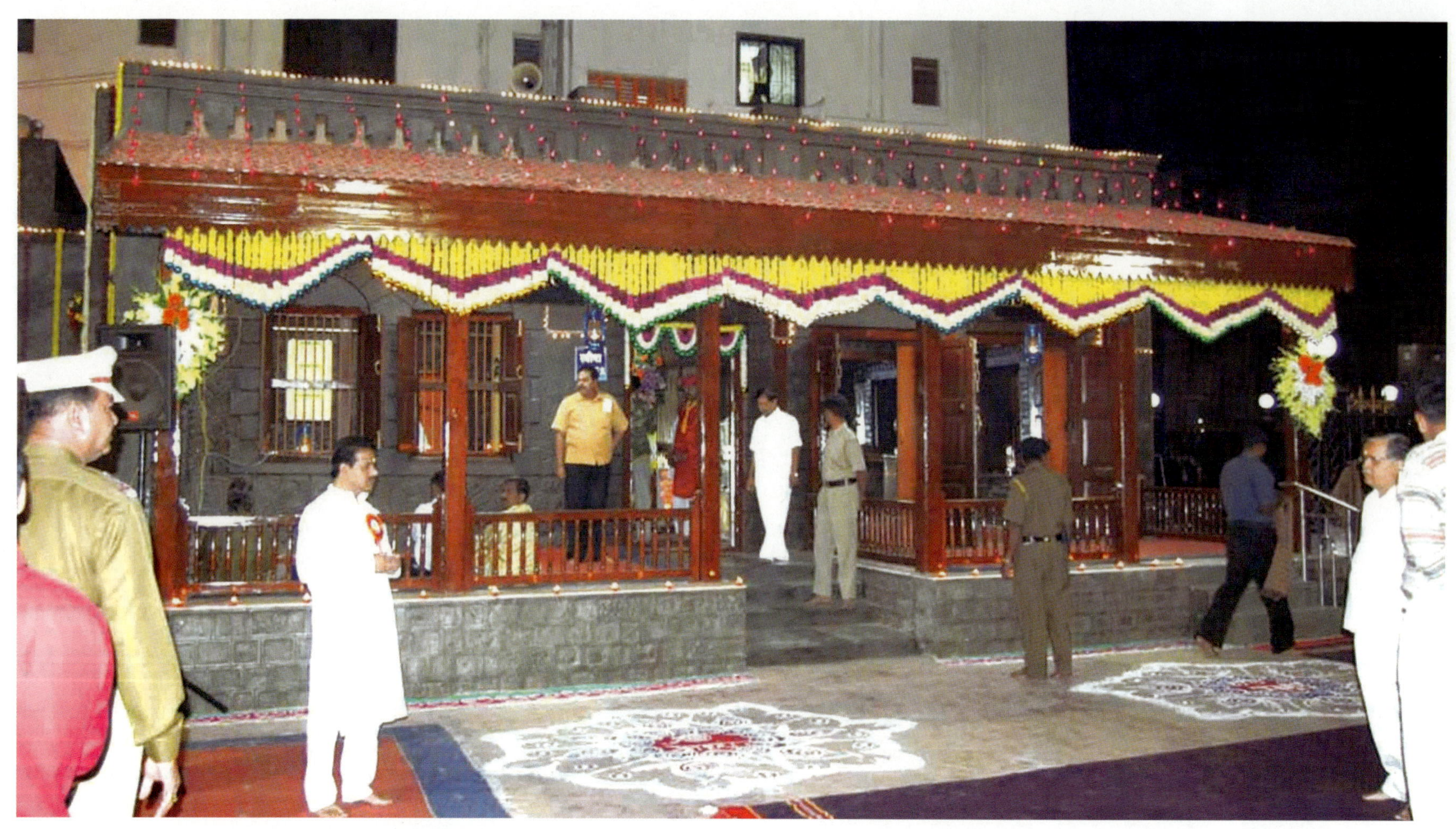

Celebration of 100 years of Chavadi procession on December 10, 2009

Samadhi Mandir standing tall celebrating each and every moment *(2011)*. →

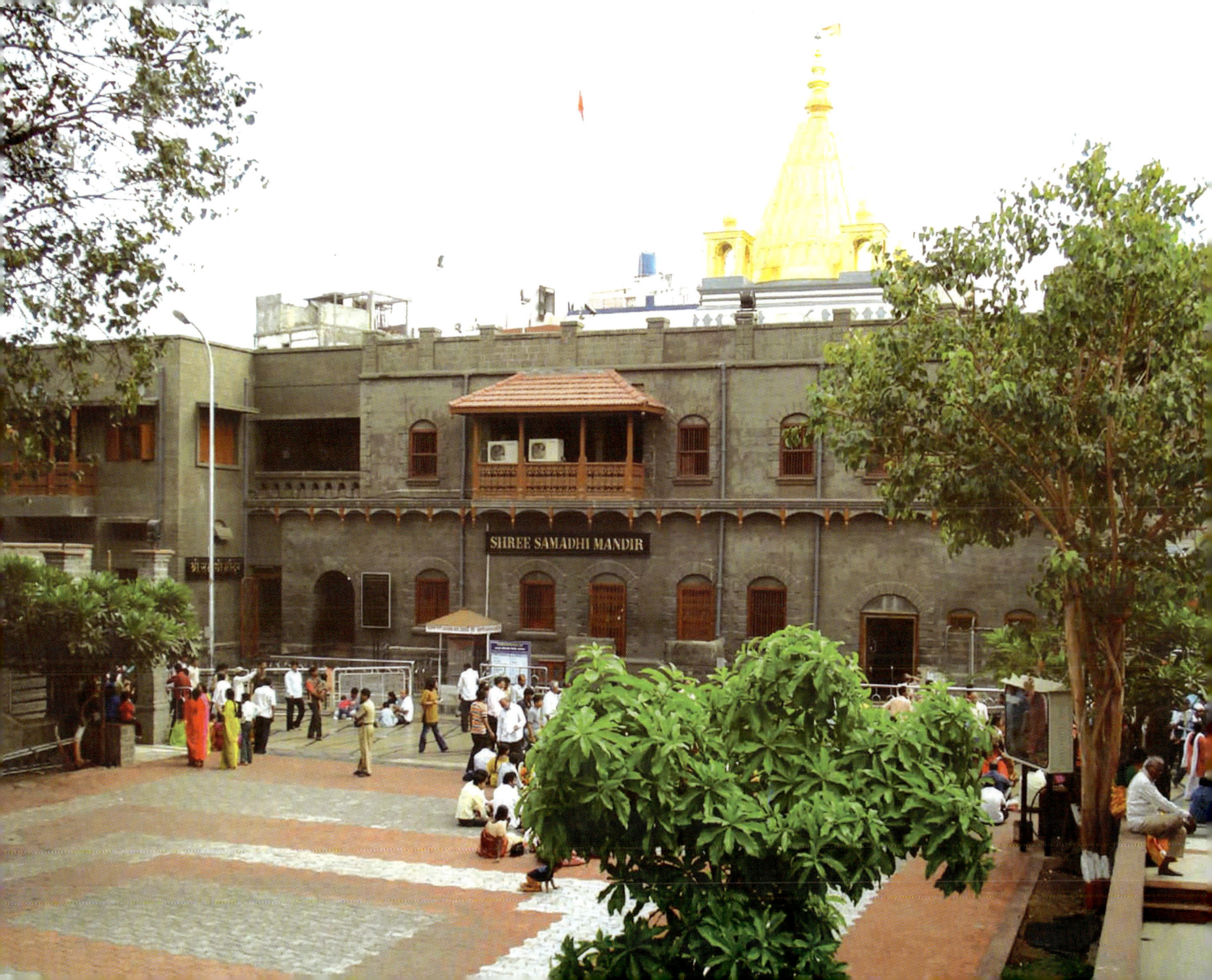
SHREE SAMADHI MANDIR

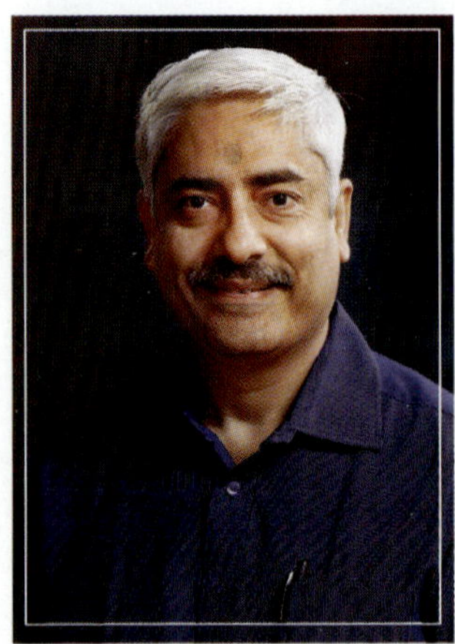

Dr Rabinder Nath Kakarya

Dr Rabinder Nath Kakarya (born 19th March 1967) is a fervent disciple of Sai Baba of Shirdi. An extremely talented scientist, he did his doctorate in Physics from Delhi University. He took up teaching as a profession so that he could channelise all his talents, energy and accomplishments in perpetuating Baba's glory to the uninitiated. His upbringing was rooted in Indian traditions and with Baba's blessings he immersed himself in religious and philosophical pursuits. Apart from teaching he is tirelessly involved in collection, compilation and translation of literary material on the life, teachings and miracles associated with Sai Baba of Shirdi. He has so far translated eighteen books on Baba and has thrown his heart and soul into this nineteenth offering in the form of a photo-essay to the Divine Soul who has immortalised the once dusty hamlet of Shirdi.

A naturally gifted singer, Dr Kakarya has released several CDs and cassettes on Sai Baba. He is a regular fixture on the Thursday bhajan sandhya in the Rohini Sai Temple, New Delhi singing paens to Baba's glory in a soul stirring mellifluous voice. His life is dedicated to the service of Baba and his greatest aspiration and contentment lies in being able to make a positive impact, no matter how inconsequential, to every Saibhakta's life.

Our Books on Shirdi Sai Baba

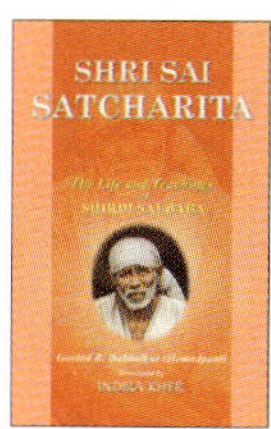

Shri Sai Satcharita
The Life and Teachings of Shirdi Sai Baba
Translated by Indira Kher
ISBN 978 81 207 2211 8
₹ 600(HB)
ISBN 978 81 207 2153 1
₹ 500(PB)

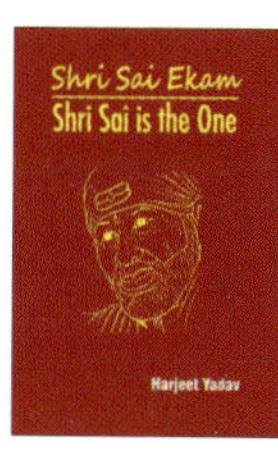

Shri Sai Ekam
Shri Sai is the One
Harjeet Yadava
ISBN 978 93 86245 38 0
₹ 900

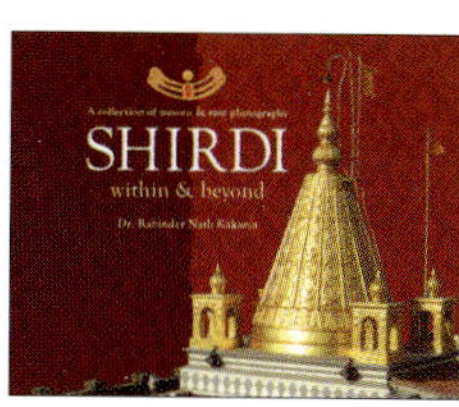

Shirdi : within & beyond
A collection of unseen & rare photographs
Dr. Rabinder Nath Kakarya
ISBN 978 81 207 7806 1 ₹ 750

Shirdi Sai Baba is a household name in India as well as in many parts of the World today. These books offer fascinating glimpses into the life and miracles of Shirdi Sai Baba and other Perfect Masters. These books will provide you with an experience that is bound to transform one's sense of perspective and bring about perceptible and meaningful spiritual growth.

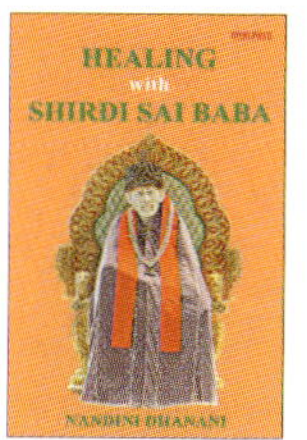

Healing with Shirdi Sai Baba
Nandini Dhanani
ISBN 978 81 947772 7 4
₹ 300

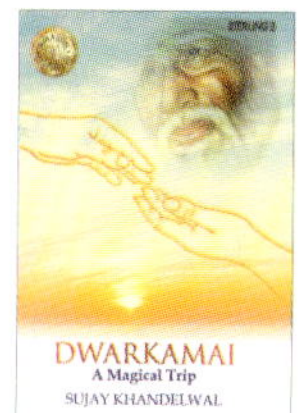

DWARKAMAI: A Magical Trip
Sujay Khandelwal
ISBN 978 93 93853 04 2
₹ 199

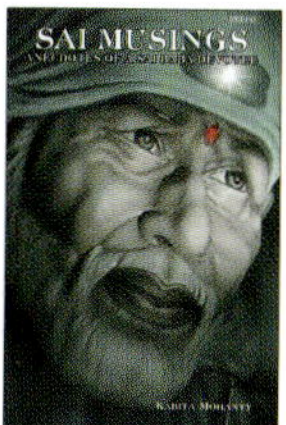

Sai Musings
Kabita Mohanty
ISBN 978 81 950824 5 2
₹ 300

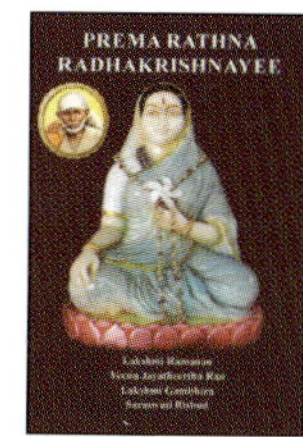

Prema Rathna Radhakrishnayee
Lakshmi Ramanan, Veena Jayatheertha Rao, Lakshmi Gambhira, Saraswati Risbud
ISBN 978 81 947772 0 5
₹ 100

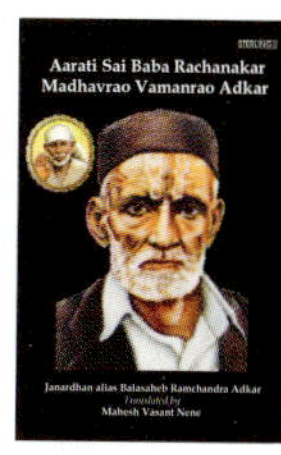

Aarati Sai Baba Rachanakar Madhavrao Vamanrao Adkar
Janardhan alias Balasaheb Ramchandra Adkar Translated by Mahesh Vasant Nene
ISBN 978 81 954046 1 2
₹ 100

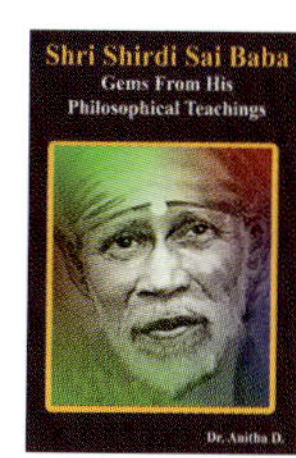

Shri Shirdi Saibaba:
Gems From His Philosophical Teachings
Dr. Anitha D.
ISBN 978 81 944007 3 8 ₹300

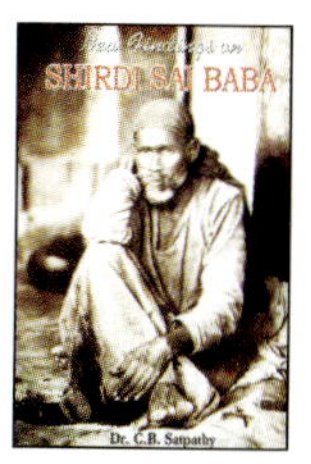

New Findings on Shirdi Sai Baba
Chandra Bhanu Satpathy
ISBN 978 93 86245 52 6
₹ 300

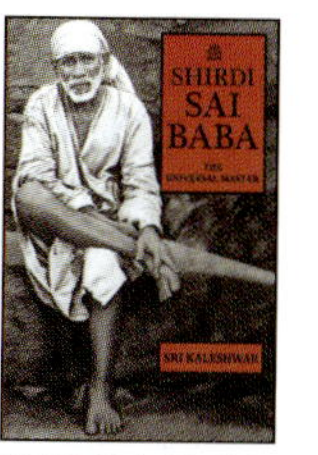

Shirdi Sai Baba: The Universal Master
Sri Kaleshwar
ISBN 978 81 207 9664 5
₹ 150

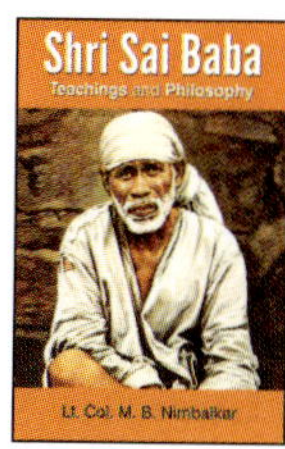

Shri Sai Baba Teachings & Philosophy
Lt Col M B Nimbalkar
ISBN 978 81 207 2364 1
₹ 150

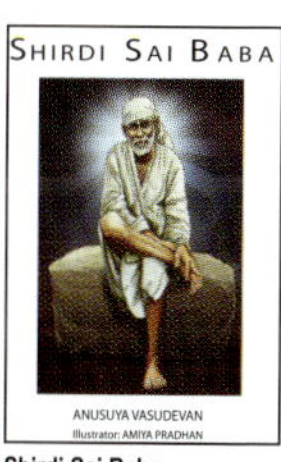

Shirdi Sai Baba
Anusuya Vasudevan
ISBN 978 93 86245 16 8
(64 pages plates)
₹ 200

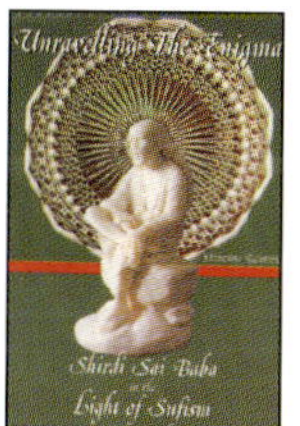

Unravelling the Enigma: Shirdi Sai Baba in the light of Sufism
Marianne Warren
ISBN 978 81 207 2147 0
₹ 400

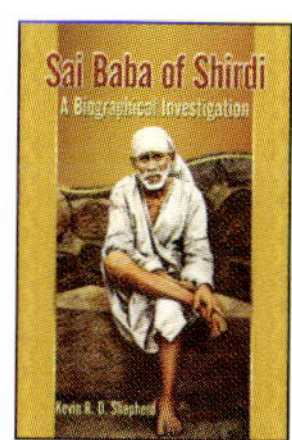

Sai Baba of Shirdi:
A Biographical Investigation
Kevin R. D. Shepherd
ISBN 978 81 207 9901 1
₹ 450

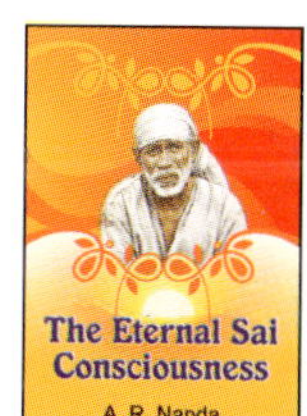
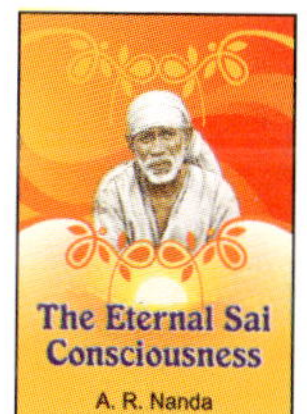

The Eternal Sai Consciousness
A. R. Nanda
ISBN 978 81 207 9043 8
₹ 200

BABA:
The Devotees' Questions
Dr. C. B. Satpathy
ISBN 978 81 207 8966 1
₹ 150

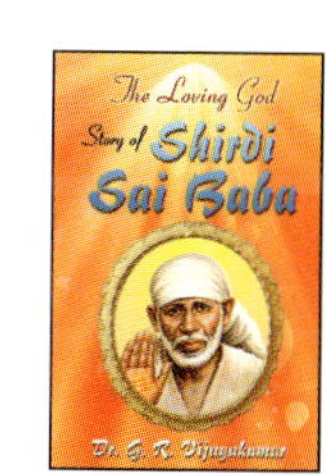

The Loving God:
Story of Shirdi Sai Baba
Dr. G. R. Vijayakumar
ISBN 978 81 207 8079 8
₹ 200

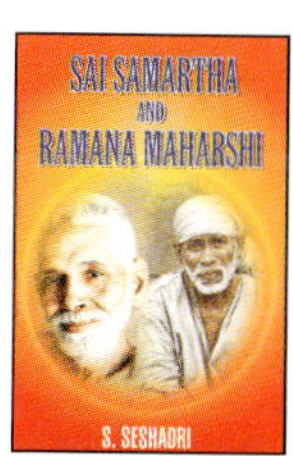

Sai Samartha and Ramana Maharshi
S. Seshadri
ISBN 978 81 207 8986 9
₹150

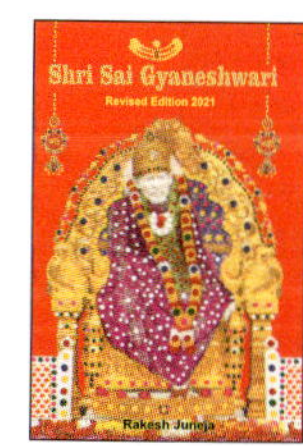

Shri Sai Gyaneshwari
Rakesh Juneja
ISBN 978 81 950824 7 6
₹300

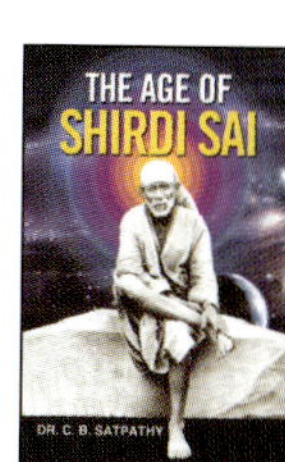

The Age of Shirdi Sai
Dr. C. B. Satpathy
ISBN 978 81 207 8700 1
₹ 300

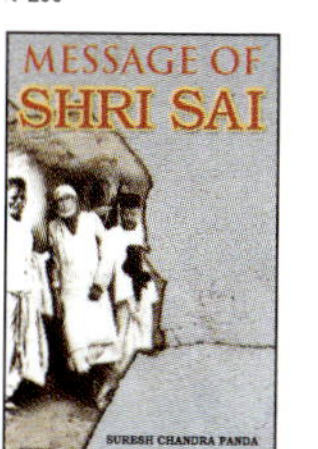

Message of Shri Sai
Suresh Chandra Panda
ISBN 978 81 207 9512 9
₹ 150

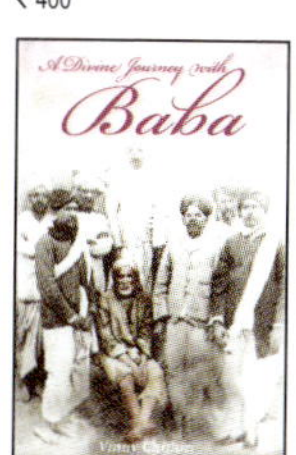

A Divine Journey with Baba
Vinny Chitluri
ISBN 978 81 207 9859 5
₹ 300

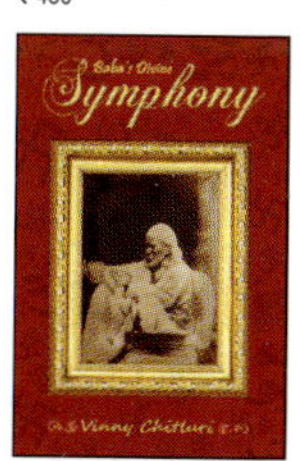

Baba's Divine Symphony
Vinny Chitluri
ISBN 978 81 207 8485 7
₹ 300

Baba's Rinanubandh
Leelas during His Sojourn in Shirdi
Compiled by Vinny Chitluri
ISBN 978 81 207 3403 6
₹ 300

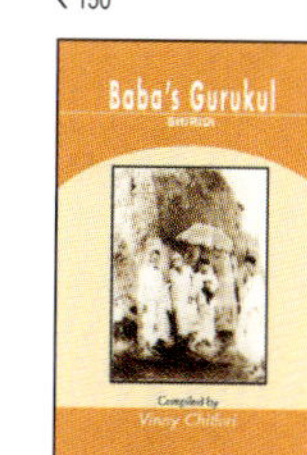

Baba's Gurukul Shirdi
Vinny Chitluri
ISBN 978 81 207 4770 8
₹ 250

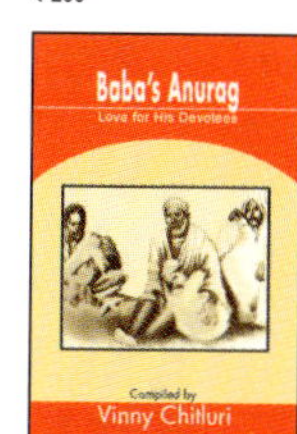

Baba's Anurag
Love for His Devotees
Compiled by Vinny Chitluri
ISBN 978 81 207 5447 8
₹ 200

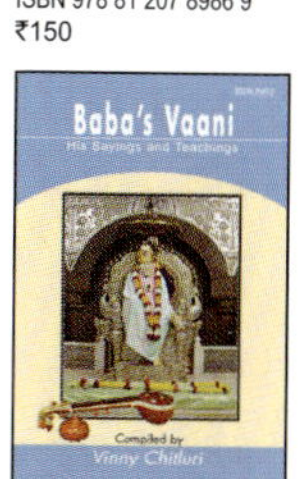

Baba's Vaani: His Sayings and Teachings
Compiled by Vinny Chitluri
ISBN 978 81 207 3859 1
₹ 250

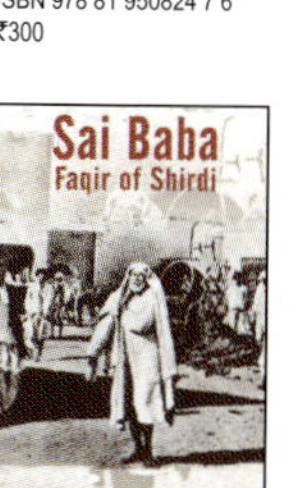

Sai Baba: Faqir of Shirdi
Kevin R.D. Shepherd
ISBN 978 93 86245 06 9
₹ 350

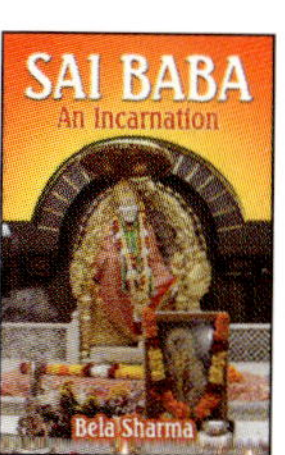

Sai Baba an Incarnation
Bela Sharma
ISBN 978 81 207 8833 6
₹ 200

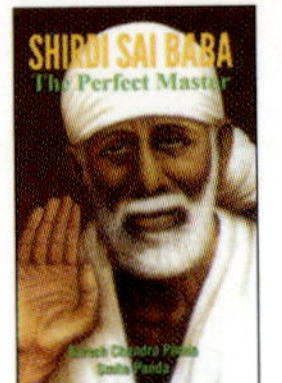

Shirdi Sai Baba: The Perfect Master
Suresh Chandra Panda & Smita Panda
ISBN 978 81 207 8113 9
₹ 200

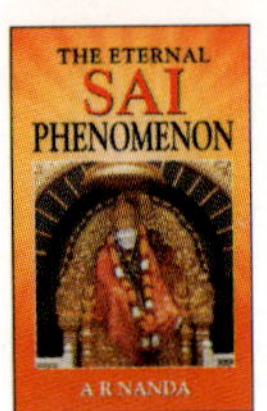

The Eternal Sai Phenomenon
A R Nanda
ISBN 978 81 207 6086 8
₹ 200

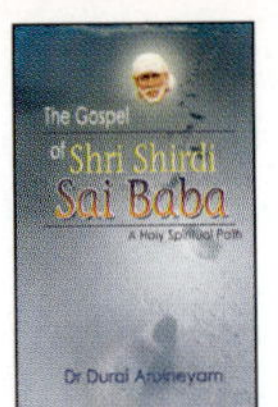

The Gospel of Shri Shirdi Sai Baba: A Holy Spiritual Path
Dr Durai Arulneyam
ISBN 978 81 207 3997 0
₹ 150

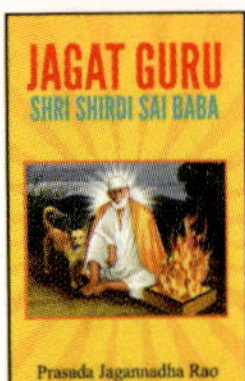

Jagat Guru: Shri Shirdi Sai Baba
Prasada Jagannadha Rao
ISBN 978 81 207 8175 7
₹ 100

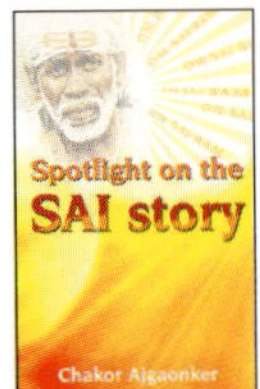

Spotlight on the Sai Story
Chakor Ajgaonker
ISBN 978 81 207 4399 1
₹ 200

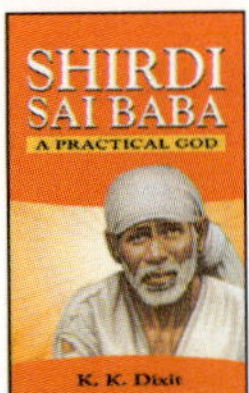

Shirdi Sai Baba A Practical God
K. K. Dixit
ISBN 978 81 207 5918 3
₹ 75

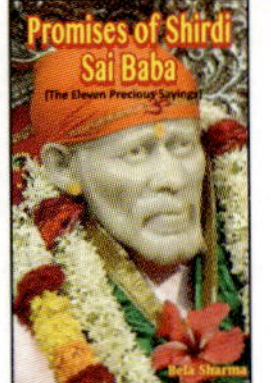

Promises of Shirdi Sai Baba (The Eleven Precious Sayings)
Bela Sharma
ISBN 978 93 85913 98 3
₹ 75

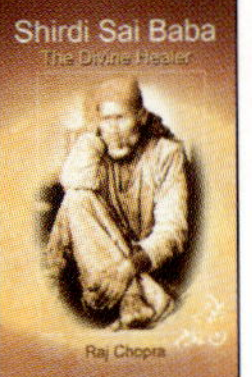

Shirdi Sai Baba The Divine Healer
Raj Chopra
ISBN 978 81 207 4766 1
₹ 150

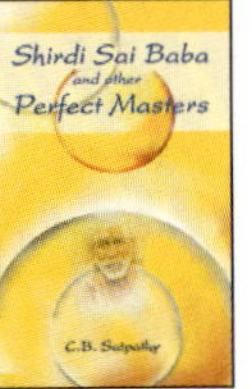

Shirdi Sai Baba and other Perfect Masters
C B Satpathy
ISBN 978 81 207 2384 9
₹ 200

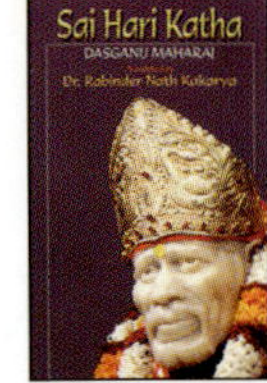

Sai Hari Katha
Dasganu Maharaj Translated by *Dr. Rabinder Nath Kakarya*
ISBN 978 81 207 3324 4
₹ 150

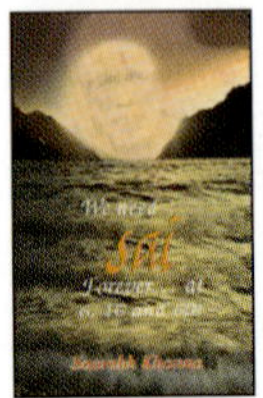

We need Sai forever... at 6, 16 and 60!
Saurabh Khanna
ISBN 978 93 86245 15 1
₹ 190

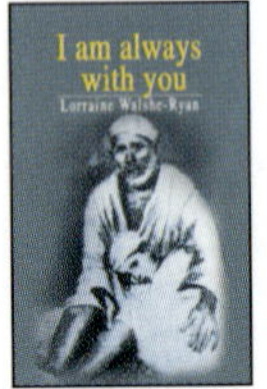

I am always with you
Lorraine Walshe-Ryan
ISBN 978 81 207 3192 9
₹ 150

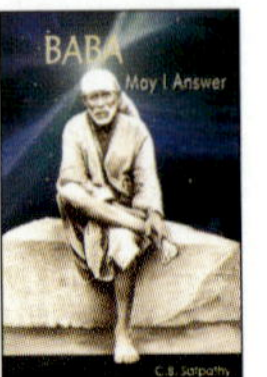

BABA- May I Answer
C.B. Satpathy
ISBN 978 81 207 4594 0
₹ 150

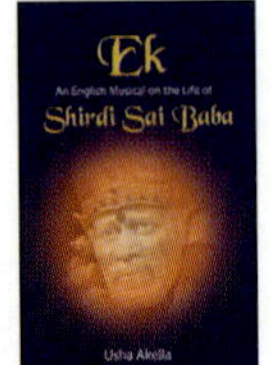

Ek: An English Musical on the Life of Shirdi Sai Baba
Usha Akella
ISBN 978 81 207 6842 0
₹ 75

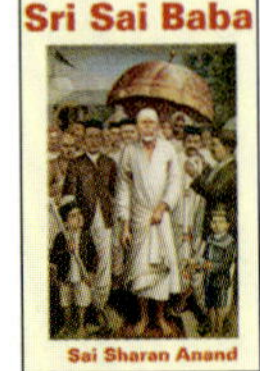

Sri Sai Baba
Sai Sharan Anand
Translated by V.B Kher
ISBN 978 81 207 1950 7
₹ 200

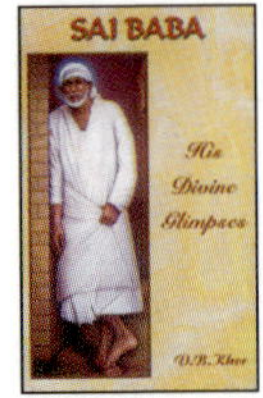

Sai Baba: His Divine Glimpses
V B Kher
ISBN 978 81 207 2291 0
₹ 95

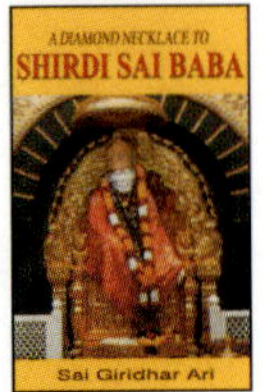

A Diamond Necklace To: Shirdi Sai Baba
Giridhar Ari
ISBN 978 81 207 5868 1
₹ 200

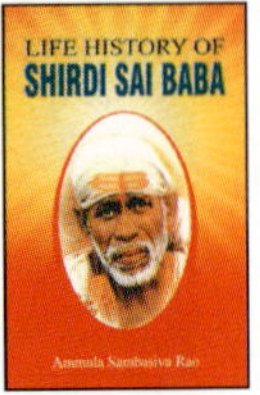

Life History of Shirdi Sai Baba
Ammula Sambasiva Rao
ISBN 978 81 207 7722 4
₹ 250

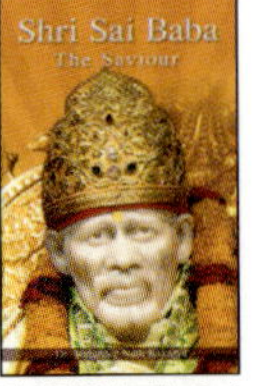

Shri Sai Baba- The Saviour
Dr. Rabinder Nath Kakarya
ISBN 978 81 207 4701 2
₹ 100

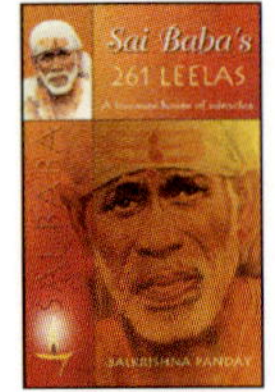

Sai Baba's 261 Leelas
Balkrishna Panday
ISBN 978 81 207 2727 4
₹ 200

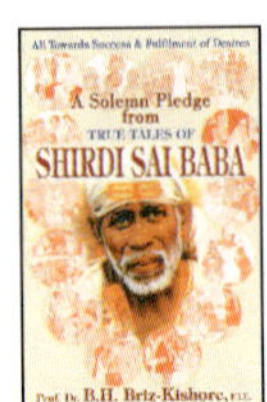

A Solemn Pledge from True Tales of Shirdi Sai Baba
Dr B H Briz-Kishore
ISBN 978 81 207 2240 8
₹ 95

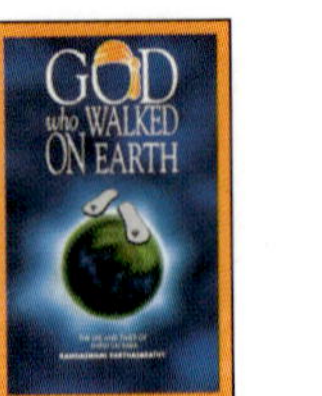

God Who Walked on Earth:
The Life & Times of Shirdi Sai Baba
Rangaswami Parthasarathy
ISBN 978 81 207 1809 8
₹ 225

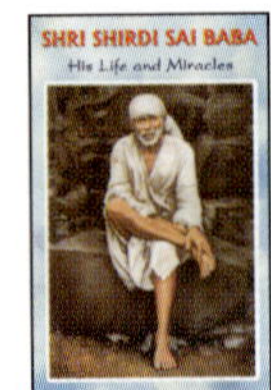

Shri Shirdi Sai Baba: His Life and Miracles
ISBN 978 81 207 2877 6
₹ 35

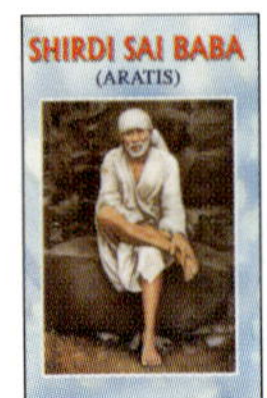

Shirdi Sai Baba Aratis
ISBN 978 81 207 8456 7 (English)
₹ 10

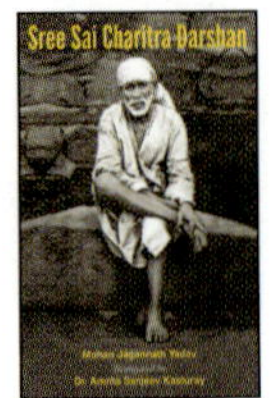

Sree Sai Charitra Darshan
Mohan Jagannath Yadav
ISBN 978 81 207 8346 1
₹ 225

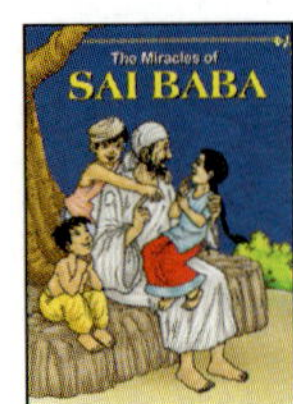

The Miracles of Sai Baba
ISBN 978 81 207 5433 1 (HB)
₹ 300

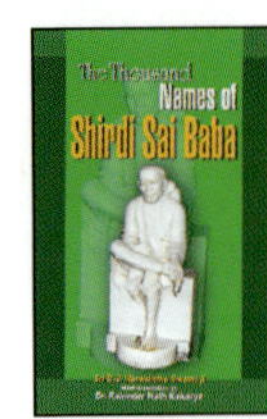

The Thousand Names of Shirdi Sai Baba
Sri B.V. Narasimha Swami Ji
Hindi translation by
Dr. Rabinder Nath Kakarya
ISBN 978 81 207 3738 9 ₹ 75

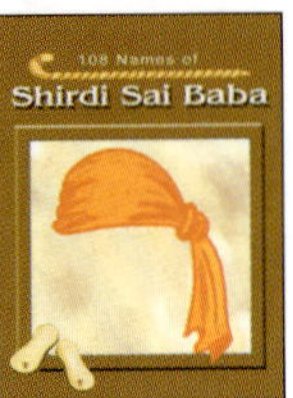

108 Names of Shirdi Sai Baba
ISBN 978 81 207 3074 8
₹ 50

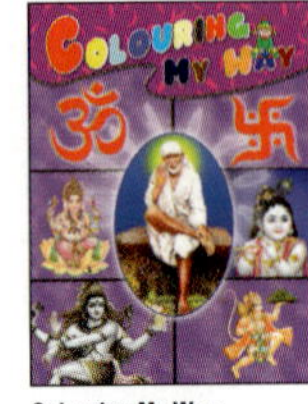

Colouring My Way
Sterling studio
978 81 207 9790 1
₹ 50

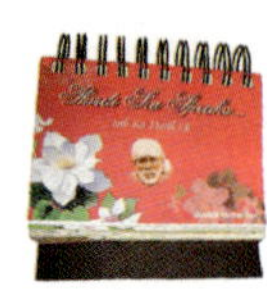

Shirdi Sai Speaks... Sab Ka Malik Ek
Quotes for the Day
ISBN 978 81 207 3101 1
₹ 200

THE THOUSAND NAMES OF GOD

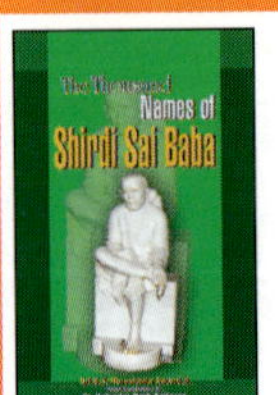

Shirdi Sai Baba
Dr.Rabinder Nath Kakarya
978 81 207 3738 9
₹ 75

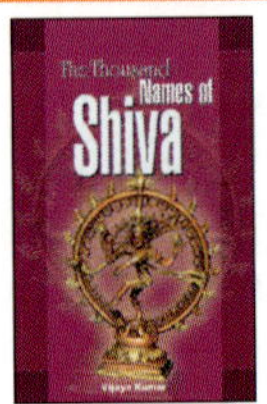

Shiva
Vijaya Kumar
978 81 207 3008 3
₹ 75

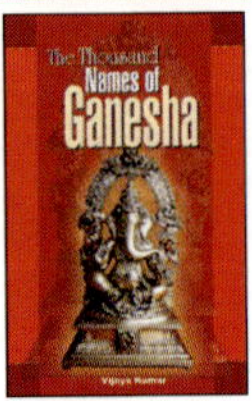

Ganesha
Vijaya Kumar
978 81 207 3007 6
₹ 75

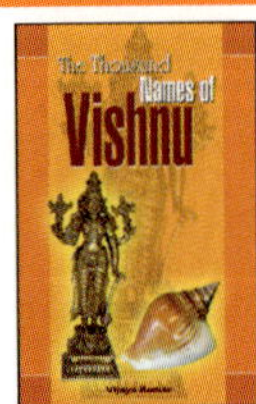

Vishnu
Vijaya Kumar
978 81 207 3009 0
₹ 75

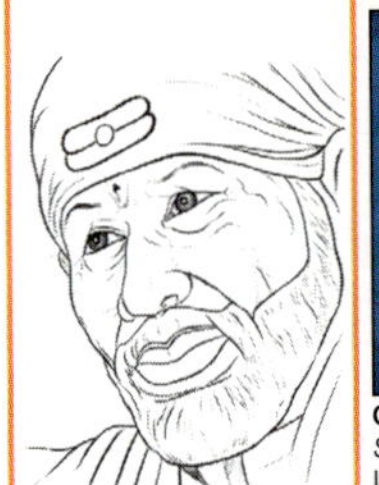

DIVINE GURUS

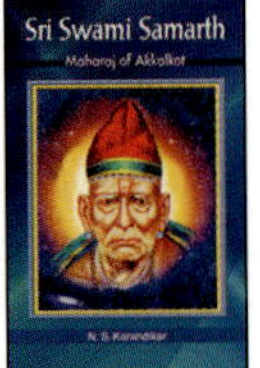

Guru Charitra
Shree Swami Samarth
ISBN 978 81 207 3348 0
₹ 300

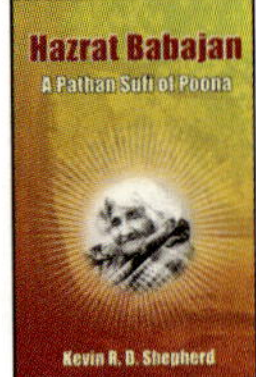

Sri Swami Samarth Maharaj of Akkalkot
N.S. Karandikar
ISBN 978 81 207 3445 6
₹ 250

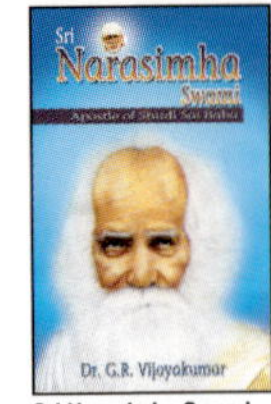

Hazrat Babajan:
A Pathan Sufi of Poona
Kevin R. D. Shepherd
ISBN 978 81 207 8698 1
₹ 200

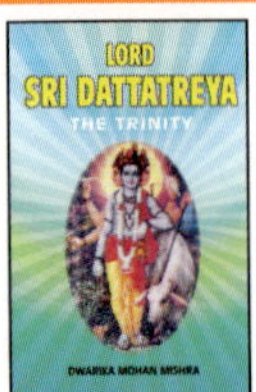

Sri Narasimha Swami Apostle of Shirdi Sai Baba
Dr. G.R. Vijayakumar
ISBN 978 81 207 4432 5
₹ 90

Lord Sri Dattatreya The Trinity
Dwarika Mohan Mishra
ISBN 978 81 207 5417 1
₹ 200

For Online order & detailed Catalogue visit our website

श्री शिरडी साई बाबा

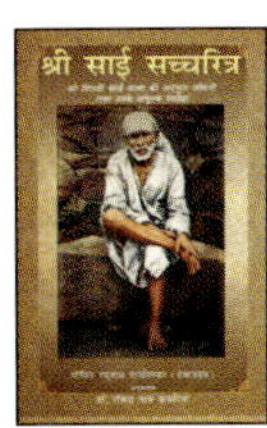
श्री साई सच्चरित्र
श्री शिरडी साई बाबा की अद्भुत जीवनी तथा उनके अमूल्य उपदेश (हेमाडपंत)
गोविंद रघुनाथ दाभोलकर
978 81 207 2500 3
₹ 400 (HB)

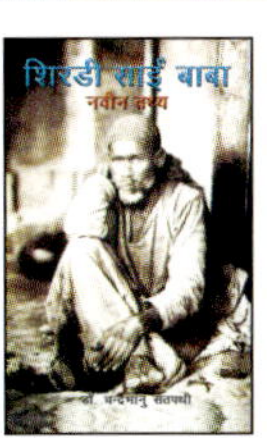
शिरडी साई बाबा
नवीन तथ्य
चन्द्रभानु सतपथी
978 93 86245 63 2
₹ 300

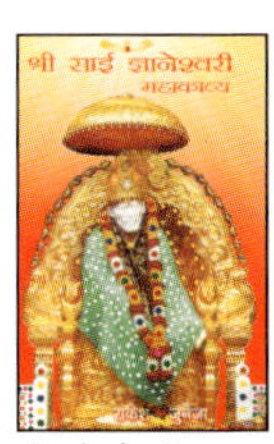
श्री साई ज्ञानेश्वरी-महाकाव्य
राकेश जुनेजा
978 93 86245 17 5
₹ 250

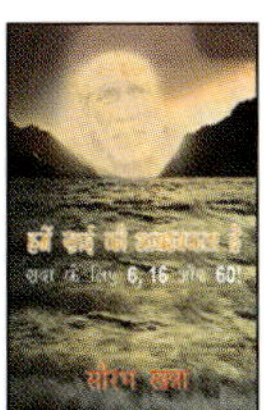
हमें साई की आवश्यकता है सदा के लिए 6, 16 और 60!
सौरभ खन्ना
978 93 86245 21 2
₹ 125

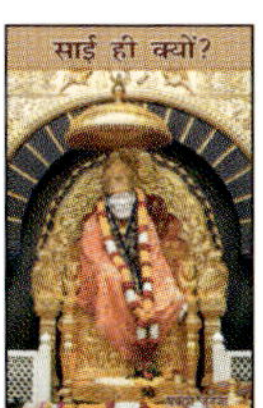
साई ही क्यों?
राकेश जुनेजा
978 81 207 9610 2
₹ 200

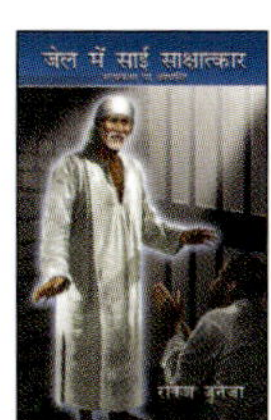
जेल में साई साक्षात्कार
राकेश जुनेजा
978 81 207 9507 5
₹ 150

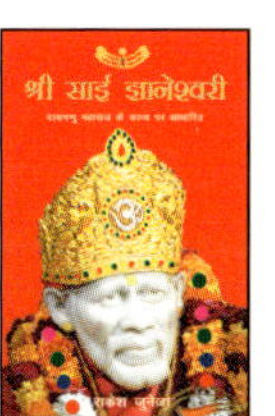
श्री साई ज्ञानेश्वरी
राकेश जुनेजा
978 81 207 9491 7
₹ 250

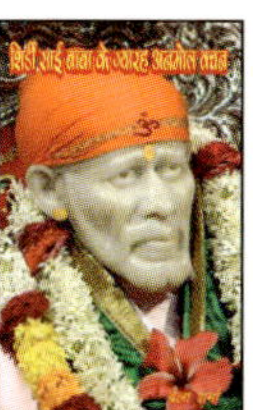
शिर्डी साई बाबा के ग्यारह अनमोल वचन
बेला शर्मा
978 93 85913 97 6
₹ 75

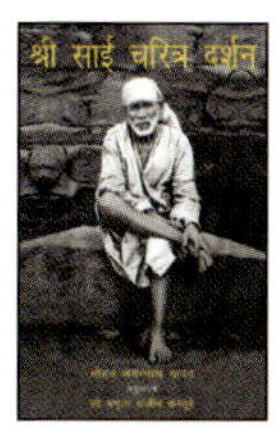
श्री साई चरित्र दर्शन
मोहन जगन्नाथ यादव
978 81 207 8350 8
₹ 200

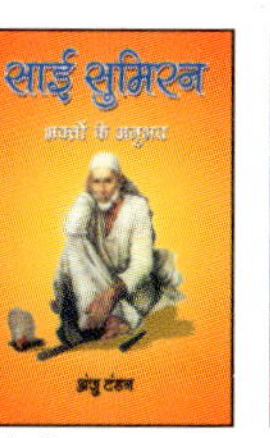
साई सुमिरन
अंजु टंडन
978 81 207 8706 3
₹ 100

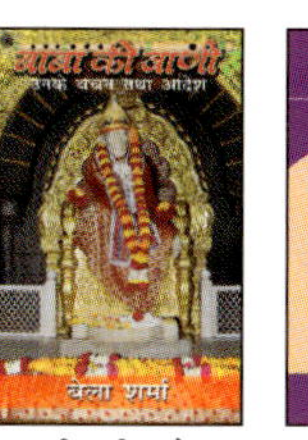
बाबा की वाणी-उनके वचन तथा आदेश
बेला शर्मा
978 81 207 4745 6
₹ 100

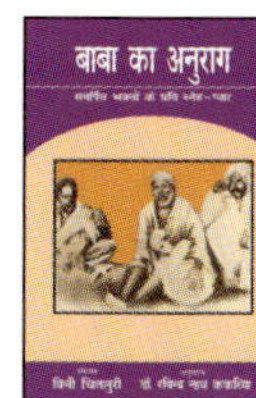
बाबा का अनुराग
विनी चितलुरी
978 81 207 6699 0
₹ 125

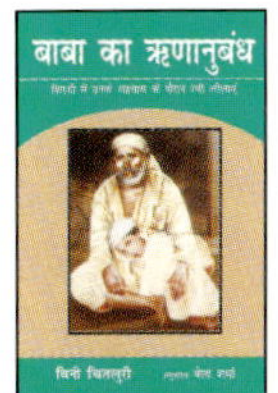
बाबा का ऋणानुबंध
विनी चितलुरी
978 81 207 5998 5
₹ 150

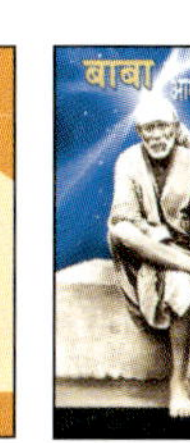
बाबा का गुरूकुल-शिरडी
विनी चितलुरी
978 81 207 6698 3
₹ 150

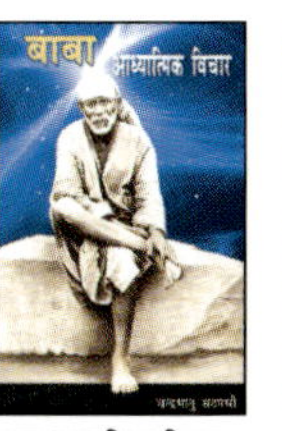
बाबा-आध्यात्मिक विचार
चन्द्रभानु सतपथी
978 81 207 4627 5
₹ 175

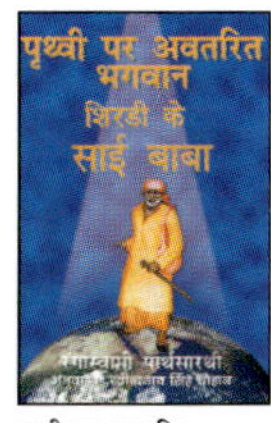
पृथ्वी पर अवतरित भगवान शिरडी के साई बाबा
रंगास्वामी पार्थसारथी
978 81 207 2101 2
₹ 200

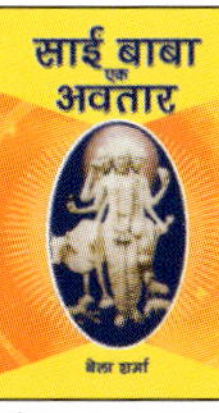
साई बाबा एक अवतार
बेला शर्मा
978 81 207 6706 5
₹ 150

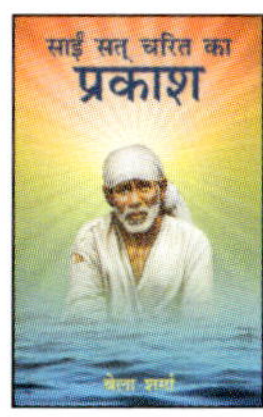
साई सत् चरित का प्रकाश
बेला शर्मा
978 81 207 7804 7
₹ 200

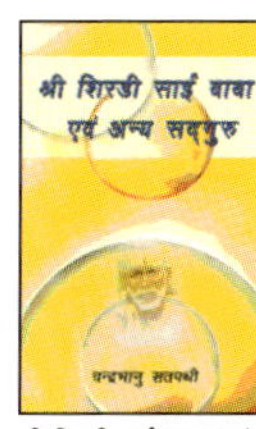
श्री शिरडी साई बाबा एवं अन्य सद्गुरु
चन्द्रभानु सतपथी
978 81 207 4401 1
₹ 90

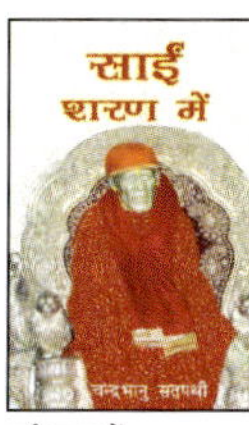
साई शरण में
चन्द्रभानु सतपथी
978 81 207 2802 8
₹ 150

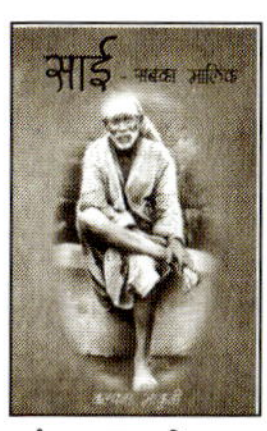
साई - सबका मालिक
कल्पना भाकुनी
978 81 207 9886 1
₹ 200

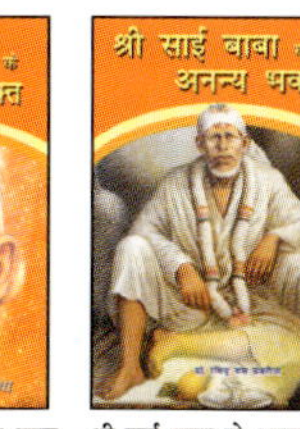
श्री साई बाबा के परम भक्त
डॉ. रबिन्द्रनाथ ककरिया
978 81 207 2779 3
₹ 125

श्री साई बाबा के अनन्य भक्त
डॉ. रबिन्द्र नाथ ककरिया
978 81 207 2705 2
₹ 100

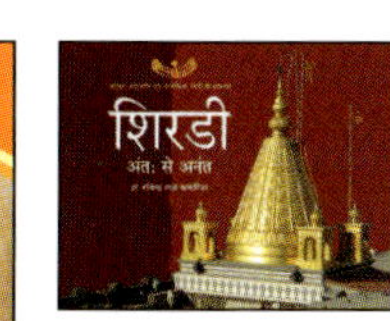
शिरडी अंत: से अनंत
डॉ. रबिन्द्रनाथ ककरिया
978 81 207 8191 7
₹ 750

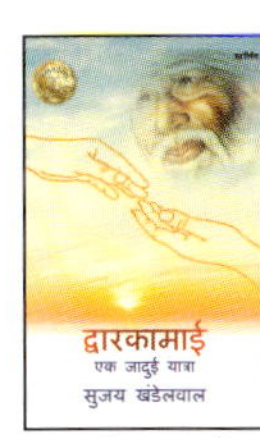
द्वारकामाई: एक जादुई यात्रा
सुजय खंडेलवाल
978 93 93853 02 8
₹ 199

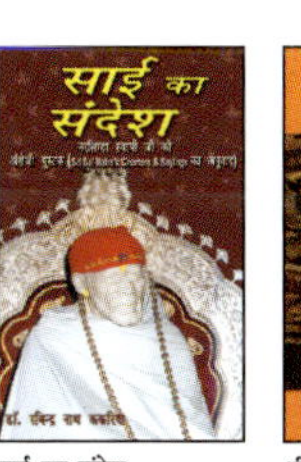
साई का संदेश
डॉ. रबिन्द्र नाथ ककरिया
978 81 207 2879 0
₹ 200

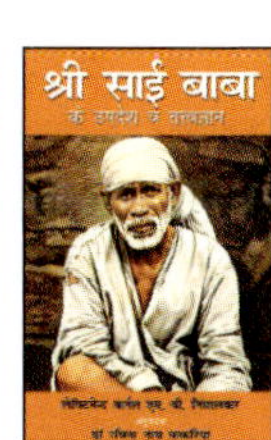
श्री साई बाबा के उपदेश व तत्त्वज्ञान
लेफ्टिनेन्ट कर्नल एम. बी. निंबालकर
978 81 207 5971 8 ₹ 100

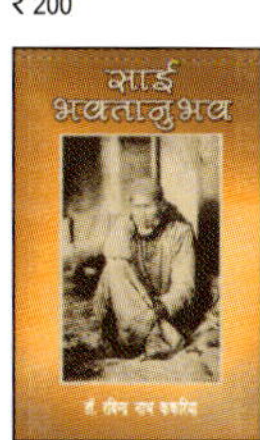
साई भक्तानुभव
डॉ. रबिन्द्रनाथ ककरिया
978 81 207 3052 6
₹ 125

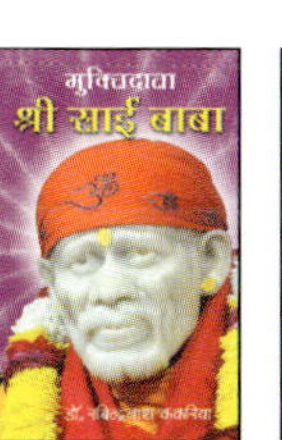
मुक्तिदाता - श्री साई बाबा
डॉ. रबिन्द्रनाथ ककरिया
978 81 207 2778 6
₹ 65

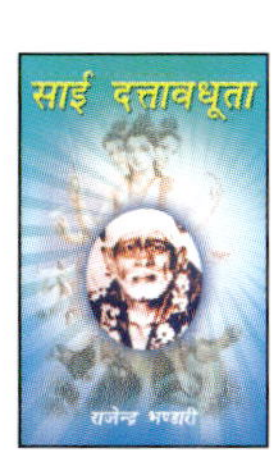
साई दत्तावधूता
राजेन्द्र भण्डारी
978 81 207 4400 4
₹ 75

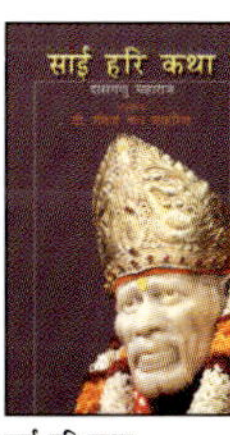
साई हरि कथा
दासगणु महाराज
978 81 207 3323 7
₹ 65

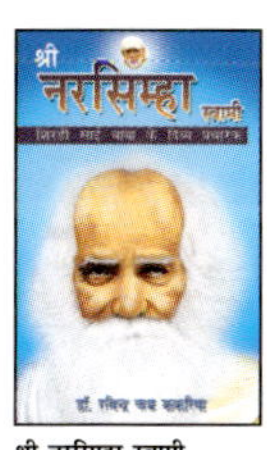
श्री नरसिम्हा स्वामी
शिरडी साई बाबा के दिव्य प्रचारक
डॉ. रबिन्द्र नाथ ककरिया
978 81 207 4437 0 ₹ 100

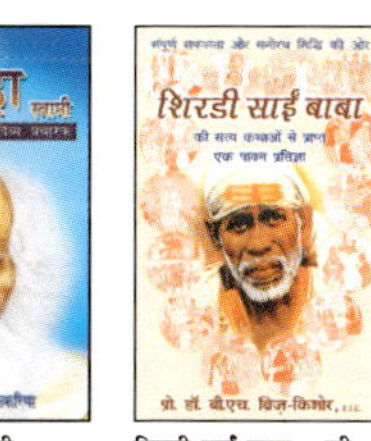
शिरडी साई बाबा - की सत्य कथाओं से प्राप्त - एक पावन प्रतिज्ञा
प्रो. डॉ. बी.एच. ब्रिज-किशोर
978 81 207 2346 7 ₹ 95

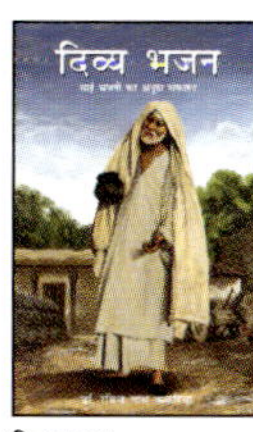
दिव्य भजन
डॉ. रबिन्द्रनाथ ककरिया
978 81 207 9505 1
₹ 125

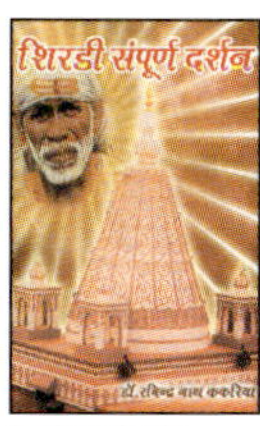
शिरडी संपूर्ण दर्शन
डॉ. रबिन्द्रनाथ ककरिया
978 81 207 2312 2
₹ 50

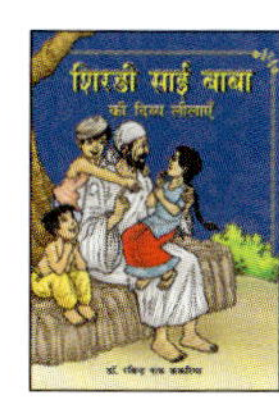
शिरडी साई बाबा की दिव्य लीलाएँ
डॉ. रबिन्द्र नाथ ककरिया
978 81 207 6376 0
₹ 150

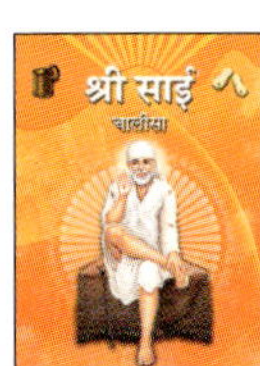
श्री साई चालीसा
978 81 207 4773 9
₹ 50

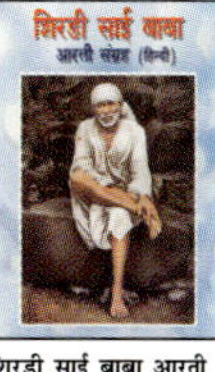
शिरडी साई बाबा आरती
978 81 207 8195 5
₹ 10

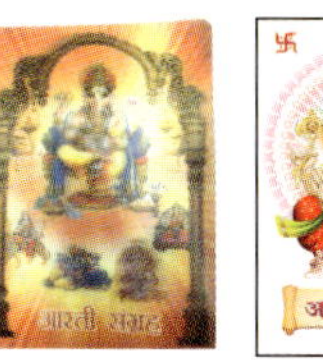
आरती संग्रह
(3D cover)
on Plastic
ISBN 978 81 207 8940 1
Size: 14.20 x 10.70 cm
₹ 50

आरती संग्रह
(Index Boardbook)
Gold/Silver Cover
ISBN 978 81 207 9057 5
Size: 10.70 x 15.45 cm
₹ 100

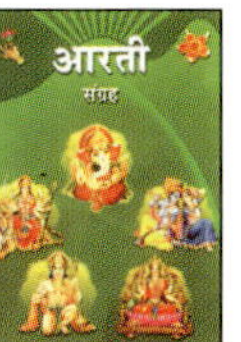
आरती संग्रह
(Boardbook)
Green Cover
ISBN 978 81 207 4774 6
Size: 11 x 15 cm (9 Leafs)
₹ 50

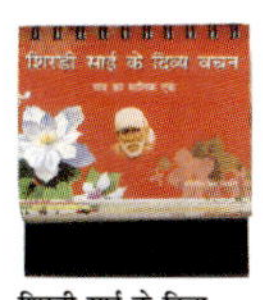
शिरडी साई के दिव्य वचन-सब का मालिक एक
प्रतिदिन का विचार
978 81 207 3533 0
₹ 200

108 NAMES OF GOD

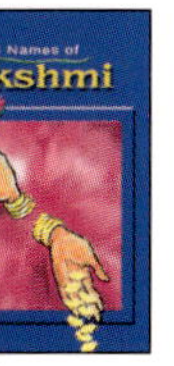
Lakshmi
978 81 207 2028 2
₹ 50

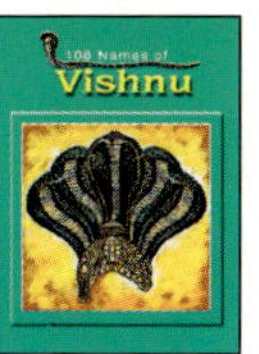
Vishnu
978 81 207 2023 7
₹ 50

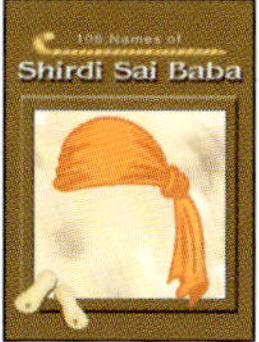
Shirdi Sai Baba
978 81 207 3074 8
₹ 50

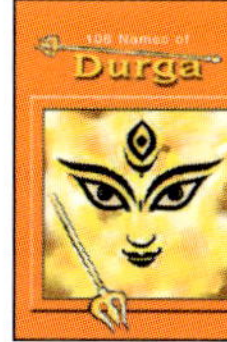
Durga
978 81 207 2027 5
₹ 50

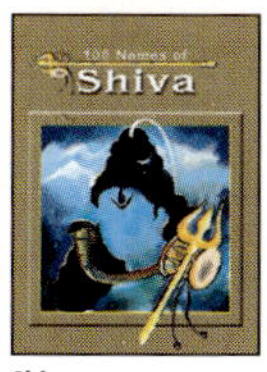
Shiva
978 81 207 2025 1
₹ 50

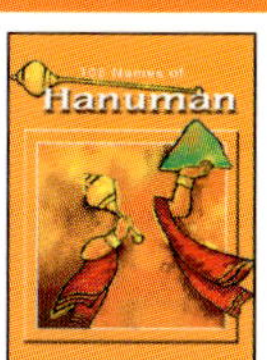
Hanuman
978 81 207 2024 4
₹ 50

Other Indian Languages

KANNAD

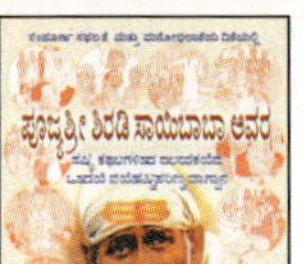

Shirdi Sai Baba Aratis
(Kannada)
₹ 10

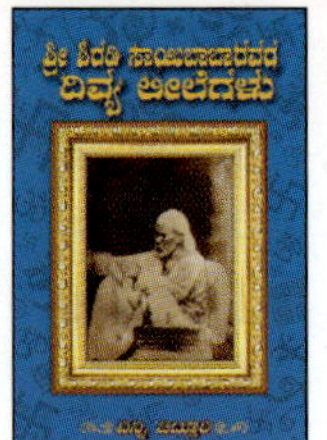

ಬಾಬಾರವರ ಋಣಾನುಬಂಧ
ವಿನ್ನಿ ಚಿಟ್ಲೂರಿ
978 81 207 9500 6
₹ 200

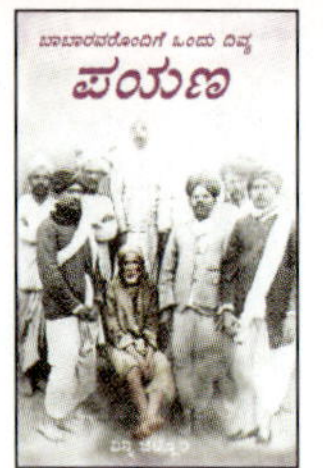

ಪೂಜ್ಯಶ್ರೀ ಶಿರಡಿ ಸಾಯಿಬಾಬಾ ಅವರ
(Kannada)
प्रो. डॉ. बी.एच. ब्रिज-किशोर
978 81 207 2873 8
₹ 95

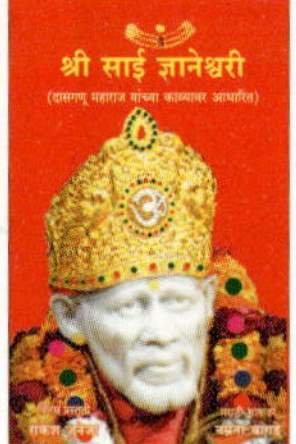

ಶ್ರೀ ಶಿರಡಿ ಸಾಯಿಬಾಬಾರವರ ದಿವ್ಯ ಲೀಲೆಗಳು
ವಿನ್ನಿ ಚಿಟ್ಲೂರಿ
978 81 207 8930 2
₹ 225

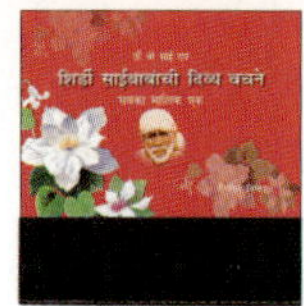

ಬಾಬಾರವರೊಂದಿಗೆ ಒಂದು ದಿವ್ಯ
ಪಯಣ
ವಿನ್ನಿ ಚಿಟ್ಲೂರಿ
978 81 207 9975 2
₹ 200

MARATHI

Shri Sai Gyaneshwari
(Marathi)
Rakesh Juneja
ISBN 978 81 947772 2 9
₹ 250

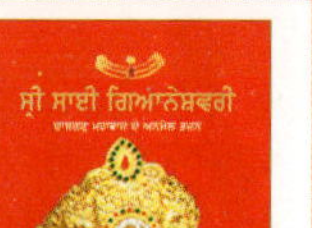

शिर्डी साईबाबांची
दिव्य वचने (Marathi)
सबका मालिक एक
दैनंदिन विचार
978 81 207 7518 3 ₹ 200

PUNJABI

Shri Sai Gyaneshwari
(Punjabi)
Rakesh Juneja
ISBN 978 81 954046 3 6
₹ 250

BENGALI

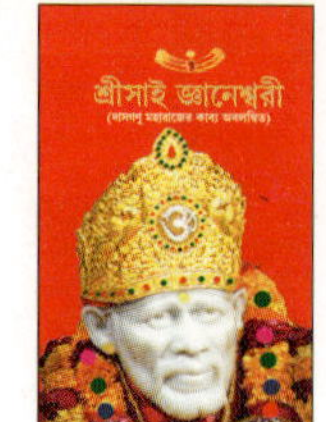

Shri Sai Gyaneshwari
(Bengali)
Rakesh Juneja
ISBN 978 81 954046 8 1
₹ 250

ORIYA

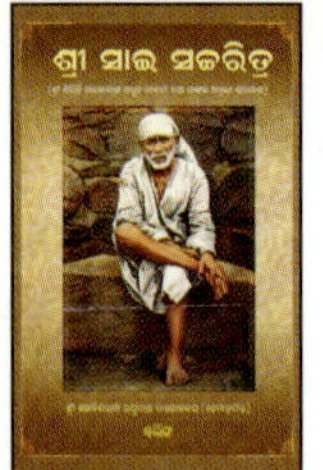

ଶ୍ରୀ ସାଇ ସଚ୍ଚରିତ୍ର
ଶ୍ରୀ ଗୋବିନ୍ଦରାଓ ରଘୁନାଥ ଦାଭୋଲକର
(ହେମାଡପନ୍ତ)
978 81 207 8332 4
₹ 350

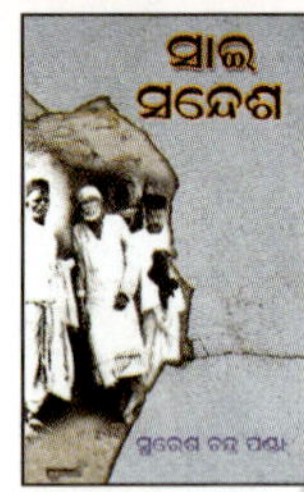

ସାଇ ସନ୍ଦେଶ
ସୁରେଶ ଚନ୍ଦ୍ର ପଣ୍ଡା
978 81 207 9534 1
₹ 100

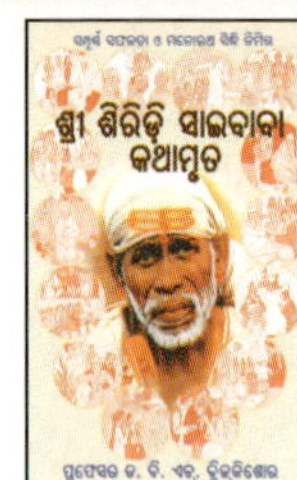

ଶ୍ରୀ ଶିରିଡ଼ି ସାଇବାବା କଥାମୃତ
ପ୍ରଫେସର ଡ. ବି. ଏଚ୍. ବ୍ରିଜ୍‌କିଶୋର
978 81 207 7774 3
₹ 95

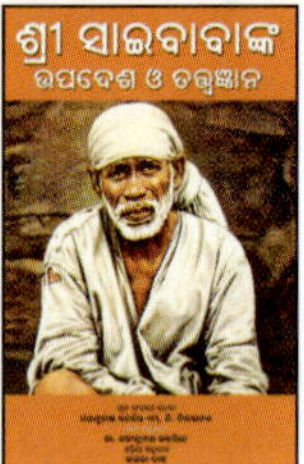

ଶ୍ରୀ ସାଇବାବାଙ୍କ
ଉପଦେଶ ଓ ତତ୍ତ୍ୱଜ୍ଞାନ
978 81 207 9982 0
₹125

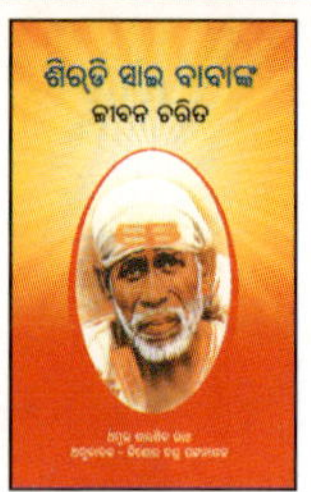

ଶିରିଡ଼ି ସାଇ ବାବାଙ୍କ
ଜୀବନ ଚରିତ (Oriya)
ଅନୁବାଦକ - କିଶୋର ଚନ୍ଦ୍ର ପଟ୍ଟନାୟକ
978 81 207 7417 9
₹125

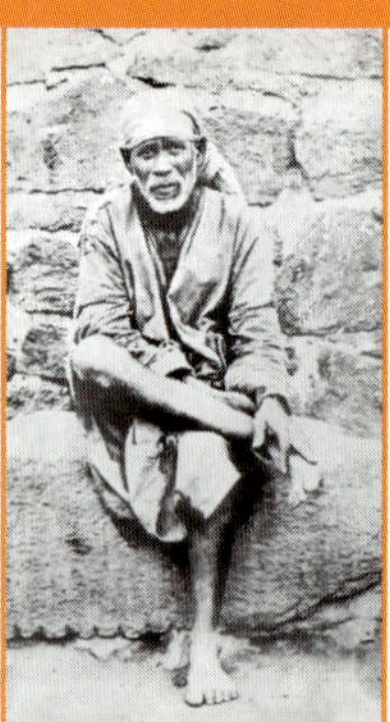

TAMIL

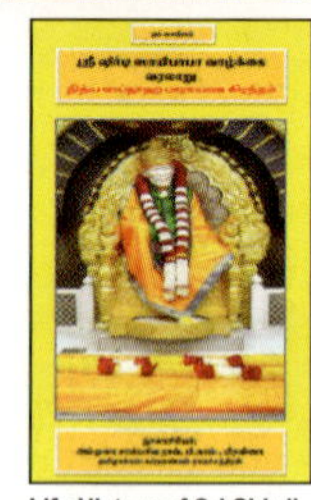

Shri Sai Gyaneshwari
(Tamil)
Rakesh Juneja
978 81 947772 5 0
₹ 250

Life History of Sri Shirdi Sai Baba
978 93 86245 77 9
₹ 250

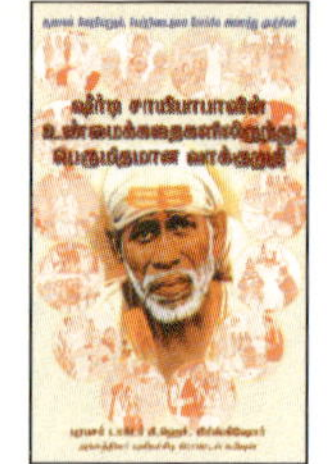

ஷீர்டி சாயிபாபாவின் (Tamil)
உண்மைக்கதைகளிலிருந்து
பெருமிதமான வாக்குறுதி
प्रो. डॉ. बी.एच. ब्रिज-किशोर
978 81 207 2876 9 ₹ 95

TELUGU

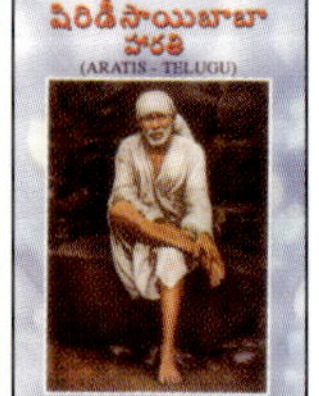

Shirdi Sai Baba Aratis
(Telugu) ₹ 10
(Tamil) ₹ 10

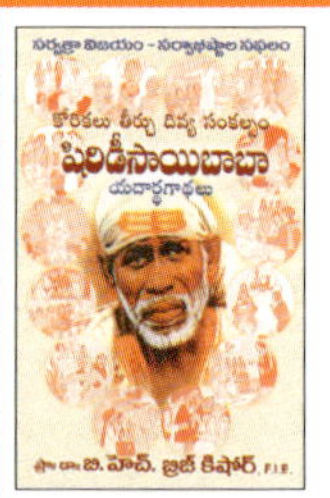

షిరిడీసాయిబాబా
(Telugu)
प्रो. डॉ. बी.एच. ब्रिज-किशोर
978 81 207 2294 1 ₹ 95

We invite established and upcoming authors to send us manuscript proposals.

STERLING

Sterling Publishers Private Limited
PLOT NO. 13, ECOTECH-III, GREATER NOIDA - 201306, U. P. INDIA
CIN: U22110DL1964PTC211907 GST: 09AACS0306C1Z1
Phone No : 00+91 82877 98380 /+91 120-6251823
E-mail : mail@sterlingpublishers.in www.sterlingpublishers.in

For Online order & detailed Catalogue visit our website